THE ISIS READER

HARORO J. INGRAM
CRAIG WHITESIDE
CHARLIE WINTER

The ISIS Reader

*Milestone Texts of the
Islamic State Movement*

HURST & COMPANY, LONDON

First published in the United Kingdom in 2020 by
C. Hurst & Co. (Publishers) Ltd.,
41 Great Russell Street, London, WC1B 3PL
© Haroro J. Ingram, Craig Whiteside and Charlie Winter, 2020
All rights reserved.
Printed in Great Britain by Bell and Bain Ltd, Glasgow

The rights of Haroro J. Ingram, Craig Whiteside and Charlie Winter to be
identified as the authors of this publication is asserted by them in accordance
with the Copyright, Designs and Patents Act, 1988.

A Cataloguing-in-Publication data record for this book is available
from the British Library.

ISBN: 9781787381971

This book is printed using paper from registered sustainable
and managed sources.

www.hurstpublishers.com

CONTENTS

CONTENTS

ACKNOWLEDGEMENTS

The authors owe a debt of gratitude to those who have shaped their thinking about the Islamic State phenomenon over the years. As researchers, our thinking has been deeply influenced by scholars and analysts such as Laith Alkhouri, Amarnath Amarasingam, Rasha al-Aqeedi, J.M. Berger, Cole Bunzel, Martha Cottam, Jon Czarnecki, Anas Elallame, Brian Fishman, Mohammed Hafez, Hassan Hassan, Samuel Helfont, Tore Hamming, Ahmed Hashim, Nibras Kazimi, Ginamarie Ligon, Charles Lister, Shiraz Maher, Will McCants, @ Mr0rangetracker, Wassim Nasr, Pieter Van Ostaeyen, Daniele Raineri, Aymenn al-Tamimi, Robert Tomlinson, Karl Walling, and Aaron Zelin. We appreciate the support from Ryan Evans and his War on the Rocks editorial team who published early explorations on our read of the group that inspired chapters in this book. We also owe particular thanks to the International Center for Counter-Terrorism (ICCT) in the Hague who have been a tremendous support to the authors. Special thanks to Dr Alastair Reed who has been a great supporter of our work over the years and continues to work tirelessly to push the field of research and practice forward. During the authors' military and national security careers, many fellow practitioners have offered their own insights into the Islamic State movement, helping to shape not only how we understood the movement but how best to confront it. Most importantly, we are grateful to the people from across the Middle East, Africa, Europe, and South and Southeast Asia who have endured the hardships wrought upon them by this movement and shared their insights and experiences with us over countless conversations. Finally, thank you to Hurst's Michael Dwyer and Farhaana Arefin for their support and patience throughout the editing process. We are grateful for all of their time and effort.

INTRODUCTION

The Islamic State (also known as ISIS, ISIL, and *Daesh*) swept into the global consciousness in 2014 with its daring seizure of territory in Iraq and Syria, before seeming to fade just as quickly back into the deserts from which it allegedly came. From its outset, it has been a source of widespread confusion—General Michael Nagata, the US Special Forces commander tasked with countering the group in late 2014, admitted in a moment of candour that he and his command did not understand 'this movement'.[1] Today, after years of bloody conflict concentrated in Syria and Iraq but also stretching across the Middle East, Africa, and Asia, there is still an alarming amount of confusion about its nature, strategy, and ultimate goals. Is it a nihilistic terrorist movement, an apocalyptic death cult, an insurgency, a terrorist army, a proto-state, or some hybrid of the above? Can the roots of this organisation, which seemingly appeared out of nowhere in 2014, really be traced back to the late 1990s, as some say? Or do the various names it has adopted since then actually refer to completely different groups? And is it really driven by Islamic principles, or is it better classified as a Sunni neo-Ba'athist restoration movement with genocidal proclivities? Confusion is rife within academic and policy circles, so it is hardly surprising that the Islamic State movement's various evolutions baffle the uninitiated, with even the most knowledgeable observers to bluring its history and strategy into tortuous catch phrases that distort more than they illuminate.

The purpose of this book is to present the Islamic State movement in its own words, through the texts and speeches that shaped its evolution from the

[1] Schmitt, Eric, 'In Battle to Defang ISIS, U.S. Targets Its Psychology', *New York Times*, 28 Dec. 2014, p. A1.

late 1990s through the second decade of the twenty-first century. To assist the reader with understanding this history, we will refer to the group by the name used in the historical period being referenced. However, we use the term 'Islamic State movement' to refer to the phenomenon holistically, encapsulating all of its historical phases and name changes. While many of the speeches and documents that appear in this text were translated from the original Arabic to make them accessible to English-speaking audiences, in many cases the Islamic State's propagandists have produced English translations and it is these, wherever possible, that have been used here. This helps to ensure that the inevitable challenges of interpretation during translation reflect the intended meanings of its authors. Where an English-language translation by the Islamic State movement itself was unavailable, the translation was subject to multiple reviews by Arabic-speaking subject matter experts and references to the original Arabic text included in footnotes.

We were motivated to write this book by both our hope of providing some clarity to readers about the historical and strategic nuances of the Islamic State movement and, perhaps more importantly, by a desire to highlight the importance of ensuring that primary sources play a central (but not singular) role in shaping our understanding of violent, non-state political actors. There has too often been a tendency for scholars and policymakers to turn to secondary rather than primary source materials.

Our intent is not to propagandise for this brutal terrorist group. Indeed, we have spent much of our professional careers working in operational, strategic, policy, and advisory roles to confront it in different parts of the world. As such, all of the original source material contained in this book is introduced with explanatory notes and followed by detailed analysis designed to support the reader's critical understanding of the sources, which are, more often than not, provided in abridged form with just enough detail for a reasoned understanding of their significance. In doing so, we hope to encourage the research and policy fields to prioritise primary sources to understand violent political movements and devise more effective strategies to undermine and ultimately defeat them. With that in mind, while this book may be of limited value to the hardened researchers and practitioners who have been monitoring and combating this group for over two decades, it was not written for this niche community but rather for a broader readership keen to learn more about this perplexing phenomenon. This said, we have found in our own research that rereading these foundational texts over and over again has helped us gain an understanding of this elusive foe.

INTRODUCTION

Given how much has been spent combating the Islamic State movement in its various iterations, perhaps the most important readers of this text will be the next generation of journalists, scholars, operators, and strategists, who will undoubtedly need to understand and confront this group, or at least its offshoots, in years to come. Since 2016, the Islamic State has weathered a series of blows. It has essentially lost all the territory it once controlled, suffered a significant decline in its overall operations, seen a large proportion of its coterie of commanders and media officials killed, including its first caliph Abu Bakr al-Baghdadi and its much vaunted propaganda machine has been largely dismantled and successive spokesmen killed. However, in the midst of such a precipitous decline and despite the continuing efforts of a US-led coalition to eliminate its remnants and hunt down its leaders, the group has remained remarkably cohesive organisationally, ideologically, and strategically—a true measure of resilience beyond mere survival. For each emerging trend that suggests it is on down and out, others spring up, hinting that it is clawing its way back. At times, these trends prove to be something more than just hints of capability. Indeed, as the chapters of this book reveal, the Islamic State's unexpected return from the brink of defeat prior to 2014 should not have come as a surprise to the global community. In learning more about the group, we can help ensure that this does not happen again.

Why Is the Islamic State Movement's Earliest History Important?

There is a misconception, even amongst scholars and practitioners, that the Islamic State movement first emerged in 2013–14. In ignoring almost two decades of its history, such a misunderstanding blinkers any attempt to understand its nuances. Indeed, even a cursory glance through its early history reveals operational and strategic patterns that emerge time and again even to this day.

The Islamic State movement began as a small group under the leadership of Abu Musab al-Zarqawi, a Jordanian jihadi who established a camp in Afghanistan that collected displaced fighters and families from the Levant in the late 1990s. He led the group into northern Iraq after US forces ejected them from Afghanistan in 2002. There, in Kurdistan, a group of Iraqi Salafi-jihadis hosted them for a time as Zarqawi worked to establish a network throughout Sunni Arab parts of Iraq and Syria.[2] His efforts continued after

---

[2] The Levant refers to Greater Syria, including Palestine, Lebanon, Syria, and Jordan. The Salafi movement is a politico-religious ideology that stresses strict adherence to

the US-led invasion of Iraq until he made his first moves late in the summer of 2003, launching attacks on the United Nations and the Jordanian Embassy in Baghdad and the Imam Ali Mosque in Najaf with large car bombs. The strikes killed the head of the United Nations mission in Iraq and the head of the Shi'a Hakim family among scores of others, a tremendous first effort that generated serious political aftershocks.[3] The attacks went unclaimed, leaving mystery and confusion in their wake.[4]

The initial political agenda of the Islamic State movement was ambitious. It intended to expand its numbers from a handful of foreign fighters and local hosts to a force that dominated the Iraqi resistance. Although Zarqawi's group had valuable experience in clandestine operations, it had to outpace the reorganising Ba'athists, rival Islamists, and a fledgling Iraqi government with one hand, while battling a very capable foreign military coalition with the other. Furthermore, while other groups had various degrees of interest in power sharing with the national government, Zarqawi's group held firm to its revolutionary goal of replacing it with a Salafi-influenced state run according to the 'prophetic method'.

To accomplish this, the Islamic State movement's political efforts were five-fold: it had to frustrate and weaken the growing power of the government and its security forces, recruit from rival resistance groups, foster an exaggerated perception of Sunni alienation, provoke an overreaction from Shi'a militias, and convince the United States to withdraw from Iraq.[5]

---

the original texts and practices of the early, pious Muslims, or Salaf. Salafi-jihadi is a general term referring to a subset of militants that adhere to the Salafi spectrum and advocate its implementation using coercive methods instead of politics. *Takfir* is a concept that supports the excommunication of apostate Muslims by certain authorities. The Islamic State movement is made up of a unique blend of Salafi/jihadi/*takfiri*/revolutionaries. For an excellent discussion on the dangers of using these terms loosely, see Hegghammer, Thomas, 'Jihadi-Salafis or Revolutionaries? On Religion and Politics in the Study of Militant Islamism', in *Global Salafism: Islam's New Religious Movement*, ed. Roel Meijer, London: Hurst, 2009, pp. 244–66.

[3] Warrick, Joby, *Black Flags: The Rise of ISIS*, New York: Anchor Books, 2015, pp. 106–114.

[4] Ghosh, Bobby, 'Twelve Years On, Remembering the Bomb that Started the Middle East's Sectarian War', *Quartz*, 28 Aug. 2015, http://qz.com/476191/remembering-the-bomb-that-started-the-middle-easts-sectarian-war/, last accessed 18 Dec. 2018.

[5] Many of these strategic objectives can be found in this publication: Abu Hamza al Baghdadi, 'Why do we fight?', Legal Committee of al-Qaida Organization in the

To this end, it kicked off its kinetic campaign with its sights set on the neutralisation of the United States' tremendous technological capabilities.[6] Ceding the day-to-day struggle (sniping and roadside bombs) to local insurgent groups, Zarqawi's forces focused on high-visibility attacks against symbolic targets using 'precision-guided' suicide bombers and special operations that attracted media attention and popularity among resistance sympathisers.[7] These ultimately served to discredit the state's authority and legitimacy, and divide elements of the population against each other.

It is a strategy reflected in al-Qaida strategist Abu Bakr Naji's *Management of Savagery*, which propagates a controversial and violent method for destroying the government and society before starting anew.[8] It is worth noting that the Islamic State disputes the influence of Naji's book on its approach, arguing:

> As for the concise but beneficial 100-page book titled *Management of Savagery*, written by an unknown author who went by the pen name Abu Bakr Naji, when Sheikh al-Zarqawi read it, he commented, 'it is as if the author knows what I'm planning.' Note: Although Naji's book describes very precisely the overall strategy of the *mujahidin*, Naji made some errors on the issue of *takfiri* elements in parties who forcefully resist sharia and its laws.[9]

Land of Two Rivers, 17 Oct. 2005, originally posted online by the Islamic Renewal Organization forum at tajdeed.org.uk.

[6] Lia, Brynjar, *Architect of Global Jihad: The Life of Al Qaeda Strategist Abu Mus'ab Al-Suri*, New York: Columbia University Press, 2008, p. 363.

[7] On the Islamic State movement's utilization of suicide bombers, see Mohammad Hafez, *Suicide Bombers in Iraq*, Washington, D.C.: United States Institute of Peace (USIP), 2007. For a comparison of Islamic State (TwJ, AQI, and ISI) claims versus others, see Katherine Seifert and Clark McCauley, 'Suicide Bombers in Iraq, 2003–2010: Disaggregating Targets can Reveal Insurgent Motives and Priorities', *Terrorism and Political Violence* 26, no. 5 (2014), pp. 803–820. For examples of special operations capturing and torturing US soldiers, read Dexter Filkins, 'Bodies of G.I.'s Show Signs of Torture, Iraqi General Says', *New York Times*, 20 June 2006, http://www.nytimes.com/2006/06/20/world/20cnd-iraq.html?_r=0, last accessed 18 Dec. 2018; and Damien Cave, 'Iraq Insurgent Group Claims it Killed Missing U.S. Soldiers', *New York Times*, 5 June 2007, http://www.nytimes.com/2007/06/05/world/middleeast/05iraq.html, last accessed 18 Dec. 2018.

[8] McCants, Will, *The ISIS Apocalypse: The History, Strategy, and Doomsday Vision of the Islamic State*, New York: St. Martin's Press, 2015, p. 82.

[9] Islamic State, 'The Revival of Jihad in Bengal', *Dabiq*, no. 12 (2015), p. 39, Jihadology,

In this disavowal of Naji's work, there is an implicit acknowledgement that Zarqawi's early military strategy bears a marked resemblance to the concepts in Naji's book. Furthermore, there is some evidence that it has been used as a teaching aid fairly recently, despite its apparent 'errors'.[10] In any case, its asymmetric logic is sound: Eliminating enemies can create opportunities to access and sway the population without interference from competing ideologies, and in this respect, the Islamic State movement was an innovator, frequently experimenting with its influence campaigns. It developed and applied a comprehensive approach to its propaganda efforts, encapsulating the political, social, military, and economic spheres, something that left the overarching, strategic logic of its media approach characterised by two distinct but often interwoven categories. The first are rational-choice appeals that present jaundiced cost-benefit arguments in favour of its ability to provide things like stability livelihood and security. Second are identity-choice appeals that exploit sectarian and other identity-related tensions to present itself as the only viable protector of Sunni Muslims.[11]

The successful deployment of this influence campaign would help the Islamic State movement alter the social fabric of Iraq as an ideological and political imperative to mobilise the Sunnis, who were a demographic minority in post-2003 Iraq. The potential this created for social conflict is what Mao Zedong referred to as a 'contradiction', and could be used by flexible practitioners for mobilisation purposes.$[12] Historically, there was a latent sectarian divide among Iraqi Muslims that had grown in salience following the Iranian revolution and the uprisings that swept through Iraq

---

http://jihadology.net/2015/11/18/newissue-of-the-islamic-states-magazine-dabiq-12%E2%80%B3/, last accessed 18 Dec. 2018.

[10] Hassan, Hassan, 'The Sectarianism of the Islamic State: Ideological Roots and Political Context', Carnegie Endowment for International Peace, 13 June 2016, http://carnegieendowment.org/2016/06/13/sectarianism-of-islamic-state-ideological-roots-and-political-context/j1iy, last accessed 18 Dec. 2018.

[11] Ingram, Haroro, 'The Strategic Logic of Islamic State Information Operations', *Australian Journal of International Affairs* 69, no. 6 (2015), pp. 729–752, http://www.tandfonline.com/doi/full/10.1080/10357718.2015.1059799, last accessed 18 Dec. 2018.

[12] Johnson, Chalmers, 'The Third Generation of Guerilla Warfare', in *Revolutionary Guerrilla Warfare*, ed. Sam Sarkesian, Chicago, IL: Precedent Publishing, 1975, pp. 357–373.

in 1991.[13] It seems likely, then, that Zarqawi's targeting of the 'dangerous' Shi'a was designed to act as a wedge, driven between Iraqi Sunnis and the government. While Zarqawi's bloodletting may have seemed like the crude manifestation of an irrational zealousness, it was much more the product of a considered strategy.[14] In addition to all this, he intended for his movement to quickly become economically independent, freeing itself of outside influence, in order to protect its credibility, legitimacy, and authority.[15]

This is the abridged but too-often dismissed founding story of the Islamic State movement, within which the characteristics that have been repeated time and again throughout its history can be observed. The movement's extreme violence may look like fanatical brutality, but it is typically deployed with the intent of achieving specific operational, strategic, and propagandistic aims. Its jurisprudential rulings, masquerading as a representation of true Islam, while broadly dismissed by Muslims around the world and even by other violent extremists, are deployed by Islamic State leadership to cloak what are typically pragmatic decisions with a religious and legal credibility. Beneath the Islamic State movement's rhetoric is a political agenda that it has consistently pursued via a range of activities, of which violence is only one. To develop a considered understanding of the Islamic State phenomenon, it is therefore necessary to not only engage with the primary source materials but to do so with an appropriate objectivity and sobriety, something that requires as broad a view of its history as possible.

Choice of Sources

The Islamic State movement's last three decades informed the choice of primary sources included in this book. We started with the speeches and videos

---

[13] Haddad, Fanar, *Sectarianism in Iraq: Antagonistic Visions in Unity*, London: Hurst, 2011.

[14] al-Zarqawi, Abu Musab, 'Zarqawi's Cry', seized document released by the CPA Iraq, trans. Haverford College Global Terrorism Research Project, 14 Feb. 2004, https://dsdrupal.haverford.edu/aqsi/aqsi-statement/596, last accessed 18 Dec. 2018.

[15] This section contains material previously published in the following journal article: Craig Whiteside, 'New Masters of Revolutionary Warfare: The Islamic State Movement (2002–2016)', *Perspectives on Terrorism* 10, no. 4 (2016), http://www.terrorismanalysts.com/pt/index.php/pot/article/view/523/html, last accessed 18 Dec. 2018.

that set the stage for the Islamic State's founding in October 2006 and feature those who self-identified with the movement to achieve a caliphate in the Levant region, ruled by the precepts of what they termed 'the prophetic method'. This includes statements by the founder, Zarqawi, and his successors, who made his vision a reality by laying the foundations for a future Islamist caliphate, one that was eventually realised with its declaration in Mosul in 2014. The majority of the speeches and videos from the period after its caliphate was declared relate to the Islamic State movement's broader strategic objectives and tactics, advice to its members, communication of its doctrine, and justification for its actions. In many ways, the primary sources selected throughout this book are thus milestones in the movement's history—the story told in the words of its own members. Together, we have assessed that this collection of documents and transcripts, many of which have never been published in English, can further our collective knowledge of the Islamic State movement in the hopes of not only assisting those charged with defeating it, but also academics, journalists, and the general public in trying to understand how this group is changing the dynamics of political violence.

The debate over what should and should not be included in this book could continue ad nauseum. For example, what about materials produced by the movement's formal and aspiring provinces around the world? Or internal administrative documents that shape the bureaucratic and organizational dynamics of the group? Ultimately, we chose the selected sources because they capture the strategic dynamics of a particular period in the movement's evolution. Many important documents and speeches are not referenced in this compendium, mostly because we felt that they did not meet the criteria listed above or that they did not capture the dynamics we were trying to highlight as strongly as those we had selected. The most obvious omissions are Naji's aforementioned text, *The Management of Savagery* and Abu Abdullah al-Muhajir's *The Jurisprudence of Blood*. Both have been highly influential on the Islamic State, despite petty differences ideologues in the group might have with the authors. First, neither Naji nor Muhajir were Islamic State members, and the influences of the texts are difficult to establish, even though they promote similar rhetoric and tactics to those employed by the Islamic State since its founding. Accordingly, we chose to focus on content authored by official, stated members of the movement (both before and after the declaration of the 'Islamic State' in 2006) and promulgated by its leadership.

INTRODUCTION

Structure of the Book

The book's fifteen chapters have been divided into four sections that cover the Islamic State movement's evolution under the banners of Tawhid wal Jihad, al-Qaida in Iraq, the Islamic State of Iraq (ISI), the Islamic State in Iraq and al-Sham (ISIS), and the Islamic State. 'Part I: Join the Caravan' traces its origins, starting with a collection of Zarqawi's earliest speeches, the first from 1994 (Chapter 1), followed by an in-depth look at the strategy behind his war in Iraq based on a letter captured by US forces in January 2004 (Chapter 2).

'Part II: *Baqiyyah!*' covers the period from the establishment of the movement's first 'state'—the Islamic State of Iraq (ISI)—its struggle to survive, and subsequent resurgence after ISI's near decimation in Iraq. Chapter 3 starts, as it should, with a look at the formative documents explaining the rationale behind the founding of ISI in its first year, including a speech by its leader at the time Abu Umar al-Baghdadi. Chapter 4 includes advice given to the leaders of the Islamic State, particularly its military commanders, by then-Islamic State in Iraq War Minister Abu Hamza al-Muhajir. Chapter 5 features a never-before-published strategy document, the Fallujah Memorandum, from late 2009 that presciently lays out ways for the movement to take advantage of the United States' departure from Iraq in 2011 and bolster its own position.

'Part III: The Caliphate' addresses the movement's second resurgence, the period in which it was most prolific. In early 2013, Abu Bakr al-Baghdadi[16] announced the expansion of the group into Syria and the adoption of the name the Islamic State in Iraq and al-Sham (ISIS). Part of this declaration, which had a significant impact on the transnational jihadi milieu, can be found in Chapter 6. Following on from this, Chapter 7 details the announcement of the caliphate in Mosul in the summer of 2014 (and the point at which ISIS became the Islamic State), featuring two speeches by Abu Bakr al-Baghdadi, who was by this point the self-declared caliph. Chapter 8 examines what is believed to be one of the driving forces behind the spread of global terror attacks at the Islamic State's behest, a speech by its charismatic spokesman Abu Muhammad al-Adnani, alongside an iconic article from the movement's English-language magazine *Dabiq* titled 'The Extinction of the Greyzone'.

---

[16] To avoid confusion with Abu Umar al-Baghdadi, in Parts I and II of this book, Abu Bakr al-Baghdadi is referred to as Abu Bakr. In Parts III and IV, Abu Bakr al-Baghdadi is referred to as Baghdadi.

Chapter 9 presents an internal document that provides instructions for the role of women in the Islamic State, and the final chapter features the Islamic State's doctrine for media jihad, which provides its operatives with guidance for how to engage in effective messaging.

'Part IV: Purification' features primary source materials that take us through the period of Islamic State's most recent decline. Chapter 11 focuses on an Islamic State video that breaks down the structure of the Islamic State in 2016, when it administered tens of thousands of square miles of territory and millions of citizens. Chapter 12 includes the final speech of the long-time spokesperson, Abu Muhammad al-Adnani, who first appears in this text in Chapter 1. In it, this veteran of the movement, who was involved since before 2003 and was an associate of founder Zarqawi, summarizes the Islamic State's past and attempts to chart its trajectory in the future. The following chapter presents Abu Bakr al-Baghdadi's August 2018 speech 'And Give Glad Tidings to Those Who Are Patient'. From the rubble of his supposed caliphate, he calls on his supporters to remain committed during this period of hardship and purification and lay the foundations for survival and future revival. The final two chapters of this book look at 2019 speeches by the Islamic State spokesperson Abul Hasan al-Muhajir, and the now-dead 'guerrilla caliph' Abu Bakr al-Baghdadi. Only months later both men were killed in targeted operations in northern Syria signaling the end of Baghdadi's reign as leader and heralding a new era in the Islamic State movement's history. In many respects, then, this book ends as it began, with the Islamic State movement again looking at long odds in gaining the traction needed to control territory and implement the 'prophetic' methodology amongst a willing population of subjects.

The Authors

The three authors of *The ISIS Reader* have all been intensive students of the movement; one since its outset, when it first transitioned from al-Qaida in Iraq (where it was part of a political front named the Mujahidin Shura Council) to the Islamic State of Iraq in October 2006. We are all academics who have written extensively on the political worldview of the Islamic State movement, leadership in militant Islamism, and Islamic State propaganda and strategic communications, respectively. Two of us are former practitioners in counterinsurgency and counterterrorism, with direct experience in combating the group and assisting others in doing so. One author has extensive Arabic language skills and developed his own translation of the documents, another was involved in counterterrorism operations before working in capacity building initiatives in communities previously controlled by the Islamic State, while the other helped raise and equip the Sahwa (Awakening) tribal auxiliaries to successfully defeat the early Islamic State in 2007, albeit temporarily, only to see the Sahwa whither away in the succeeding years. Between us, we have lived in or been deployed to the Middle East several dozen times as well as to other corners of the world where the Islamic State movement has appeared in various forms. It is through the lens of practitioner-scholars that we now embark on an exploration of the Islamic State movement's history from the inside.

A note on translation and transliteration

There are a number of inconsistencies in translation and transliteration style in the texts appearing in the course of this book. This is due to the fact that they were derived from a number of sources—among them the Islamic State movement itself, the United States Department of Defense, one of the authors, and an additional two translators, Anas Elallame and Aymenn Jawad al-Tamimi. Where they were acquired from the movement and the Department of Defense, no effort was made to standardise terminology or approaches to transliteration. A note at the beginning of each primary source excerpt outlines the origins of the transcript and how it has been edited.

PART I

JOIN THE CARAVAN

'Part I: Join the Caravan' focuses on the speeches and writings of the Islamic State movement's founder Ahmad Fadil al-Nazal al-Khalayleh—better known by his *kunya* (nom de guerre) Abu Musab al-Zarqawi. Although Zarqawi did not live to see the declaration of the Islamic State of Iraq in October 2006, the group has always designated him as the father of the movement and the leader of its vanguard. Chapter 1 contains two largely unread speeches that mark pivotal moments in the development of the insurgent leader: one from his prison sentencing in Jordan in 1994 that got the attention of the wider Salafi-jihadi movement, and his first speech as a commander in Iraq ten years later. Chapter 2 presents the most famous document in the movement's early history, a letter Zarqawi wrote to his prospective leaders in al-Qaida, petitioning them to become an affiliate, penned at around the same time as his first speech. The insights from these texts convey a real sense of the challenges the movement faced in mobilising 'good Muslims' to fight against the injustices of authoritarian Muslim regimes and the presence of foreign occupiers on Muslim soil. They blend emotional appeals with sober, clear-thinking strategic vision, both elements which endure and continue to impact the trajectory of the movement to this day.

1

THE FIRST SPEECHES

In this first chapter, we present two speeches by the Islamic State movement's founder Abu Musab al-Zarqawi. The first dates from 1994 and contains evidence of him adopting the unique framework of ideas, largely inspired by his perspective as an Islamist in Jordan, that would become very familiar to students of the current Islamic State. The second speech, from 2004, allows us a glimpse of Zarqawi's worldview as his insurgency in Iraq is poised to transition from a small network to a nationwide movement with an expanding global reach.

1.1a. 'Deposition of a Captive: "O My People, Why Am I Calling You to Salvation and You Are Calling Me to Hell!"', 15 April 1994[1]
Abu Musab al-Zarqawi

We begin with an excerpt from Zarqawi's first public speech, read as he and Abu Muhammad al-Maqdisi were sentenced by a Jordanian court for activities against the state. Zarqawi, born Ahmad Fadil Nazzal al-Khalayilah, was a little-known petty criminal turned reformed religious zealot from Zarqa, just north of Amman. Maqdisi was Zarqawi's spiritual and ideological mentor, and

---

[1] The title is derived from a line in the Quran, Surah 40. This speech was found in an online collection of Zarqawi speeches (Arabic) in 2019 and translated for the authors by Anas Elallame, the Middlebury Institute of International Studies, Monterey, California.

remains an influential proponent of the Salafi-jihadi ideology.[2] *According to the historian Shiraz Maher, this spectrum of political thought consists of five tenets: monotheism* (tawhid), *Allah's rule as the political system* (hakimiyya), *association and disavowal* (al-wala wal-bara), *struggle* (jihad), *and excommunication of apostates* (takfir).[3] *Zarqawi's speech made a splash—it was noticed by Osama bin Laden's lieutenants in far away Afghanistan because of its bold defiance in the face of an autocratic regime* (taghut, *as Zarqawi called it*).[4] *It also appealed to other Islamists of all stripes who had been chafing under the allegedly un-Islamic and corrupt rule of the region's autocrats, seeking to undermine them, and, in some cases, rebel. The speech demonstrates that even ten years before he gained notoriety as the leader of Jama'at Tawhid wal-Jihad (the Society of Monotheism and Struggle) and later the Tanzim Qa'idat al-Jihad fi Bilad al-Rafidayn (Organisation of the Base of Struggle in the Land of the Two Rivers, more commonly known as al-Qaida in Iraq, or AQI), Zarqawi was an outspoken advocate of Islamist revolution.*

[Zarqawi]: This is not about 'bombs, weapons, and explosives', [the charges against Zarqawi and Maqdisi] rather, it is a call for unification and a call to religion ... we have been pushed away [jailed] for a while now only because our brothers started spreading this honourable call to Islam, the call of our prophets. Our brothers hosted lessons and classes in mosques and houses to help draw people out of disbelief and bring them towards monotheism, from a temporary life towards a permanent one, from injustice to fairness and to security, from hell to delightful gardens. His greatness said, 'O our people, respond to the Messenger of Allah and believe in him; Allah will forgive for you your sins and protect you from a painful punishment' (Verse 46:31). We have all heard and read about the [Jordanian] secret service, the people of hell,

---

[2] Abu Muhammad al-Maqdisi's real name is Essam Muhammad Tahir al-Barqawi. He was born in Nablus, Palestine, and is considered to be one of the most influential Islamists alive today. See Wagemakers, Joas, *A Quietist Jihadi: The Ideology and Influence of Abu Muhammad al-Maqdisi*, Cambridge: Cambridge University Press, 2012; and McCants, Will, 'Militant Ideology Atlas', CTC West Point, November 2006.

[3] Maher, Shiraz, *Salafi-Jihadism: The History of an Idea*, New York: Oxford University Press, 2016.

[4] al-Adel, Sayf 'Jihadist Biography of the Slaughtering Leader Abu Musab al-Zarqawi, by the Military Commander of Qaedat al-Jihad', *Global Islamic Media Front*, 2005.

physically assaulting people, as in the 'Mu'tah case', in which they physically tortured and violated the dignity of the Brothers [unknown dissidents against the regime].

In the Hadith of the Prophet (peace be upon him):

A man asked the Prophet: Oh Prophet of Allah, if a man comes and takes my money, should I give it to him?
The Prophet said: No, don't.
The man: What about if he fights me for it? Should I kill him?
The Prophet: You should.
The man: And what if I kill him?
The Prophet: He goes to hell.
The man: What if he kills me?
The Prophet: Then you are a martyr.

The Sheikh of Islam Ibn Taymiyyah said, 'if an enemy decides to attack the religion, then repelling that enemy will become the personal duty of all.' Thanks to Allah, we are people of a *dawa* [great call to Islam], one sounded by prophets who came before us. Those that carry on this call have dignity and honour. I promise you that we would rather die than watch our honour be violated. We would rather die rather than watch the soldiers of the *taghut* (apostate dictator) attack our houses and arrest us in front of our families and children.

We, O judge, we say this not only to tell you who we are, but also because, as his Majesty said, 'and thus do We detail the verses, and [thus] the way of the criminals will become evident' (Verse 6:55). We know—thanks to Allah—the price we will have to pay for this *dawa* to Islam and that there may be harmful consequences. His greatness said: 'You will surely be tested in your possessions and in yourselves. You will surely hear from those who were given the Scripture before you, and from those who associate others with Allah [idolaters], you will hear much abuse. But if you are patient and fear Allah—indeed, that is among the matters [worthy] of determination' (Verse 3:186).

Clearly, you are calling for democracy—a heretic modern religion. You kill people, permit alcohol, adultery, and corruption, all in the name of democracy. Your media works hard to polish the image of this modern religion, which it describes as just, balanced, and predicated on the freedom of the individual and the dignity of the citizen. The killing of Mohammed al-Awalmeh [it is unclear to us who this is] is evidence of this dignity [sarcasm]. In the name of this heretic democracy you throw people behind bars in their masses. These people have been accused of many things, including 'offensive speech.' Anyone who stands against your wrongdoings, you punish for 'offensive speech' against the regime and its evil followers. What is the definition of 'offensive speech' under your laws?

His Majesty said in his book, 'And do not insult those that invoke other than Allah, lest they insult Allah in enmity without knowledge' (Verse 6:108). Ibn Kathir explained this verse as, 'If an insult leads to significant harm, then it is forbidden.'

This *dawa* [call to religion] that we have broken down for you and explained, that your laws consider 'offensive speech', is our moral law and our duty. The Prophet (peace be upon him) said 'the master of the martyrs is Hamza ibn Abdul Muttalib, and a man who stands [in front of] an oppressive ruler and enjoins the good and forbids the evil and so is killed for it.' Speaking the truth and uncovering the wrongs is a duty of our laws. The Prophet's follower said, 'We swore allegiance to Messenger of Allah (peace be upon him) to hear and obey him in times of difficulty and in prosperity, in hardship and in ease, and to say what was right wherever we were, and to fear reproach from no one.' His Highness said, commending these people, 'Allah praises those who convey the messages of Allah and fear Him and fear no one but Allah. And Allah is sufficient in keeping account' (Verse 33:39). The monotheist will express his beliefs according to the Quran and the Sunnah of the Prophet; he calls people to monotheism and warns against polytheists. A monotheist will prove his point using the Quran and the Sunnah of the Prophet. As his Greatness said, 'And whoever does not judge by what Allah has revealed— they are the disbelievers' (Verse 5:44). And so, if someone stands against and changes Allah's laws, are they not an infidel?

Is stating Allah's laws and rules, as revealed in the Quran, considered 'offensive speech' under your man-made laws?

The Prophet (peace be upon him) was right when he said: 'The end times will come when your leaders are unjust, your ministers are immoral, your judges are traitors, and your imams are liars. Whoever lives during these times, you shall not work with them.' This is a verified hadith, one that we are only recounting to advise you. You said [ours was] 'offensive speech?' Nowadays, the right is wrong and the wrong is right.

The Prophet (peace be upon him) and the other prophets before him broke their pagan statues and pagan gods. His Highness said, referring to Ibrahim, 'Then, instead of Allah, do you worship that which can neither benefit you nor harm you? Woe to you and to what you worship instead of Allah. Will you not use reason?' (Verse 21:66–67). In the Hadith, the Prophet (peace be upon him) was asked by the leaders and the *tawaghit* of Quraysh: 'Are you the one who insults our gods and our dreams?' He said: 'Yes, I am.' Although in his *dawa*, he never used insult or obscene language. This is the Sunnah of our prophets, which you will follow by Allah's will.

Those who insult the Creator get lesser sentences and punishments than those who insult your ruler! Tell me, O you the one judging me, who is your god then?

Your slogan is: 'Allah, the homeland, and the king.' Allah's book should come before 'the Homeland, and the King.' Too, the punishment for 'offensive speech' against the king is harsher than the punishment for 'offensive speech' against Allah, his Highness! Who, then, is the right god, according to your laws?

1.1b. Analysis

The themes present in Zarqawi's courthouse speech do not reflect the widely held perception of him as a simple street thug and a drug-dealing pimp. He may have been all of those things, but that was long before he found himself leading the group that would one day evolve into the Islamic State and he made a considerable effort to learn and espouse the doctrine of Salafi-jihadism. This excerpt from his first public speech demonstrates Maqdisi's influence over his protégé, which is particularly present in the rhetoric against democracy. The statement is an indictment of secular Arab rule based in man-made law, with Zarqawi, Maqdisi, and others strongly believing that guidance should come from Islamic rule. Their decision to take up jihad against a regime that deferred to man's law over Allah's law is in keeping with the heart of the Salafi-jihadi doctrine of disavowing apostates. The speech also reveals Zarqawi's preference for undermining local secular Arab regimes by force, instead of focusing on the far enemy—the United States. His strategic inclinations and those of his successors would strain the relationship between Islamic State movement leaders and al-Qaida, to which Zarqawi would pledge allegiance later down the line, in 2004.

Zarqawi's relationship with al-Qaida, never close to begin with, was not the only one corroded by his vision of how to bring about an Islamic State in the region. Ten years after this speech, Zarqawi's campaign in Iraq drew criticism from Maqdisi—who was once again imprisoned in a Jordanian jail—over the industrial use of suicide bombing against Shi'a Muslims in Iraq. At the time, Zarqawi's religious and spiritual guide was one of Maqdisi's favourite students, Abu Anas al-Shami. Killed in 2004, Shami's death in the name of jihad against the occupier and apostates was later used by Zarqawi to counter the criticism levelled by his former mentor and teacher. In a 2005 statement defending his tactics and broader strategy, Zarqawi argued that he was fully embracing the tenets of Salafi-jihadism—particularly those he had been unable to actualise in 1994 out of weakness—by enforcing principles of disavowal (*al-bara*) and the verdict of apostasy (*takfir*). The justifications he gave for targeting the Shi'a as a people (for their apostasy and 'innovations'—religious practices) and apostate Sunnis who rallied to the Iraqi government (itself partnered with infidel Americans) were straight from the writings and ideology of his mentor Maqdisi. As Nibras Kazimi wrote in 2005, 'Today, something new has emerged as the cutting-edge, hardcore version of jihad, and Zarqawi is its master. It is a sign that even the most radical notions of Salafi-Jihadism are entering new, uncharted ideological territory.'[5]

Kazimi wrote at the time that 'Zarqawism' was a new offshoot of Salafi-jihadism, and in some ways a more pure embrace of the principles of the ideology than Maqdisi's more pragmatic balancing act, which saw him tolerating and operating on the fringes of autocratic regimes that were prone to jailing him periodically. Rather than sourcing Zarqawism's ideas in Saudi Arabian Wahhabism or Qutbian thought, Kazimi instead points to Juhayman al-Utaybi—the Saudi rebel who seized the Grand Mosque in Mecca in 1979 and whose followers embraced the tenet of disavowal of 'anyone and any state that does not rule through the laws of sharia, or that introduces legal elements from beyond the realm of sharia in administering the public and private lives of Muslims'.[6] Certainly this impulsiveness, the celebration of brazen acts like Juhayman's occupation of the Grand Mosque, can be seen in the philosophy of the Islamic State today—particularly after the battles for Mosul and Marawi. 'Zarqawism', a distinct offshoot of Salafi-jihadism, seems to be the dominant element of the larger movement today, as demonstrated in the brutal administration of the caliphate (2014–17). What would otherwise be an insular discussion among a small group of experts became required knowledge for sizeable elements of the world's general population, after the Islamic State successfully exported its hardline ideology to would-be affiliates and indi-

[5] Kazimi, Nibras, 'A Virulent Ideology in Mutation: Zarqawi Upstages Maqdisi,' *Current Trends in Islamist Ideology*, Hudson Institute, 6 July 2005, p. 59. This article covers the split in excellent detail and quite accurately predicts the contagious effects of this full and literal embrace of Salafi-Jihadi doctrine.

[6] Ibid., p. 61.

vidual supporters who would go on to embrace and enact hundreds of terror attacks around the globe.

Zarqawi's first speech was similar in tone and content to his future efforts: strident, defiant, peppered with Quranic verses to support the Salafi-jihadi doctrine, and moralistic. Largely overcoming a substantial educational deficit in a community where religious knowledge is a requirement for effective leadership, Zarqawi's ability to repetitively and simply communicate the core tenets of Salafi-jihadism to Iraqis in the post-invasion period would help swell the movement from dozens to thousands of dedicated adherents.

1.2a. Untitled Speech, 4 January 2004
Abu Musab al-Zarqawi

The second text is an excerpt from Zarqawi's first public speech in a decade, this time as the amir of Jama'at Tawhid wal-Jihad (Monotheism and Struggle)— which was also the name of Zarqawi and Maqdisi's group in Jordan.[7] The group carried out large suicide truck bombings in the summer of 2003 that rocked the Iraqi landscape and stunned the American occupiers, but Zarqawi avoided claiming responsibility for the operations just yet. In the eulogy of Abu Anas al-Shami (d. 2004), then-amir of Anbar Province Abdullah Abu Azzam al-Iraqi admits that

> initially we were operating as a nameless group, and we were not keen on making the group, or its name public.[8] But Sheikh Abu Anas was seeing the rug pulled out from under the feet of the real mujahidin, and placed under the feet of those who had no connection to jihad [meaning nationalist and neo-Ba'athist groups]. So he

---

[7] This speech had no title and was found in an Islamic State-produced online collection of Zarqawi speeches (Arabic) in 2019 and translated for the authors by Anas Elallame, Middlebury Institute of International Studies, Monterey, California.

[8] Abu Azzam appears masked in the video. His real name was Abdallah Najim Abdallah Muhammad al-Juwari. A native Iraqi from Fallujah and early joiner of the group, he was the military commander of Anbar province and, along with Umar Hadid, led the fight in Fallujah. He later became the amir of Baghdad in 2005 and was blamed for a surge in violence before he was killed in a raid on his hideout. He was also responsible for running the group's growing financial enterprise. See U.S. Department of Defense, 'IED Kills Marine; Coalition, Iraqi Forces Kill al Qaeda Leader', Armed Forces Press Service, 27 Sept. 2005; Roggio, Bill, "The Demise of Abu Azzam', *FDD's Long War Journal*, 26 Sept. 2005, https://www.longwarjournal.org/archives/2005/09/the_demise_of_a_2.php

suggested that the sheikh announce the name of the group as Jama'at al-Tawhid wal-Jihad. The sheikh [Zarqawi] wanted to wait for a while, hoping that other qualified brothers might appear to whom the group could pledge allegiance, and under whose banner they could work. But Sheikh Abu Anas persevered until Allah opened the heart of Sheikh Abu Musab al-Zarqawi and an announcement was made [after consultation with the Shura Committee of the group].[9]

On 4 January 2004, the group released an audiotape of Zarqawi, the first recording of him as 'amir of the mujahidin *in Iraq'. In spite of Shami's words of encouragement, the tape did not mention the group's name, nor did it claim credit for its influential 2003 bombing campaign, for which everyone already assumed Zarqawi to be responsible. The group was buying time as it built a functioning media department which would help synchronize a careful influence campaign to rally Sunnis to their banners.*

[Zarqawi opens with the standard religious sayings and his own testament of faith, before beginning the task at hand: addressing the *umma* publically for the first time as the amir of a fighting group.]

'Allah will unite the divided parties when these parties think that they will never be joined.'

To the brothers who follow our path and share the same spirit of Islam, I address you today in the hope that Allah will unite us all to obey him and to adhere to jihad in his name.

I address you today as I wait for us to band together and restore that which our ancestors built.

[Poetry:] 'O brothers: my love for you is no longer a secret. How can it be a secret when my two eyes speak of this love? With the love of the Almighty Allah, I love you. I harbour for you a love that is shining on the sides of my heart. Each individual has a place in my heart. Even though the heart is small, it has space for everybody.'

I address you now at a time where there is a shortage of new recruits, and when many intrepid knights have passed in the name of our cause. Our wounds have multiplied and misfortune worsened. But we promise Allah, and we guarantee to you, that we will remain a constant threat to the oppressors—a sword ready to cut off the heads of the unjust, soldiers prepared to sacrifice anything to defend Islam until the word of Allah is victorious—or we will die doing so.

---

[9] Media Section of Jama'at al-Tawhid wal-Jihad, 'The Lion of al-Rafidayn, al Sheikh al-Mujahid Abu Anas al-Shami', video, posted on jihadi websites on 30 Nov. 2004.

I address you as a compassionate man and an admonisher. A sad man who is puzzled as to why some of you failed to join this caravan of jihad. Some of you have lagged behind, preferring to live a healthy life away from jihad, failing to mobilise as the crusaders come in unison to kill you. Where is the talk of old? The nightly chats, the daily wounds, and the sighs of those who yearn for jihad, paradise, and black-eyed maidens? Have your embraced your failure to carry out jihad?

Are you content with this sad situation?

His Greatness [The Almighty Allah] stated:

Have you not seen those who were told, "restrain your hands [from fighting], establish prayer and give *zakat* [alms]?" But then, when fighting was ordained for them, they grew to fear men as they fear Allah, perhaps even more. They said, "Our Lord, why have You decreed upon us fighting? If only You had postponed [it for] us a short time." Say [to them], "brief is the enjoyment of this world, and the Hereafter is better for him who fears Allah. And injustice will not be done to you, [even] as much as a thread [inside a date seed]." Wherever you may be, death will come for you, even if you should be hiding in lofty towers (4:77–78).

Now, America is clearly presenting itself to you in all its pride and haughtiness, challenging Allah and his Messenger. Are you coming to their [the ummah] defense, O you lions of Islam, knights of the battlefields, heroes of monotheism, and men of the creed?

His Greatness said, 'So fight [O Muhammad] for the cause of Allah. You are responsible for no one but yourself. Encourage the believers [to join you] and perhaps Allah will restrain the [military] might of the disbelievers. And Allah is greater in might and stronger in [exemplary] punishment.' (4:84). His Greatness also said, 'O Prophet, urge the believers to battle.' (8:65). Then He said:

O you, who have believed, shall I point you to a transaction that will save you from painful punishment? To believe in Allah and His Messenger and strive in the cause of Allah with your wealth and your lives—that is best for you, if you only knew. He will forgive you your sins and admit you to gardens beneath which flow rivers, and to pleasant dwellings in those gardens of eternity. That is the great achievement. And [you will obtain] another [blessing] that you love—victory from Allah and an imminent conquest. So give good tidings to the believers (61:10–13).

According to Ibn Maja:

Usama bin Zaid said: 'The Messenger of Allah (peace be upon him) said one day to his companions: "Who will strive sincerely for Paradise? For there is nothing like it. By the Lord of the Kaba, it is all sparkling light, sweet basil blowing in the breeze, a lofty palace, a flowing river, abundant ripe fruit, a beautiful wife, and many fine garments, in a palace of eternal abode, in ease and luxury, in beautiful, strongly built, lofty houses." They said: "We will strive hard for it, O Messenger of Allah." He said: "Say: In sha'Allah [if Allah wills]." Then he spoke of jihad, encouraging them to take part in it.'

Ali [ibn Abi Talib]—may Allah be pleased with him—cited Prophet Muhammad as saying 'Whoever encourages his brother to engage in jihad will receive the same reward as the person he helped. Each step will be equivalent to a year worshipping Allah.'

[Poetry:] 'O my people, the clouds of victory will not yield rain without an extremely generous and audacious generation. Take up arms and respond to the call, for there is no comfort in a life of misery. Mecca is the trunk and the Ansaris [supporters] the branches. The banner of monotheism still flutters and the edge of the sword is honed sharp.'

When we saw that the signs of jihad had disappeared, that its lights were no longer seen by mankind, and that its nights, once moonlit, had become dark, we grew pained and our livers ulcerated. The days of jihad have become dark, though once they were illuminated. Its branches, once leafy, have dried up. Its beauty, which was splendid, has diminished. Its doors have been closed and no one is knocking. The reasons for jihad have been ignored and left unheeded. Its horses have been standing with one foot slightly raised, but they are not running. Its lions are lying down, chests on the ground—they are not getting up. The servile infidels reached out their hands to hurt Muslims, but these hands were not [harshly] grasped [by any defenders of the Muslims]. The swords were returned to their scabbards instead of being turned against the enemies of the religion, prompted by a desire for a life of meekness and security. The general call to arms, though directed towards believers, was muted and the bride of the martyrs is almost a widow because nobody has asked for her hand in marriage. People have ignored jihad, as if they are not being called upon take part. People have either ignored jihad, or espoused their dislike for it, having become burdened with the ephemeral bliss of the worldly life, or renounced it out of fear. Some may have shunned it because they do not want to spend money on it or because they are greedy. Maybe they are ignorant of the generous rewards, or perhaps they prefer the worldly life to the afterlife. Nowadays, we only see those who are avoiding jihad, choosing to enjoy their short lives, fearing death, or because they are greedy and do not wish to donate to it. Some of the people are also avoiding jihad because they do not realise the greatness of the reward that

Allah will grant them. They are pleased with current life rather than being happy with the eternal afterlife. 'But what is the enjoyment of the worldly life compared to the Hereafter, except a [very] little' (9:38).

O brothers, you who share the same belief, what is your excuse? Are you a people of the right path? What is stopping you from jihad, O people of the truth? Is it that you may lose your families, children, and homes? His Greatness said, 'If your fathers, your sons, your brothers, your wives, your relatives, the wealth which you have obtained, the commerce wherein you fear decline, and the dwellings with which you are pleased are more beloved to you than Allah and His Messenger and jihad in His cause, then wait until Allah executes His command. Allah does not guide the defiantly disobedient' (9:24).

[Omitted: long section with excerpts from the Quran and hadith, all concerning jihad as a duty, and the benefits of heaven over hell.]

The martyr is spared these sufferings. The Messenger (peace be upon him) said, 'When slain, the martyr experiences no more pain than you feel when stung by an ant.' Why do you not adhere to jihad, dear brother? This is your chance to avoid the punishment of the grave and obtain Allah's blessing. The martyrs belong to heaven and they are happy with whatever Allah has given to them. You should choose wisely between the glory and benefits that come with dying a martyr and the suffering and pain that accompany a natural death.

His Greatness said:

> O you who believe, whoever of you should turn away from his religion—Allah will bring forth in your place a people who He will love and who will love Him in turn. A people who are humble towards the believers and resolute against the disbelievers; they strive in the name of Allah and do not fear reproach from any critic. That is the gift of Allah; He bestows it upon whom He wills. And Allah is all-encompassing and all-knowing (5:54).

These verses reveal to us something about those who ally themselves with the disbelievers and obey them. ...

... I warn you against failing to join the caravan of jihad. You should consider yourself, brother in faith, to be among those who love Allah and who He loves. If the caravan of jihad starts to move forward, those who have not committed will never be able to invest. Then, Allah will show us who is righteous and who is wrong.

Abu Hurairah asked, 'Can anyone fast throughout his whole life?' And the people replied, 'O Abu Hurairah, who do you think can do this?' Abu

Hurairah replied, 'by Allah, a *mujahid* obtains more rewards in his sleep than someone who fasts his whole life.' If this is the reward for a *mujahid* who is sleeping, can you imagine the recompense for an active *mujahid*?

By Allah, this is clearly a gift that Allah has bestowed upon his people and they must be ready for such a reward before it is too late. May those who are hesitant heed Allah's call.

[*Nashid* (musical lyrics) in the background]: 'America is here among us. So come, take revenge on it and slake your thirst with its blood. Come and defend the honour of Muslim women and reap this generous reward.'

O Allah, how many of our beloved have you taken beside you? Please, Allah, reward us as you rewarded them and have us join them [in paradise]. Even if I may sometimes forget, I will never forget about our brothers, the martyrs who were with us and who supported us during our ups and downs—most importantly my beloved and precious brother Abdel Hadi Daghles, who we called Abu Ubaydah, may Allah accept him as a martyr. By Allah, the loss of this brother is the greatest I have suffered since Allah guided me toward his path. This brother sacrificed everything and showed courage, will, patience, and ethical behaviour. For people like Abdel Hadi, we should mourn his loss ... we should mourn his loss.

When the *mujahidin* were routed by the incessant bombing, Abdel Hadi refused to retreat and committed himself to dying in the name of Allah, alongside a handful of the brothers. They engaged the enemy, and we ask Allah to accept them as martyrs.

[Poetry:] 'They died and their bodies were buried in earth. Bones decay, but victory is sweet smelling.'

By Allah, he was a lion, a worshiper, and someone who committed to the religion. You could see on his face that he was among the righteous ones. He could handle war and was unaffected by adversity. He was relentless against the enemies of Allah and merciful with his brothers.

May Allah gift you his mercy. By Allah, you were a true brother and a dear friend. You listened and advised me well. By Allah, your place with us is still empty and no one can replace you—losing you was like losing a part of myself. Even if I may sometimes forget, I will never forget the day you told me, 'I pray to Allah for your sake more than I pray for my parents.'

What an enormous loss—I lost you when I needed you the most. I ask his greatness Allah to accept you among his highest ranks and to have us join you as righteous martyrs alongside the prophets and the true believers. I ask him to accept you, and your brothers [slain with Daghlas], those that I did not have time to mention.

His Greatness said, 'And when Allah took a covenant from those who were given the Scripture, he said, "You must make it clear to the people and not conceal it." But they cast it behind their backs, exchanging it for a small price. And wretched is that which they purchased' (3:187).

You pledged to me that you would adhere to the word of Allah, his orders to prevent vice, promote virtue and jihad in the path of Allah, preserve sharia, and direct the utmost efforts towards following the path of His religion. Unfortunately, however, instead of heeding the call of Allah, you chose to relax in safety, to commit yourself to your people, money, and children. In doing so, you left the *mujahidin* to face the strongest power in the world, as it came with mercenaries to fight them.

[*Nashid* in the background]

Where are the scholars of our nation? How long will you stay quiet and avoid righteousness? Are corruption and personal gain still your method? When are you planning on coming back to your religion? The fact that the prophet said 'until you return to your original religion' is proof that to leave jihad, to refuse to commit to it in favour of enjoying life is heresy and a definite sin. Isn't time for you to wake up from your dreams? Isn't time for this dark cloud to leave? What *fitna* [infighting] are you talking about? What benefits are you talking about?

Can there be a greater *fitna*, O *ulama* [religious scholars] of the nation, than the one we already live in? The greatest *fitna* occurs as heresy and wrong-doing win out over righteous acts, as Allah's rule on earth diminishes, and as the lions of jihad are thrown in jail in Cuba [Guantanamo]. Some of you are now in your thirties, forties, fifties—or even older—and have not committed one day of jihad! You do not walk the path of Allah because you do not want to get your feet dirty. You spend your life seeking knowledge from a couch, pledging peace to Allah's enemies. You have not suffered even a day in jail in Allah's name.

By Allah, this is happening for one of two reasons: because Allah loves you and praises you more highly than his Messenger—who suffered all manner of pain—or because you are not following the path of the Prophet. Allah, let it not be the first one ... Allah, let it not be the first one. 'By Allah, no one can commit to what I have come to you with without being hurt' [hadith].

To whom did you leave this nation? To the *tawaghit* in the east and west who abuse it, allow for sons of the *mujahidin* to be slaughtered and killed, and confiscate the country's resources? Is this the way our righteous ancestors used to be? Where are the sacrifices, O *ulama* of the nation?

Now, our nation is living with disasters, setbacks, and [Muslim] countries that forbid the law of Allah. The *ulama* of our *umma* [Muslim community] removed the notion of sacrifice from their commitments and the duty of jihad has become irrelevant to them. They did not join the caravan of jihad. It is because they have forgotten that our nation will not stir unless the scholars sacrifice their blood. It is a natural process, left to the scholars by our prophetic heritage.

As for you, *ulama*—you who made peace with the *tawaghit* and surrendered the country and its people to the Jews and crusaders by supporting apostate rulers—it is because you decided to keep quiet about their crimes, acting like cowards instead of facing them. You failed to raise the flag of jihad and monotheism, assigned to you by Allah, when you crushed the youth's desire to defend Allah's religion and honour by prohibiting them from joining the battlefront. Now, these fronts are empty and only a few, guided by Allah, are among us.

Aren't you afraid of not supporting the *mujahidin*? You gave us up to our enemies when you betrayed us and refused to support us, O *ulama* of the nation. *Ulama* of the nation! You should know that one day we will face Allah, 'and every pregnant woman will abort her pregnancy' (22:2). 'On that Day a man will flee from his brother, from his mother and father, and from his wife and children. Each one of them, on that Day, worries about his own destiny' (80:34–36). On this difficult day, you should be prepared to meet Allah of all. He will ask what you gave to the nation, what you gave to the *mujahidin* and how you supported them, and he will ask about the enemies of Islam, how you opposed them and hated them. Was it with your sword, your teeth, your heart, or with your word?

Allah will ask you about those imprisoned in the jails of the Jews, the crusaders, and the apostates—those whom you could not liberate. Have you not heard what Abdel Rahman bin Umrah asked when the [Caliph] Umar bin Abdel Aziz sent him to rescue the Muslims in Constantinople? He asked Umar, 'O amir of the believers! What will we do if they refuse to exchange one of our people, who they have imprisoned, for one of theirs, imprisoned by us?' Umar replied: 'then offer to release more of their people in order to rescue ours.' So he asked, 'but what if they want one prisoner exchanged for four?' To this, Umar replied, 'give them whatever they want. By Allah, a Muslim man is more valuable to me than any imprisoned apostate. Whatever it takes to rescue a Muslim is a win—indeed, we are not rescuing only one person but saving Islam itself.'

Allah will ask you what did in Afghanistan and Iraq. Allah will ask you about Mullah Umar [the Taliban's leader in Afghanistan] and why you betrayed him, when he was only following the path of Allah and his Prophet and obeying them. He refused to exchange life for his religion.

[Imam] Ibn al-Jawzi (may Allah have mercy upon him) stood in the mosque and spoke, calling the people to jihad, the preservation of religion, and to expel infidels from Muslim lands.[10] People back then had fallen short of committing to Jihad, and he said,

> O people! Have you forgotten your religion? Abandoned your honour and failed to support the rule of Allah? You act as if honour is only for apostates, when Allah has given honour only to his Prophet and to the believers. How dare you! Doesn't it trouble or hurt you to see the enemies of Allah walking on your land, which was watered with the blood of your fathers? The enemy humiliates and enslaves you. You, who were once the masters of this earth [reference to the early caliphate]. Aren't you bothered or shaken to know that the enemy has trapped your brothers and is massacring them? Are you able to eat, drink, and enjoy life while your brothers go through hell in battles as we speak? O people! This is the time for war and jihad. The skies have opened their gates to the *mujahidin* and if you do not want to be among the knights in this war then allow your women to take part. O women! Join the battlefield and fight like men, ride the horses, and lead them by the reins or the bit. Do you know, O people, how these reins and bits were fashioned? They were made by women from their hair, as that is all they have. The time of love is over and now it is time for a holy war in the name of Allah. If you cannot ride the horses, then take them by the reins, as they are made of women's hair [*shu'ur*] and you—you should take them as you have no compassion [*shu'ur*].

Then, he then threw reins to the people and cried, 'hearts are broken like ashes in water. Men have lost their manhood.'

Indeed, by Allah, men have lost their manhood!

What do we say about why we lack support these days, when all the nations are against us. By Allah, we do not need men like Abu Bakr, Umar, Othman, Ali, Sa'd, Meqdad, Talha, or Zubayr [the Rashidun and other leaders]. We want men like Safiyyah [a woman]. Yes, like Safiyah, who defended Muslim honour when she stood against a cunning Jew who tried to enter and look upon Muslim women. O Allah help us, things have come to a head.

---

[10] Ibn al-Jawzi was a religious legal scholar in the twelfth century from the Hanbali school of jurisprudence, Baghdad, who was extensively studied by Ibn Taymiyah, a favorite scholar of Salafis.

O *ulama*, preachers, and youth of the nation: be mindful of Allah, and be aware of Allah. Make up for what you have already missed—bond yourselves to Allah through the sword.

Leave the enemies of sharia behind and, before you die, extend your support to your brothers with everything you have got and become a part of our history. Yes! Become a part of our heritage before the test of life is over and He chooses the winners and losers [judgment day].

When I address the *ulama* of the nation, I speak to those who fear Allah, not those who preach through their television and satellite channels, who are already sinful enough. When the graves complained to Allah about the rotten smell of the bodies of the infidels, Allah told them that the stench of wicked scholars is even worse, for they make their wages from religion.

And you! The *mujahidin*, the patient ones, despite every disaster we face and the hardships we suffer, by Allah, our enemies will only see in us everything they hate. We will commit jihad against them with all available means. We will sacrifice everything to fight them. To stand against the *tawaghit* in the name of Allah is one of the greatest deeds. Be patient for only a few days and Allah will bring reprieve, then victory. And if victory is delayed, it does not mean that Allah will not hold fast to his promise.

Be careful not to retreat or abandon this path. By Allah, its toughness, bitterness, and hardship will yield excellent rewards. To be chosen to bring victory to religion and commit to jihad in his path is a blessing.

Ibn Taymiyyah (may Allah have mercy upon his soul) said:

> He is blessed who is allowed to live until that time when Allah renews religion, revives the spirit of Islam, and improves the situation of believers and *mujahidin*, making them again like the early the *Ansar* [first supporters] and *Muhajirin* [first converts who migrated with Muhammad to Medina]. Believers should thank Allah for this trial, which is a truly generous gift, and for this call to arms, which is a great blessing. If members of the *Ansar* and *Muhajirin* like Abu Bakr, Umar, Uthman, and Ali, among others, were here now, the best thing they could do is engage in jihad. This opportunity would only be wasted by those with poor judgement, whose trade is losing. They will enjoy few benefits in this world or in the afterlife.

No amount of gratitude or anything else can stand in the place of this commitment. Extend your *dua* [prayers] to Allah and ask him to direct us towards this path.

[Omitted: poetry verses in which Zarqawi asks Allah for the honour of being a martyr in His cause]

O Allah, empower and strengthen the *mujahidin* and the monotheistic people in this land. O Allah, bolster their armies, send their battalions to battle, enhance their faith, and remind others to follow their example.

O Allah, make it easy for them to perform your good deeds and strengthen their will. Support them and bring them victory, for they are strong with your help, O Lord.

O Allah, America has brought its horses and knights to challenge you and your Prophet. O Allah, destroy them soon and swiftly, and end the kingdom of Bush as you did with Caesar.

O Allah, weaken their ranks and make their possessions *ghanima* [spoils] for the Muslims.

Oh Allah, damn the Arab and foreign *taghut*. By Allah, kill and destroy every one of the apostate rulers. Praise be to Allah.

Abu Musab al-Zarqawi.

1.2b. Analysis

Zarqawi's first speech as amir of Jama'at al-Tawhid wal-Jihad, released to the pubic in January 2004 after he had kept his presence in Iraq a secret for the better part of a year, has the sound of the leader whose group is foundering. It is hard to read it and not sense the bitter rejection that Zarqawi personally felt in the face of minimal enthusiasm for the jihad in Iraq, especially having survived the US invasion of Afghanistan, an airstrike in Kandahar that wounded him, a trip across Iran which saw many of his small group apprehended, and a near miss in another US bombing in Kurdistan. Despite a solid influx of foreign fighters into Iraq from neighbouring Syria, the Muslim *umma* had not embraced the jihad against the infidel invader and rallied to defend their fellow Muslims under occupation.

This speech was not the first message Zarqawi sent from Iraq, however. In May of 2003, he wrote a public letter to his tribe in Jordan and warned them to stop supporting the Jordanian regime that was assisting the US in Iraq and suppressing jihadi movements like his own. Zarqawi's organisation had already conducted operations in Jordan in 2002, and if not for the invasion of Iraq, this and other Levantine countries may have been his primary focus.[11] He revealed his intentions clearly when he told his Bani Hasan tribesmen: 'The truth is that our war today to establish an Islamic State is not only against the

---

[11] Fishman, Brian, *The Master Plan: ISIS, Al Qaeda, and the Jihadi Strategy for Final Victory*, New Haven: Yale University Press, 2016, p. 23.

leaders and rulers, but also their aides and accomplices such as the soldiers, police forces, and secret services, whom Allah described as "Owner of the Stakes" [powerful leaders with large followings].' He signed the letter, 'the amir of Jama'at al-Tawhid wal-Jihad, Iraq-Mesopotamia'.[12]

The message in Zarqawi's audio release almost a year later struck a very different tone, and is accurately described by Western analysts as a rebuke of Muslims who failed to join the fight in Iraq. The anger manifested in Zarqawi's speech stemmed from the group's frustration with a lack of progress against the occupation and the fledgling democratic government growing in Iraq. Abu Anas al-Shami, the chair of Zarqawi's sharia council, wrote in his diary that the group had struggled to accomplish anything in its first year of jihad and projected a gloomy outlook for the future.[13] Zarqawi submitted a report to al-Qaida leadership around the same time (see Chapter 2), appealing for acceptance into bin Laden's group and hinting at the possibility that the rebellion could end badly. In it, he acknowledged that the consequence of failure would be to 'pack our bags and search for another land, as is the sad, recurrent story in the arenas of jihad, because our enemy is growing stronger and his intelligence data are increasing day by day'.[14]

The bitter note in Zarqawi's rebuke of his fellow Muslims differs in tone from the message of the grandfather of global jihad, Abdallah Azzam, who he tried to mimic. The Palestinian Islamist famously argued that Muslims had a duty to protect other Muslims from attack, and helped inspire thousands of Muslim men to travel to Afghanistan as part of the jihad against the Soviets.[15] His most famous book went by the name *Join the Caravan*.[16]

---

[12] al-Zarqawi, Abu Musab, 'A Message to the Bani Hasan Clan; Oh People Answer the Call of Allah's Preacher,' 1 May 2003. This letter was found in an Islamic State-produced online collection of Zarqawi speeches (Arabic) in 2019 and translated for the authors by Anas Elallame, Middlebury Institute of International Studies, Monterey, California.

[13] Hallberg Tønnessen, Truls, 'The Islamic Amirate of Fallujah', ISA conference paper, Montreal, March 2011, p. 4.

[14] al-Zarqawi, Abu Musab, 'CPA English Translation of Terrorist Musab al-Zarqawi letter obtained by USG in Iraq,' US State Department Archive, Feb. 2004, https://2001–2009.state.gov/p/nea/rls/31694.htm

[15] Hegghammer, Thomas, 'Abdallah 'Azzam and Palestine', *Welt des Islams*, 53–3–4 (2013), pp. 353–387; Hegghammer, Thomas, *The Caravan: Abdallah Azzam and the Rise of Global Jihad* (Cambridge University Press, 2020)..

[16] Azzam, Abdullah, *Join the Caravan*, self published, 1987.

Zarqawi, who had been to Afghanistan twice himself, had ideas of replicating this flow of foreign fighters to his cause, but numbers were stagnating by the end of 2003. He even deliberately used the phrase 'join the caravan' in his opening paragraphs, while describing his sadness at the fact that the majority of Muslims preferred to save their own loves over joining jihad. His shaming tactics, asking for 'cowardly' men to replicate the example of Safiyyah, a woman, was something he would try again and again in the next few years. Zarqawi never lost his sense of outrage at being abandoned, but this did not necessarily hurt the movement. This same emotional investment in the cause is what made him essential as a charismatic leader and forged tight bonds between him and his close group of followers.[17]

This focus on emotional appeal might have been the impetus for including the eulogy of Zarqawi's close companion three quarters of the way into the speech. Certainly it reinforced his point that jihad was a duty and good men were dying in upholding its ideals. Abdel Hadi Daghlas was a Jordanian member of the network who left for Afghanistan with Zarqawi—his amir—upon his general amnesty, granted by the new king of Jordan in 1999.[18] The men went to Pakistan and quickly on to Afghanistan, where al-Qaida leaders, eager to recruit the group into their fold, sponsored them, providing money and vehicles. Setting up an Islamic commune in Herat in western Afghanistan, Daghlas served as Zarqawi's deputy and was in charge of the camp in his absence.[19] The Jordanian also served as the group's point person in establishing a foothold in the autonomous region of Kurdistan for future operations in the Levant after their idyllic existence in Herat was ended by the US invasion in 2001. He was killed in the early days of the Iraq War after the US military fired 40 missiles into the Ansar al-Islam compound in Iraqi Kurdistan where Daghlas was operating, a key part of Zarqawi's new network in the Levant.[20] Speaking about the death of his friend, a portent of things to come, might

[17] Ingram, Haroro and Craig Whiteside, 'Don't Kill the Caliph! The Islamic State and the Pitfalls of Leadership Decapitation', *War on the Rocks*, June 2, 2016 https://warontherocks.com/2016/06/dont-kill-the-caliph-the-islamic-state-and-the-pitfalls-of-leadership-decapitation/

[18] Warrick, Joby, *Black Flags: The Rise of ISIS*, New York: Anchor Books, 2016, pp. 43–45.

[19] al-'Adel, 'Jihadist Biography of the Slaughtering Leader Abu Musab al-Zarqawi', 2005.

[20] Fishman, *The Master Plan*, p. 8.

have made the speech especially difficult to deliver, with Zarqawi saying, 'what an enormous loss—I lost you when I needed you the most'. The impact such losses have on militant leaders might play a bigger role for those with skin in the game, as opposed to political leaders who can take a more appropriately detached and insulated perspective. In Zarqawi's case, it likely hardened his and his advisors' desire to do whatever was necessary to have a greater impact in post-invasion Iraq.

Including Daghlas' eulogy in Zarqawi's speech a year after his death served an important function for the organisation beyond facilitating a process of grieving—something we can see in texts as far back as the Iliad. It replicated a pattern of idealising martyrdom, a key tactic for the men who would successfully industrialise suicide bombing as a terror tactic.[21] The caravan of martyrs, a notion popularised by Azzam during the Afghanistan jihad, also inspired the creation of a numbered series published by Tawhid wal-Jihad's media department after 2004 called 'Biographies of the Eminent Martyrs', which continued uninterrupted until 2011.[22] Anas al-Shami's death later in 2004 merited its own video, complete with testimonies from the newly proclaimed al-Qaida in Iraq's most prominent members. Zarqawi's voice can be heard in the background of one section as a snippet from his first public speech plays, referencing *dawa*, jihad, and sacrifice— elements of a cycle that would repeat itself endlessly for the members of the group. Today, it is a rare video that does not have background audio of Zarqawi, Abu Umar al-Baghdadi, Abu Muhammad al-Adnani, or other famous leaders killed in the struggle to create an Islamic State.

Significantly, Zarqawi did not mention the name of his group in his first speech, nor did he claim the massive attacks from the previous summer, the effects of which still reverberated across the country. In particular, the attacks on Shi'a targets had stirred a long dormant sectarian dynamic that gained even more momentum in the weeks after the speech, when nine coordinated bomb-

---

[21] Hafez, Mohammad, *Suicide Bombers in Iraq: The Strategy and Ideology of Martyrdom*, Washington DC: USIP, 2007; and Bloom, Mia, *Dying to Kill: The Allure of Suicide Terror*, New York: Columbia University Press, 2007.

[22] Whiteside, 'Lighting the Path', 2016, p. 9. In fact, the Mujahidin Shura Council began a video series, continued under al-Furqan Media under the Islamic State, called 'Caravan of the Martyrs'. See https://news.siteintelgroup.com/Jihadist-News/the-caravan-of-martyrs-part-two-video-compilation-of-martyr-biographies-from-al-furqan-foundation-of-the-islamic-state-of-iraq.html

ings killed 178 Shi'a pilgrims in Karbala commemorating Ashura—the most important Shi'a celebration alongside Ramadan. Despite clues that pointed to Zarqawi, including the use of foreign suicide bombers and coordination and planning strategies that had become the group's trademark, the previous summer's attacks went unclaimed, as did many carried out between 2003 and 2007.[23] Zarqawi eventually came out into the open on 26 April 2004, when he announced the group's name in its first official statement (while the group had referred to itself internally as Tawhid wal-Jihad, it did not publicly do so until April) and claimed that it was responsible for the controversial August and September attacks on the United Nations and the Jordanian Embassy, and the bombing of the Imam Ali Mosque in Najaf that killed Ayatollah Muhammad Baqir al-Hakim and 84 others. This last attack, which had a personal connection as it was carried out by Zarqawi's father-in-law, was the most controversial as it targeted Iraqi Muslims at the Shrine of Imam Ali, one of Muhammad's companions and one of the Rashidun (first four rightly guided caliphs). Master bomb maker Abu Umar al-Kurdi, who belonged to the Salafi-jihadi group Ansar al-Islam before he defected, alongside many others, to Zarqawi's group, later confessed that this was among the countless bombs he made during this wave of terror.[24] The attack on a revered holy site earned Zarqawi the first rebuke of many from his prospective bosses in al-Qaida. However, this did not deter him from igniting the ever-smouldering coals of Sunni-Shi'a violence by destroying the golden dome of the revered al-Askari Mosque in Samarra in 2006.

Following this speech, Zarqawi, Shami, and other lieutenants like Umar Hadid, Abu Azzam, and Abu Muhammad al-Lubnani took a risk and focused their efforts on the creation of a mini-emirate in the city of Fallujah. This move, which resulted in the temporary, shared governance of the conservative city for about six months, was a boon to recruitment efforts across the country.[25]

[23] Burns, John F., and Jeffrey Gettleman, 'Blasts at Shiite Ceremonies in Iraq Kill More Than 140', *New York Times*, 2 Mar. 2004, https://www.nytimes.com/2004/03/02/international/middleeast/blasts-at-shiite-ceremonies-in-iraq-kill-more-than.html?_r=0

[24] Farrell, Stephen, 'Iraq Hangs Insurgent Who Killed Shiite Leader in Bombing of Shrine in 2003', *New York Times*, 7 July 2007, https://www.nytimes.com/2007/07/07/world/middleeast/07iraq.html

[25] For a better understanding of the importance of territory to the Islamic State, something that has been constant since 2004, read Burak Kadercan, 'Territorial logic of

The local momentum the group had built up was soon expanded to reach a global audience when, at around the same time, Zarqawi and many of these same lieutenants released footage of the beheading of an American captive— creating the movement's first viral video.[26] There was also an uptick in the inflow of foreign fighters after the First Battle of Fallujah, and this progress might have convinced al-Qaida that, despite its negatives, Zarqawi's group was the only element in Iraq that had earned the right to carry al-Qaida's banner.[27] Negotiations dragged on for the better part of 2004, until the jihadis in Pakistan agreed to accept Tawhid wal-Jihad as its Iraqi affiliate ahead of the Second Battle of Fallujah in October.[28]

---

the Islamic State: an interdisciplinary approach', *Territory, Politics, Governance* (2019). A shorter, ungated version can be found here: Kadercan, Burak, 'Defeat as Victory? How the Islamic State Will Rely on Hijrah to Claim a Win', *War on the Rocks*, 13 Oct. 2017, https://warontherocks.com/2017/10/defeat-as-victory-how-the-islamic-state-will-rely-on-hijrah-to-claim-a-win/

[26] Breslow, Jason, 'The Secret History of ISIS; Nada Bakos: How Zarqawi Went From 'Thug' To ISIS Founder,' *Frontline*, PBS, 17 May 2016, https://www.pbs.org/wgbh/frontline/article/nada-bakos-how-zarqawi-went-from-thug-to-isis-founder/. According to researcher Danielle Raineri, the men in the infamous video were all top lieutenants of the group except for one: Abu Usama al-Tunisi, Abu Muhammad al-Lubnani, Abu Anas al-Shami, Zarqawi (who was the murderer in the video), and Lubnani's driver Manaf al-Rawi, who later became the amir of Baghdad in 2009. See Twitter thread: https://twitter.com/DanieleRaineri/status/821315966663585793

[27] Tønnessen, 'The Islamic Amirate of Fallujah', pp. 5, 20.

[28] al-Zarqawi, Abu Musab, 'Pledge of Allegiance to al-Qa'idah and its amir, Sheikh Osama bin Laden', Tawhid wal-Jihad Media Section, online statement, 17 Oct. 2000.

2

ZARQAWI'S STRATEGY

It is far too simplistic to see the extraordinary violence perpetrated by Abu Musab al-Zarqawi's group as the inevitable product of bloodthirsty ideologues unleashed on a society in flux. There was a clear operational and strategic rationale for it. Within its ranks, Tawhid wal-Jihad had predatory, strategic thinkers who understood the importance of soberly assessing their own capabilities and those of their adversaries while identifying opportunities to be exploited and, at times, created through targeted and timely actions, all feeding into an overarching campaign plan. While this may seem obvious with hindsight, especially in light of events since 2013, there was ample evidence of this even in the movement's most nascent stages. The focus of this chapter is a letter written by Zarqawi to al-Qaida leaders and intercepted by coalition forces on 23 January 2004.

Zarqawi's letter reveals much, and not only about the logic that drove his bloody campaign in Iraq and the strategic principles that largely continue to inform the movement's manhaj *(methodology) to this day. It also reflects a strategic culture, especially amongst the Islamic State's leaders, that seems to encourage surprisingly critical and considered assessments of its theatre of operations through not only political, military, and informational lenses, but demographic, sociocultural and psychological ones too. The letter also hints at another side to Zarqawi that stands in stark contrast to that of the brutal, street-tough criminal turned brutal street-tough terrorist. While the letter's contents likely reflect the collective wisdom of his inner circle, it offers a glimpse into his mind as field commander and aspiring commander-in-chief. In less than two and a half years after writing this letter,*

Zarqawi would be dead, but not before he had risen to the forefront of the global jihadi milieu, turning Iraq into a sectarian killing field and laying the foundations for a movement that made ruthless brutality one of its trademarks.

2a. Abu Musab al-Zarqawi's Letter to al-Qaida Leadership
Captured by United States forces on 23 January 2004[1]

...Even if our bodies are far apart, the distance between our hearts is close.

Our solace is in the saying of the Imam Malik. I hope that both of us are well. I ask Allah the Most High, the Generous, [to have] this letter reach you clothed in the garments of health and savoring the winds of victory and triumph. Amen.

I send you an account that is appropriate to [your] position and that removes the veil and lifts the curtain from the good and bad [that are] hidden in the arena of Iraq.

As you know, God favored the [Islamic] nation with jihad on His behalf in the land of Mesopotamia. It is known to you that the arena here is not like the rest. It has positive elements not found in others, and it also has negative elements not found in others. Among the greatest positive elements of this arena is that it is jihad in the Arab heartland. It is a stone's throw from the lands of the two Holy Precincts and the al-Aqsa [Mosque]. We know from God's religion that the true, decisive battle between infidelity and Islam is in this land, i.e., in [Greater] Syria and its surroundings. Therefore, we must spare no effort and strive urgently to establish a foothold in this land. Perhaps God may cause something to happen thereafter. The current situation, o courageous shaykhs, makes it necessary for us to examine this matter deeply, starting from our true Law and the reality in which we live.

Here is the current situation as I, with my limited vision, see it. I ask God to forgive my prattle and lapses. I say, having sought help from God, that the Americans, as you know well, entered Iraq on a contractual basis and to create the State of Greater Israel from the Nile to the Euphrates and that

---

[1] al-Zarqawi, Abu Musab, 'February 2004 Coalition Provisional Authority English-translation of terrorist Musab al-Zarqawi letter obtained by United States Government in Iraq', *US Department of State Archive*, Jan. 2004, https://2001–2009.state.gov/p/nea/rls/31694.htm, last accessed 13 April 2019. Some sections of the translation have been excised. Texts in square and round brackets are from the original translation published by the US Department of Defense.

this Zionized American Administration believes that accelerating the creation of the State of [Greater] Israel will accelerate the emergence of the Messiah. It came to Iraq with all its people, pride, and haughtiness toward God and his Prophet. It thought that the matter would be somewhat easy. Even if there were to be difficulties, it would be easy. But it collided with a completely different reality. The operations of the brother mujahidin began from the first moment, which mixed things up somewhat. Then, the pace of operations quickened. This was in the Sunni Triangle, if this is the right name for it. This forced the Americans to conclude a deal with the Shi'a, the most evil of mankind. The deal was concluded on [the basis that] the Shi'a would get two-thirds of the booty for having stood in the ranks of the Crusaders against the mujahidin.

First: The Makeup [of Iraq]

In general, Iraq is a political mosaic, an ethnic mixture, and scattered confessional and sectarian disparities that only a strong central authority and an overpowering ruler have been able to lead, beginning with Ziyad Ibn Abihi [tr. note: seventh century CE] and ending with Saddam. The future faces difficult choices. It is a land of great hardships and difficulties for everyone, whether he is serious or not.

As for the details:

1. The Kurds

In their two Barzani and Talabani halves, these have given the bargain of their hands and the fruit of their hearts to the Americans. They have opened their land to the Jews and become their rear base and a Trojan horse for their plans ....

3 [sic]. The Shi'a

[They are] the insurmountable obstacle, the lurking snake, the crafty and malicious scorpion, the spying enemy, and the penetrating venom. We here are entering a battle on two levels. One, evident and open, is with an attacking enemy and patent infidelity. [Another is] a difficult, fierce battle with a crafty enemy who wears the garb of a friend, manifests agreement, and calls for comradeship, but harbors ill will and twists up peaks and crests (?). Theirs is the legacy of the Batini bands that traversed the history of Islam and left scars on its face that time cannot erase. The unhurried observer and inquiring onlooker will realize that Shi'ism is the looming danger and the true challenge ....

These [have been] a sect of treachery and betrayal throughout history and throughout the ages. It is a creed that aims to combat the Sunnis. When the repulsive Ba'thi regime fell, the slogan of the Shi'a was 'Revenge, revenge, from Tikrit to al-Anbar'. This shows the extent of their hidden rancor toward the Sunnis. However, their religious and political 'ulama' have been able to control the affairs of their sect, so as not to have the battle between them and the Sunnis become an open sectarian war, because they know that they will not succeed in this way. They know that, if a sectarian war was to take place, many in the [Islamic] nation would rise to defend the Sunnis in Iraq. Since their religion is one of dissimulation, they maliciously and cunningly proceeded another way. They began by taking control of the institutions of the state and their security, military, and economic branches. As you, may God preserve you, know, the basic components of any country are security and the economy. They are deeply embedded inside these institutions and branches. I give an example that brings the matter home: the Badr Brigade, which is the military wing of the Supreme Council of the Islamic Revolution, has shed its Shi'a garb and put on the garb of the police and army in its place. They have placed cadres in these institutions, and, in the name of preserving the homeland and the citizen, have begun to settle their scores with the Sunnis. The American army has begun to disappear from some cities, and its presence is rare. An Iraqi army has begun to take its place, and this is the real problem that we face, since our combat against the Americans is something easy. The enemy is apparent, his back is exposed, and he does not know the land or the current situation of the mujahidin because his intelligence information is weak. We know for certain that these Crusader forces will disappear tomorrow or the day after.

He who looks at the current situation [will] see the enemy's haste to constitute the army and the police, which have begun to carry out the missions assigned to them. This enemy, made up of the Shi'a filled out with Sunni agents, is the real danger that we face, for it is [made up of] our fellow countrymen, who know us inside and out. They are more cunning than their Crusader masters, and they have begun, as I have said, to try to take control of the security situation in Iraq. They have liquidated many Sunnis and many of their Ba'th Party enemies and others beholden to the Sunnis in an organized, studied way. They began by killing many mujahid brothers, passing to the liquidation of scientists, thinkers, doctors, engineers, and others. I believe, and God knows best, that the worst will not come to pass until most of the American army is in the rear lines and the secret Shi'i army and its military brigades are fighting as its proxy. They are infiltrating like snakes to reign over the army and police apparatus, which is the strike force and iron fist in our Third World, and to take complete control over the economy like their tutors the Jews. As the days pass, their hopes are growing that they will establish a Shi'i state stretching from Iran through Iraq, Syria, and Lebanon and ending in the Cardboard Kingdom of the Gulf. The Badr Brigade entered carrying the slogan of revenge against Tikrit and al-Anbar, but it shed its garb and then put on the emblem[s] of the army and police to oppress the Sunnis and kill the people of Islam in the name of law and order, all under cover of smooth talk ....

The Qur'an has told us that the machinations of the hypocrites, the deceit of the fifth column, and the cunning of those of our fellow countrymen whose tongues speak honeyed words but whose hearts are those of devils in the bodies of men—these are where the disease lies, these are the secret of our distress, these are the rat of the dike. 'They are the enemy. Beware of them.' Shaykh al-Islam Ibn Taymiyya spoke with truth and honesty when he said—after he mentioned their (Shi'a) thinking toward the people of Islam—'For this reason, with their malice and cunning, they help the infidels against the Muslim mass[es], and they are one of the greatest reasons for the eruption of Genghis Khan, the king of the infidels, into the lands of Islam, for the arrival of Hulagu in the country of Iraq, for the taking of Aleppo and the pillage of al-Salihiyya, and for other things ....'

2 [sic]. As regards the Sunnis

They are more wretched than orphans at the tables of the depraved. They have lost the[ir] leader and wandered in the desert of artlessness and negligence divided and fragmented, having lost the unifying head who gathered the scattered [pieces] and prevented the egg from shattering. They also are [various] kinds.

1. The Masses

These masses are the silent majority, absent even though present. 'The hooligans following everyone and his brother hungered. They did not seek enlightenment from the light of science and did not take refuge in a safe corner.' These, even if in general they hate the Americans, wish them to vanish and to have their black cloud dissolve. But, despite that, they look forward to a sunny tomorrow, a prosperous future, a carefree life, comfort, and favor. They look ahead to that day and are thus easy prey for cunning information [media] and political enticement whose hiss rings out. In any event, they are people of Iraq.

2. The Shaykhs and 'Ulama'

These are mostly Sufis doomed to perdition. Their part of religion is an anniversary in which they sing and dance to the chanting of a camel driver, with a fatty banquet at the end. In truth, these are narcotic opiate[s] and deceitful guides for an [Islamic] nation that is feeling its way on a pitch-black night. As for the spirit of jihad and the jurisprudence of martyrdom and disavowal of the infidel, they are innocent of all of that ....

3. The [Muslim] Brothers

As you have observed, they make a profession of trading in the blood of martyrs and build their counterfeit glory on the skulls of the faithful. They have debased the horse, put aside arms, said 'no jihad' and lied.

Their whole effort is to extend political control and seize the posts of Sunni representation in the government cake whose creation has been decided, while taking care in secret to get control of the mujahidin groups through financial support for two purposes. The first is for propaganda and media work abroad to attract money and sympathy, exactly as they did during the events in Syria, and the second is to control the situation and dissolve these groups when the party ends and the gifts are distributed. They are now intent on creating a Sunni shura body to speak in the name of the Sunnis. It is their habit to grab the stick in the middle and change as the political climate changes. Their religion is mercurial. They have no firm principles, and they do not start from enduring legal bases. God is the one from whom we have sought help.

D. [sic] The Mujahidin

These are the quintessence of the Sunnis and the good sap of this country. In general, they belong to the Sunni doctrine and naturally to the Salafi creed. The Salafis splintered only as the bend curved, and the people of the [distant] regions fell behind the caravan. In general, these mujahidin distinguish themselves by the following:

1 – Most of them have little expertise or experience, especially in organized collective work. Doubtlessly, they are the result of a repressive regime that

militarized the country, spread dismay, propagated fear and dread, and destroyed confidence among the people. For this reason, most of the groups are working in isolation, with no political horizon, farsightedness, or preparation to inherit the land. Yes, the idea has begun to ripen, and a light whisper has arisen to become noisy talk about the need to band together and unite under one banner. But matters are still in their initial stages. With God's praise, we are trying to ripen them quickly.

2 – Jihad here unfortunately [takes the form of] mines planted, rockets launched, and mortars shelling from afar. The Iraqi brothers still prefer safety and returning to the arms of their wives, where nothing frightens them. Sometimes the groups have boasted among themselves that not one of them has been killed or captured. We have told them in our many sessions with them that safety and victory are incompatible, that the tree of triumph and empowerment cannot grow tall and lofty without blood and defiance of death, that the [Islamic] nation cannot live without the aroma of martyrdom and the perfume of fragrant blood spilled on behalf of God, and that people cannot awaken from their stupor unless talk of martyrdom and martyrs fills their days and nights. The matter needs more patience and conviction. [Our] hope in God is great.

E [sic.] The Immigrant Mujahidin

Their numbers continue to be negligible as compared to the enormity of the expected battle. We know that the convoys of good are many, that the march of jihad continues, and that only confusion over the banner and a muffled reality keep many of them from [answering] the call to battle. What prevents us from [calling] a general alert is that the country has no mountains in which we can take refuge and no forests in whose thickets we can hide. Our backs are exposed and our movements compromised. Eyes are everywhere. The enemy is before us and the sea is behind us. Many an Iraqi will honor you as a guest and give you shelter as a peaceable brother. As for making his house into a base for launching [operations] and a place of movement and battle, this is rarer than red sulphur. For this reason, we have worn ourselves out on many occasions sheltering and protecting the brothers. This makes training the green newcomers like wearing bonds and shackles, even though, praise be to God and with relentless effort and insistent searching, we have taken possession of growing numbers of locations, praise be to God, to be base sites for brothers who are kindling [the fire of] war and drawing the people of the country into the furnace of battle so that a real war will break out, God willing.

Second: The Current Situation and the Future

There is no doubt that the Americans' losses are very heavy because they are deployed across a wide area and among the people and because it is easy to procure weapons, all of which makes them easy and mouth-watering targets for the believers. But America did not come to leave, and it will not leave no matter how numerous its wounds become and how much of its blood is spilled. It is looking to the near future, when it hopes to disappear into its bases secure and at ease and put the battlefields of Iraq into the hands of the foundling government with an army and police that will bring the behavior of Saddam and his myrmidons back to the people. There is no doubt that the space in which we can move has begun to shrink and that the grip around the throats of the mujahidin has begun to tighten. With the deployment of soldiers and police, the future has become frightening.

Third: So Where Are We?

Despite the paucity of supporters, the desertion of friends, and the toughness of the times, God the Exalted has honored us with good harm to the enemy. Praise be to God, in terms of surveillance, preparation, and planning, we have been the keys to all of the martyrdom operations that have taken place except those in the north. Praise be to God, I have completed 25 [operations] up to now, including among the Shiʻa and their symbolic figures, the Americans and their soldiers, the police and soldiers, and the coalition forces. God willing, more are to come. What has prevented us from going public is that we have been waiting until we have weight on the ground and finish preparing integrated structures capable of bearing the consequences of going public so that we appear in strength and do not suffer a reversal. We seek refuge in God. Praise be to God, we have made good strides and completed important stages. As the decisive moment approaches, we feel that [our] body has begun to spread in the security vacuum, gaining locations on the ground that will be the nucleus from which to launch and move out in a serious way, God willing.

Fourth: The Work Plan

After study and examination, we can narrow our enemy down to four groups.

1. The Americans

These, as you know, are the most cowardly of God's creatures. They are an easy quarry, praise be to God. We ask God to enable us to kill and capture them to sow panic among those behind them and to trade them for our detained shaykhs and brothers.

2. The Kurds

These are a lump [in the throat] and a thorn whose time to be clipped has yet to come. They are last on the list, even though we are making efforts to harm some of their symbolic figures, God willing.

3. Soldiers, Police, and Agents

These are the eyes, ears, and hands of the occupier, through which he sees, hears, and delivers violent blows. God willing, we are determined to target them strongly in the coming period before the situation is consolidated and they control arrest[s].

4. The Shi'a

These in our opinion are the key to change. I mean that targeting and hitting them in [their] religious, political, and military depth will provoke them to show the Sunnis their rabies and bare the teeth of the hidden rancor working in their breasts. If we succeed in dragging them into the arena of sectarian war, it will become possible to awaken the inattentive Sunnis as they feel imminent danger and annihilating death at the hands of these Sabeans. Despite their weakness and fragmentation, the Sunnis are the sharpest blades, the most determined, and the most loyal when they meet those Batinis (Shi'a), who are a people of treachery and cowardice. They are arrogant only with the weak and can attack only the broken-winged. Most of the Sunnis are aware of the danger of these people, watch their sides, and fear the consequences of empowering them. Were it not for the enfeebled Sufi shaykhs and [Muslim] Brothers, people would have told a different tale.

This matter, with the anticipated awaking of the slumberer and rousing of the sleeper, also includes neutralizing these [Shi'a] people and pulling out their teeth before the inevitable battle, along with the anticipated incitement of the wrath of the people against the Americans, who brought destruction and were the reason for this miasma. The people must beware of licking the honeycomb and enjoying some of the pleasures from which they were previously deprived, lest they surrender to meekness, stay on the[ir] land, prefer safety, and turn away from the rattle of swords and the neighing of horses.

5. The Work Mechanism

Our current situation, as I have previously told you, obliges us to deal with the matter with courage and clarity and to move quickly to do so because we consider that [unless we do so] there will be no result in which religion will appear. The solution that we see, and God the Exalted knows better, is for us to drag the Shi'a into the battle because this is the only way to prolong the fighting between us and the infidels. We say that we must drag them into battle for several reasons, which are:

1 – They, i.e., the Shi'a, have declared a secret war against the people of Islam. They are the proximate, dangerous enemy of the Sunnis, even if the Americans are also an archenemy. The danger from the Shi'a, however, is greater and their damage is worse and more destructive to the [Islamic] nation than the Americans, on whom you find a quasi-consensus about killing them as an assailing enemy.

2 – They have befriended and supported the Americans and stood in their ranks against the mujahidin. They have spared and are still sparing no effort to put an end to the jihad and the mujahidin.

3 – Our fighting against the Shi'a is the way to drag the [Islamic] nation into the battle. We speak here in some detail. We have said before that the Shi'a have put on the uniforms of the Iraqi army, police, and security [forces] and have raised the banner of preserving the homeland and the citizen. Under this banner, they have begun to liquidate the Sunnis under the pretext that they are saboteurs, remnants of the Ba'th, and terrorists spreading evil in the land. With strong media guidance from the Governing Council and the Americans, they have been able to come between the Sunni masses and the mujahidin. I give an example that brings the matter close to home in the area called the Sunni Triangle—if this is the right name for it. The army and police have begun to deploy in those areas and are growing stronger day by day. They have put chiefs [drawn] from among Sunni agents and the people of the land in charge. In other words, this army and police may be linked to the inhabitants of this area by kinship, blood, and honor. In truth, this area is the base from which we set out and to which we return. When the Americans disappear from these areas—and they have begun to do so—and these agents, who are linked by destiny to the people of the land, take their place, what will our situation be?

If we fight them (and we must fight them), we will confront one of two things. Either:

1 – We fight them, and this is difficult because of the gap that will emerge between us and the people of the land. How can we fight their cousins and their sons and under what pretext after the Americans, who hold the reins of power from their rear bases, pull back? The real sons of this land will decide the matter through experience. Democracy is coming, and there will be no excuse thereafter.

2 – We pack our bags and search for another land, as is the sad, recurrent story in the arenas of jihad, because our enemy is growing stronger and his intelligence data are increasing day by day. By the Lord of the Ka'ba, [this] is suffocation and then wearing down the roads. People follow the religion of their kings. Their hearts are with you and their swords are with Bani Umayya (the Umayyads), i.e., with power, victory, and security. God have mercy.

I come back and again say that the only solution is for us to strike the religious, military, and other cadres among the Shi'a with blow after blow until they bend to the Sunnis. Someone may say that, in this matter, we are being hasty and rash and leading the [Islamic] nation into a battle for which it is not ready, [a battle] that will be revolting and in which blood will be spilled. This is exactly what we want, since right and wrong no longer have any place in our current situation. The Shi'a have destroyed all those balances. God's religion is more precious than lives and souls. When the overwhelming majority stands in the ranks of truth, there has to be sacrifice for this religion. Let blood be spilled, and we will soothe and speed those who are good to their paradise. [As for] those who, unlike them, are evil, we will be delivered from them, since, by God, God's religion is more precious than anything and has priority over lives, wealth, and children ....

If you knew the fear [that exists] among the Sunnis and their masses, your eyes would cry over them in sadness. How many mosques have been converted into Husayniyyah (Shi'i mosques), how many houses have they demolished on the heads of their occupants, how many brothers have they killed and mutilated, and how many sisters have had their honor defiled at the hands of these depraved infidels? If we are able to strike them with one painful blow after another until they enter the battle, we will be able to [re]shuffle the cards. Then, no value or influence will remain to the Governing Council or even to the Americans, who will enter a second battle with the Shi'a. This is what we want, and, whether they like it or not, many Sunni areas will stand with the mujahidin. Then, the mujahidin will have assured themselves land from which to set forth in striking the Shi'a in their heartland, along with a clear media orientation and the creation of strategic depth and reach among the brothers outside [Iraq] and the mujahidin within.

1 – We are striving urgently and racing against time to create companies of mujahidin that will repair to secure places and strive to reconnoiter the country, hunting the enemy—Americans, police, and soldiers—on the roads and lanes. We are continuing to train and multiply them. As for the Shiʿa, we will hurt them, God willing, through martyrdom operations and car bombs.

2 – We have been striving for some time to observe the arena and sift those who work in it in search of those who are sincere and on the right path, so that we can cooperate with them for the good and coordinate some actions with them, so as to achieve solidarity and unity after testing and trying them. We hope that we have made good progress. Perhaps we will decide to go public soon, even if in a gradual way, so that we can come out into the open. We have been hiding for a long time. We are seriously preparing media material that will reveal the facts, call forth firm intentions, arouse determination, and be[come] an arena of jihad in which the pen and the sword complement each other.

3 – This will be accompanied by an effort that we hope will intensify to expose crippling doubts and explain the rules of shariʿa through tapes, printed materials, study, and courses of learning [meant] to expand awareness, anchor the doctrine of the unity of God, prepare the infrastructure, and meet [our] obligation.

5. [sic] The Timing for Implementation

It is our hope to accelerate the pace of work and that companies and battalions with expertise, experience, and endurance will be formed to await the zero hour when we will begin to appear in the open, gain control of the land at night, and extend it into daylight, the One and Conquering God willing. We hope that this matter, I mean the zero hour, will [come] four months or so before the promised government is formed. As you can see, we are racing against time. If we are able, as we hope, to turn the tables on them and thwart their plan, this will be good. If the other [scenario happens]—and we seek refuge in God—and the government extends its control over the country, we will have to pack our bags and break camp for another land in which we can resume carrying the banner or in which God will choose us as martyrs for his sake.

6. What About You?

You, gracious brothers, are the leaders, guides, and symbolic figures of jihad and battle. We do not see ourselves as fit to challenge you, and we have never striven to achieve glory for ourselves. All that we hope is that we will be the spearhead, the enabling vanguard, and the bridge on which the [Islamic] nation crosses over to the victory that is promised and the tomorrow to which we aspire. This is our vision, and we have explained it. This is our path, and we have made it clear. If you agree with us on it, if you adopt it as a program and road, and if you are convinced of the idea of fighting the sects of apostasy, we will be your readied soldiers, working under your banner, complying with your orders, and indeed swearing fealty to you publicly and in the news media, vexing the infidels and gladdening those who preach the oneness of God. On that day, the believers will rejoice in God's victory. If things appear otherwise to you, we are brothers, and the disagreement will not spoil [our] friendship. [This is] a cause [in which] we are cooperating for the good and supporting jihad. Awaiting your response, may God preserve you as keys to good and reserves for Islam and its people. Amen, amen.

Peace and the mercy and blessings of God be upon you.

2b. Analysis

The purpose of Zarqawi's letter is to provide al-Qaida's leadership with a strategic assessment of Iraq and its operational implications. It is upon this basis that Zarqawi presents the core principles of a campaign that fuses political, military, and informational activities that are calibrated to fuel a Sunni uprising as part of a Sunni-Shi'a-coalition war.[2] Zarqawi's project was fundamentally political in nature, with the use of violence being merely a means towards ultimately political ends. As highlighted in Chapter 1, the fundamental challenge he faced was how to mobilise Iraq's minority Sunni population and, in doing so, cultivate the friendly networks that were so crucial to establishing safe havens. From these, bases could be established, governance implemented, and gains consolidated. Tawhid wal-Jihad would play the role of vanguard in

[2] For more on Zarqawi and the impact of his leadership on the foundations of the Islamic State movement, see Brisard, Jean-Charles, *Zarqawi: The new face of Al-Qaeda*, New York: Other Press; McCants, Will, *The ISIS Apocalypse: The history, strategy, and doomsday vision of the Islamic State*, New York: Picador, 2015; Warrick, Joby, *Black Flags: The Rise of ISIS*, New York: Anchor Books, 2016.

Zarqawi's strategy, its actions and propaganda helping shape conditions conducive to winning the support of Iraq's Sunnis and, ultimately, mobilising them towards action. Zarqawi strategized that extreme violence partnered with sacrifice—irrefutable demonstrations of the vanguard's commitment to the cause—would be essential for polarising and mobilising all sides of the conflict in self-perpetuating cycles of violence. These themes are the focus of the following analysis.

Safety and Victory Are Incompatible

Despite opening his assessment with the acknowledgment that 'Iraq is a political mosaic, an ethnic mixture, and scattered confessional and sectarian disparities', Zarqawi focuses his strategy on two populations that he sees as crucial to the success of his campaign planning. The first is Iraq's Shi'a population, which he describes as 'the most evil of mankind' and 'the insurmountable obstacle, the lurking snake, the crafty and malicious scorpion, the spying enemy, and the penetrating venom'. Zarqawi devotes the longest passage in his letter—only some of which appears in the excerpt above—drawing out contemporary, historical, and jurisprudential arguments to justify the targeting of Iraq's Shi'a. From his perspective, in early-2004, Iraq's Shi'a wanted to avoid a sectarian war 'because they know that they will not succeed in this way' and instead sought to exert control over Iraq by 'maliciously and cunningly ... taking control of the institutions of the state and their security, military, and economic branches'. Dismissing American forces as 'the most cowardly of God's creatures' destined to 'disappear tomorrow or the day after', there are several reasons why the militant leader chose to cast Iraq's Shi'a as the greatest threat facing his movement. For one, as Iraqis, the Shi'a population had a better understanding of the operating environment's geographical, sociopolitical, and ethno-tribal nuances than any outsiders. Equally troubling to Zarqawi was the possibility that fighting Iraq's Shi'a, especially amidst the US and coalition forces' drawdown, would look increasingly like a war against fellow Iraqis. His solution was the use of extreme violence against the Shi'a in the hope that they would respond in kind, targeting the second essential demographic in his strategy: Iraq's Sunni population.

Zarqawi paints a picture of Iraq's Sunnis as a pitiful and misguided people, 'more wretched than orphans at the tables of the depraved', but with a great revolutionary potential that his strategy sought to unleash. Of his five types of Iraqi Sunnis, 'the Shaykhs and "Ulama"' ('narcotic opiate[s] and deceitful guides') and 'The [Muslim] Brothers' ('their religion is mercurial') were largely dismissed as, at best, inept, or at worst, obstacles to Sunni empowerment. The Sunni component of his strategy was instead focused on bringing together 'The Mujahidin' ('the good sap of this country') and 'The Immigrant Mujahidin' ('their numbers continue to be negligible') as the core of a vanguard to inspire and mobilise 'the [Sunni] masses' ('silent majority, absent even though present') while seeking to 'provoke them [Iraq's Shi'a] to show the Sunnis their rabies'. For this to work, Zarqawi assessed that Iraq's Sunni insurgents needed to not only be better organised and operationally coherent but more willing to engage in the types of high-risk/high-reward operations necessary to favourably transform strategic conditions. In one of the most powerful passages of the correspondence, he presents the case for extreme violence and sacrifice as potent pillars of his strategy:

> We have told them in our many sessions with them that safety and victory are incompatible, that the tree of triumph and empowerment cannot grow tall and lofty without blood and defiance of death, that the [Islamic] nation cannot live without the aroma of martyrdom and the perfume of fragrant blood spilled on behalf of God, and that people cannot awaken from their stupor unless talk of martyrdom and martyrs fills their days and nights.

Extreme violence was to be deployed as an instrument of destruction and provocation. In doing so, sacrifice would serve not only as a powerful rallying cry and propaganda tool but a means to maximise operational efficiencies and strategic impact. In the months and years that followed the 2004 letter, the trademark of Zarqawi's war on Iraq was an unprecedented wave of suicide operations. The use of human- or vehicle-borne improvised explosive devices meant that significant planning, time, or resources devoted to safely extracting operatives post-attack were unnecessary. That people were willing to sacrifice themselves for the sake of this cause made suicide operations the ultimate 'propaganda of the deed'; a powerful symbol of the campaign's *raison d'être*.[3]

---

[3] For detailed analyses of Zarqawi's tactics and operations circa. 2004–06, see al-Shishani, Murad, 'Al-Zarqawi's rise to power: Analyzing tactics and targets', *Terrorism Monitor* 3/22 (2005); Brock, Gary, *Zarqawi's sfumato: Operational art in irregular warfare*, research monograph prepared for the United States Army Command and General Staff College, Fort Leavenworth, 2013; Hafez, Mohammed, 'Suicide Terrorism in Iraq: A Preliminary Assessment of the Quantitative Data and Documentary Evidence', *Studies in Conflict and Terrorism* 29/6 (2006); and Palmer, Kate, 'Zarqawi's reign of terror', *Foreign Policy*, 8 June 2006.

The overarching purpose of Zarqawi's proposed strategy was to polarise Iraq along Sunni and Shi'a divides and mobilise both sides to engage in a self-perpetuating cycle of escalating violence. If the strategy worked, Iraq's Sunnis would be plunged into a dire predicament of stark choices; bear the brunt of Shi'a reprisals unprotected, seek protection from coalition forces who would likely 'disappear tomorrow or the day after', or seek protection from their fellow Sunnis. According to Zarqawi's calculations, such a dynamic would render his vanguard the only viable option for a Sunni population cornered amid a tripartite war:

> This is what we want, and, whether they like it or not, many Sunni areas will stand with the mujahidin. Then, the mujahidin will have assured themselves land from which to set forth in striking the Shi'a in their heartland, along with a clear media orientation and the creation of strategic depth and reach among the brothers outside [Iraq] and the mujahidin within.

By Zarqawi's reckoning, the time for restraint had passed and so a sense of extreme urgency is palpable in his letter. He clearly had deep concerns about the diminishing space and time afforded to his forces and the need for swift, targeted actions: 'As the decisive moment approaches, we feel that [our] body has begun to spread in the security vacuum, gaining locations on the ground that will be the nucleus from which to launch and move out in a serious way, God willing.' The support of local Sunni populations was essential for Zarqawi's strategy because, with 'no mountains in which we can take refuge and no forests in whose thickets we can hide', safe havens would have to be established in urban areas and, most importantly, Iraq's rural townships. It was here that Zarqawi's men could strengthen their relationships with the people, consolidate gains, and train foreign *mujahidin* to help swell the ranks.

Striving Urgently and Racing Against Time

The situation was no doubt precarious for Zarqawi but there were still opportunities ripe for exploitation, which, if taken in a timely and targeted manner, would help to create more opportunities. Zarqawi hints that his group was responsible for over two dozen operations, suggesting that his assessment of the risks and opportunities facing his nascent movement was informed by active engagement in the operating environment, not just his own musings. It also seems clear that Zarqawi was exercising restraint at this time, again indicating his appreciation for appropriately timing speech and action for maximum impact: 'What has prevented us from going public is that we have been waiting until we have weight on the ground and finish preparing integrated structures capable of bearing the consequence of going public so that we appear in strength and do not suffer a reversal.' Having operated largely underground in Iraq up to this point, he proposes a strategic pivot characterised by self-reinforcing lines of effort that include engaging in operations designed to violently destabilise enemies while building relationships with Iraq's Sunni communities via public outreach. Of course, propaganda is afforded a central role in this new campaign via a multi-medium endeavour to shape the perceptions of friends and foes in line with Zarqawi's vision.

With hindsight, the 2004 letter represents the end of one definable strategic period in the evolution of the Islamic State movement and the beginning of another. Its story prior to this point is that of a movement in its earliest formative phase. The small group surrounding Zarqawi that found its way to Afghanistan in the late 1990s and were reluctantly given a training facility by the figureheads of the transnational jihad, only to be forced to flee years later, were now seeking to impose themselves on what promised to be the land of jihad for the twenty-first century with the approval of those same senior figures. While Zarqawi's letter did not make it to bin Laden (at least not directly),[4] it soon became clear that a campaign eerily similar to the one Zarqawi proposed was being unleashed on Iraq. At the time, the letter was misinterpreted by some as a sign of poor morale and desperation, written by a man weary and blinded by sectarian hatred. Such commentaries reflected the biases and insecurities of the time. With hindsight—if one is willing to consider the xenophobic rants and ideological ravings largely as distractions (at least for understanding the strategic dynamics at play)—this letter sketches the portrait of a calculating, if predatory, pragmatist willing to critically weigh up risk and opportunity to turn precariously balanced strategic conditions to the advantage of his campaign. Zarqawi recognised the challenge before him as a competition for control and meaning, one that did not require perfection but the outcompeting of opponents on these two most vital of fronts.

Any questions regarding the extent to which this letter reflects Zarqawi's own thinking[5] versus that of his inner circle are largely secondary to these

---

[4] The letter was publicly released by the Coalition Provisional Authority in February 2004.

[5] A retrospective debate emerged questioning Zarqawi's role in shaping the movement's strategy, see Bunzel, Cole, 'Understating Zarqawi', *Jihadica*, 6 Dec. 2018; Hassan, Hassan, 'The true origins of ISIS', *Atlantic*, 30 Nov. 2018.

considerations: since its foundation, the Islamic State movement has had a culture of strategic thinking and a blueprint embedded deep into its DNA directing how its core strategic pillars should be operationalised.[6] Zarqawi was already a celebrity in the global jihadi milieu thanks, in part, to then Secretary of State Colin Powell's address to the UN a year earlier.[7] Zarqawi would position himself as the face of his group's propaganda campaign, and while this arguably propelled him to the forefront of the global jihad, it ultimately would cost him his life on 7 June 2006. In the months prior to his death, he arguably became more of a hindrance than an asset to the movement he founded. But his death cleared the stage for two highly capable leaders who would take the reins, focusing on internally rebuilding for the future and laying the foundations for what would become the most infamous militant group in recent times.

[6] This strategic culture being present in the nascent stages of the Islamic State movement is perhaps best evidenced by the production of a 'lessons learned' document by a commander in the aftermath of the Sunni Sahwa (awakening) in Iraq that almost decimated the organisation through 2006–07. For a detailed analysis of this document, see Fishman, Brian, *Dysfunction & Decline: Lessons learned from inside al-Qaʿida in Iraq*, West Point, NY: West Point's Combating Terrorism Center, 2009.

[7] Powell, Colin, 'Remarks to the United Nations Security Council,' *US Department of State Archive*, 5 Feb. 2003, https://2001–2009.state.gov/secretary/former/powell/remarks/2003/17300.htm

PART II

BAQIYA!

'Part II: *Baqiya*!' examines a seven-year period, beginning with Abu Umar al-Baghdadi's defence of the nascent proto-state in 2007 (Chapter 3), while Abu Hamza al-Muhajir's 2009 advice provides a leadership guide for commanders on how to transform the movement's doctrine into real-world action (Chapter 4). Next, a largely unknown strategy document, the Fallujah Memorandum, outlines the Islamic State's plans to reemerge in the aftermath of its near annihilation in Iraq (Chapter 5). The picture that emerges from Part II is of a movement that leveraged strategy, opportunism, and the missteps of its adversaries to make a seemingly impossible comeback from devastating defeats in the aftermath of the Sunni-dominated Sahwa uprising in Iraq.

3

THE FIRST YEAR OF THE ISLAMIC STATE

This chapter presents four public strategic communications from the newly formed Islamic State of Iraq, and a fifth from 2011 that echoes a memorable phrase from the fourth source—baqiya! (remaining)—which was used to rally supporters during the bust periods of the movement. The first source is a 2006 statement from official spokesperson Muharib al-Jubouri, announcing the formation of the Islamic State of Iraq, as read in a video released by the Mujahidin Shura Council's (MSC) media department before the movement's name and logo were changed to what we are familiar with today. The second source is the introductory speech of the Islamic State's newly elected leader Abu Umar al-Baghdadi (Hamid Dawud Muhammad Khalil al-Zawi). In it, he gives some of the only publicly available details about the transformation of the MSC—the political front that created the Islamic State of Iraq—into something more unified and coherent. The third source is an excerpt of a letter containing a critique of the previous two communications, written by Chief Sharia Judge of the Islamic State Abu Sulayman al-Utaybi in the spring of 2007 to al-Qaida leaders in Pakistan. Al-Qaida leaked the full contents of this and other communications in 2013 after the falling out with the Islamic State, in an attempt to retroactively delegitimise its original foundation. The following source is an excerpt from Abu Umar's fourth speech, commemorating the fourth anniversary of the jihad in Iraq since the US-led invasion. The speech defends the Islamic State's achievements and celebrates the setbacks of its opponents, and would have been unremarkable except for the ending. This speech contains his defiant mantra, responding to those pre-dicting the downfall of the 'state': 'The Islamic State is remaining (baqiya) ....' The fifth and final source is an excerpt from Islamic State spokesperson Abu Muhammad al-Adnani's inaugural speech in 2011, as he reflects back on Abu Umar's musings about the insurgency's resiliency during a period of renewed growth for the movement, and the fulfilment of his slogan of 'baqiya'.

3.1a. Statement and Video Message Announcing the Formation of 'The Alliance of al-Mutayyabin', 12 October 2006
Mujahidin Shura Council in Iraq[1]

[Opening scene: The logo of the MSC in Iraq is accompanied by text that reads, 'The Media Committee Presents the Announcement of the Hilf al-Mutayyabin (Alliance of the Scented Ones)'. The first scene depicts six masked figures dressed in white and kneeling in a circle, one of whom holds a piece of paper in his hand. The following statement is read by a blurred-out Muharib al-Jubouri, a professor of Islamic Studies who is soon to be revealed as the official spokesman of the new Islamic State in Iraq.[2]]

In the name of Allah, the Merciful, the Compassionate.

All praise be to Allah, who united the hearts of His faithful worshippers, and prayers and peace be upon the one who was sent as a mercy to all humankind and his honourable and blessed family and companions.

Allah, His Almighty, said: 'And cooperate in righteousness and piety, but do not cooperate in sin and aggression' [5:2]. His Almighty and Glorious also said in a *hadith qudsi*, 'O My servants, I have forbidden oppression for Myself

---

[1] The Alliance of al-Mutayyabin (the scented men) was formed during the Prophet's time and included the Prophet and a number of tribes. It was called al-Mutayyabin because they dipped their hands in a bowl of scented liquid to symbolize the sealing of their agreement. The audio version can be listened to on Aaron Zelin's Jihadology website: https://jihadology.net/2006/06/12/release-from-majlis-shura-al-mujahi-din-in-iraqs-shaykh-mu%E1%B8%A5arib-al-jaburi-announcing-%E1%B8%A5ilf-al-mu%E1%B9%ADayibin/, last accessed 18 December 2018. The audiotape was transcribed and translated for this chapter by Anas Elallame, Middlebury Institute for International Studies, in July 2019.

[2] The first spokesperson of the movement was Abu Maysara al-Iraqi (2004–6), and, after an interim, Muharib was appointed as his successor. A popular academic in Salafi circles, he gave some heft to the expansion of the group in 2006–7. See Craig Whiteside, 'Lighting the Path: the Evolution of the Islamic State Media Enterprise (2003–2016)', International Centre for Counter-Terrorism—The Hague 7, no. 11 (2016).

and have made it forbidden amongst you, so do not oppress one another.' And the imam of the *mujahidin*, Muhammad, prayers, and peace be upon him, said during the Farewell Pilgrimage, 'Verily your blood, your property, and your honour are as sacred and inviolable as the sanctity of this day of yours, in this month of yours and this town of yours' and, prayers and peace be upon him, he said: 'A Muslim is a brother of (another) Muslim, he neither wrongs him nor does hand him over to one who does him wrong. If anyone fulfills his brother's needs, Allah will fulfill his needs; if one relieves a Muslim of his troubles, Allah will relieve his troubles on the Day of Resurrection; and if anyone covers the faults of a Muslim [his sins], Allah will cover his faults on the Resurrection Day.' And as the honest and trusted [Muhammad] said: 'Injustice will appear as darkness on the Day of Resurrection.' Therefore, Majlis Shura al-Mujahidin [the Mujahidin Shura Council in Iraq, including AQI], Jaysh al-Fatihin [Army of the Conquerors], Jund al-Sahabah [Soldiers of the Companions], Katib Ansar al-Tawhid wal-Sunnah [The Supporters of Monotheism and Sunnah Brigades], many of the faithful tribal sheikhs, and others who will announce himself thereafter, decided to form an alliance named Hilf al-Mutayyabin, named so after the saying of the Messenger of Allah, prayers and peace be upon him, as mentioned in *Musnad Ahmad* and *al-Mustadrak*: 'I took part in the Hilf al-Mutayyabin with my uncles when I was a boy, and I would not renege on it for any price.' And in the *Mursal Hadith*, narrated by Talha bin 'Auf, 'If I were invited to it in Islam today, I would have answered.' Therefore, we call all the *mujahidin* factions, the scholars, the chiefs of the clans, and the notables to put their hands in the hands of their brothers from the Hilf al-Mutayyabin to establish the law of the Lord of all mankind, expel the occupiers, and support the servants of Allah—the oppressed ones. Allah is Great. Honour belongs to Allah, his messenger, and the believers; but the hypocrites know not.

And now, we dip our hands in the pleasant scent [at this point, the men dipped their hands into a bowl containing a yellowish oil] and we endorse the covenant of Allah by taking this oath:

> We swear by the Mighty Allah; We swear by the Mighty Allah; We swear by the Mighty Allah to work hard to free the prisoners, lift the injustice suffered by the Sunnis overpowered by the hateful rejectionists and the occupying crusaders, and to assist the oppressed, and restore his rights to him, even if it costs our lives; not to disappoint a Muslim who comes to us with a just cause, and to implement Allah's law on earth, and reinstate the religion to its glory. Prayers be upon the one who was sent as a mercy to all mankind, and upon all his family and companions.

[This oath was repeated back to the speaker (Jubouri) in sequence by the other men before the video ends.]

3.1b. Analysis

This mysterious announcement references the joining of insurgent groups and tribes, especially those belonging to the MSC—a political front that included al-Qaida in Iraq (AQI) and other smaller groups. The intent was to sublimate the prominence of al-Qaida and promote the joining of smaller Salafi-jihadi groups and the allegiance of tribal groups to a new Islamic State. Three days later, Jubouri, the 'official spokesperson', announced the establishment of the Islamic State of Iraq. Nibras Kazimi correctly noted at the time that the group was obviously laying out the groundwork for Zarqawi's ultimate political goal—the establishment of an Islamic state in the region.[3]

The choice of a pre-Islamic tribal ritual used to sanctify the merger of groups into the Islamic State is interesting, but likely reflected a growing fear that stemmed from the previous month's announcement of the Sahwa (awakening)—a tribal alliance dedicated to fighting al-Qaida—just one month earlier. The challenge presented by the tribal alliance and the death of founder Zarqawi accelerated plans to declare the Islamic State. The involvement of Jubouri in the video and his appointment as the spokesperson tells us a great deal about some of the hidden dynamics behind the politics of the formation of the new group.

Jubouri's predecessor was a young man named Abu Maysara al-Iraqi, who held the job for over two years. A Shi'a convert to Sunni Islam, he had been a religious student at the Faculty of Islamic Sciences in Saddam University of Baghdad and studied under Jubouri and Subhi al-Badri—considered the founder of the underground Salafi movement in Iraq.[4] Badri was a relative and

---

[3] Kazimi, Nibras, 'The Caliphate Attempted: Zarqawi's Ideological Heirs, Their Choice for a Caliph, and the Collapse of Their Self-Styled Islamic State of Iraq', *Current Trends in Islamist Ideology* 7 (2008), pp. 5–49. The 15 October 2006 announcement of the Islamic State of Iraq can be found on Aaron Zelin's Jihadology website: https://jihadology.net/2006/10/15/video-message-from-majlis-shura-al-mujahidin-in-iraqs-shaykh-mu%E1%B8%A5arib-al-jaburi-announcement-on-the-establishment-of-the-islamic-state-of-iraq/, last accessed 18 Dec. 2018.

[4] Malik, Abu Abdel, 'Biographies of the Eminent Martyrs, 46th Issue: Abu Maysara al-Iraqi', originally released by the Islamic State of Iraq (al-Furqan Media, 18 Aug. 2010),

teacher of Abu Bakr al-Baghdadi, who had worked for Muharib in the new Islamic State's media department as an adjunct.[5] Abu Maysara had served as Zarqawi's spokesperson since the very beginning, posting statements for the group online (including those in Chapter 1) and managing its outreach before he was killed in the spring of 2006 while serving as spokesperson for the MSC, the umbrella political front serving AQI and other groups. Abu Maysara, Abu Bakr, and Muharib came from the same network of Salafi religious students, and both Abu Maysara and Muharib's biographies recount that their subjects had been tortured by Saddam's intelligence services prior to 2003.[6] The US occupation wanted Jubouri for several high-profile kidnappings and the killing of several Westerners, but up until this announcement he had never been affiliated directly with Zarqawi's organisation. Within a year, the Islamic State's amir would be eulogising Jubouri as one of the founders of the 'state of Islam in Iraq'.[7]

The US military had a slightly jaundiced take on the Mujahidin Shura Council: '[The MSC] are a few guys and a dog and an Internet connection. Al Qaeda really drives the agenda.'[8] There is no doubt that al-Qaida militants were the driving force compared with the smaller allied groups involved in the MSC, but it is also obvious that it transitioned into a wider, more inclusive Iraqi organisation, a process that started with its founding in January 2006 and ended with the announcement of the Islamic State's formation in October of the same year. The Iraqis running the MSC were mostly AQI veterans who had been promoted to the board of the larger political front, like spokesperson Abu

---

translated and published by the Ansar al-Mujahidin English Forum; Barber, Matthew, 'Meet the Badris', *Syria Content* (blog), 13 March 2015, https://www.joshualandis.com/blog/meet-the-badris/

[5] Hashem, Ali, 'The Many Names of Abu Bakr al-Baghdadi', *Al-Monitor*, 23 March 2015.

[6] The Islamic State's press release announcing Jubouri's death described his past with the Salafi movement as one 'who fought vice since the mid-eighties until today'. Islamic State of Iraq, 'The Islamic State of Iraq Brings the Good Tidings to the Muslim Nation of the Martyrdom of its Official Spokesman', al-Fajr Media Center, 3 May 2007.

[7] al-Baghdadi, Abu Umar, 'For the Scum Disappears Like the Froth Cast Out', audio recording, al-Furqan Media, Islamic State of Iraq, distributed by the al-Fajr Media Center, 5 Dec. 2007.

[8] Murphy, Dan, 'Jill Carroll's captor claims to be insurgency chief', *Christian Science Monitor*, 21 Aug. 2006, https://www.csmonitor.com/2006/0821/p01s03-woiq.html

Maysara, and Abu Ali al-Anbari (using the pseudonym Abu Abdullah al-Rashid al-Baghdadi) as the political leader. When Anbari was captured in an April 2006 raid—part of the efforts to find Zarqawi—he was with senior MSC members, according to the subsequent interrogations. Following Zarqawi's death, a little known insurgent leader named Abu Bakr (then known as Abu Dua) joined the MSC and pledged to the new amir in October.[9]

The official US take on the announcement of the Islamic State in Iraq was that it was merely a ploy to shake perceptions that the group was a collection of outsiders killing Iraqis, and went so far as to claim that Abu Umar, the newly declared 'commander of the faithful' (*amir al-muminin*),[10] was a fictitious persona.[11] Despite killing Zarqawi earlier that year and kicking the man-hunting campaign of its much-vaunted special operations forces into high gear, the US never fully grasped the movement's evolution into an 'Islamic State'. It would continue to describe the group as 'al-Qaida in Iraq' until 2013, despite the fact that there wasn't a single pronouncement or letterhead that used that name after the 2006 announcement. There are a variety of reasons for this, but in the end, the reality of the group's political transformation never really took hold in US intelligence thinking.[12]

To review the cartoonish official Iraqi and US reports of Jubouri's death, in one three-day period (1–3 May), false reports circulated claiming that the dead man was Abu Hamza al-Muhajir (Zarqawi's Egyptian lieutenant), then Abu Umar, and finally that it was Jubouri, who had in fact been the secretive Abu Umar all along, who was killed. Clearly, with the benefit of hindsight, the only accurate report was the Islamic State of Iraq's own press release on 3 May 2007.[13] Some of this confusion came from this very video. Iraqi intelligence officers analysed the voice in the Hilf al-Mutayyabin announcement and identified it as Jubouri's, but then it seems they mistakenly assumed that meant he

---

[9] Atwan, Abdel Bari, 'A Portrait of Caliph Ibrahim,' *Cairo Review* (Fall 2015), https://www.thecairoreview.com/essays/a-portrait-of-caliph-ibrahim/

[10] Kazimi, 'Caliphate Attempted', 2008.

[11] Yates, Dean, 'Senior Qaeda figure in Iraq a myth: U.S. military,' Reuters, 18 July 2007, https://www.reuters.com/article/us-iraq-qaeda-idUSL1820065720070718.

[12] The US and Iraqi press conferences can be watched on the Associated Press archive: http://www.aparchive.com/metadata/youtube/134a4062860b1a4c4a22e6b7b6c1fdae

[13] Sanders, Edmund, and Tina Susman, 'Key Al Qaeda in Iraq figure slain in U.S. raid,' *Los Angeles Times*, 4 May 2007, https://www.latimes.com/archives/la-xpm-2007-may-04-fg-iraq4-story.html

was Abu Umar. The group's security measures were too effective for this to be the case, however, and it was another four years before Abu Umar and Muhajir were finally caught and killed.

In retrospect, taking the group at its word would have been helpful in understanding not just the evolution of AQI into the Islamic State, but also the resilience that would later help keep the organisation together after the beating it took at the hands of US 'surge' brigades, Iraqi security forces, tribal auxiliaries working for the government, and the rival resistance groups that rallied to the government in 2007. Despite its reputation as a group that did not play well with others, the Islamic State's consistent political project and its firm stance against both the occupation and the democratic government won over adherents from many other groups in the Salafi-jihadi milieu. Although al-Qaida veterans dominated the new Islamic State, many of its new 'cabinet' members were from other organisations and, like Jubouri, who ran his own independent group up until late 2006, they were Iraqis.[14] In fact, the majority had not initially embraced the early Tawhid wal-Jihad, but instead brought small groups to the Islamic State, came from Ansar al-Islam—the occasionally rudderless Salafi-jihadi group[15]—or were recruited in prison from mainstream Iraqi resistance groups like the Islamic Army in Iraq, Jaysh al-Mujahidin, and the 1920 Revolution Brigades.[16] Anbari (who, despite what his *kunya* suggests, was from Tal Afar) exemplified this as a Salafi adherent from the 1980s who left Ansar al-Islam in 2004 and joined Zarqawi, rising to the rank of MSC political leader before his capture in April 2006. He would return to the Islamic State movement after his amnesty in 2012 to continue his service as

---

[14] Another example of this was Abu Ali al-Anbari, who was an Iraqi Salafi.

[15] Hallberg Tønnessen, Truls, 'Heirs of Zarqawi or Saddam? The relationship between al-Qaida in Iraq and the Islamic State', *Perspectives on Terrorism* 9, no. 4, Special Issue on the Islamic State (August 2015), p. 50.

[16] One such prison convert was the infamous Haji Bakr (Samir Abd Muhammad al-Khlifawi), who, as Iraqi Senior Interior Secretary Adnan al-Asadi said on an Al-Arabiyah television show called 'Death Industry,' (1830 GMT 14 February 2014), was recruited in Camp Bucca by Ziyad al-Hadithi (Abu Zinah), an Iraqi close to Zarqawi lieutenant Abu Muhammad al-Lubnani. If accurate, this account dates his oath sometime between 2006 and 2008. Before this he was an insurgent in the nationalist and nominally Salafi-leaning Islamic Army in Iraq. The large elements of this group that allied with the Sahwa against the Islamic State might have been the impetus behind his defection.

the head of its religious and financial committees, and then serve as the highest military commander in Iraq and Syria.[17]

This trend of absorbing members from other Salafi groups accelerated after 2007, when many of these same groups splintered and partnered with the Sahwa movement, effectively reconciling with the government. This left Sunni resistance fighters who refused to accept an Iranian influenced, Shi'a dominated government with fewer and fewer places to turn. By 2010, the Islamic State was a true network of networks, which helped it compartmentalise and protect itself from the American man-hunt machine.

The next source is from Abu Umar, who the US military spokesperson called—as late as July 2007—the 'fictional' leader of an organisation that was in actuality led by foreign fighters (specifically the Egyptian Muhajir, also referred to as Abu Ayyub al-Masri). Once again, history proved this notion to be very wrong.[18]

3.2a. 'Truth has Arrived, and Falsehood Perished', 22 December 2006
Abu Umar al-Husayni al-Qurayshi al-Baghdadi, al-Furqan Media

The Islamic State of Iraq's media production unit al-Furqan Media posted a statement on jihadi websites that included the first speech of Abu Umar al-Husayni al-Qurayshi al-Baghdadi, the newly selected amir of the Islamic State of Iraq, on 22 December 2006. This translated excerpt is taken from a more recent online

---

[17] For the story of Abu Ali al-Anbari, see Whiteside, Craig, 'A Pedigree of Terror: The Myth of the Ba'athist Influence in the Islamic State Movement', *Perspectives on Terrorism* 11, no. 3 (2017). Hassan Hassan argued more recently that Abu Ali al-Anbari was the central individual influence on the evolution of the Islamic State in 'The True Origins of ISIS', *Atlantic*, 30 Nov. 2018.

[18] Brigadier General Kevin Bergner cited the prison interrogation of Khaled al-Mashadani, the Islamic State Media amir and a former member of Ansar al-Islam who defected to Zarqawi, as claiming 'the Islamic State of Iraq is a front organisation that masks the foreign influence and leadership within al-Qaida in Iraq, in an attempt to put an Iraqi face on the leadership.' Mashadani also claimed Abu Umar did not exist. See Yates, 'Senior Qaeda figure in Iraq a myth,' *Reuters*. The group was almost overwhelmingly Iraqi at the time, and this obvious deception worked, at least for a spell, as it was simply telling the Americans what they wanted to hear. In reality, Mashadani was a shura council member and most likely voted for Abu Umar al-Baghdadi to be the amir, as described in the next source.

Islamic State compendium of Abu Umar's speeches. The statement was titled 'Truth has Arrived, and Falsehood Perished,' derived from a verse in the Quran.[19]

O Muslim Umma [global community]; O my beloved Umma: Your men have resolved to establish a state for Islam, in which its shar'iah [system of law derived from the Quran] is enforced, in which its injunctions are enforced, and in which its soldiers assemble. That is why they offered their blood after sacrificing their money. Accordingly, they shunned each and every lust and endured each and every hardship, seeking death where they expect to find it and looking for either victory or martyrdom. Hence came the blessed step of laying down a strong foundation for the Islamic state in the Land of the Two Rivers, drawing on the example set by the master of prophets and messengers. And here is the edifice reaching greater heights, visible to friends and rancorous people alike. The blessed inception of this state prompted Bush, the enemy of God, to say: 'They seek to establish an Islamic state extending from China to Spain.' He was telling the truth even though he is a liar.

I thank God and praise Him for granting success to His soldiers in taking this blessed step. The initial move stemming from this step was the fact that more than thirteen factions and jihadist groups came together under one banner, following their good declaration manifested in the appearance of *Hilf al-Mutayyabin.*[20] Then, the good yield appeared quickly when dozens of brigades and thousands of brother fighters operating in the ranks of the Mujahidin Army, the Islamic Army, the 1920s Revolution, Ansar al-Sunnah, and other groups made their oaths of allegiance.[21] This happened in Fallujah, Karmah, Amiriyah, al-Ramadi, Gharbiyah, Tarmiyah, Siniyah, Tikrit,

---

[19] The title of the speech, like all of Abu Umar's speeches, comes from religious texts, in this case Sura verse 17:81. A complete version of the speech can be found on Kyle Orton's website for reference: https://kyleorton1991.wordpress.com/2018/03/18/the-announcement-of-the-islamic-state-in-2006/, last accessed 18 Dec. 2018.

[20] According to classical Islamic sources, *hilf al-mutayyabin* was an oath of allegiance taken in pre-Islamic times by several clans of the Quraysh tribe, in which they pledged to protect the oppressed and the wronged. The name 'oath of the scented ones' apparently derives from the fact that the participants sealed the oath by dipping their hands in perfume and then rubbed them over the Ka'ba. This practice was later adopted by the Prophet Muhammad and incorporated into Islam.

[21] An underappreciated factor in the growth of the Islamic State movement since 2003 has been its cannibalisation of other Islamist groups, particularly in stealing its leadership away.

Samarra, Ba'qubah, Uzaym, and then in Mosul, Kirkuk, Tal Afar, and beloved Baghdad.

The manifest prize and the great harvest took place when some 70 percent of Sunni tribal chieftains in the Land of the Two Rivers hastened to join *Hilf al-Mutayyabin* and bless the oaths of allegiance made to the state of Islam and Muslims. Hence, I thank and hold in high esteem my brothers the tribal chieftains of al-Dulaym, al-Jubur, al-Ubayd, Zawba, Qays, Azzah, Tayy, al-Janabi-yin, al-Lihyaliyin, al-Mashahidah, al-Dayniyah, Bani-Zayd, al-Mujamma, Bani-Shammar, I'nizah, al-Sumayda, al-Nu'aym, Khazraj, Bani-Luhayb, al-Bu-Hayyat, Bani-Hamdan, al-Sa'dun, al-Ghanim, al-Sa'idah, al-Ma'adid, al-Kara-bilah, al-Salman, and al-Kubaysat.

Based on what was said, it has become clear that those who said that we are not strong are liars. God's word is the higher word and the mujahidins' word is what is applied in several areas, as the enemy itself admits. It is said that the al-Qa'idah Organization [AQI] has controlled al-Anbar and has gained popularity.[22] Al-Qa'idah is but one of the groups of the Islamic state. We in Ninawa, Salah al-Din, and Diyala are in a better position than this. As for Baghdad, those who are far and near know that the state's sons are the God's soldiers who repelled and amputated the hands of the malicious Magus [Iranians literally, but likely a reference to Shi'a militias] a long time ago. What prevents us from fully taking over things there are reasons that this is not the right time to mention now, and God will eliminate these reasons with His might and will.[23] God knows that I repeatedly refused this thing—I mean the leadership of Muslims—because my dream had been only to be a soldier among the ordinary people to fight those who do not believe in God until God alone is worshipped. I have never been a leader of one of these groups, but the people agreed on us and thought that something good is expected from us.[24] I pray God to be better than what they think of me.

---

[22] This is almost surely a reference to a *New York Times* report of a leaked US military intelligence report that wrote off Anbar province as lost to 'al-Qaida'. It is also a defence against rival resistance group claims that 'al-Qaida' was trying to dominate the resistance despite being weaker than others.

[23] Quite possibly a reference to the Sahwa, or Awakening, in Baghdad, which upended the Islamic State's presence in the urban setting and likely forced them to flee to more rural and secure environments.

[24] Abu Umar was a high-ranking member of AQI, but was not the amir of the group when it was part of the MSC. He was chosen because he was high ranking (the chief

Therefore, I resolutely decided not to make a decision on anything before consultations with my brothers. For that purpose, we have formed an expanded shura council that includes three members of every group that joined the state of Islam regardless of the number of its soldiers and the size of its operations. The council will also include a representative of every main tribe, in addition to a number of those who have experience and specialization. A smaller shura council of five members was formed to decide on important issues that require quick decisions. We pray to God to lead us to the right path.

O Umma of Islam: We have been slaughtered by the knife of pan-Arabism, then have been divided by lancet of nationalism, and later we have been fragmented by the alleged tribalism, and feasts have been held for purposes that are against God.

O Muslim Umma: We do not need anyone today to shed tears or devise slogans. Today, we need sacrifices. We need those who would respond to God's order 'Go ye forth, whether equipped lightly or heavily.' We need those who would desert their beds and wives, shake off their cowardice and fearfulness, and embrace the course of jihad. We need those whose deeds are a reflection of their beliefs. Hence, we—as a first step—call upon a group of the former Iraqi Army who hold the ranks from first lieutenant to major, to join the army of the Islamic State, provided that those who like to join memorize at least three parts of the holy Koran and pass a test in Islamic faith put by the religious committee in each area so that they can prove their disavowal of the Ba'ath and its tyrant [Saddam]. We, in turn, will provide them with a car, residence, and a good salary that can secure them decent life just like the rest of the mujahidin who are fighting under the banner of the Islamic State of Iraq. God Almighty said: 'Those who believe fight in the cause of Allah, and those who reject Faith Fight in the cause of Evil—So fight ye against the friends of Satan. Feeble indeed is the cunning of Satan.'

3.2b. Analysis

Abu Umar's goal in his first speech was to communicate the breadth and diversity of the coalition that formed the new Islamic State. The tribal back-

---

of staff and former *wali* of Diyala province), an Iraqi (unlike many of the foreign fighters at the top like Abu Hamza al-Muhajir and Abu Usama al-Tunisi), and he belonged to a tribe that had Qurayshi lineage, which was Muhammad's tribe and something the Islamic State decided would be the criteria for the caliph in waiting. Abu Bakr has a similar lineage and background.

lash, or Sahwa, had publicly announced its formation at this point, but had yet to take hold in many places in a context solidly in the grasp of a brutal civil war between insurgent elements, government forces, and overseen by an exhausted occupation force. Of particular interest in this primary source is Abu Umar's description of the shura council, a deliberative body that determined policy for the new coalition. In addition to the growing tribal backlash, which most likely inspired Abu Umar's extended description of the alleged tribal support for the new political entity, rival Sunni insurgent groups—also named by Abu Umar as among ISI's supporters—were increasingly turning their weapons against the budding caliphate.

Questions about Abu Umar's identity still reverberate today, and it is possible to read entire books about the formation of 'ISIS' without finding so much as one paragraph on the leader that connected Zarqawi and Abu Bakr, its caliph from 2014–2019. According to his semi-official biography, written by a member of the movement, he was recruited by foreign fighters travelling through the Iraqi-Salafi networks, specifically Abu Muhammad al-Lubnani and Abu Anas al-Shami—two legendary lieutenants mentioned in previous chapters who served under Zarqawi. Abu Umar sheltered Zarqawi on several occasions in Haditha before joining Tawhid wal-Jihad, probably around the time of the battles of Fallujah. Up until this point, he had run his own small insurgent group in his hometown on the Euphrates River.[25]

Abu Umar was not a product of Saddam's infamous Faith Campaign, which pushed a conservative Islamist agenda, but had been a member of the underground Salafi movement since the 1980s, meaning he was in good company among the movers and shakers of the transitioning Islamic State in 2006. He had been fired as a police officer in 1993 for his outspoken Salafi viewpoint, which, in the conservative areas of Anbar Province, must have made his views quite extreme.[26] After the invasion, he changed his *kunya* (nom de guerre) each time he changed positions, which meant that few outside of the leader-

[25] al-Iraqi, Abu Usama, 'Stages in the Jihad of Amir al-Baghdadi', post on Global Jihad Network, 12 May 2012.

[26] An excellent analysis of the intent of Saddam's Faith Campaign, also based on primary source documents and the Ba'athist rivalry with Islamist competitors in Iraq (especially the Salafis) can be found here: Helfont, Samuel, *Compulsion in Religion: Saddam Hussein, Islam, and the Roots of Insurgencies in Iraq*, New York: Oxford University Press, 2018.

ship circle knew his true identity.[27] As with Anbari, who had many *kunyas* and kept his multiple identities in play until his death in 2016, the confusion about Abu Umar's identity contributed significantly to the United States' inclination to believe rumours that he was not a real person.[28] The Iraqi police chief in Haditha exposed Abu Umar's real identity—Hamid Dawud Mohamed Khalil al-Zawi—in 2008, two years after his selection as amir.[29]

After proving himself in Haditha and Baghdad in various security and sharia roles, he was selected to be the amir of Diyala, whose capital Baqubah was one of the jewels in the new al-Qaida franchise's crown. By late 2005 and early 2006, he was serving as the organisation's chief of staff, personally screening the selection of all senior members, and he was a voting member of the group's shura council.[30] It was from this position that the council voted him to be the amir of the newly proclaimed Islamic State of Iraq in October 2006, favouring him over Muhajir, an Egyptian veteran of al-Qaida and long-time Zarqawi deputy.[31]

The reasons for choosing an Iraqi over other members with more seniority have been discussed in the previous source analysis, but additional factors likely weighed in. The council picked an Iraqi with a claim to Qurayshi tribal affiliation—which imbued the leaders with a traditional legitimacy that the Islamic State decided to embrace, making it a requirement for its amirs or proto-caliphs.[32] One other interesting dynamic is that the different groups that joined with AQI to make up the MSC were equally represented on the shura council, meaning that it was mostly Iraqi. Abu Umar states in his first speech that he was humbled and surprised to be chosen, since he had never

---

[27] In Haditha, he was known as Abu Mahmud; in Baghdad, Abu Marwah, according to Abu Usama al-Iraqi; 'Stages in the Jihad of Amir al-Baghdadi.'

[28] Abu Ali might have had ten names, and was a complete mystery to his opponents who granted amnesty to him in 2012 without guessing his role as the leader of the MSC in 2006. See Hassan, 'The True Origins of ISIS', 2018; and Whiteside, 'The Myth of the Ba'ath Influence', 2016.

[29] CBS News, 'Report: True Identity of 'Islamic State of Iraq' Leader Revealed, Photos Aired', *Al Arabiya*, 7 May 2008.

[30] al-Iraqi, 'Stages in the Jihad of Amir al-Baghdadi'.

[31] For more on this, see Wing, Joel, 'Who Was Al Qaeda In Iraq's Abu Omar al-Bagh-dadi?' *Musings on Iraq* (blog), 13 June 2016, http://musingsoniraq.blogspot.com/2016/06/who-was-al-qaeda-in-iraqs-abu-omar-al.html

[32] For more on the importance of the Quresh tribal lineage, see Kazimi, 'Caliphate Attempted', 2008.

been one of the original leaders of these groups, and certainly not the ranking member of the clearly dominant faction (AQI)—like Muhajir. Nonetheless, Muhajir, who was made leader of the AQI 'faction' of the MSC after Zarqawi's death, quickly pledged allegiance to Abu Umar and they ran the organisation in close coordination and cooperation, one of them responsible for the political aspects of management (Abu Umar) and the other military (Abu Hamza). In fact, they were frequently mentioned in correspondences within and outside of the organisation as 'the two sheikhs.'[33] They were killed together in 2010, but not before building and sustaining the group that we know today.

The next source presents a critique of the new Islamic State by someone who was there and witnessed its creation as a newly arrived migrant and adherent: the Saudi Utaybi.

3.3a. Letter from Abu Sulayman al-Utaybi to al-Qaida leadership, April/May 2007

Abu Sulayman al-Utaybi was a Saudi religious student selected to be the first chief sharia judge of the Islamic State. He was selected by Muhajir, the Egyptian who replaced Zarqawi as the leader of al-Qaida in Iraq, most likely appointing a Saudi as their chief religious figure for propaganda purposes. This turned out to be a big mistake, as Utaybi and the Islamic State leadership were not a good fit. He was unceremoniously replaced late in the summer of 2007. This excerpt is from a letter written that spring, detailing his complaints to the al-Qaida leadership in Pakistan.[34] After his dismissal, he went to Pakistan and was killed in 2008 by a US drone strike.

[33] The tribal engagement official for Baghdad's Southern Belt was an Iraqi who referred to 'the sheikhs'. See Abu Khaldun, 'Synopsis of the Relations Committee in Baghdad's Southern Belt', CRRC document AQ PMPR-d-001–717 (2009). After the death of Abu Umar and Abu Hamza, the training camp in Anbar that hosted the training force that would conduct the raid on Haditha in 2012 was named 'Sheikhayn', or the two sheikhs, in their honour.

[34] al-Utaybi, Abu Sulayman, letter to al-Qaida leadership (dated April–May 2007), posted on Ana al-Muslim network, 24 Nov. 2013. This document was found in Arabic on Just Paste It and translated in July 2019 by Anas Elallame, Middlebury Institute for International Studies, Monterey, California. A discussion about this letter from the perspective of captured al-Qaida responses to Abu Umar and Abu Hamza in 2008 can be found in: Roggio, Bill, Daveed Gartenstein-Ross, and Tony Badran, 'Intercepted Letters from al-Qaeda Leaders Shed Light on State of Network

There is no good in brotherhood without truthfulness. I am not exaggerating if I say: al-Qaida is now the only faction, according to my limited knowledge, that was established based on honesty and advice, and it won't succeed otherwise. This is what drove me, by Allah, to join this group in the Land of Two Rivers [Iraq], which is victorious. Its leader used to be the champion of Islam, the patient Abu Musab al-Zarqawi, may Allah accept him as a martyr. Based on this principle, I am writing this message to carry on the advice that the *al-Salaf* [first generation of Muslims] of this nation gave to amirs, and so as not to discuss this problem [publicly] among the soldiers to avoid spreading *fitna* [discord]. It is to highlight the actual state of the jihad in the Land of the Two Rivers. While it used to be robust and almost reached *tamkin* [consolidation], it has become weak and regions are falling one after the other. Ramadi, for example, was the first city the brothers were able to capture and declare as an Emirate (I am not saying that we completely controlled the city, but at least the word of the *mujahidin* was the only one, no other flags were raised, and Sheikh Abu Musab stayed there for a few months before being killed). After the declaration of the State [Islamic State of Iraq in October 2006], the city became a haven for apostasy [referring to the Sahwa tribal forces], Allah forbid. It was encircled by about thirty checkpoints of the pagan guards [Iraqi Army] and the Americans. There is no power or strength save in Allah, I say may Allah bring harmony.

The main reason for this [failure] was the way in which the establishment of the State was declared. People believe that the establishment of the State [Islamic State of Iraq] was settled after groups within the Mujahidin Shura Council pledged allegiance to Tanzim al-Qaida and the allegiance of Hilf al-Mutayybin. This was absolutely not the case. It was only the heads of groups like Saraya al-Jihad, Saraya al-Ghuraba, Jaysh Ahl al-Sunnah, Kataeb al-Ahwal, and Jaysh al-Taefah al-Mansourah. These people are not related to true jihad. Some of them have never even carried a weapon, and some do not even have followers. These are just names who pledged a verbal or written allegiance on the condition that they would be given [high ranking] positions once the State was declared. This became reality, as these groups wished. And I swear by Almighty Allah, I witnessed this process as I was close to Abu Hamzah al-Muhajir.

in Iraq', *The Long War Journal*, Foundation for Defense of Democracies (FDD), 12 Sept. 2008, https://www.fdd.org/analysis/2008/09/12/intercepted-letters-from-al-qaeda-leaders-shed-light-on-state-of-network-in-iraq/, last accessed 18 Dec. 2018.

The deviation away from the [al-Qaida] *manhaj* [methodology] resulted in many severe methodological mistakes due to courtesies [inter-group politics]. It also led to numerous security breaches, as we lost many brothers who were killed or captured. It also resulted in the loss of the right way to work and the theft of people's money in the name of the State. I witnessed incidents similar to those carried out by a previous Amir of *Saraya al-jihad* alongside the current Vice Amir of the Faithful Abu Abdel-Rahman al-Fallahi. His group looted twenty-six trucks, with the value of each truck, except one, measuring two and a half *daftar* ['books', colloquial term with a book/ *daftar* equalling around US$10,000].[35] When I received a complaint from the owner of one these trucks, I called out this man [Fallahi, deputy to Abu Umar], and he apologetically told me that the money belonged to the rejectionists [he was saying it was Shi'a money and therefore *ghanima* (booty)], which was not the case. When it was proved that the money belonged to the people of Sunnah [a Sunni Iraqi], he told me: 'Yes, indeed it is money from a Sunni man who had a debt to the Islamic State.' When I asked him to count the amount of the debt, we found out that this debt was not even equal to the value of one truck, never mind the twenty-six vehicles looted. This man [Fallahi] told me: 'I took this money to enforce the order I received from Muhajir to take away any merchant's money going to Baghdad.' I then asked him [Abu Hamza] about this order, and he denied it, saying he never issued it. He told me, and I quote him: 'Sheikh Abu Sulayman, you are the general judge of the State. Do not get involved in a case until we refer it to you so that you don't lose your veneration.' I then understood that avoiding confrontation with this man was an example of the weakness [of the Islamic State's approach] brought about by these new allegiances to the group. The merchant is a well-known man who previously helped the brothers in Tanzim al-Qa'idah with smuggling explosive materials, devices, and remote detonators. His name is Abu____. Everybody knows him in Anbar [province], and he is known to be in debt because of this incident.

One of the reasons behind the deteriorating situation are the many mistakes, some of which are dangerous and, if left untreated, will lead to serious catastrophe. Among them are mistakes related to the methodology, for example, his [Abu Hamza, the military commander of the new Islamic State of Iraq] leniency with a clan that burned three brothers [Islamic State fighters]

---

[35] Hassan, Hassan, researcher at the Center for Global Policy assisted with the translation of the term *daftar*, August 2019.

because they assaulted a police station in Salah ad-Din [province, northwest of Baghdad]. The *wali* [Islamic State governor] of Salah ad-Din negotiated with them [the tribe], even though he could have simply exercised *hudud* [the rule of Allah] on them. We took the matter to Muhajir, and he backed his *wali's* decision to negotiate. Then I, the poor servant of Allah, the general judge of the State, went and discovered that the *wali* of Salah ad-Din agreed with this clan not to strike a police station unless they received approval from the clan. *In reality, it became so that the Islamic State was the one who pledged allegiance to the clan, not the opposite, as Muhajir claims* [sarcastic tone, emphasis added]. It is also worth mentioning that the main reason for all this is Muhajir's absence from the scene. He is satisfied with little more than the reports that are passed to him. The *walis* and the amirs of the Dawla do not send truthful reports—they only send the good news. Among these people are the *wali* of Salah ad-Din province Abu-Safa, whose [real] name is Najm ...

3.3b. Analysis

The Utaybi episode is insightful to outsiders because it has been one of the few glimpses we have had into the inner workings of the early Islamic State movement's leadership. This letter was utilised by al-Qaida six years later to delegitimise the original founding of the Islamic State of Iraq, although it had given it full support at the time, following the Islamic State and al-Qaida split in 2013. Utaybi was critical of almost all aspects of the group that he had left his schooling in Saudi Arabia to join, and this critique extended to the leadership,[36] its new flag (unknown at the time but infamous now), its strategy, and its involvement in taxing and extorting Sunni businesses for revenue.[37] In this

---

[36] Utaybi was highly critical of Abu Umar's leadership, and felt both Muhajir and his lieutenants were weak. He singled out Jubouri before his death for espousing a corrupt Salafi methodology counter to al Qa'ida, and he felt the new black flag was an innovation—the ultimate Salafi critique, meaning it wasn't something done in the days of the al-salaf al-salih (pious ancestors). In truth, the Islamic State has always hewn a careful balance between tradition and creating new methods to be an effective insurgency.

[37] According to a RAND analysis, 'The records show that AQI was a bureaucratic, hierarchical organisation that exercised tight financial control over its largely criminally derived revenue streams' (p. iii); Utaybi's naiveté on issues of insurgency funding is only exceeded by the level of his extremism in reaction to the tribal resistance to the Islamic State of Iraq. Bahney, Benjamin, Howard J. Shatz, Carroll Ganier,

short excerpt of the letter, Utaybi accuses the Islamic State amir in Salah ad-Din province of erring in its approach to tribal leaders who resisted Islamic State sovereignty over Sunni areas. This is an important issue in 2007, when the Sahwa movement had taken root in Anbar and was working with the Americans to destroy the provincial capital where the Islamic State had declared the Islamic Emirate of Ramadi.

Utaybi, who at one point had to be directed by Muhajir to stop playing the roving ombudsman and only adjudicate cases assigned to him as sharia judge, uses events in Salah ad-Din province as the most glaring example of leadership failure in the group—they were what prompted him to reach out to his superiors in Pakistan. The Saudi sharia judge's investigations revealed that the Islamic State's *wali* in Salah ad-Din had authorised a practice whereby the group warned tribes about upcoming attacks on government targets, in order to allow them to pull their tribesmen out of police stations ahead of time. This system had failed in the case under investigation, as the tribes retaliated and killed three Islamic State soldiers. The Salah ad-Din *wali* recommended negotiation with the tribes, and Utaybi felt this was an egregious ideological error. After all, the tribes lived in an area 'controlled' by the Islamic State, and they owed their fealty to the amir—not vice versa, as Utaybi caustically remarks in his letter. Worse, in his eyes, this kind of delegation of responsibility was a prime example of Abu Umar's poor leadership.

In the remainder of the letter, Utaybi describes how he took the matter into his own hands (as supreme judge) and burned three tribal fighters alive in retaliation, attaching a CD for proof. Clips from this footage somehow found their way onto the internet, without clearance by official Islamic State of Iraq media.[38] Certainly this was the cause for his subsequent dismissal in August 2007, and the leadership decided they had had enough of foreign ideologues and replaced him with an Iraqi, a choice they explained in a very brief statement.[39]

Renny McPherson, and Barbara Sude, 'An Economic Analysis of the Financial Records of al-Qa'ida in Iraq', *RAND Corporation*, 2010.

[38] Thanks to Fanar Haddad who verified this video existed in 2007 and watched it, and @Mr0rangetracker who made us aware of its existence.

[39] The statement reads: 'the Office of the Amir of the Believers, Abu-Umar al-Baghdadi (God render him victorious) has decided to dismiss Judge Abu Sulayman al-Utaybi and to replace him with al-Shaykh Abu-Is-Haq al-Juburi as the chief judge for the Islamic State of Iraq'; Ministry of Information, Islamic State of Iraq, 'Two Announcements from the Office of the Amir of the Believers', al-Fajr Media, 25 Aug. 2007.

Brian Fishman calls Utaybi the 'first defector,'[40] but in truth, he was the first extremist of the group (relatively speaking, of course), one they got rid of just in time. Conflict with the tribes was building to a head in 2007, as we shall see in the next source and subsequent chapter. Attitudes towards the Shi'a or occupying infidels are rarely a controversial issue within this group. How to deal with rebellious tribes and Sunnis that reject the authority of the Islamic State, however, is a much bigger problem and the source of endless debate and sometimes serious conflict within its upper echelons. As we have seen in more recent events, the matter of extremists in its ranks is something the Islamic State pays careful attention to, and occasionally struggles with, during periods of downturn and defeat.[41]

It is also important to note that despite Utaybi's high rank as the chief judge of the Islamic State, his letter penned to al-Qaida leaders in Pakistan over his superior's heads contradicts the publication of his own Ministry of Sharia Organizations, 'Informing the People About the Birth of the Islamic State'. Published in January 2007 and written by a team of writers from the ministry led by Uthman Bin Abd al-Rahman al-Tamimi (who was killed prior to its release by US soldiers), the 87-page pamphlet released online was a passionate defense of the need to establish an Islamic State.[42] According to Tamimi:

[40] Fishman, Brian, 'The First Defector: Abu Sulayman al-Utaybi, the Islamic State, and al-Qa'ida', *CTC Sentinel* 8, no. 10 (2015), pp. 24–26.

[41] For details on the current ideological splits, which don't sound very different to Utaybi's concerns that the Islamic State was too pragmatic in its dealings with dissenting tribes (ironic, to be sure, to use the term pragmatic), see Bunzel, Cole, 'Caliphate in Disarray: Theological Turmoil in the Islamic State', *Jihadica*, 3 Oct. 2017, http://www.jihadica.com/caliphate-in-disarray/; Bunzel, 'A House Divided: Origins and Persistence of the Islamic State's Ideological Divide', *Jihadica*, 5 June 2018, at http://www.jihadica.com/a-house-divided/; Hafez, Mohammad, 'Al-Qa'ida Losing Ground in Iraq', *CTC Sentinel* 1, no. 1 (Dec. 2007), https://ctc.usma.edu/al-qaida-losing-ground-in-iraq/; and Hafez, 'Fratricidal Jihadists: Why Islamist Keep Losing their Civil Wars', *Middle East Policy* 25, no. 2 (Summer 2018), pp. 86–99.

[42] al Tamimi, Uthman bin abd al-Rahman, 'Informing the People About the Birth of the Islamic State of Iraq', al-Furqan Media, Islamic State of Iraq, 7 Jan. 2007, posted online at *World News Network*. An excellent synopsis of this pamphlet can be found in Brian Fishman, 'Fourth Generation Governance—Sheikh Tamimi defends the Islamic State of Iraq', CTC West Point, 23 Mar. 2007, https://ctc.usma.edu/fourth-generation-governance-sheikh-tamimi-defends-the-islamic-state-of-iraq/, last accessed 6 Aug. 2019.

This work will explain the theory followed by the *mujahidin* in establishing the blessed state in accordance with sharia and the actual political context. It uncovers the reasons and needs that provided the suitable circumstances for the emergence of this project and the increase of its strength at this time, as well as the necessity of its adoption in accordance with sharia, political, and logical requirements. The work also discusses the ideas and the opposition that will confront the young Islamic state. It also aims at dispelling many of the doubts raised about the blessed Islamic state and the way it is established. The research project for the Islamic state is a search for the destiny of the *umma* and its future generations. The *umma* must learn its rules and connect them to reality. The topic of the Islamic state is not a theoretical luxury that ends with the conclusion of conferences and forums resulting in little. The research in our hands is chiefly practical research that benefits from the fruits of a contemporary jihadi experience, which has recently become apparent. Its conclusion is that it is a source of legitimacy for the Islamic state project announced by the Mujahidin Shura Council [and the Alliance of the Mutayyabin—referenced frequently in this document].

How could this massive disconnect exist between key figures in the same ministry? When it dismissed Utaybi, ISI did not go into any detail about why he was replaced, and it seems like the group's leadership decided his appointment had been an error of judgement and decided to quietly move on. Tamimi's work, which interestingly happens to contain parts of the Ibn Jawzi address quoted in Zarqawi's first speech as the amir of the movement (2004), also includes many talking points that Abu Umar used in the next primary source presented, celebrating the fourth anniversary of jihad in Iraq.

3.4a. 'The Harvest of the Years in the Land of the Monotheists', 17 April 2007
Abu Umar al-Husayni al-Qurayshi al-Baghdadi, al-Furqan Media

Al-Furqan Media posted a 42-minute audiotape of Abu Umar on jihadi websites on 17 April 2007. The recording was titled 'The Harvest of the Years in the Land of the Monotheists'.[43] *The speech by the group's relatively new amir celebrated four years since the beginning of jihad in Iraq, which had brought the movement all the opportunity it needed to try and achieve its political project—the establishment of a caliphate in the heart of the Arab world.*

[Standard religious opening comments omitted for brevity]

---

[43] The statement can be viewed online at Haverford's Global Terrorism Research Project: https://scholarship.tricolib.brynmawr.edu/bitstream/handle/10066/4432/AOB20070417.pdf, last accessed 18 Dec. 2018.

It has been four years since the start of this blessed jihad [referencing the invasion of Iraq in the spring of 2003], God willing. These were years of opulence and blessing, years of grace and paradise, and years of glory and pride. These years call for quick reflections on our situation in order to announce what we expect, with the help of God, in terms of dividends and losses. The dividends are for the Sunnis in Iraq, for the mujahidin, and for all Muslims. The losses are for the world infidelity with its three heads, the cross, the sickle, and the star.

First: What have the Sunnis gained out of the jihad of four years? It is a clear goal. Allah created heavens, the earth, and all people for this goal. 'I have only created Jinn and men, that they may serve Me.' So, what are the dividends on the side of monotheism, morals, and worship in general?

A. The issue of monotheism: It is the head of worship for the sake of which Allah sent messengers, revealed Books, and created Paradise and Hell. Praise be to God first and foremost for helping us to make the people of Iraq today among the greatest peoples on earth in terms of safeguarding monotheism. There is no propagation of polytheist Sufism, no mausoleums to be visited, no heretical days, no candles to be lit, or an idol to be worshipped. This is particularly true since the people of Iraq have destroyed these mausoleums with their own hands so that worship be only to God. Governance has also begun with the implementation of the law of God so that the legal origin, God's shari'ah, prevails instead of the lowly misshapen midgets; namely, the man-made constitutions of the infidel West.

B. The issue of morals and good manners: Jihad has brought back to the Land of the Two Rivers the memories of the early conquerors, Khalid and al-Muthanna, as well as the breezes of the Orthodox Caliphate, which has long shadows. So, go throughout the country to search for how many places are left calling for vice and corruption, and how many unveiled women remained of those who tempt youths and seduce middle-aged men, and of those who are grabbed with the teeth of wolves and look like a commodity in a slaves market. Search to see: Does your ear hear a dancing party that angers God in the highest seven heavens? Praise be to God, there is nothing of this kind.

C. The issue of worship and social life: We praise God for the people have returned to their God. It is an irreversible return, God willing. A few people used to go to mosques in the past. We only used to see old people in them. Today, however, the visitors of mosques are the youths, the hope of the future. We have seen a shepherd taking some of his sheep and giving it as alms to the mujahidin to distribute them in accordance with the shari'ah. This is out of a religious devotion and love. This is exactly what the farmers and merchants do. Before this and that, it is needless to say that the Sunnis in Iraq are the people of jihad and endurance. Jihad is the peak of religion and the top of the pyramid of worship. You cannot find a house without having one of its members was martyred to be an intercessor and witness to them on the Day of Judgment, waiting a prisoner in the enemies' prisons, or treating a person who was injured by the tyranny of the infidel occupier.

O our people in the Land of the Two Rivers, for a poor and impoverished person to go to Paradise is for God much better and loved than a tyrant, rich, haughty ruler who goes to Hell. So, what counts is the end result, whether one goes to Paradise or to Hell. We have promised you to sacrifice our pure blood before your blood, sacrifice ourselves before you, and send our sons to battle before your sons. 'If ye take a dislike to them it may be that ye dislike a thing, and Allah brings about through it a great deal of good.' Perhaps, bodies could become healthier through sickness. As al-Bukhari said: 'Ye are the best of peoples evolved for mankind. He said, the best of peoples are those who are good to people. You bring them with the iron chains around their necks until they embrace Islam.' Although we have not promised you with the fruits from heaven, but the very best of God is coming, God willing.

Second: What have the mujahidin gained in four years? The situation of the mujahidin has developed tangibly on the ideological, organizational, military, and political levels:

On the ideological level: In a record time, a large generation of the youth was trained on the forgotten ideology of loyalty (to Muslims) and disavowal (of non-Muslims). At a time when we used to read the books of history and biography and term Ibn-al-Jarrah's [one of the military commanders in early Islam] killing of his father as strange, and the waiting by Abdallah of a signal from the prophet to kill his father, Ubayy Ibn Abi Salul, we now see with our own eyes and hear with our own ears something very strange from the Land of the Two Rivers. This is despite suspicions and desires. Here is a father killing his spy son with his own hands, and here is a tribe disavowing its son, the policeman of [Prime Minister Nouri] al-Maliki. The strangest thing is that a woman has abandoned her husband because he reneged on the [Islamic] state, instead supporting al-Maliki and his party. The strangest of all these things, which Bush and those who planned for him his useless war did not expect, is that [people of] the Land of the Two Rivers are now competing, not in presenting flowers and expressing obedience, but in martyrdom in the cause of

God. Hundreds of people seek death to live in the presence of God. Why not, considering they are the people of generosity and courage, and generosity and courage are twin brothers? In fact, the women of Iraq shed tears demanding martyrdom operations. However, we save them from doing anything men can do, except under special circumstances that are difficult men. What a pity for anyone whose courage was less than that of women.

On the organizational level: It has greatly developed, in quality, quantity, and nature. The area of the land on which the mujahidin apply the law of God has also expanded. Unity among the mujahidin and the nation was bolstered. The nation began to go back to its normal status as a nation of jihad. Take as an example al-A'zamiyah, al-Fadhil, Haifa [Street in Baghdad], al-Miqdadiyah, Balad Ruz, Mosul, Tal Afar, and many other areas.

On the military level: One of their devils was right when he said: 'If Afghanistan was the school of terrorism, then Iraq is the university of terrorism.' Here we are announcing the graduation of the largest batch in the history of Iraq of the officers of jihad in the cause of God, and based on the highest international standards. Study is continuing without interruption, during summer and winter, and day and night. Praise be to God for granting us success. As with regard to equipment, you just name it. As for the field of electronics, the making of explosives, and the manufacturing of explosive charges, this [expertise] was admitted by the enemies. The world has seen the hunters of mine sweepers. Concerning aircraft, the worshipped idol was broken. It is that lethal weapon with which they have terrorized the world and toppled the state of the atheist Ba'ath. Yes, the mujahidin have downed a number of spy aircraft and helicopters. We carry good tidings to the nation that pleases its hearts and angers the enemies. In the field of weapons and equipment, we carry the good news to all the mujahidin all over the world in general and to the people of jihad in the Land of the Two Rivers in particular that the al-Quds 1 missile has now entered the stage of military industrialization and production. With its high specifications in terms of length, weight, range, and accuracy, it can compete with what was made by the world states for the same military targets. 'And those who strive in our cause, we will certainly guide them to our paths; for verily Allah is with those who do right.'

On the political level: Four years have passed without mentioning the mujahidin except by speaking ill of them. However, the world today waits for their surprises, statements, and the speeches of its leaders.[44] This is only as a result of the glory of jihad, and not the result of peaceful solutions, parliamen-

---

[44] This does not seem to have changed over a decade later.

tary meetings, or meetings with the rulers of Arab states. It is true to say that any people who abandon jihad will be humiliated. As for the sake of contrast, any people who adhere to jihad will triumph. Indeed, if the mujahidin today speak they will be heard, if they threaten they scare others, and if they achieve reconciliation they will be obeyed. This is the logic of politics at our time. The world only respects the strong.

Third: What has the Islamic world gained from the jihad of four years in the Land of the Two Rivers? They have gained materially and morally. If our war was a moral war, then we would be satisfied with the fact that the alleged US giant has collapsed under the strikes of the mujahidin during day and night. The fear from the US Marines and technology has disappeared from the hearts of all peoples of the world. The veil of what they call the deceptive Western civilization has also fallen. The hostility to all the institutions of the evil world order was consolidated in the hearts of the nation's sons, particularly to the so-called United Nations, which is united only on basis of injustice and aggression. All this was achieved thanks to God and then to the mujahidin. As on the material level, the Iraqi jihad has restored vigor to jihadi areas where there was a lull for some time after they were active. It has also paved the way for invading the Jewish state and the restoration of Jerusalem. This is like seeing Iraqi groups leave here to search for al-Mahdi who is near the curtains of the Kaaba. Vigor was restored and the number of mujahidin has doubled many times. Their number has reached many thousands after they were a small group shortly after the fall of the state of the infidel Ba'ath.

[A long description of the travails of the adversaries of the Islamic State is omitted here for the purpose of brevity.]

Let everyone know that our aim is clear: the establishment of God's law and the path to that is jihad in its wider sense. That is not achieved as it should be, except through the community. We know its requirements. Consequently I address calls:

The first such call is to all Muslims throughout the world. The Prophet said: 'Any person who lets down a Muslim in a matter in which his honor is disparaged and his sanctities are violated is bound to be let down by Almighty God in a matter in which he wants to be supported. Any person who comes to the support of a Muslim in a matter in which his honor is disparaged and his sanctities are violated is bound to be supported by God in a matter in which he likes to be supported.' The Muslim is the brother of the Muslim, and they are united by brotherhood in faith. 'Believers are brothers.' However many the homelands may be, Muslims are equal in the inviolability of their blood; the lowest among them enjoys their protection, and they are united against others.

The second call: O Sunnis in Iraq in particular, know that the mighty oppressor of the age, America—and its allies—have known your strength and intrepidity, and they have sought to win you over so that you leave your mujahidin brothers, or at least to neutralize you. Had it not been for the mujahidin, the descendants of Ibn-al-Alqami [reference to a Shi'a vizier blamed for betraying the last Abbasid Caliph] would have tortured you. You are not unaware of what they are doing in their prisons.

The third call is addressed to the tribal shaykhs in particular: Know—may God set me and you on the right path—that every one of you is a shepherd, and all of you are responsible for their herd. Let each one of you consider what key he is: There are people who are keys that let in what is good and ward off what is bad, and there are people that ward off what is good and let in what is bad. Blessed are those who God has made keys to what is good, and woe to those who God has made keys to what is evil. Take the same stand as that taken by the Prophet's Companion, Urwah al-Thaqafi: When the Prophet Muhammad died, the Thaqif wanted to renounce Islam, and Urwah Bin-Mas'ud al-Thaqafi said to them: 'O Thaqif, you were the last to converts to Islam, do not be the first to become apostates.' They refrained from becoming apostates and he was a good leader for them. 'Be a man, so that those who come after him will say: He has passed and that is the trace.'

My brothers, know that reneging on the pledge that is between us is a big sin. God says: 'Those who break their covenant with God after it has been confirmed, who sever the bonds that God has commanded to be joined, who spread corruption on the earth—there is the curse and their is the ill abode.' Brothers, do not follow those occupiers and their criminal lackeys, for it is better to die than to follow any of them. Let not the seeking of a living or the harvesting of crops make you disobey God, for attaining what God has to give is achieved only by obeying Him. What is destined to be attained is bound to be attained. Eat in dignity, not in humiliation.

I say to you and to Muslims in general what Abu Bakr al-Siddiq said: 'Obey me as long as I obey God in running your affairs. If I disobey Him you do not owe me any obedience.'

The fourth call is to those among our sons and clans who stood with the occupier and his collaborators: Know that the Prophet Muhammad said: 'A band of my nation will be fighting in the cause of God, repulsing their enemy, undaunted by those who disagree with them, until Judgment Day.'

Do you, O worshippers of God, know who are the worst of people? Among the worst people are those who lost their hereafter for the sake of another person's temporal world. Let no enemy make you against your religion, by finding an excuse for every sin, and seizing on a fatwa to justify every offense. What is permissible is clear, and what is wrong is clear. 'We patch our temporal world by tearing up our religion, and the result is that we lose both our religion and our temporal world. Blessed is he who has preferred to obey God and gave his life in return for what he expects.' You still have the chance, O you who rebel against God's law and against His mujahidin worshippers and pious men, those who defend your honor, homeland, property, and above all your religion.

O worshippers of God, it is not we who have violated the honor of your mothers, sisters, and daughters in Abu Ghurayb and voluntarily broadcast that on television in order to humiliate you. We are not the ones who raped the free and chaste Abir al-Janabi and set her corpse on fire.[45] We are not those who raped Sabrin in broad daylight.[46] The culprits are the ones that you, who stand with the regime and the occupiers, are with.

On the contrary, some days after that we arrested 39 apostates among those people, and we killed them to avenge your honor, and we launched a campaign to avenge our honor as well, a campaign that is continuing to this day until God decides their fate.

God has pointed to the cause of our weakness when He said: 'and do not quarrel with one another, or you may lose heart and your spirit may desert you.' The Prophet—according to Abi Dawud and al-Tirmidhi—has prohibited us from setting animals against each other, but is not the setting of human beings against each other worse, and the setting of Muslims against each other worse, and the setting of mujahidin against each other even worse?

I remind you of the stance of Mu'awiyah Bin Abi-Sufyan. It is said that Heraclius offered him assistance when he heard of his disagreement with Ali, the latter answered him in words that can be written in gold: 'Dog, if you

[45] This reference is to the rape and murder of Abir al-Janabi in Mahmudiya in 2006, a war crime perpetrated by American soldiers and described in the book *Black Hearts: One Platoon's Descent into Madness in the Triangle of Death* by Jim Fredrick. See Dao, James, 'Soldier Gets Life Sentence for Iraq Murders', *New York Times*, 21 May 2009.

[46] Almost one year later, Sabrin al-Janabi (a Sunni from west Baghdad) accused three Shi'a policemen of raping her, starting a sectarian row in the parliament and across the nation. The Islamic State and other Sunni insurgent groups used the case to rally Sunnis to their cause. See Daragahi, Borzou, and Ruaa Al-Zarary, 'New rape allegation adds to Iraqi uproar', *Los Angeles Times*, 23 Feb. 2007.

advance one inch, you will see me a soldier under Ali's banner.' Hold on to the community, for what you hate in being in a community and in obedience is better than what you like in division, as Ibn Mas'ud said.

O brothers in the Ansar al-Sunnah Army and in the Mujahidin Army: The friendship between us is deep. The bonds of faith and love are too great and strong to be harmed. O my sons in the Islamic Army, know that I am prepared to shed my blood to spare yours, and offer my honor to protect yours. By God, you will hear from us only what is good, and you will see from us only what is good. Rest assured, for what is between us is stronger than what some people think, may God forgive them.

O soldiers of the 1920 Revolution: Yes, the devil has resorted to sowing discord and incitement between us and you, the devil of the Islamic Party [Muslim Brotherhood in Iraq] and its henchmen. However, the reasonable among your battalions have averted deterioration in the situation and have sat down with their brothers in the State of Islam, in order to diffuse the sedition and to sow the seeds of amity. We pin our hopes on them, God willing. We owe it to God to protect your blood and the blood of every Muslim who has not committed an act of open idolatry or shed blood when he is forbidden to do so. Fear God and do not forget the lofty goal, namely that the word of God prevails, not abhorrent nationalism. You have only one soul and you are responsible for it on Judgment Day. O worshippers of God everywhere. Know and teach others that we are bound by the Prophet's guidance in the matter of blood. In the farewell pilgrimage, the Prophet Muhammad said: 'Your blood, property, and honour are inviolable to you, just as this day is inviolable, in this country, in this month.' The Prophet said: 'The Muslim's blood, property, and honor are inviolable for the Muslim.' Ibn Mas'ud is quoted as saying, 'The Prophet, may God's prayers and peace be upon him, said: The first thing on which people are judged on Judgment Day is the shedding of blood.' Ibn Umar said when he looked at the Ka'bah: 'How great you are and how great is your inviolability. Yet for God, the believer is more inviolable than you are.' Ibn Umar also said: 'Among the predicaments from which there is no way out for those who have become embroiled in them is the shedding of inviolable blood without justification.'

Therefore, we turn to God and cite you as witnesses that we do not deliberately shed the blood of a protected Muslim, as long as he has prayed as we do, and turned toward our Qiblah, and ate our slaughtered food. By God, if I hear of anything to the contrary I will stand to be judged, in humility before God, in the presence of the weakest Muslim in the Land of the Two Rivers, until he takes his right from me even if it is by shedding my blood. By God, we have not abandoned the worldly life in order to go to hell, for the sake of a leadership in which we do not know what God will do with us tomorrow, let alone the blood of the mujahidin and the good people who were the first to volunteer, which is even dearer to us....

...I do not exonerate my brothers among the soldiers of the State of things of which I do not know, but I expect them to be among the most God-fearing in this matter. We have known and tested them, and I am just a soldier among them. They are not better than Khalid (Ibn al-Walid) when he killed people who did not express well their Islamic faith, and the Prophet Muhammad said: 'O God, I ask you to absolve me of what Khalid has done.' Yet the Prophet did not dismiss him and did not defame him. Fear God when talking about those who have risen to champion God's religion, God rewards them.

My last call is addressed to my sons, the soldiers of the Islamic State: O mujahidin, do not stop a river you caused to flow by making sacrifices, or demolish an edifice you have raised by your efforts. Do not consider everyone who disagrees with you an adversary, and do not consider everyone who accompanies you a friend. Those who disagree with you may be among your best friends. Be like the sea that is not unsettled by buckets, and be forgiving, for God gives strength and pride to the forgiving.

O nation of Islam. When we proclaimed the State of Islam, a state of *hijrah* (migration) and jihad, we did not lie to God and to the people, and we were not talking about dreams. However, praise be to Almighty God, we are more capable of understanding God's tradition in this jihad. The source of such understanding is the blood of the mujahidin, both *muhajirin* (migrants) and *ansar* (supporters), after looking into their morals and path.

When we proclaimed the State of Islam, we were not only trying to pick the fruit after it ripened, but the fruit fell on its own, and we picked it before it fell into the mud, and it came into our hands safe and clean. What happened after the fall of the Soviet Union, and the scattering of Muslim peoples far from the communist center? They fell prey to communism and secularism. What happened after the mujahidin, migrants and supporters, stopped at the gates of the Serbian capital in the Bosnia war? Simply it is the Dayton Agreement for an alleged peace. What happened after the fall of the fruit in Afghanistan, and the enemy's defeat at the time of the parties? Killing, ruin, and destruction, which remain a stigma for all those who took part in it. O nation of Islam. We have resolved not to repeat the tragedy, and resolved that the fruit must not be lost, for once bitten a believer is twice shy.

The State of Islam will *baqiya* (remain). It will remain because it has been built by the bodies of martyrs and has been irrigated by their blood, and the preparations for going to heaven were made in it.

It will remain because God's granting of success to this jihad is as clear as daylight.

It will remain because it has not been polluted by unlawful gains or a perverted course.

It will remain because of the truthfulness of the leaders who have sacrificed their blood, and the truthfulness of the soldiers who established it with their efforts, and God will reward them.

It will remain because it is land of the mujahidin, and it is the haven of the oppressed.

It will remain because Islam has begun to rise, the cloud has begun to dispel, and unbelief has begun to retreat and to be exposed.

It will remain because it is the call of the wronged, the tear of those who have been bereaved of a child.

It will remain because unbelievers of all kinds have banded against us, and every coward with a whim or an innovation has begun to defame and malign it, and therefore we became certain that the goal and the path are right.

It will remain because we are confident that God will not break the hearts of the monotheist oppressed, and will not allow the oppressors to gloat over us. It will remain because in His Book God has promised: 'God has made a promise to those among you who believe and do good deeds: He will make them successors to the land, as He did those who came before them; He will surely establish their religion, which He has approved for them; and He will grant them security to replace their fear.' 'God always prevails in His purpose, though most people do not realize it.'

Your brother...

3.4b. Analysis

Abu Umar's speech on the anniversary of the invasion of Iraq is typical of the group, which marked this date and the October 2006 founding of the Islamic State for several years with commemorative speeches. In this one, Abu Umar celebrates the benefits that jihad brought to his Iraqi (Sunni) society: a rise in the practice of monotheism, a more conservative culture, the embrace of the Salafi tenet of association and disassociation, and the advent of women martyrdom operations. Nonetheless, it is clear from what follows in the speech that the group is facing stiff headwinds, and Abu Umar addresses several key groups that would have a large impact on the Islamic State in the following six months.

This speech spends a great deal of time dealing with Sunni actors, and this is the area in which the group was struggling most, just six months after the announcement of its founding.[47] The leader of a small group of tribes that declared the formation of the Sahwa movement in September of 2006, Abu Risha al-Rishawi, had created a force that was now threatening the safety of Islamic State cells and units around the country,[48] and so Abu Umar warns the tribes not to renege on their pledges to his new 'state'. This acknowledgement in the speech of the fluid nature of tribes and their ability to shift quickly as fortunes wax and wane was prophetic, given the coming catastrophe.

Worse, the Islamic State's insurgent rivals saw the Anbar tribal uprising in Ramadi as an opportunity to pile on a dangerous organisation that had the very distinct and open political objective of creating and monopolising a caliphate in their midst. Fighting broke out between smaller units of the Islamic State group and their local rivals over their failure to join, as other groups had.[49] Abu Umar singles out the most dangerous group, the 1920 Revolution Brigades, in his speech because of its ties to the Iraqi version of the Muslim Brotherhood (the Iraqi Islamic Party). The 1920 Revolution Brigades would ultimately join the Sahwa movement in its associated forms in large numbers and help push the Islamic State out of its sanctuaries. Sunni elites, realising that their side was losing the sectarian civil war in Iraq by 2007, were moving carefully towards reconciliation with the government.[50]

This speech was given at the zenith of the Islamic State of Iraq's power, but its amir was obviously worried. Should the centripetal forces described become too much for the group to handle, Abu Umar warns his followers that whatever happens, the Islamic State project would remain. It would remain

---

[47] This speech is from about the same time as Utaybi's letter to al-Qaida in Pakistan, in the previous source in this chapter.

[48] Benraad, Myriam, 'Iraq's Tribal "Sahwa": Its Rise and Fall', *Middle East Policy* XVIII, no. 1, Spring 2011.

[49] al-Muhajir, Abu Hamza, 'Letter from Abu Hamza al-Mujahir to Abi 'Abdullah al-Shafi'I', Harmony document NMEC-2007–636898, (2007), CTC West Point archive.

[50] Ollivant, Douglas A., 'Countering the New Orthodoxy: Reinterpreting Counter-insurgency in Iraq', *New America Foundation*, June 2011, p. 2.

because of the sacrifices made to date, and because no one would give up on the quest considering how far it had come since the early days of 2003.

Abu Umar didn't reveal it, of course, but the group had a plan to change its fortunes. The amir of Baghdad, Jarrah al-Shami, was made responsible for putting together an out-of-sector force, to be trained and equipped for a counterattack into the former Islamic State emirate of Ramadi, which, as Utaybi wrote in his 2007 letter, Sahwa tribal forces now controlled with US support.[51] Highly trained and extravagantly equipped, the commando unit of 100 Islamic State fighters was tasked with breaking the Sahwa in Ramadi, and keeping it from spreading to other Sunni areas. Not only was this effort probably too late, it was also ill fated. The unit was discovered by a US patrol in its final assault preparations in a camp just south of the city along the Euphrates (in a place called Donkey Island), and in the ensuing battle American air power and ground forces crushed it.[52] This defeat was a signal for the Islamic State to begin its first transition from an expansive guerrilla army that controlled cities to a retreating guerrilla force that moved out into the desert to regroup and try to survive.

Whether the counterattack into Ramadi would have been successful is hard to know. What we do know is that the tide had already turned against the Islamic State. Just a month after Abu Umar's speech, emissaries from the Islamic Army of Iraq and the Janabi tribal federation—to which the two women who were raped, as mentioned in Abu Umar's speech, belonged—approached the US army unit stationed in the town of Jurf ah-Sakhr in north Babil province and asked to form a Sahwa unit. Their goal was to clear the area of Islamic State fighters and start to establish local governance functions, like policing, water filtration, and the election of a mayor. After several months, the pressure they put on Abu Umar's group culminated in the death of Abu Usama al-Tunisi, its amir in the southern Baghdad belt, who was flushed from cover just south of Jurf ah-Sakhr and killed by a US special operations task force.[53] The veteran

---

[51] al-Qahtani, Mu'awiyah, 'The Biography of the Brave Leader and Lion of Epic Battles: Jarrah al-Shami, May God Rest Him in Peace', posted on the Ana al-Muslim Network, Aug. 26, 2012. One picture of him exists from archived Islamic State of Iraq videos, Daniele Raineri, 'And many others, included Ibn Jarrah al Shami, Abu Hamza al Muhajir and this old one I don't know', Twitter, 19 Aug. 2016 https://twitter.com/danieleraineri/status/766700879500181504, last accessed 10 Oct. 2018.

[52] Scott Tyson, Ann, 'A Deadly Clash at Donkey Island', *Washington Post*, 19 Aug. 2007.

[53] One of the authors witnessed these events first hand in the summer of 2007 in

foreign fighter had been an early Zarqawi lieutenant and was present in the Nick Berg execution video in early 2004.[54]

The next source presents, in brief, an example of how the survivors of this traumatic period for the Islamic State movement used Abu Umar's refrain 'baqiya' to endure the tribulations of defeat and work to restore the fortunes of the group.

3.5a. 'The Islamic State of Iraq Will Remain', 7 August 2011
Abu Muhammad al-Adnani, al-Furqan Media

Abu Muhammad al-Adnani was the Islamic State's official spokesperson from 2011 until he was killed in a 2016 airstrike in Syria. This was his first speech, and the title he chose reflects the previous source, Abu Umar's April 2007 speech, which ended with a section that used 'baqiya' (remain) as a refrain, justifying why the Islamic State would outlast its many enemies in 2007. On 7 August 2011, the Islamic State of Iraq's al-Furqan Media Department released an audio file on the Shumukh al-Islam Network titled 'The Islamic State of Iraq Will Remain'.[55]

Poetic verse [chanted]:

We are not weakened by what life might bring us; we are the steady mountains that do not fall...

Iskandariyah, Iraq, as part of the 1–501st Parachute Infantry Regiment (Geronimo), 4th Brigade (Airborne), 25th Infantry Division.

[54] Tunisi was killed after Sahwa pressure forced him to relocate several times. His death was reported by both the coalition and the Islamic State of Iraq, see the DOD briefing slides here: https://archive.defense.gov/DODCMSShare/briefingslide/314/070928-D-6570C-001.pdf; and research puts him in the Berg video: Raineri, Daniele, 'Update: Abu Usama al Tunisi, Manaf al Rawi, Abu Musab al Zarqawi, Abu Anas al Shami, Abu Muhammad al Lubnani–murdering Berg, May 2004 Iraq', Twitter, 17 Jan. 2017, https://twitter.com/DanieleRaineri/status/821315966663585793

[55] For a description of Adnani's involvement with the media department post-Bucca, see Whiteside, 'Lighting the Path', *ICCT* (2016). Adnani's full speech was found at Haverford's Global Terrorism Research Project: http://gtrp.haverford.edu/statement/ADN20110807/, last accessed 18 Dec. 2018. The audiotape for this speech was given to the author by Laith Alkhouri, @MENAanalyst, the senior director of Flashpoint Intel, and was translated by Anas Elallame of the Middlebury Institute of International Studies in July 2019.

We will defend our tradition and sanctuaries, we will not submit nor give up and we will be victorious...

Our armies will remain on all the frontlines, blowing up the strongholds of the infidels;

We will cut the throats of all the tyrants, and they will not live in peace, even the Antichrist...

To protect the religion of Allah, and a nation; we proudly and happily seek death;

We generously and lovingly seek death—can we be excused?

Our faces reject indignity, but it gladly goes into the mud after battle...

Fighting is our ethos; we are honest, and the cowards know it...

None of our leaders have died in his bed—nor hiding in the bushes on the battlefields...

If one of our leaders dies, his soul ascends and the horse continues...

Death for free men is not a disgrace—the Prophet, peace be upon him, wished to be killed several times...

Death forAllah's sake is a dignity, martyrdom cleanses all sins...

Death is better than a life of humiliation where the rulers are unjust and malicious...

O Allah, give us the courage until you see our dead bodies scattered as a pious deed.

[End of the poetic verses. The voice of Abu Muhammad al-Adnani, spokesperson of the Islamic State of Iraq, begins]:

Be delighted and assured that the Islamic State is remaining, Allah willing, despite the hateful people. As its amir Abu Umar, may Allah have mercy on his soul, said: 'The Islamic State will remain because it was founded on the bodies of martyrs, irrigated with their blood, and it became a market [of opportunities] for Paradise.' It will remain because Allah is clearly, with his blessings, making this a land of jihad. It will remain because it was not corrupted by sinful earnings or a broken methodology. It will remain because of the sincere leaders who sacrificed their blood and the soldiers who built it with their arms—we consider them martyrs and Allah is the best judge. It will remain because it unites the *mujahidin* and shelters the weak. It will remain because Islam has begun to ascend, and infidelity is disappearing. It will remain because of the supplications of the oppressed people, the tears of the mothers who lost their children, the scream of the prisoners, and the hope of the orphans. It will remain because infidelity in all its factions has united against us, and every sedition started to doubt us, so we know for a fact that we are on the right path and that our objective is a righteous one. It will remain because we know without a doubt that Allah will not break the hearts of the weakened monotheists and he won't allow the oppressors to gloat over us. It will remain because Almighty Allah promised us in the Quran:

> Allah has promised, to those among you who believe and work righteous deeds, that He will, of a surety, grant them in the land, inheritance of power, as He granted it to those before them; that He will establish in authority their religion—the one which He has chosen for them; and that He will change their state, after the fear in which they lived, to one of security and peace [24:55].

3.5b. Analysis

Adnani was the third official spokesperson of the group. After Abu Maysara and Jubouri were killed in 2006 and 2007 respectively, the Islamic State movement decided to do away with the position, most likely due to the risk involved. For a time, it recycled Zarqawi and Jubouri speeches and simply relied on strategic communications from 'the two sheikhs', Abu Umar and Abu Hamza. Adnani, a Syrian who had joined Zarqawi in 2002 before the invasion in Iraq, had fought in the Second Battle of Fallujah. He was later wounded and captured in combat in Anbar province sometime in 2005.[56] He spent four years in Camp Bucca, longer than most, before being paroled. When he re-joined the organisation, Abu Umar appointed him to the media department, most likely due to their past association in Anbar province and Adnani's religious zeal, which has always been a prerequisite of Islamic State spokespersons.[57] Adnani, a self-taught religious student, was noted for his recitations of the Quran and had performed for Zarqawi and Abu Umar before his imprisonment.[58] By January 2010, he was narrating Islamic State media releases.[59]

[56] al-Binali, Turki, 'A Biography of IS spokesman Abu Muhammad al-Adnani as-Shami', ed. and trans. Pieter Van Ostaeyen, 1 Nov. 2014, https://pietervanostaeyen. com/2014/11/02/a-biography-of-is-spokesman-abu-muhammad-al-adnani-as-shami/

[57] As noted earlier in this chapter, both of Adnani's predecessors were religious students and scholars who were educated by the premier Salafi teacher in the country. Adnani was not, but he was self-taught and had combat experience—much like Zarqawi's partner Abu Anas al-Shami, the sharia judge killed on the battlefield.

[58] Binali, 'Biography of Adnani'.

[59] Whiteside, 'Lighting the Path'.

After working in the media department for almost two years, the decision was made to 'unmask' Adnani's work and make his role official. The choice of Abu Umar's 'baqiya' wording exemplified not only the defiance Adnani often displayed in his speeches, but, more broadly, the group's sense of permanence after having survived on a very tough battlefield for close to a decade by 2011. With the US on its way out of the country, the new leadership and Adnani may have sensed that the tide was turning in their favour.

The resilience of the Islamic State in 2019 is still difficult for many observers to comprehend, and it is especially so without an understanding of the movement's history and how it sees its own ebb and flow, its successes and failures. Adnani's long tenure in the organisation allowed him to summarise why the phrase 'baqiya' would act as an anchor for the group in the boom and bust period that lay ahead—shortly before his death in 2016, he said:

> Or do you think, O America, that victory is killing one leader or another? Indeed, it would then be a falsified victory. Were you victorious when you killed Abu Mus'ab, Abu Hamzah, Abu 'Umar, or Usamah? Would you be victorious if you were to kill ash-Shishani, Abu Bakr, Abu Zayd, or Abu 'Amr? No. Indeed, victory is the defeat of one's opponent. Or do you, O America, consider defeat to be the loss of a city or the loss of land? Were we defeated when we lost the cities in Iraq and were in the desert without any city or land? And would we be defeated, and you victorious, if you were to take Mosul or Sirte or Raqqah, or even all the cities, and we were to return to our initial condition? Certainly not! True defeat is the loss of willpower and desire to fight. America will be victorious and the mujahidin defeated in only one situation. We would be defeated and you victorious only if you were able to remove the Quran from the hearts of Muslims.[60]

---

[60] For more see Chapter 12: Defining Success and Failure.

4

ADVICE TO THE LEADERS OF THE ISLAMIC STATE

On 24 January 2018, a social media group affiliated with the Islamic State's central media office circulated an e-book titled Advice for the leaders and soldiers of the Islamic State. *It was attributed to Abd al-Munim bin Izz al-Din al-Badawi, better known as Abu Hamzah al-Muhajir, the former prime minister and minister of war for the Islamic State of Iraq (ISI). First officially published in Arabic and made available online by the organisation's printing press, the* Himmah Library, *in the* Hijri *year 1428 (which spanned the Gregorian year 2007), the volume has two sections, 'Advice for the Leaders of the Islamic State' and 'Advice for the Soldiers of the Islamic State', which offer thirty pieces of 'advice' to leaders and thirty-one to soldiers about how best to pursue the aims of the Islamic State's insurgency. The first half follows below.[1]*

4a. 'Advice for the Leaders and Soldiers of the Islamic State', 2007
Abu Hamzah al-Muhajir

Introduction

Praise be to Allah, and may blessings and peace be upon the Messenger of Allah, and upon his family and those who support him. As for what follows...

---

[1] This is the Islamic State's own translation and formatting, entirely without edits, though the honorifics *radi allahu 'anhu* (رَّضِيَ اللّٰهُ عَنْهُ—May Allah be pleased with them) and *'azz wa jal* (زوَجَلَّ—the Mighty and Majestic) have been typed in Arabic, as has *sallallāhu 'alayhi wa sallam* (ﷺ—peace be upon him).

My dear mujāhid brother, these are some pieces of advice that I've gathered from the mouths of men and the pages of books, although I do not claim to be a man of wisdom. I ask Allah to make you and me benefit from these pieces of advice. And Allah knows all intentions.

Abu Hamzah al-Muhajir
1 Ramadan 1428

Advice for the leaders of the Islamic State

[1] Have sincerity towards Allah, for it will lead to salvation in the worldly life and the Hereafter. Allah's Messenger ﷺ said, 'Allah has guaranteed the one who performs jihād for His cause, having left his home for no reason other than to perform jihād for His cause and to affirm the truth of His words, that He would enter him into Jannah or return him back home with all the rewards he has attained or the ghanīmah he has acquired.'

Let the goal of your deed be that the word of Allah becomes the highest, for Abū Mūsā (عَنْهُ رَّضِيَاللهُ) said, 'Allah's Messenger ﷺ was asked about a man who fights out of bravery, out of zeal, or out of riyā' (showing off), which of these is fighting for Allah's cause? So Allah's Messenger ﷺ said, "Whoever fights so that the word of Allah is the highest is fighting for Allah's cause."'

[2] Be just and sincere towards your subjects, for 'No man is appointed to lead ten people except that he will be brought forth in shackles on the Day of Judgment, and will either be set free on account of his justice or destroyed as a result of his oppression.' Likewise, 'Any leader who takes charge of the affairs of the Muslims and then doesn't strive for them and advise them, will not enter Jannah with them.' And likewise, 'Allah does not give one of His slaves leadership, who then dies having cheated his subjects, except that Allah will make Jannah prohibited for him.'

[3] Seek consultation and hold discussions, for discussion is the partner of consultation. One should sit in a gathering to exchange ideas, then each person comments on the opinions put forth by the others, or puts forth a new opinion, and at the end of the gathering the correct opinion will become clear. Allah (وَجَلَّ عَزَّ) said, {And consult them concerning the matter} [Āl 'Imrān: 159]. Allah has directed His Prophet to consult those under him despite the Prophet's prudent intellect. So what about you?

And as was reported, 'One who seeks consultation will have no regret, and one who prays istikhārah will not go wrong.' And it's been said, 'He who relies exclusively on his intellect will go astray, and he who is content with his own opinion will slip up, and he who consults intelligent men will take the correct path, and he who seeks the help of a man with insight will attain what is hoped for.'

So let every leader have a true consultative council beginning with the general leader and ending with the detachment commanders. But do not consult a person who has a certain need that he is seeking to fulfill, nor a person whom you sense desires to be consulted, nor a person who doesn't think his opinions through, for it's been said, 'Leave your opinion until it ripens.' It was reported that 'Alī said, 'The opinion of an elder is better than the view of a young man,' meaning with regards to battle. And don't consult anyone unless he's alone, meaning that you should consult him in private, for this ensures more secrecy and is a greater deterrent to anyone who might otherwise disclose the issue. It is true! 'Consultation and discussion are two doors to mercy, and two keys to blessings. No opinion that's been reached with the help of these two things will go wrong.'

[4] Beware of only consulting a person who always agrees with your opinion, and beware of bad company. Get accustomed to being patient with any advisers who disagree with your opinion, and swallow the bitterness of their words and their criticism. But don't be casual in that regard except with people who are virtuous, intelligent, chivalrous, senior in age, and trustworthy with secrets.

[5] There's nothing more destructive towards the religion and dunyā than for a leader to become unaware of the actual circumstances that his subjects are in. So don't seclude yourself from them, for you are only a human being and you don't know what the people are concealing from you. And beware of using security as an excuse, thereby ensuring your personal security and neglecting your subjects in the process, for what a terrible leader you would then be!

And follow up on everything yourself even after appointing sincere and reliable individuals over areas of responsibility, for even a reliable person can betray you, and even a sincere person can deceive you, so be sure to verify things yourself. Allah (عَزَّوَجَلَّ) says, {O Dāwūd, indeed We have made you a successor upon the Earth, so judge between the people in truth and do not follow [your own] desire, as it will lead you astray from the way of Allah} [Sād: 26].

'So Allah did not suffice with a broad implication and thereby avoid an explicit address. Nor did He accept busyness as an excuse, being content with the delegation of duties, but instead He linked such to misguidance.'

And don't hasten to believe a person who seeks to spread corruption, for such an individual is deceitful even if he makes himself out to be sincere.

Likewise, don't just dismiss his words, for he may be telling the truth. Give your brothers the benefit of the doubt, for doing so will save you a lot of hardship.

[6] The leader is required to ensure that he and his soldiers are held responsible for the rights that Allah (عَزَّ وَجَلَّ) has made obligatory and the limits that He has set, 'For he who fights for the religion is more deserving amongst the people of being held to its rulings.' But you will not reform anything when you yourself are corrupt, nor will you guide anyone when you yourself are astray. For how can a blind man guide others, and how can a disgraceful person give honor? And there's nothing more humiliating than the disgrace of sin, and nothing more honorable than the honor of righteousness. So keep yourself above having poor character and befriending immoral people.

[7] Beware of letting your dire need of something cause you to acquire it in an unlawful manner, for having patience in the face of dire need, while hoping for improved circumstances and a better outcome, is greater than committing a sin and then fearing its consequences. And the religion revolves around patience.

[8] Beware of standing out from others by way of the vehicle that you ride or the clothes that you wear, for indeed 'Umar wrote to Abū Mūsā al-Ash'arī saying, '...and it has reached me that word is going around that your and your family's clothing, food, and means of transport are of a different standard than that of the Muslims. So beware, O servant of Allah, of becoming like an animal that passes by a fertile valley and has no concern other than to fatten itself. Indeed its fatness will be what kills it. And know that if the leader goes astray, so too will his subjects. And the most wretched of people is he whose subjects are unhappy with him.'

[9] Know that war is just as they say, its burdens lie in being patient, its axis is comprised of craftiness and good judgment, its backbone is endurance, and its reins are caution. Each of these has its fruit: the fruit of patience is support [from Allah], the fruit of craftiness is triumph, the fruit of good judgment is success, the fruit of endurance is prosperity, and the fruit of being cautious is safety. 'Amr Ibn Ma'diyakrib (رَضِيَ اللّٰهُ عَنْهُ) was asked about war, so he said, 'Whoever is patient in war becomes prominent, and whoever abstains from it perishes.' So beware of hastiness, for an act of hastiness may lead to regret.

[10] Put the harsh and courageous men forward against the enemy during the heat of the battle, and distribute them amongst the various detachments

so that they can be a source of strength for the weak and a source of courage for the coward. Beware of letting your brothers be accompanied by one who will cause them to abandon the fight or will say things that will harm their morale. Furthermore, beware of spies, for how many small forces have defeated large forces by Allah's permission. And don't select the strong fighters for the battle while leaving out the weak ones who are eager to attain the rewards of Allah, for the Prophet ﷺ said, 'And are you given victory or sustenance except through the weak amongst you?' Indeed, Allah grants victory to a people through the weakest amongst them.

[11] Don't neglect to take what you can of equipment, such as armor and helmets. Doing so is not cowardice, for Allah's Messenger ﷺ, the bravest of all people, had armour. And this doesn't mean you can't fight without armour when it's appropriate to do so. Habīb Ibn al-Muhallab said, 'I have not seen any man in war wearing armor except that he was worth two men to me. And I have not seen two men going without armor except that they were worth one man to me.' A knowledgeable man heard this statement and said, 'He spoke the truth! Indeed, weapons have virtue. Can't you see that when they hear someone scream for help, they call out "Grab your weapons! Grab your weapons!" not "Gather the men! Gather the men!"'

[12] One who provides his brothers with a supply of food and drink that will strengthen them throughout their day is undoubtedly a wise leader. Indeed, when we searched the pockets of some fighters who were under the command of an Afghan leader that was fighting the Taliban, we found raisins.

[13] The leader should appoint a commander for each squad, and should inspect their vehicles, weapons and supplies, especially prior to a battle. Nothing should be taken that will become too much of a burden when the situation becomes serious and difficult, and nothing should be left that you will need when something breaks down or when the distance is very long, especially if the leader anticipates a long battle.

[14] You should not have more than three fighters in any car, unless there's an overriding benefit in doing so. The leader should establish a secure, elaborate method of communication between each of the detachments, and establish code words for them to use when communicating, and slogans to shout when they're fighting.

[15] The leader must let his subjects and soldiers hear things that will strengthen them and cause them to feel that they will triumph over their enemy. He should narrate to them from the causes of victory that would make them belittle their enemy. Allah (عَزَّ وجَلَّ) says, {(And remember) when Allah

showed them to you in your dream as few; and if He had shown them to you as many, you would have lost courage and would have disputed in the matter [of whether to fight]} [al-Anfāl: 43].

[16] The leader must study the battlefield very well. He should not fight from a position that will be easy for the enemy to surround without ensuring that the vulnerable points are guarded. And he should not take his soldiers out to a place so far that it's impossible to bring them back safely.

[17] The Prophet ﷺ said:

Al-Muhallab said, 'You must use deception in war, for it is more effective than reinforcements.' Some methods of deception include:

a. Planting spies.

b. Reconnaissance.

c. Feigning an intent to attack an area other than the actual target, for when the Prophet ﷺ wanted to attack one area, he would give his army the impression they were going to attack another.

'If a man's chest is too narrow to hold his own secret, then the chest of the one with whom he stores the secret is even narrower' [Poetry].

And be on guard against your enemy at all times so that he doesn't:

a. Pounce on you from near.

b. Assault you from far.

c. Ambush you when you're inattentive.

d. Or follow you when you're returning home.

[18] Among the signs of a leader's experience and sophistication is that he takes advantage of opportunities, 'For indeed they come and go as the passing of clouds. And do not only seek the traces of the enemy left behind after the main body is gone.' Pounce when the opportunity first arises and not when it's already gone.

'When your wind blows take advantage of it, for everything that flutters becomes calm' [Poetry].

[19] It's permissible for the leader of an army to let one eager for shahādah expose himself to it if the leader knows that seeing him killed will be an incitement for the Muslims to fight zealously to avenge him. The opposite is also correct; he should protect any person whose killing will break the strength of his brothers, such as a distinguished commander. For this reason, know that the center is the most fortified and furthest from the enemy.

[20] Don't allow your brothers to kill or take captive anyone on account of whom they would dispute and become disunited, even if it's permissible from a certain angle, for unity during the course of battle is a predominant interest that cannot be superseded by anything else.

[21] Beware of blood. Beware of blood. Beware of shedding blood unjustly. For nothing is quicker to draw wrath or cause blessings to disappear than shedding blood unjustly. And beware of strengthening your authority and your soldiers through unlawful bloodshed, for this would be a short-term gain whose long-term consequences are weakness and helplessness. If you were to do so, you would have no acceptable excuse, neither before Allah nor before us. And by Allah, no case is reported to us involving the bloodshed of an innocent person from Ahlus-Sunnah that isn't backed up by clear evidence of what he did to deserve his blood being shed, or supported by reasonable doubt, except that we will bring justice for the one wronged.

[22] Don't be deceived by the ease of any operation, for a downhill slope can be followed by rough terrain. So give careful thought to both the present and the future, for nothing is more harmful to the people than a leader who only thinks about the present.

[23] Reward those who perform very well, be generous to a detachment that achieves victory, and honor a brave person publicly. In contrast, punish those who do wrong for their actions, even if by boycotting them, since it's permissible for a leader to punish those who disobey his orders. If you don't do so, those who perform well will begin to slack, and those who do wrong will become emboldened, things will get worse and your work will be ruined.

Furthermore, when rewarding those who perform well, do so publicly and when punishing those who've done wrong, do so privately, especially when it comes to the virtuous ones amongst them. As for the corrupt amongst them, then punish them publicly, for this is what the Sharī'ah has come with.

Be extremely cautious of over-punishing a soldier, or of pardoning him and then regretting it. And beware of letting your harshness become repulsive, for indeed the purpose of punishment in the Sharī'ah is to bring reform, not to quench one's thirst for revenge. Likewise, be careful not to say something when you're angry that you won't be able to take back, for how often does a statement say to the one who wants to speak it, 'Discard me.' And don't make your statement inconsequential, O leader, when either punishing or pardoning someone. And when punishing someone, don't go beyond the limits that Allah has set for you through your transgression and desires, for 'transgression will be darkness on the Day of Judgment.'

So you need to be gentle, dear brother, in all of your affairs, even when it comes to punishment. Allah (عَزَّ وَجَلَّ) says, {And had you been severe and harsh-hearted, they would have dispersed from around you} [al 'Imrān: 159].

The Prophet ﷺ said, 'Whoever has been given his share of gentleness has been given his share of all goodness. And whoever has been deprived of his share of gentleness has been deprived of his share of all goodness.' He ﷺ also said, 'Indeed, this religion is firm, so delve into it with gentleness.'

[24] Know that your brothers listen and obey out of eagerness for Allah's rewards, so their compliance is due more to their good character and adherence to the Sharī'ah, than it is due to fear of authority. So you should only discipline those whom you know will accept it due to their strong adherence to the religion. As for one whom you believe won't be deterred by his religious commitment, then beware of punishing him. Rather, be lenient with him and win his heart, for those fittest to pardon others are those most capable of punishing them, and those who are least in worth and intelligence are those who oppress people under their authority. So be sincere towards Allah and be just towards the people as it relates to yourself, your family, and those whom you love from amongst your brothers and your subjects. Otherwise, you would be oppressing them. And whoever oppresses the servants of Allah, will have Allah as his opponent. And whoever has Allah as his opponent, will find Allah at war with him until he repents and desists. And fear the supplication of the oppressed, for there's no screen between it and Allah, and the doors of the heavens are opened for it. And set aside an hour of your day to think carefully as to whether you've oppressed anyone, or whether there's an oppressed person whom you could support. And if one wishes to hasten the anger of Allah, he should commit oppression!

[25] Reign over your brothers and over the people with kindness and you'll win their hearts, for long-lasting love is due to kindness, and its disappearance is due to tyranny. If you show affection to the general public, their love for you will be sincere and you will win their esteem. Indeed, affection from a powerful person is humbleness.

'Umar Ibn 'Abdil-'Azīz would be extremely kind to the people. If he wanted to order the people with something from the orders of Allah that he thought they would dislike, he would wait until something came that the people would love, and would then announce both of them together. It was reported that he said, 'Indeed, Allah disparaged alcohol twice in the Qur'ān and prohibited it the third time it was mentioned. And I fear that I would impose the truth upon the people all at once, so they would leave it and it would become a tribulation for them.'

[26] Recognize each person's individual value, know their ranks, and give preference to men who are:

a. From the people of knowledge and virtue. The verses and narrations concerning their virtue are numerous.

b. Older in age, for 'He who does not respect our elders, have mercy towards our young, and recognize the rights of our scholars, is not one of us.'

c. From a noble and prestigious family, at the forefront being the family of the Prophet ﷺ.

[27] Check up on the families of the shuhadā' and prisoners, and give them preference over others. Visit the sick and act as a servant for your brothers, for aside from carrying a heavier burden and having a lot more to be accountable for in front of Allah, you're just a man from amongst them, so work for tomorrow.

[28] Choose well when selecting a messenger to communicate with tribes and armed groups, and likewise when selecting someone to take control over checkpoints and bring the people to account, for to the people they are the face of the State. If they do well then we've done well, and if they do wrong then we've done wrong. To summarize, 'Send a wise person who doesn't need advising.'

[29] Beware, O leader, of jāhilī partisanship, for nothing destroys a firmly established structure other than extreme partisanship. Use intelligence and ploy to dismantle partisanship, not just strength, for indeed, the people of Iraq revolted with Ibn al-Ash'ath against 'Abdul-Malik Ibn Marwān, and amongst them were a large number of the best of the tābi'īn, such as Sa'īd Ibn Jubayr and his likes. But al-Hajjāj defeated them at Dayr al-Jamājim using ploy more so than strength. And know that it is wise policy to deal with these partisans quickly, especially their leaders.

[30] You must be serious, hardworking, and very ambitious. Beware of incompetence, for by Allah there's no ride more humiliating. No matter how many times you stumble, keep trying, for we've seen through experience that there's no work in which Allah granted success, except that there were many stumbles along the way.

4b. Analysis

Abu Hamzah's advice is strikingly reminiscent of doctrinal texts attributed to jihadis like al-Qaida in the Arabian Peninsula's Abd al-Aziz al-Muqrin as well as the likes of Carlos Marighella and Ernesto 'Che' Guevara.[2] When one strips

---

[2] Cigar, Norman, *Al-Qā'ida's Doctrine for Insurgency: Abd al-Aziz al-Muqrin's 'A Practical Course for Guerrilla War'*, Dulles, VA: Potomac Books, 2008; Guevara, Ernesto Che, *Guerrilla Warfare*, La Vergne, TN: BN Publishing, 2008 (1961); Marighella, Carlos, *Minimanual of the Urban Guerrilla*, Scotts Valley, CA: CreateSpace, 2011 (1969).

back its theological window-dressing, the pragmatic principles at its core are distinctly recognisable. In part, the presence of these shared, seemingly pan-ideological instincts were simply borne out of revolutionary intuition. However, they are also likely to be the result of tactical plagiarism—Abu Hamzah notes, after all, that his guidance is 'gathered from the mouths of men and the pages of books', and this would certainly not be the first time a jihadi commander has borrowed from his putative adversaries.[3] In any case, whether instinctual or learned, his advice can be usefully grouped into four broad themes—perception, discipline, morale, and planning. Each of these is discussed in greater detail below.

Regarding the first issue, perception, Abu Hamzah is unequivocal. He holds that, if the Islamic State project is to succeed, public perceptions regarding what it is and why it is must be enduringly positive. To this end, he states that the leader should try to remain close to the people whom they are leading and/or ruling over: early on in the text, for example, he warns that there is 'nothing more destructive towards the religion and *dunyā* than for a leader to become unaware of the actual circumstances that his subjects are in'. As such, even if this puts them at risk, they should still endeavour to position themselves as men of the people—naturally, this means not eating better food, wearing superior clothes or enjoying special luxuries. Essentially, then, he is advising his readers to keep image management at the forefront of their minds, making sure that the idea of the movement they represent is sustainably amenable to their immediate and potential support base.

In the context of military expansion, when new constituents are being brought into the ideological fray of the Islamic State, Abu Hamzah's guidance again centres the issue of perception. First, he holds that the leader must not allow his soldiers to engage in excesses. 'Beware of blood', he warns, reiterating, 'Beware of blood. Beware of shedding blood unjustly.' Given the Islamic State's track record, this statement may, at face value, be counterintuitive. However, in the context of its 2014 and 2015 offensives, it does ring true. At that time, when the group attempted to consolidate control over newly captured territories, its first recourse to action was to claim a monopoly over the

---

[3] The personal library of Usama bin Laden, the late leader of al-Qaida Central, famously stocked dozens of books on military and political doctrine that originated in the West. See: 'November 2017 Release of Abbottabad Compound Material', *CIA*, Nov. 2017, https://www.cia.gov/library/abbottabad-compound/index_documents.html, last accessed 18 Dec. 2018.

use of violence, something that itself required the deployment of violence.[4] In so doing, its local commanders would purge the local population of actual or potential threats, usually through a highly public amnesty campaign supplemented with arrests and executions. Its consolidation of power in this form was violent, but also marked by restraint.

The Islamic State was thus unambiguous: resistance was futile and would result in death, but acquiescence and support would be a guarantee of safety. It had clearly calculated that, by killing a few publicly in the short term, it could communicate its resolve to the many in the long term.[5] Perhaps this is what Abu Hamzah is referring to when he states: 'Beware of strengthening your authority and your soldiers through unlawful bloodshed, for this would be a short-term gain whose long-term consequences are weakness and helplessness.'

If the threat of bloodshed is the stick brandished by Islamic State leaders, Abu Hamza also recommends they offer the carrot of 'affection'. This could comprise anything from displays of kindness to 'the general public' to the sugar-coating of unfavourable policies. Exemplifying the latter, he recalls the experience of caliph 'Umar, who, 'if he wanted to order the people with something from the orders of Allah that he thought they would dislike, [would] wait until something came that the people would love, and would then announce both of them together'. Countless times in recent years, the Islamic State put this gradualist advice into practice, operationalising it in the context

---

[4] See Phillips, Vaughan, 'The Islamic State's Strategy: Bureaucratizing the Apocalypse through Strategic Communications', *Studies in Conflict & Terrorism* 40, no. 9 (2016), pp. 731–757; Winter, Charlie, 'Totalitarian Insurgency: Evaluating the Islamic State's In-Theater Propaganda Operations', *Center on Irregular Warfare and Armed Groups* (CIWAG) Case Study, Naval War College, https://digital-commons.usnwc.edu/ciwag-case-studies/154, last accessed 18 Dec. 2018; Zelin, Aaron, 'The Islamic State's Territorial Methodology', Research Note 29, *Washington Institute for Near East Policy*, Jan. 2016, https://www.washingtoninstitute.org/policy-analysis/view/the-islamic-states-territorial-methodology, last accessed 18 Dec. 2018.

[5] This violent manifestation of the Hobbesian social contract is directly alluded to by a member of the Islamic State's domestic intelligence service in a Nov. 2016 video, in which he states that the group's brutal executions are strictly intended to deter individuals from cooperating with its enemies. See: The Islamic State, 'And Allah Will Be Sufficient For You Against Them', Wilayat al-Furat Media Office, 1 Nov. 2016, Jihadology, https://jihadology.net/2016/11/01/new-video-message-from-the-islamic-state-and-Allah-will-be-sufficient-for-you-against-them-2-wilayat-al-furat/, last accessed 18 Dec 2018.

of everything from smoking and clothing to taxation and satellite television.[6] The principle continues to characterise its governance operations even now.

Abu Hamzah's next theme ties in closely with the above. Specifically, it relates to the issue of discipline in the rank and file. Noting that the leader must 'choose well when selecting a messenger to communicate with tribes and armed groups, and likewise when selecting someone to take control over checkpoints and bring the people to account, for to the people they are the face of the State', he urges them to ensure that their men do not perpetrate excessive violence in the name of the Islamic State. To this end, he holds that they should work to encourage a reciprocal atmosphere of discipline at all times, on the one hand, 'reward[ing] those who perform very well, be[ing] generous to a detachment that achieves victory, and honour[ing] a brave person publicly' and, on the other, punishing those 'who do wrong for their actions'. Without a system in place to encourage this form of obedience, a quality that has repeatedly been fetishised by the Islamic State in recent years, Abu Hamzah warns that there could be a gradual breakdown of authority, such that 'those who perform well will begin to slack, and those who do wrong will become emboldened, things will get worse and your work will be ruined'.[7]

Later, while ruminating on this same issue, he returns to the communicative function of violence. In the context of reward and punishment for good or bad conduct, he suggests that, 'when rewarding those who perform well, [the leader should] do so publicly and when punishing those who've done wrong, [they should] do so privately, especially when it comes to the virtuous ones amongst them' (emphasis added). Again, image management is a priority: leaders are advised to amplify the good and minimise the bad.

Moreover, while wrongdoers must be punished, the punishment should not discredit the image of the Islamic State, nor should it alienate the individual

---

[6] See Abdul-Ahad, Ghaith, 'The Bureaucracy of Evil: How Islamic State Governed A City', *Guardian,* 29 Jan. 2018, https://www.theguardian.com/cities/2018/jan/29/bureaucracy-evil-isis-run-city-mosul, last accessed 18 Dec. 2018; Muir, Jim, '"Islamic State": Raqqa's Loss Seals Rapid Rise and Fall', *BBC News,* 17 Oct. 2017, https://www.bbc.co.uk/news/world-middle-east-35695648, last accessed 18 Dec. 2018; Palazzo, Chiara, 'Islamic State Calls for Destruction of Satellite Dishes Ahead of Ramadan', *Telegraph,* 1 June 2016, https://www.telegraph.co.uk/news/2016/06/01/islamic-state-calls-for-destruction-of-satellite-dishes-ahead-of/, last accessed 18 Dec 2018; Winter. 'Totalitarian Insurgency', CIWAG, pp. 28–35.

[7] See, for example: al-Muhajir, Abu Hamzah, 'Paths to Victory', *Rumiyah III*, al-Hayat Media Center, 4 Oct. 2016, pp. 20–23.

who did wrong in the first place. They should be treated with leniency, only being disciplined if the leader knows that they 'will accept it'. Abu Hamzah goes on to note that the same cannot be said for 'the corrupt amongst them'— that is, people who have committed unforgivable sins or acts of treason against the Islamic State. This class, he writes, is to be punished 'publicly, for this is what the Sharī'ah has come with', but in a manner that is not 'repulsive'. The latter part of this item has not aged well.

The third cluster of advice relates to the maintenance of morale in the rank and file. Abu Hamzah discusses this at length, first advising that 'harsh and courageous men' should be selected to be at the forefront of the battle and distributed equally among 'the various detachments so that they can be a source of strength for the weak and a source of courage for the coward'. He also states that it is acceptable to allow someone to kill themselves out of reckless intent—that is, commit suicide on the battlefield—even if it has little or no material impact on the outcome of the battle.[8] This is because, in certain circumstances, the death of one will incite others to 'fight zealously to avenge him'.

For Abu Hamzah, morale is something in need of constant attention. The man that 'provides his brothers with a supply of food and drink that will strengthen them throughout their day is undoubtedly a wise leader', and the same is true of he who tells his unit stories 'that will strengthen them and cause them to feel that they will triumph over their enemy'. Here, he is alluding not only to the importance of pre-battle speeches, but also to the Islamic State's propaganda, which has been distributed and screened to those on the frontlines on a continual basis for over a decade now.[9]

The final portion of guidance relates to tactical planning. For the most part, Abu Hamzah keeps his advice general, something that is to be expected—after all, a publicly disseminated field-guide is not the place for disclosing operational secrets. When tactics do come up, there is nothing particularly groundbreaking; indeed, his remarks tend to just be jihadi rewordings of military principles that have been around for millennia.[10] He encourages leaders to be

---

[8] For more on the Islamic State's use of suicide tactics, see Winter, Charlie, 'War by Suicide: The Islamic State's Martyrdom Industry', ICCT-The Hague, vol. 8, no. 3 (2017), https://icct.nl/wp-content/uploads/2017/02/ICCT-Winter-War-by-Suicide-Feb2017.pdf., last accessed 18 Dec. 2018.

[9] See Chapter 5: On Propaganda.

[10] See, for example, 'Attack by stratagem', 'Tactical dispositions', 'Energy', 'Weak points

wary, noting that 'war is just as they say, its burdens lie in being patient, its axis is comprised of craftiness and good judgment, its backbone is endurance, and its reins are caution', putting significant emphasis on the need for planning and preparedness. The leader must know 'the battlefield very well', he states, so that they can avoid 'fight[ing] from a position that will be easy for the enemy to surround without ensuring that the vulnerable points are guarded'.

Abu Hamzah also contends that they must be confident in their ability to delegate. Specifically, leaders 'should appoint a commander for each squad, and should inspect their vehicles, weapons and supplies, especially prior to a battle', so that they can ensure that nothing 'will become too much of a burden when the situation becomes serious and difficult'. Finally, he advises them to be patient, 'pounc[ing] when the opportunity first arises and not when it's already gone' but to avoid being 'deceived by the ease of any operation, for a downhill slope can be followed by rough terrain'. Considering the Islamic State's experiences in Mosul and Raqqah in 2017, it would appear that this advice was internalised on a short- but not long-term basis.

Beneath its jihadi veneer, Abu Hamzah's advice is strikingly familiar. Throughout this text, he borrows from and builds upon many long-established norms of symmetric and asymmetric warfare. While this is interesting, what sets his guidance apart is not its focus on military affairs but its focus on the need for image management. It seems that for Abu Hamzah, a successful insurgency must be built on the notion that local non-combatants are the most precious of commodities—their hearts and minds are a decisive battlespace. It is the insurgent's first priority to win them over and its second priority to sustain their support, a dichotomous principle that has long characterised the Islamic State's approach to proto-statehood.

and strong', 'Manoeuvring', 'The army on the march', and 'Terrain' in Sun-Tzu, *The Art of War*, Saint Louis, MO: Pax Librorum, 2009 (fifth century BC).

5

THE FALLUJAH MEMORANDUM

The dark years of the Islamic State movement, which came after it was flattened by the Sahwa uprising, fellow Sunni resistance rivals, and the US surge brigades in 2007, are characterised by a healthy dose of soul-searching. While the movement in its various forms has shared tremendous details about its people through biographies, strategy documents are harder to come by for operational security reasons. Published at a time when the group was in dire straits—a period it describes as being 'in the desert'—this document was paid little heed and not taken very seriously. The limited curiosity and analysis was largely fuelled by a general belief that the group was bereft of public support and finished.[1]

The Fallujah Memorandum, or the Khoutah Istratigya li Ta'aziz al-Moqif al-Siyasi al-Dawlat al-Islamyiah fi al-Iraq *(A Strategic Plan to Improve the Political Position of the Islamic State of Iraq), was dated the month of Muharram, 1431 (18 December 2009–15 January 2010). The author's identity is unknown, which means there is a possibility they could still be alive today. Western analysts*

---

[1] al-Shishani, Murad Batal, 'The Islamic State's Strategic and Tactical Plan for Iraq', *Terrorism Monitor* 12, no. 16 (2014), pp. 6–7; scholar Marc Lynch is the first to report on this document, which he found on a jihadist website forum and downloaded. See Lynch, Marc, 'AQ-Iraq's Counter Counterinsurgency Manual', *Foreign Policy,* 17 March 2010, https://foreignpolicy.com/2010/03/17/aq-iraqs-counter-counter-insurgency-manual/, last accessed 18 Dec. 2018.

have largely ignored the impact of the memorandum to date, perhaps because it has not yet been made publicly available in English.[2]

5.1a. The Fallujah Memorandum, December 2009/January 2010
Untitled introduction

The establishment of the Islamic State in Iraq [abbreviated as ISI for the remainder of the text] was the crusaders' worst nightmare. It was the strongest blow to the new crusade wars in the land of Islam. The purpose of the war in Afghanistan was to topple the Islamic Emirate and to utterly remove the Islamic political model. The collapse of the emirate in Afghanistan and its reestablishment in Iraq with the help of the crusaders who had removed the Ba'athist regime facilitated our mission. The crusaders came to establish a Western political model in the Islamic nations. The fact that 'the terrorists' stole the crusaders' dream enraged them fully. The dirty war led by the Americans was at its peak when ISI was also at its peak. The bombings in the markets, public stores, and mosques that killed those who opposed ISI were meant to frame the *mujahidin* as having carried them out.[3] On the other hand, when ISI's influence was diminishing due to the apostate Sahwa forces, these bombings lessened. These dishonourable actions make for easy goals. It is the strategy of the weak rather than the strong, because it does not require preparation or planning. There are some videos that show American soldiers planting explosive devices by the road, one of which exploded in the hand of a crusader soldier in a famous video. Even the people who were dissidents of ISI assured us afterwards that these criminal acts were the deeds of the crusaders. People who once believed the crusaders' media broadcastings then realised that they were a lie and that ISI was falsely accused of many other acts.

The *dawla* [state, shortened version of the Islamic State] was mocked because, according to those mocking it, it was only exercising its power over

---

[2] Fishman (2017), McCants (2015), and Hashim (2018) all briefly mention this document in their histories of the movement, but without quotes or extensive analysis. Hassan Hassan graciously shared a copy with us. Dr. Mohammad Hafez, US Naval Postgraduate School, shared his thoughts on the document with us as well. Thanks to Anas Elallame, Middlebury Institute of International Studies, who expertly translated the document for the authors as part of another research project.

[3] This is an odd statement detached from reality. The Islamic State regularly claimed these killings and explosions and it is a matter of public record. Its leaders' strategic communications were clear on the rationale behind the killigs.

the internet and so only exists if the internet exists. However, these people who mocked the State also mocked its collapse, implying that they acknowledge the State's existence and that it is not a delusion.[4]

The Islamic State Baqiya [remains][5]:

The State collapsed after its first establishment, but it will come back with Allah's permission. This is the universal divine way of Allah and will not change, as Allah is only testing the believers.[6] This early trial ISI is experiencing is, in fact, a mercy from Allah. It is better for this trial to come earlier instead of later, as it did when the Taliban pushed people into committing sedition by claiming that an Islamic State cannot be established in Iraq based on the example of the Taliban. This trial and test from Allah will only continue.[7] However, thanks to the universal divine way, this trial will not be as intense or enormous. The fact that there are one hundred thousand apostate Sahwa, who are dramatically diminishing, is proof that the trial and test will not be as intense.[8]

---

[4] While the author(s) are quite sensitive of the fun poked at the Islamic State for being a 'paper state', as Cole Bunzel calls it in his authoritative history of its ideology by the same name, they are in the process of writing a strategy document focused on returning its past glory from 2006–7. They are also notably dismissive of the idea of a 'virtual caliphate', popularised in 2009.

[5] The authors use the phrase *baqiya*, two years after Abu Umar's speech in the last chapter. The impact of this speech would be magnified when the group later added the term *tatamaddad* (expanding) for its unofficial motto after 2014: '*baqiya wa tatamaddad*' (remaining and expanding). Today the use of expanding is muted due to the loss of territory in what was the caliphate, but in some ways with the global spread of affiliates, it remains a partial truth. See al-Tamimi, Aymenn, 'The Islamic State: Baqiya?' *Bicom*, 16 May 2017, http://www.aymennjawad.org/19918/the-islamic-state-baqiya

[6] The phrase 'testing the believers' was already in use again from 2017 on, as the caliphate faded and returned to a uniform insurgency in its core and outlying provinces.

[7] Note the resentment toward the Taliban (and by extension al-Qaida's allegiance to Mullah Omar) that the Islamic State never openly admitted, but seems to have harboured during this period. By 2009, these leaders in the Islamic State were continuing with the state project in Iraq, one that was, in some ways, quite independent from al-Qaida and foreshadowed the split in 2013 over control of al-Nusrah Front in Syria.

[8] This is an accurate number of the original Sahwa recruitment, as well as their declin-

Here is a simplified examination that will address—if Allah wills it—how to reinforce the position of ISI in current times. This will put ISI in a better political and military position two years from now, when the majority of the enemy forces withdraw. When this happens, the Islamic project will be ready to take over all matters in Iraq. It is obvious that everyone is getting ready for when the majority of the enemies' crusader forces withdraw from Iraq. The other people—the nationalists and technocrats, among others—are also getting ready to reinforce their political position. Some of them are aiming for the recognition of the enemy crusader, so they can take power. This recognition comes with well-known concessions that these people give to the crusaders. Some other people aim to get the recognition of the Arab countries—puppets of the crusaders—in order to avoid the intimidation that can accompany direct cooperation with the crusaders. There are also other people who trust in Allah, follow what Allah allows, and use the right ways to become empowered. This empowerment is only given to the people of belief and of righteous deeds. It is to this last group that we address the text you are currently reading, because all the other groups have followed obscure and lonesome roads, the results and reasons of which are known, dangerous, and have consequences.[9]

Following the righteous path requires the adoption of new methods, such as clear strategic planning. It is a duty that Allah ordered of his monotheistic servants when He said in His Quran: 'And prepare against them whatever you are able of power,' power that includes work and knowledge.

The Phenomena of the Apostate Sahwa Forces

The crusaders and the traitors and Muslims who ally with them often speculate about unjust acts committed by the State while it is in control of certain regions. They also claim that the clans would not have taken up arms against

---

ing numbers by the end of 2009. This happened for a variety of reasons: people quit, got other jobs, were persuaded to quit by the Islamic State, or were disillusioned with pay or the lack of government support. This prediction of the demise of the Sahwa was an accurate one.

[9] Our best guess is that this cryptic allusion refers to other Islamist groups (not including the Iraqi Islamic Party/Muslim Brotherhood), and the remnants of Sunni resistance groups that are still estranged from the government, in the attempt to convince them to come join the Islamic State movement over other groups that are reconciling with the government.

the State if it had not killed Muslims and accused them of apostasy. This is not entirely true.[10] For example, during the era of the first Caliph Abu Bakr Siddiq, may Allah be pleased with him, the majority of Arab tribes committed apostasy. This was not because the caliph was unjust, confiscated their money, or killed them. This is an historic example that shows the Islamic state was not to blame in Medina at that time—the tribes were to blame for committing apostasy. The tribes [that rebelled against Abu Bakr, the successor to Muhammad] were more numerous than the official numbers of the Sahwa forces of today. This is rational, reasonable proof. Theoretically speaking, the issue of Sahwa forces fighting ISI can easily be explained through sociology.[11] Both the clans in Iraq today and the tribes that committed apostasy during the era of Abu Bakr Siddiq did not choose to fight the state because the latter was unjust, but because these tribes and clans had certain customs and traditions that control and affect them enormously, such as:

a) Clan and tribe members will always support their own, even if they are unjust. This is, in fact, because the tribe's members abide by clannishness and tribalism, which allows a member to support his fellow no matter what. Ibn Khaldun—mercy upon him—said: 'Kinship is a natural desire among humans, it bonds the close ones and relatives together during a catastrophe or when they are going through hard time.' Azhari also mentioned that tribalism is characterised by a tribe member supporting his fellow tribe member, even if he is practicing injustice. Therefore, the advocacy of tribe members is not a proof that there is something wrong or unjust, as the crusaders are trying to show the world through their media and research centres.[12] The example we gave earlier of Abu Bakr's tribes rebelling against him although he was a fair ruler is a good example that proves the problem is tribalism and not ISI. There are many other examples that also can be cited in the Islamic Maghreb and Andalusia. As a result, we cannot claim that the rise of the Sahwa forces was caused by the bad deeds of ISI. This is a false accusation by

---

[10] In fact, this is completely true, although there are other reasons why tribes fought the rising power of the Islamic State, including economic and social reasons, and even tribal feuds.

[11] The attempt to use a social science explanation of tribal behaviour to exculpate the Islamic State from 'causing' the tribal backlash is the focus of an upcoming article by one of the authors, 'The Islamic State's Tribal Engagement Experiment', *Small Wars and Insurgencies* (Fall 2019/Winter 2020).

[12] As the Abbottabad documents have shown regarding Usama bin Laden, the Islamic State also pays close attention to what is written about them, including some of it in their more recent glossy magazines *Dabiq* and *Rumiyah*.

the crusaders' media ... The purpose of labelling ISI and other groups that carry out the mission of jihad terrorist organisations and extremists was to turn people against these jihadi groups and make them join the Sahwa forces to fight against ISI and delay the Islamic project.

b) Most of the Sahwa forces are young. These young people tend to like project-ing power, engaging in adventure, and being leading members. This is well known, especially among the youth of the tribes and clans. These young people lack faith. The fact that other members of their clans are joining the Sahwa forces is enough to convince them to join as well. There is also the financial aspect of getting paid to join the Sahwa forces and the apostate clan leaders, who receive money to send youth to fight, issuing commands. The young people are also afraid of the consequences of not submitting to a com-mand from the clan leader. These factors are enough to make the youth of the clans and tribes contribute to the swelling numbers of the Sahwa forces. These acts are encouraged by the lack of an ethics of self-conscientiousness, invigorated by the media that keeps falsely accusing the *mujahidin* of crimi-nal, unjust, and oppressive deeds, and by some mistakes made by the *muja-hidin*. The mistakes of the *mujahidin* do not include blowing up mosques, as the media claims.[13] All these elements paved the way for the rapid rise of the Sahwa forces.

All these reasons prove to us that the rise of the tribal Sahwa forces was not a result of actions allegedly carried out by the *mujahidin*, such as forcing peo-ple to pledge allegiance to Islam or accusing people of apostasy if they disagree with the *mujahidin*. This is especially clear now that we know the first of the Sahwa forces—created in Qaim [in 2004] under the name of Hamza—was a secret police unit formed by the Americans, the interior ministry of Iraq and the criminal [Iraqi] Islamic Party, according to the recently leaked documents from the interior ministry of Iraq.[14] This occurred even prior to the establish-

---

[13] This is untrue, as the Islamic State has not had any compunction about destroying the mosques of apostates (Sunni or not), of killing their wives and children, and claiming it in their operational statements. The Islamic State has killed Shi'a pilgrims indiscriminately since 2003, and after 2007, regularly claimed it; see Whiteside, Craig, 'A case for terrorism as genocide in an era of weakened states', *Dynamics of Asymmetric Conflict*, 8:3 (2015), pp. 232–250, DOI: 10.1080/17467586.2015. 1104418

[14] This precursor to the Sahwa movement took place in 2004 and genuinely was an indigenous tribal uprising (not the work of the secret police) that surprised the Americans, who eventually adapted. See William Knarr, 'Al-Sahawa: An Awakening in al-Qaim', *Combatting Terrorism Exchange (CTX)* 3, no. 2 (2013), https://glo-balecco.org/al-sahawa-an-awakening-in-al-qaim#18, last accessed 18 Dec. 2018.

ment of ISI. This first Sahwa force claimed to fight against the crusaders, which led some *mujahidin* to support them with weapons and money. However, this force started organising assassinations of the *mujahidin* in the region of Qaim, while the real *mujahidin* avoided confrontations with the Sahwa force because they wanted to concentrate on the confrontation with the Americans and did not want to provoke popular discontent.[15]

Some *mujahidin* told us that one of the biggest mistakes they committed was not to fight the Hamza Sahwa force in its early stages.[16] This mistake occurred because the *mujahidin* were worrying about the will and happiness of the people rather than the will and pleasure of Allah, which was to kill these apostates after the leaked documents were revealed. When the *mujahidin* delayed achieving the will of Allah, they lost the battle and the apostates confiscated the city of Husaybah, followed by Qaim, with the aerial help of the Americans, the military, and the police. That is how the Sahwa apostate forces began to spread through the rest of Anbar region and over all of Iraq.[17]

---

[15] The assassinations of Islamic State members by Sahwa tribal fighters is documented in many instances in eulogies and captured documents, although these have been largely ignored due to the Sahwa's alliance with the US and the problems that accompany acknowledging these extra-judicial killings. This played a large part in the Sahwa's defeat of the Islamic State, but had limited impact after the Islamic State retreated, watched, and waited.

[16] Note that this Hamza force was a tribal one not affiliated with the Sahwa movement, but the Islamic State has evolved to calling all Sunni armed groups that oppose it a 'Sahwa of apostasy'. See Whiteside, Craig, 'Nine Bullets for the Traitors, One for Crusaders; the Slogans and Strategies of the Islamic State's Counter-Sahwa Campaign', ICCT-The Hague, vol. 9 (2018), https://icct.nl/wp-content/uploads/2018/09/ICCT-Whiteside-Nine-Bullets-For-The-Traitors-September–2018.pdf., last accessed 18 Dec. 2018.

[17] This is a distorted history of the Sahwa. Al-Qaida in Iraq crushed the 'Desert Protectors' of Qaim in 2005, with a special appearance by Abu Musab al-Zarqawi. Zarqawi mentioned in a later speech that it was a necessity, and a warning to Sunni tribes considering rebelling against his group. See al-Zarqawi, Abu Musab, 'Leader of al-Qaida in Iraq al-Zarqawi Declares "Total War" on Shi'ites, States that the Sunni Women of Tel-Afar Had "Their Wombs Filled with the Sperm of the Crusader"', al-Qaida in Iraq Media Battalion, 14 Sept. 2005, Haverford al-Qaida statements collection. The Sahwa that formed in 2006 was the third uprising against al-Qaida, and the one that stuck. See Cottam, Martha, and Joe Huseby, *Confronting al Qaeda: The Sunni Awakening and American Strategy in al Anbar*, Lanham MD: Roman & Littlefield Publishers, 2016.

Everybody can be a witness of the good deeds and good behaviour of the *mujahidin* in Qaim. These witnesses in the region protected the *mujahidin*, especially the *muhajirin* [non-Iraqi emigrants to the Islamic State movement], as they are loved by these people. Qaim was only a bridge for the *mujahidin* to reach other regions. All this success was due to huge local popular support. At that time, there were no explosions or any other issues, contrary to some people's claims that bombings were the reason for the rise of the Sahwa forces. This is confirmation that the accusations made by the traitors and national resistance groups that the Sahwa forces' rise was due to ISI and the jihadi organisations are malicious and false.[18]

The issue facing the *mujahidin* was due to something they themselves were not able to do, which was to stop worrying about the local population and concentrate their efforts against the occupiers.[19] This is why the *mujahidin* no longer abide by the preferences of the people, but rather abide by their objective to satisfy Allah's will. This is why we now see the blessing of our actions, satisfying Allah by imposing the prescribed penalties of sharia law on the apostate Sahwa forces.[20] Allah's blessing has resulted in the obvious, gradual return of ISI to its previous status, strength and power.

Preface

The critical period, in which the Sahwa forces rose and endangered ISI and the jihad project, is over and we are recovering from its circumstances. That was also the period when the crusaders played their national resistance movements [trick] card, so these movements are obviously allies to the crusaders rather than resistance movements. For example, the political wing of the national resistance signed a secret protocol with the crusaders. This protocol will allow this political wing to take over the matter of Iraq once the crusader troops leave the country in two years.[21] After this period came another period of

---

[18] In this case, 'national' resistance groups is a disparaging term, since Salafi-Jihadism disparages the idea of nationalist sentiment for artificial states and instead advocates for a different form of nationalism: that for the Muslim nation or *ummah*.

[19] This is also not true, as the Islamic State admittedly prioritized killing Shi'a and apostates over Americans, as seen in Chapter 2 in Zarqawi's letter to Zawahiri.

[20] This is a subtle switch, admitting that the Islamic State has been killing Sahwa members in accordance with its interpretation of sharia.

[21] This protocol does not exist in any form, nor has anything like it come to light in

planning and preparing for the time post-American withdrawal from Iraq. This period would see some American troops stay under the pretext of training and preparing the Iraqi forces. This is just a pretext crusaders use so that their forces can re-enter Iraq to provide help to the traitor regime that supports them. It also serves as a pretext to push away anything that might endanger the existence of this traitor regime by claiming to defend American interests in the region.

We can claim that the next war will be primarily a political and a media war. The winner of this war will be the one who can prepare and plan for the period after American troops' withdrawal. This will allow the winner to promote themselves among people and to completely take charge of guiding Iraq, directing it towards either the winner's approach or a betrayal, a nationalistic approach or an Islamic approach.

We see two political paths for Iraq's future. One of them is a nationalistic project, represented by the empowerment factions and the political council. Although there are differences between the factions and the political council, they are still easy to deal with as most of them are just differences of interests and vision that can be surpassed. The nationalistic project will form a government in which all Iraqi factions will be represented regardless of any Islamic criteria. Therefore, Christians and Devil worshipers [Yazidi] and Shi'a *rafidites* [literally rejectionists, meaning of the first three Rashidun/caliphs] will be represented.[22] This government will abide by international laws, United Nations resolutions, and Arab League laws, which is what a national government is supposed to do.

The second project is an Islamic one that follows the prophet's methodology, a project that understands the law of the *salaf* [the ancestors] and their *fiqh* [jurisprudence], and that cherishes Islam and is represented by ISI, which

---

the ten years since the Sahwa. The group mentioned is most likely the 1920 Revolution Brigades or the Islamic Army in Iraq, both national resistance groups that fragmented and had significant elements fight the Islamic State after 2007. They also reconciled with the government in return for political power over Sunni areas. This power was ephemeral.

[22] The Islamic State refers to the Yazidi as 'devil worshippers', due to the Zoroastrian influence on Yazidi practice and the presence of a fallen angel figure in the deities. The Yazidis are subject to genocide largely because the Islamic State sees the group as a polytheist group and not subject to certain protections for monotheist religions/people of the book.

will implement its promises and abides by sharia law. ISI does not believe in anything that opposes sharia and it will not compromise its values under any circumstances, such as by exercising modern day jurisprudence. Modern day jurisprudence deconstructs the foundations of the religion.

It is well known to all Muslims that the right project is the one that accepts the Islamic methodology, unlike the nationalistic projects that are not a part of Islam—even if they try to ally themselves with Islam and Salafism.[23] If they were a part of the Islamic project, then the companions of the prophet and the followers that came after the prophet would have been nationalists as well and we, ISI, would have promoted a nationalist government as well and Islam would have told us that nationalism is the right way. Nationalists claim their method is based on the gradual implementation of sharia to preserve their interests, which is the excuse of losers. It is known that Allah said: 'This day I have perfected for you your religion and completed My favour upon you and have approved for you Islam as religion.'

The project of the Islamic State in Iraq is a project for the whole nation of Islam. It is without a doubt the goal of all the truthful *mujahidin* in Iraq. What we will introduce is a strategic plan for this coming period, which we believe will be crucial for preparation and planning, and profitable to the other truthful *mujahidin* who have a different point of view and methodology than ours. We also ask Allah to empower the Islamic State in Iraq and unify the Muslims under its flag to become victorious and a source of pride for all Muslims everywhere.

This plan will have 5 chapters:
First: A Serious Quest to Unite Efforts
Second: Balanced Military Planning
Third: Establishing Awakening Jihadi Councils
Fourth: Considering the Importance of the Political Symbol
Fifth: Reassuring the Dissidents [Christians and Jews]

5.1b. Analysis

This section serves less as an introduction to the strategy document itself, and more as an opportunity for movement veterans to vent the raw emotions still felt by the end of 2009 over the betrayal of the tribes and the other resistance

---

[23] The author(s) are venting about their Sunni nationalist rivals (IAI, Mujahidin Army, JRTN) who profess to be Salafi but do not share the *takfir* concept (particularly against majority Shi'a) and participate in democratic governance.

groups three years earlier. They blamed dirty tricks by the Americans and a hostile media that disapproved of the group's attempts to dominate the resistance, its intensive suicide bombing campaign (that targeted not only Shi'a civilians and the security forces), and its killing of prominent tribal members. In fact, the Islamic State did all of these, and admitted so in its press releases at the time. This Part is mostly full of false claims and justifications for why the collapse of the Islamic State of Iraq in 2007 was due to inherent tribal dynamics and not a popular backlash against its cause. Strangely, they claim at the end of this discussion, 'This is why the *mujahidin* do not abide by the preferences of the people anymore but rather abide by their objective to satisfy Allah's will.' This is always the crux of the Islamic State dilemma: whether to follow religious law in dealing with Muslims that do not live up to the dictates of its *manhaj* (method), or to be pragmatic in its dealing with them. The reality is that the Islamic State movement became much more pragmatic after its popular decline, as the ideas in the subsequent chapters of this document will attest.[24] Yet, here they are claiming the opposite—that tolerating the tribes led to the Sahwa uprising—and so now they are simply following Allah's instructions by letting the chips fall where they may. Many of the author's protestations here are not truthful, but it is important to note what the group is lying about in order to identify its vulnerabilities.

The end of the introduction really highlights what this document is ostensibly about: how the authors foresee the creation of an Islamic State that actually governs according to the prophetic method, drawing guidance from the Prophet and his companions—a state for the best of the Muslims. The authors accomplish this by drawing a contrast between their vision and one that is against everything they believe in—that of a democratically and multi-ethnic Iraq, one subject to international (read non-Muslim) influence and globalised norms.

5.2a. The Fallujah Memorandum, December 2009/January 2010
Chapter 1—A Serious Quest to Unify Efforts

Some people might get bored of talking about this subject because they already know how important it is to the overall jihad project for which every-

---

[24] This is not to say that once successful, they would slip into their ideological trap of treating non-supporters so harshly that they inspire many to fight them to the death. This will always be the group's vulnerability, as argued by Mohammed Hafez and others.

body is calling. It is absurd that we have to mention the Quranic verses and Hadith that call for unity regardless of differences. Although everybody recognises these verses and Hadith and calls for their use in practice, there are differences in people's understanding of unification and how to establish it. The differences of opinion are not about the legitimacy of unification per se; we all believe we should remind, warn, and teach people about it. Our way of going about this shortened study of the obstacles preventing unification will be to examine statements made about unification by jihadi groups. There are two main important statements made on this matter by two different jihadi groups. We will analyse the causes of the obstacles preventing unification in order to know the truth behind them.

Generally speaking, the best-known argument about whether an Islamic state is realistic is that the Islamic State does not have complete control over a geographic location. But what about the B1 heavy bombers based in military bases outside of Iraq? The crusaders and their traitorous agents could not even partially invade the land under our control and that is why they used these heavy bombers. What about the court systems we have established? What about these large regions in Anbar that were filmed by the Sahwa forces, who admitted that they were fully under the control of IS? Or what about the any other things the cameras could not film? The fact that some little battalions still use guerrilla warfare strategies does not mean we can blow the whole Islamic project away.[25]

Even if we say that the project of a state is currently unrealistic, it will be realistic in the future. The claim of unrealistic project is just a barrier and is not true, because the Islamic project is a realistic one and I do not think the brothers in this group think an IS project is unrealistic.

The issue of [jihadi] unification does not need consultation because all jihadi groups already have only one project: the establishment of an Islamic state in Iraq. Therefore, there is no need to consult each other. Since the point of origin and the goal are agreed upon, the other little details can be agreed upon as well. In fact, the [other jihadi] group's first requirement for unification—to agree on a common point of reference—already exists. Even if there was a disagreement about the point of reference, as this particular group

---

[25] Emphasis added by the original authors. The guerrilla warfare remark refers to the smaller groups still fighting the Iraqi government and the occupation but not under ISI banners. The authors are saying that they are irrelevant to the larger picture and the need for unification.

claims, the disagreement should not stop us from merging, because doing so is a legal duty of Islam and our ultimate goal. Therefore, we cannot avoid this duty over a disagreement. If the goal was only consultation [then fine], but consultation is not the ultimate goal. Unification is. Therefore, a duty (in this case unification) has priority over what is not a duty (consultation). Umar and Abu Ubaidah [companions of Muhammed] pledged allegiance to Abu Bakr—Allah's mercy be upon them—without consulting the other companions of the prophet.

The case in today's Iraq is even more important than the issue that Abu Bakr—Allah's mercy be upon him—had to deal with, because now in Iraq there are many thieves and mercenaries waiting for the chance to take advantage of the situation to impose their misguided doctrines and perverted methodologies. They [the Muslim Brotherhood] will prohibit sharia law as their brothers in different places did, while the worst that could have happened during Abu Bakr's time was for them to fight and kill each other. Allah said, 'disorder, or *fitna* (civil unrest) is worse than killing'. Therefore, removing sharia law and replacing it with democratic laws and evil systems is *fitna* and is the worst possible outcome.

There is no proof that consultation between all the factions involved is required because they have two choices only:

1. Either they want to impose a true Islamic state that abides by sharia law, which is being done by their brothers, so why not join them since they have this goal in common?
2. Some people do not want sharia law and want to remove it. Those people have no dignity and it is impossible for the people of Islam to allow these unbelievers in their midst.

Many tribal, group, and battalion leaders, among others, pledged allegiance [to the Islamic State]. Even the enemy and the apostates know we are in control and that is why they are bombing our regions and mentioning us in their press conferences, which pushed the Christians to pay us *jizyah* [the tax on Christians and Jews] to protect them. Ten days after this [jihadi] group's statement [criticising the Islamic state], Sheikh Abu Hamza al-Muhajir held a meeting where he answered a question about whether reaching out to other groups before declaring the state was an obligation. He—may Allah protect him—answered: 'Everyone can witness that we put an effort into communication with other groups and they all know it, with the exception of one group that was completely involved in the political scene [Islamic Party/Muslim

Brotherhood].' Some groups we contacted two months ahead of the declaration and others we contacted even four months ahead. Unfortunately, we were not able to meet with each other prior to the declaration. Some of them said they were outside the country and others said they were busy doing something else, which is sadly funny. Hilf al-Mutayyabin was the first to be invited. We thought this group would comply wholly with our request to join forces. A few of them did not, but the majority did. Even after the declaration of the state we contacted them again and told them: 'Fellow servants of Allah, the Islamic State is also your project and the project of the whole nation of Islam. It is not exclusive to us only. We even changed the name of our group and left our Emirate [al-Qaida in Iraq] to be a part of this big project.'

The reason that we did not wait for the people outside of the country to come back or for others to join us is that we feared that the Islamic Party in Iraq would declare an independent Sunni region, as was the case with the Kurds. This would have hijacked the jihadi project to bring all the Sunnis together. That is why the declaration of the Islamic State had to happen—to stop the Islamic Party from making such a move.[26]

Whoever claims that the Islamic project will be a failure and, based on that, decides not to join, we say to this type of person that the circumstance and reason that pushed us into establishing a state in Iraq is the fact that the crusaders are trying to install traitors as the government. We saw this happening in other experiences where Islamic efforts and projects were hijacked.[27]

The crusaders have now established a traitor government [originally] under the leadership of the traitor Ayad Allawi. This government does not have control over any land, and even the crusaders can barely protect themselves within their military bases. We saw how they failed to break into Fallujah [in 2004] and in many other regions they were also unable to stay for a long time. This traitor government was faced by many challenges such as the refusal of

---

[26] This is as convincing a reason as you will find for the 2006 declaration of the Islamic State of Iraq—that the founders (which seems to include the author(s) here) were afraid of their Brotherhood rivals getting the jump on consolidating Sunni power into an autonomous region, which might be popular with the average Sunni Iraqi and therefore detrimental to the 'state project.' Yet, the narrative is often about Islamic State impatience and arrogance. This is not a political perspective.

[27] This reveals some expeditionary jihadi experience in the ranks of the leadership, and their observation that jihad in the Balkans, Afghanistan, and Algeria was hijacked by political parties, and those against the establishment of an Islamic State.

some hypocrites and semi-traitors to be a part of it. They claimed that this government did not represent all the factions of the Iraqi people and served the occupation forces. The crusaders wanted to form a traitor government when they came to Iraq and Afghanistan and then, after they had made sure that there was no one who might endanger this government that served their interests, they would organise parliamentary and presidential elections to make it into an [permanent] ally government to execute their plans. However, their plan cannot be executed in the presence of real Muslims who fight injustice. Their optimistic planning will be for naught because such Muslims will not accept occupation of their land or traitors who serve their masters' interests. That is the reason why the crusaders use other plans to overcome these people [faithful Muslims] who form an obstacle to the crusaders' control of the land of Islam.

The second of the crusaders' plans can be described thus: jihad has no symbolic leader.

Therefore, people only have the option of choosing the symbolic leader the crusaders choose for them, the crusaders' loyal traitor, [who leads] a fake government that is empowered by the media. This government will slowly get people's attention and people will see that now they have a new president. In fact, this president was only forced into people's awareness because of the media. For example, at first, people condemned Iraq's government when this government only had control over the Green Zone, not all of Iraq, under the leadership of Allawi then [Ibrahim] al-Ja'fari and finally [Nouri] al-Maliki. The general feeling of contempt changed and a good part of these people now accept the reality that these traitors are their leaders.

Further along in the crusaders' plan, they will change these loyal traitors into indirect traitors who will not accept jihad anymore—the weak ones. People will be attracted to these political symbols since they can provide money and jobs for them and these symbolic leaders will have a larger circle of sympathisers. As a result, the jihadi project will become an unwanted burden and useless according to them, as it only represents killing people, destruction, and insecurity. And so the jihad project would lose its value among people or it will be forgotten, lose its popular support, and fail to move forward. This is what the crusaders are trying to do in Afghanistan and Iraq. They want to reach this previous level of analysis we mentioned, in which Allah said, 'and they were scheming, and Allah was scheming; and Allah is The Most Charitable of schemers.' In fact, the crusaders are following the second plan, although it is harder and more expensive to achieve, because the first plan was stopped by the jihad awakening all over the *umma* and the *umma* is immune to all the schemes of the crusaders and the schemes of the traitors. Therefore, we conclude that the Islamic State project, which even those who oppose it will admit, remains steadfast in opposing the crusaders' project and will destroy their plan. The Islamic project will be victorious but the crusaders' project is doomed to fail. Allah said, 'and Allah will surely support those who support Him.'

It has been proven that waiting for the crusaders to achieve their plan's objective—that of establishing a loyal government—before implementing our IS project is a weak strategy. The blood and sacrifices of the *mujahidin* would be wasted. There is no doubt in our mind that limiting jihad to military efforts alone is foolish, especially in Iraq. Everybody is getting ready to benefit from the day the occupiers leave the country. Sticking only to military jihad is extremely naïve and will leave the righteous *mujahidin* out of the equation after the occupiers leave. Mullah Umar realised this and wanted to ensure his emirate—considered unrealistic by the occupiers—would be ready when the enemy left Afghanistan. The traitors and others following the wrong methodology in Iraq also realised this situation and now they are preparing their political and media programs.[28] They are working hard to get recognition and gain political currency to qualify them to lead and gain experience in negotiating with the crusaders to serve their own interests. That is why we see them attacking each other. The righteous people of clean faith also realised this and they are preparing for it by establishing a state to demolish what the crusaders are planning.

Sheikh Abu Hamza al-Muhajir said:

> The time when the occupiers leave will be the worst time ever. We are aware that there are [former resistance] factions stockpiling weapons and preparing security groups for the day the occupier leaves. They will use one rocket and save ten others. We know this from people who repented and pledged allegiance to us.[29] They claimed that the day of fighting us is approaching.

---

[28] This is not a reference to Shi'a Iraqis, rather to Sunni resistance groups and Islamist political parties all participating in the political system. The author(s) are proposing something interesting here—that beyond the military effort, politics will decide who runs the Sunni areas of Iraq. This fits well into insurgency literature about the primacy of politics in revolutionary warfare.

[29] Abu Hamza's reference echoes a similar remark by a senior member of the Shura Council in 2011 (who is still alive at the time of publication), about the steady recruitment of formal rivals in the 2008–12 period, including those that repented from

These honest words show that some people are working to completely eradicate the *mujahidin*, who according to them [non-IS resistance factions] are 'terrorists'.

Some say the deeds of the crusaders do not make [our project] legitimate, because an Islamic state has its own rules set by Islamic jurists; the ends do not justify the means. The response to this statement is this: the means, as long as they do not oppose Allah's sharia law, can be judged by the intended ends. The texts that some Islamic jurists are using to support the illegitimacy of the establishment of IS under the current circumstances are not obligatory to follow, because what is obligatory can be found in the Quran, the deeds and saying of the Prophet Muhammad, and the consensus of the *umma*. Which correct texts recounting deeds prove that the establishment of an Islamic state is forbidden under these circumstances? Of course there are none, the people that reject the establishment of an Islamic state do so on the basis of opinion, not the true sharia law.

Additionally, the *fatwa* [regarding the establishment of an Islamic state] can change according to time and place. Ibn al-Qayyim—mercy upon him—said, 'The *fatwa* changes when the time, place, and circumstances change. This is a part of the religion.' The jurists—mercy be upon them—did not have, at that time, the so-called international conventions and international political circumstances that do not want Islam to be preeminent. Therefore, using the old rules and legislation to judge today's circumstances no doubt appears ignorant to those who are considered jurists.

We summarised our opinion to target viable differences that we thought important to analyse. The aim of this analysis is to prove that these barriers are not big enough to stop us from a unification that is also being watched carefully by our enemy. A unification of the righteous people of the jihad [should have happened], especially after the Mujahidin Shura Council was established and some of the *mujahidin* still refused to unify, which was unacceptable. That is why we say that the most important thing the Islamic State in Iraq and its brothers from other different jihadi groups should look for, especially during this important and crucial time, is complete unification among them. It

---

apostasy (meaning opposed the Islamic State in the *sahwa* elements) and then decided to join them. See Abd-al-Hakim, Abu Ubaydah, 'Press Conference with the member of the Islamic State of Iraq's Shura Council,' al-Furqan Media, 11 Apr. 2011, posted on *Ana al-Muslim Network*.

should be their priority and primary concern, because if it happens, it will with no doubt disturb the crusaders' plans.

To sum up this very important strategic plan of the *mujahidin* in Iraq during this period, I will convey Sheikh Ayman al-Zawahiri's proclamation to the jihadi groups, through which we ask Allah to unify us:

> I, Ayman al-Zawahiri, direct my message and the message of my brothers to all the *mujahidin* in the land of Mesopotamia. I want to ensure to the brothers in the jihadi groups, those with clean and faithful methodology, especially the brothers in the group Ansar al-Islam and their Amir the brother sheikh Abu Abdullah al-Shafi'i—may Allah preserve him to serve the cause of Islam—and to the rest of the brothers, the protectors of Islam in Iraq, to them I say: All the *mujahidin* are impatiently waiting for the unification between you and the Islamic State in Iraq to empower the righteous jihadi project. This project wants to liberate all the lands of Islam and to establish the caliphate. To them, I also say: the Islamic State in Iraq is your state, it is your emirate, and it is your government. With whom will you unify, if not with them? Then hasten for the good with your brothers and reach the glad tidings for which the believers are impatiently waiting.[30]

5.2b. Analysis

The focus of this Part is on the political unification of the remnants of the jihad against the occupying forces and, more importantly, in the post-occupation period, rallying all legitimate jihadi groups around the Islamic State. In some ways, it is relitigating a long-lasting dispute about why some groups refused to join the Islamic State after it was declared in October 2006, and why certain groups chose to ally with the government and fight the movement. Here, the Islamic State is presenting its argument, backed by al-Qaida deputy Zawahiri, for the political unification of all Salafi-jihadis in Iraq under their banner. Interestingly enough, the discussion does not centre on the Shi'a-led Iraqi government, focusing instead on Sunni political rivals like the Iraqi Islamic Party—the Muslim Brotherhood in Iraq. The Salafi-jihadis prohibition on participating in politics makes it difficult for the Islamic State to pre-

---

[30] The full text of this speech, in which the al-Qaida deputy requests that Ansar al-Islam join the Islamic State can be found at: al-Zawahiri, Aymenn, 'Review of Events', 16 Dec. 2007, Al-Sahab Media Production, available at Haverford Al-Qaeda statement collection [registration required] https://scholarship.tricolib.brynmawr.edu/bitstream/handle/10066/4671/ZAW20071216.pdf

sent its case to a public intrigued by democracy, something that was not an obstacle to its Islamist rival. Nonetheless, it is interesting that the first chapter in their strategy document is about politics, a nod to the idea that insurgency is more politics than fighting.[31] There is little evidence to date that proves that it was successful in unifying the majority of Sunni dissidents against the Iraqi government, but it is interesting to note that by 2014, when it began to seize territory and hold it in Sunni Iraq, all of its jihadi resistance rivals either collapsed or eventually joined the Islamic State. It is highly possible that many former rivals joined the Islamic State in small groups in the years before 2014, rendering this chapter, documenting the group's focus on political unification as a first priority of the new strategy, particularly interesting. The idea that the Islamic State prioritises terror and military action over politics is not supported by texts such as this, which remind us that insurgency is best understood as 'armed politics'.[32]

5.3a. The Fallujah Memorandum, December 2009/January 2010
Chapter 2—Balanced Military Planning

The start of the military planning of jihadi work was a reaction to the crusaders' invasion, and every *mujahid* was asked to strike the crusaders' forces and their allies to inflict the greatest possible damage. As the situation evolved, ISI started targeting the Sahwa forces councils in order to get rid of them. This new political and military strategy greatly impacted the Sahwa councils and almost demolished them. This is a great achievement that shows that ISI now has enough military and political power to allow it to be able to deal with internal conflicts.[33]

Therefore, this period needs a balanced confrontation plan to impact the near future. The leaders of the battalions and higher-level amirs should recon-

---

[31] Galula, David, *Counterinsurgency Warfare: Theory and Practice*, Westport, CT: Praeger Security International, 2006, p. 4.

[32] Staniland, Paul, 'Armed Politics and the Study of Intrastate Politics', *Journal of Peace Research* 54, no. 4 (1 July 2017), pp. 459–467, https://doi.org/10.1177/00223 43317698848

[33] It is interesting that the Islamic State claims to have been successful in its counter-Sahwa campaign by 2010, a notion that is at odds with their assassination campaign of Sahwa leaders, which, depending on the province, runs long after this date, see Whiteside, Craig, 'The Islamic State and the Return of Revolutionary Warfare', *Small Wars & Insurgencies* 27, no. 5 (2016), pp. 743–776.

sider military efforts, because they might be counterproductive if they are directed towards the wrong cause, especially in this period when we have different targets and multiple fronts of confrontation. That is why we believe it is necessary for the military plan of this period to consider three main fundamental strategies and functions, which are:

1) For every ten bullets, nine should be directed toward the apostates and one toward the crusaders.[34]
2) Cleansing.
3) Targeting. .

1) For every ten bullets, nine should be directed toward the apostates and one toward the crusaders.

The crusader forces are counting on the power of their local allies, the traitors, such as the Iraqi military and police. The crusaders are working hard to build a powerful force that can completely control the scene without their help. In this way the crusaders will be able to leave the country and leave behind a force that will take over as their ally. Since the crusader forces agreed to leave the scene, it will be a waste of time and effort to focus on fighting them, especially since they are well protected in their bases. That is why it is important to demolish what the crusaders build instead, namely the military and the Iraqi police. This way, the crusader forces will try to save themselves while trying to build up these Iraqi forces, which will face a slow, eventual death.

The goal of our policy is to increase the fear of injury and death within the people in the Iraqi forces. As a result, we can minimise the desire of individuals to join them. This strategy will not bear fruit within a month or two, but it needs continuous work until this matter becomes reality.

In order to reach this goal, we must target the police and the military all over Iraq until no region is safe for them to serve and nothing might encour-

---

[34] This phrase, 'nine bullets directed towards the apostates (traitors) and one towards the crusaders' has an unknown provenance. An Islamic State billboard in Mosul used this quote and attributed it to Abdallah Azzam, the author of *Join the Caravan*, but Azzam's son disputes that his father ever said this, nor does it fit in with his philosophy of jihad (personal correspondence with author via Twitter). al-Tamimi, Aymenn Jawad, 'The Islamic State Billboards and Murals of Tel Afar and Mosul', blog, 7 Jan. 2015, http://www.aymennjawad.org/2015/01/the-islamic-state-billboards-and-murals-of-tel. Nevertheless, this phrase accurately describes an important element of the Islamic State strategy of attrition and exhaustion.

age them to join. We must keep attacking them until the numbers of deaths and injuries are such that even friends and families of the individuals in the military and police also fear for their lives because they are related to them.

It is also very important that a propagandistic media strategy should also be a part of this project to criminalise joining such forces. Additionally, we should enhance the fear of the danger of joining these forces by sending death threats and carrying them out. We should also diversify our speech and messages to differentiate between different people, depending on their orientations and ideologies. We should do that to follow Allah's advice of combining fear with persuasive tactics. That is why we should consider a strict military tactic alongside awareness raising efforts, using softer rhetoric based in sharia justifications.[35]

When it comes to the crusader forces, the *mujahidin* should attack their bases from time to time with some concentrated attacks even if these attacks are rare. The goal of these attacks would be to make sure that the crusaders do not feel safe so they will not change their minds and decide to stay longer to build stronger Iraqi forces.

2) Cleansing Strategy.

The Chinese military leader Sun Tzu said, 'Reduce the hostile chiefs by inflicting damage on them; and make trouble for them, and keep them constantly engaged; hold out specious allurements, and make them rush to any given point.'[36] Cleansing areas where the traitor Iraqi forces are present can be done by targeting the centres and the places where they gather. This is a very important strategy that benefits the jihadi project. In addition to this, the Iraqi forces will stay busy trying to rebuild these centres or looking for others. These forces will also live in insecurity, which will be a persistent feeling among them. This will minimise their power and ability to [go out from these bases to] control these regions.

This strategy is similar to a scorched-earth policy, but it more precisely targets a specific faction, namely the apostate forces. The benefits of such a

---

[35] This mixing of military action and propaganda (or awareness following a soft speech as the authors say) is how militaries try to achieve effective influence operations.

[36] The quote from Sun Tzu is a rare use of a non-jihadi or Arab source for reference, but an indication that they read the classics. It is rare because these authors are usually polytheists or atheists, anathema for the strict monotheism of Salafis.

strategy are not limited to the exhaustion of these forces' resources; it will also empower the presence of ISI within these regions and will give the *mujahidin* better ease of movement to launch bigger attacks. Also, we must not forget to try to turn the capabilities of the enemy to the benefit of the *mujahidin*. It is better to put these capabilities to use than to destroy them. The destruction of the enemy's capabilities is key only when we cannot put them to use in a way that might contribute to the power of ISI.

3) Targeting Strategy.

It is very crucial to target the leaders and the well-trained battalions during this period. This strategy will demolish the crusaders' hopes. We received reports that showed that the majority of Iraqi troops are not capable or qualified to launch operations alone without the help of the crusader forces. Therefore, targeting the well-trained and capable minority of Iraqi forces should be our priority all over the region, in addition to targeting all the qualified officers, engineers, trainers, and others. This is how we can target the most effective parts of these forces, which will make it hard for the crusaders and the Iraqi forces to replace them, especially since they spent a lot of money on these leaders during this time. This will prevent the Iraqi forces from being able to launch any effective operations and cause the crusaders' efforts to fade away. If we can concentrate and follow this strategy, it will be maddening to the crusaders' forces because their efforts will fade away. Therefore, they will be unable to build the forces they hope to build. Although this might take some time and effort to achieve, it is still valuable. A small amount of concentrated effort is better than a lot of effort with no target.

The other strategy is to target strong political symbols. The symbols that, if targeted and removed, will have a real impact, creating a power vacuum within the political process. This gap will feed the confusion and conflict among other political leaders. Long-term planning is very important in this case. If we do not have the intelligence capabilities to immediately target the leaders, we will have to draft martyrs from within their own personal security guards, no matter how long it takes us, or draft people who work for these leaders. These martyrs will be able to kill one or many of these leaders, which will significantly affect the stability of the political scene that the crusaders created. It will show the world and the Muslim community within Iraq that their government is weak and unable to protect even itself—so how can it protect the citizens?

This strategy will prompt people to think that choosing such a government is not the right choice. It will also impact the crusaders, pushing them towards hopelessness, as all their hopes of establishing a strong government able to stand by itself are dashed. This will be because the *mujahidin* were able to infiltrate their security at a high level. They will lose their strong symbols, those capable of carrying on the crusaders' mission. Replacing such powerful people quickly will not be easy.

5.3b. Analysis

This short chapter on the military strategy follows the description of the political environment and challenges laid out in the previous chapter in a fashion that Carl von Clausewitz would argue is the proper sequencing in crafting strategy. The Islamic State movement's problem is, as Ahmed Hashim succinctly writes, '1) how does the weak fight the strong, and 2) how does the weak defeat the strong'.[37] Once decided upon, this strategy must be clearly articulated to dispersed and clandestine cells across Iraq. The end point—political hegemony over Sunni Iraq in the Islamic State's case—can only be accomplished through a long and patient campaign of attrition and exhaustion to 'hollow out' the security forces. The most attention would be paid to high-ranking officers, those with specialised skills, and local politicians—the Islamic State movement's version of a decapitation campaign. There is no timeline attached to the strategy, nor a follow-up plan of exploitation for when it proves to be successful, both of which are definite deficiencies. It is possible this document relates a sanitised version of the strategy, or perhaps it was deliberately left open ended.

The Fallujah Memorandum presents a clear insight into Islamic State military strategy at a time when the movement was very weak, but also had experienced cadres of leaders and was gaining even more back from Camp Bucca on prison paroles, as the Americans wound down their role in Iraq and began to tie up loose ends.[38] This military strategy, quite particular to the Islamic

---

[37] Hashim, Ahmed, 'The Islamic State's Way of War in Iraq and Syria: From its Origins to the Post Caliphate Era', *Perspectives on Terrorism* 13, no. 1 (Feb. 2019), pp. 29–30, https://www.universiteitleiden.nl/binaries/content/assets/customsites/perspectives-on-terrorism/2019/issue-1/hashim.pdf; for further reading on the Islamic State way of war, see Hashim, *The Caliphate at War: Operational Innovations and Realities of the Islamic State*, NY: Oxford University Press, 2018.

[38] The US had difficulty in passing prisoners to the Iraqi government's detention sys-

State's context in Iraq, benefits not only from its experience in the country since 2003 but also the experiences of the larger jihadi movement that impacted its original leaders. Michael Ryan highlights how al-Qaida's strategies of conflict with the West are highly influenced by the famous canons of revolutionary warfare literature based on his analysis of the writings of Muqrin, Suri, Naji, and Qurashi.[39] Revolutionary or 'people's' war is defined as a form of irregular war that utilises 'peasant armies that are drawn upon for an integrated and protracted politico-military phase strategy of eventual state takeover. A shadow or proto-state is created in parallel to the pre-existing one being targeted for elimination.'[40] Mao, the first proponent and theorist of this type of warfare, believed that victory was only possible once the population is mobilised to support the guerrillas, whose goal is to attack the enemy when advantaged and to shy away from conflict otherwise. The part-time fighters and their supporters are to be indoctrinated in the political philosophy of the movement to motivate them to fight and persevere through a protracted struggle. The campaign progresses through three phases of blended guerrilla activities and increasing conventional strength: the building/preservation phase, the expansion phase, and the decisive phase. These periods are fluid and conditions vary from location to location, usually dependent on enemy strength and efforts. The keys to success are developing experienced and disciplined soldiers that bond well with a supportive population, the utilisation of a strong influence campaign with propaganda units at the lowest levels, and an integrated set of political goals that are synchronised with military efforts at all levels.[41]

---

tem, usually because much of the information that triggered raids to detain Islamic State members was classified at a very high level due to the technical means of acquiring the evidence as well as the top-tier SOF units that usually executed the raids. See Whiteside, Craig, 'Catch and Release in the Land of Two Rivers', *War on the Rocks*, 18 Dec. 2014, https://warontherocks.com/2014/12/catch-and-release-in-the-land-of-two-rivers/

[39] Ryan, Michael, *Decoding Al Qaeda's Strategy: The Deep Battle Against America*, New York: Columbia University Press, 2013.

[40] Bunker, Robert J., *Old and New Insurgency Forms*, Strategic Studies Institute, U.S. Army War College, Mar. 2016, p. 36. [14] Crenshaw, Martha, 'The Concept of Revolutionary Terrorism', *Journal of Conflict Resolution* (1972), p. 384.

[41] Tse Tung, Mao, *On Guerrilla Warfare*, trans. Samuel B. Griffith II (Baltimore: The Nautical & Aviation Publishing Company of America, 1992).

Revolutionary war is more than military action, since those who utilise it blend 'military, political, economic, social, and psychological' efforts to achieve their goals.[42] The military objectives are twofold: a slow defeat of the government's military and the use of terror to debilitate the existing social organisation, which, prior to the conflict, served to 'restrict or minimize violence among the people'. Once the violence reaches a certain level, these barriers collapse.[43] Martha Crenshaw notes in her study of revolutionary warfare in Algeria that terrorism almost always acts as a 'principal instrument' in this form of political violence.[44] This instrument is 'not aimed, as war is, at the annihilation of the enemy's coercive forces, but seeks to wound him politically and psychologically'.[45] Finally, the movement taxes the population under its influence in order to fund operations and derive legitimacy for the shadow state.[46]

Chapter 2 of the Fallujah Memorandum faithfully mentions several of these precepts, dressed in the Islamic State's own terminology. First, weakness forces the insurgents to prioritise targets, and any effort against a well-protected US force that is already dedicated to leaving is wasted energy. Instead, the goal is to destroy the specialised Iraqi units the US is grooming to carry on the fight after they leave. Thus the intuitive slogan for its first tenet: 'nine bullets for the apostate (traitors), one for the enemy (US)'.

The second tenet mentions a 'cleansing strategy', a strategy of 'exhaustion' with the goal of stretching the resources of the state by busying its forces with what Mao referred to as 'constant activity and movement'.[47] The end result is insecurity and fear among the members of the security forces and their families, as the areas in which they are targeted are endless, from the home to the mosque to the city street. The third and final tenet is a 'targeting strategy', emphasising quality over quantity—the idea is to select the very best men,

---

[42] Griffith, Samuel, ed., 'Introduction to First Edition', in Mao Tse-Tung, *On Guerilla Warfare*, p. 56.

[43] Johnson, Chalmers, *Revolutionary Change*, Stanford: Stanford University Press/ Longman Group, 1983, p. 3.

[44] Hutchinson, 'The Concept of Revolutionary Terrorism', p. 384.

[45] Johnson, *Revolutionary Change*, p. 153.

[46] Andrews, William, *The Village at War: Vietnamese Communist Revolutionary Activity in Dinh Tuong Province 1960–1964*, Columbia, MO: University of Missouri Press, 1973, p. 96.

[47] Tse Tung, Mao, *On Guerrilla Warfare*, trans. Samuel B. Griffith II, Baltimore: The Nautical & Aviation Publishing Company of America, 1992, p. 78.

officers, and technicians in the Iraqi security forces for elimination. This mirrors the Viet Cong strategy of leaving corrupt officials in place to discredit the incumbent government, while targeting honest political officials and virulent anti-communists who could never be co-opted into acquiescence.[48] The authors of the Fallujah Memorandum say it best: 'A small amount of concentrated effort is better than a lot of effort with no target.'

The three principles that guide the Islamic State's military efforts from 2009 on are a clear indication that, at this time, they saw themselves in Mao's 'building/persevering' phase, as described above. This is not the first time the group has been in this phase; during the early battles of Fallujah, Mosul, Tal Afar, Qaim, and Ramadi, the group's leadership learned many lessons about how to execute this phase of preservation carefully and build power for the next phase—'expansion'. We can see from the first chapter that as early as 2009, the group saw opportunity on the horizon with the US withdrawal, which was already being felt by Iraqi forces. The group would transition to the 'decisive' phase in 2014 with the campaign to control territory in Iraq and Syria, before regressing back to the first phase—preserving—again in 2016–7 as it retreated 'out into the desert', as Hassan Hassan writes.[49]

The cycle continues today, as the group builds on its past to create conditions to exploit political dysfunction, corrupt governance, and coalition fracturing. A four-part series in the Islamic State's *al-Naba* weekly newsletter reviewed the 2019 version of the Islamic State's current military strategy, and the parallels with the Fallujah Memorandum, published a decade before, are striking. The group is once again in 'the first phases of guerrilla warfare', which 'rely on surprising enemy forces in weak areas', followed by planned withdrawals. The temporary seizure of lightly defended population centres by jihadis facilitates the arrest of high-ranking security or political leaders and the seizure of wealth as *ghanima* (booty), necessary to fund the insurgency.[50] These kinds of operation build in impact through what J.C. Wiley

---

[48] Pike, Doug, *Viet Cong: The Organization and Techniques of the National Liberation Front of South Vietnam*, Boston: MIT Press, 1966; Andrews, *The Village at War*, 1973.

[49] Hassan, Hassan, 'Out of the Desert: ISIS's strategy for a long war', Middle East Institute, 6 Sept. 2018, http://education.mei.edu/content/out-desert-isiss-strategy-long-war

[50] Islamic State, 'Bringing Down the Towns Temporarily as a Method of Operation for the *Mujahidin*', *al-Naba* #179, 25 April 2019, translated by Aymenn al-Tamimi and available at: http://www.aymennjawad.org/2019/04/islamic-state-insurgent-tac-

refers to as 'cumulative strategies' of operation, seeking to produce a combination of exhaustion and attrition until an operation like Mosul (2014) takes place, and a 'temporary' raid leads to catastrophic success.[51] In *al-Naba* #179, the authors of the article mention the Haditha raid of 2012 as an ideal example of a raid (a military attack with a planned withdrawal),[52] and consider Mosul the exception—with the *mujahidin* 'adopting the decision to broaden the assault to include the left side [East Mosul] to catch the fleeing remnants of the enemy.'[53]

Subsequent *al-Naba* issues build on tactical goals for 'fleeting attacks',[54] executed to inflict *nikaya* (damage), free prisoners, and accrue *ghanima*. These attacks could also be used as bait to ambush reinforcing elements, or to target key leaders. But the strategic impact of the raids was to fix enemy forces in static positions, 'raise the zeal of the Muslims', and cause the enemy to cede territory that is too unsafe or difficult to control due to high costs.[55]

---

tics-translation, original available at Aaron Zelin's Jihadology https://jihadology. net/2019/04/25/new-issue-of-the-islamic-states-newsletter-al-naba-179/

[51] This is much in line with strategist Wylie's concept of control as the object of war and his two sets of operational patterns: sequential and cumulative; Milevski, Lukas, 'Revisiting J.C. Wylie's Dichotomy of Strategy: The Effects of sequential and Cumulative Patterns of Operations', *Journal of Strategic Studies* 35, No 2. (2012), pp. 223–242.

[52] The Haditha raid of 2012 was a special operation that featured a company-sized element of fighters dressed as Iraqi Golden Division fighters fooling police and taking over the city. The policemen were executed on camera for propaganda purposes, as was the initial target of the raid: a Sahwa commander in the area. See Whiteside, Craig, Ian Rice, and Daniele Raineri, 'Black Ops: Islamic State and Innovation in Irregular Warfare', *Studies in Conflict and Terrorism*, 2019.

[53] Islamic State, 'Bringing Down the Towns Temporarily', *al-Naba* #179.

[54] Islamic State, 'Bringing Down the Towns Temporarily as a Method of Operation for the *Mujahidin*', *al-Naba* #181, 9 May 2019, translated by Aymenn al-Tamimi and available at: http://www.aymennjawad.org/2019/04/islamic-state-insurgent-tactics-translation; original available at Aaron Zelin's Jihadology https://jihadology. net/2019/05/09/new-issue-of-the-islamic-states-newsletter-al-naba-181/

[55] Islamic State, 'Bringing Down the Towns Temporarily as a Method of Operation for the *Mujahidin*', *al-Naba* #180, 2 May 2019, translated by Aymenn al-Tamimi and available at: http://www.aymennjawad.org/2019/04/islamic-state-insurgent-tactics-translation original available at Aaron Zelin's Jihadology https://jihadology. net/2019/05/02/new-issue-of-the-islamic-states-newsletter-al-naba-180/

The contemporary explanation of the Islamic State's irregular war doctrine in *al-Naba* is just a better articulation of what we see here in its early stage. Both the Fallujah Memorandum and the *al-Naba* series serve as instructions to a dispersed network of guerrilla units that are carefully isolated from each other in order to protect against any catastrophic failure (intelligence penetration, captured members who talk, and so on). The online dissemination to supporters allows it to serve as an educational tool for new commanders in charge of new formations, as the movement works to advance to further stages of revolutionary warfare in its quest to build and maintain a caliphate.

5.4a. The Fallujah Memorandum, December 2009/January 2010
Chapter 3—Establishing Jihadi Sahwa Councils

The idea of drafting tribal leaders to exterminate the *mujahidin* is, without a doubt, something any future occupier would try to do, because such a plan would make the occupiers' work easier and shield them from *mujahidin* strikes. Therefore, the protection such as that of the tribal Sahwa forces would limit the damage and casualties incurred by the occupiers.

The tribal Sahwa forces failed because the *mujahidin* targeted their leaders. Another reason why these traitor forces failed is because of the traditional tribal principles that criminalise cooperation with a foreign occupier. Two main factors that aided the [original] establishment and spread of the Sahwa councils were (1) financial motives and (2) ideological motives, the latter of which revolved around hating anything related to Islamic sharia law and commitment to its principles, and placing value on the freedom to pursue one's desires. This was obvious in Anbar after these councils seized the region and spread an atrocious liberation of ethics that frightened honest people—practices that ended when ISI was in charge [in 2006–7].

It is impossible for these councils to continue with the strength they had before because these [two] factors have dangerous outcomes that impact the cohesiveness of tribal society itself. When these councils were in control, people noticed a lack of security because the leaders of these tribes are mercenaries and criminals who exercise control and power through the money and weapons they receive from the crusaders. They will also push away the righteous tribal leaders and youth, removing opposition to the new councils.

This is why the crusaders—with good reason—[eventually] gave up on supporting the Sahwa councils. Such a project is characterised by failure and disintegration. They were established as a temporary shield for the installation of an allied government that would serve to protect crusader military bases in the region. Therefore, we, the Islamic State, call for establishment of [our own] jihadi *sahwa* [awakening] councils, similar to the ones the Prophet—peace be upon him—convened at the Medina delegations. The idea is to cooperate with righteous and honourable tribal leaders to develop security forces from among their youth to protect their regions from traitor police and the crusaders' forces and to completely cleanse the region. In addition to this, these forces will protect people from theft and mercenaries and impose sharia rules, to be legislated by a sharia judge. Their leader should preferably have experience with the State so we are able to deal with the tribal youth.

The financial support for these forces could come through their tribe in collaboration with ISI. This, of course, can be done by convincing the leaders of the tribes, who will in turn convince the other people who live in the region of the authority of tribal traditions. They will kick out the apostates and traitors to implement sharia [the law], as our religion of Islam is telling us to do. The financial support can also be obtained through the Islamic State's *bayt al-mal* [treasury house] or *ghanima* taken from the enemy, similar to how commercial companies pay employees based on commission. This force can also be financed through the people who earn enough money, such as the merchants, who are convinced that these forces are important for their security. Allah will have a reward for these donations and the donors can join these jihad councils if their intention is to support Islam and defend it against criminals and apostates. This can be easily done when the honourable and righteous leaders of the tribes understand and are convinced by the project.

This process won't be easy because we will face security, social, and other barriers. However, it is worth the effort. We saw how the crusaders were able to remove many obstacles before them in developing their apostate councils in every region by paying money. Therefore, the difficulty of achieving this project does not mean we should give it up.

There are many important gains to be made through this project:

1. The easy expansion of ISI control and domination: This can be done by instituting a sharia judge and an ISI military leader to guide these tribal forces. This way, these regions under the control of ISI will become more powerful and secure. Unlike any regular kind of military force, which tend to be weak, these tribal forces are more powerful because they have support of the locals, who protect the region.

2. Gaining the loyalty of the tribal leaders: When ISI negotiates with the leaders of these tribes, they recognise their importance and value within

ISI. This project will also give these leaders something they can give to their own people and their country, which will make them more motivated [to participate], once they understand the importance of this project. This is the best opportunity to foster agreement and strengthen the popular support for these leaders, which will give the project a better chance of success.

3. Including tribal society in building an Islamic state in Iraq: This project helps build public awareness of the importance of living within an Islamic state. It also helps make people realise how easy it is to build an Islamic state in Iraq away from the media trying to defame the project. Also, the endorsement and contributions of some people will inspire loyalty in others, so that the public will become a part of ISI by protecting their own regions and expelling apostates. ISI will become larger and able to embrace more people. Living under sharia law might seem frightening to some, but once they actually experience it, they will see that it positively impacts their lives and the state.

4. Reassuring those who are fearful of ISI: The people in some regions and villages harbour resentment against the *mujahidin*, either because some of the *mujahidin* made mistakes, because these people believed some of the lies the media spread, or because some members of the criminal Sahwa forces imposed their side of the story. When these regions join the sovereignty of ISI, they will feel reassured because they will become part of our project through the establishment of a security force comprising their youth, which will protect them and cleanse their land by expelling the apostates, the police, and the Sahwa forces. The objective of this is that they will implement the rule of sharia through the power of these new security forces. Therefore, the illusions and ideas they once had of the *mujahidin* will be expelled from their thoughts when they see that our project will benefit them. This project might appear to be primarily a security model, but its ideological roots are more important. It will only be presented as a security model so that it will be more readily accepted and executed. This is why such a project needs people with clean backgrounds and local popularity.

We have a good example in the deeds of the Prophet—peace be upon him. When he received delegations, he would honour their leaders and hold them responsible for their people. He sent judges and jurisprudence leaders to teach them Islam so they could rule according to sharia law. This is how the land under the control of the Islamic state during the time of the Prophet expanded to include all of the Arabian Peninsula. The only difference in Iraq now is that it is the *mujahidin* who will be presenting this expansion plan and who will benefit people in their lives and afterlives.

5.4b. Analysis

The revelation from this document is that the Islamic State is supremely confident in late 2009 that the Sahwa project is already a failure, abandoned by the Americans (and, by default, the Iraqi government). The Islamic State watched the Sahwa councils almost destroy their political project years before, as we saw in Abu Umar's speech in Chapter 3, and the group counterattacked viciously to dismantle the sociopolitical barriers that stood between them and the Sunni population of Iraq. As they explain, the Sahwa councils failed because the Islamic State 'targeted their leaders', a forthright claim, considering that Sunni tribal sheikhs are esteemed members of the Iraqi society.

Understanding this chapter of the Fallujah Memorandum requires a short review of the Sahwa movement's history. As the Islamic State movement's influence and control grew after 2003, its local leaders began a campaign to intimidate tribal sheikhs, contesting their power, which included the killing of tribal authorities. The killing of influential Ramadi Sheikh Khalid Araq al-Ataymi—who had proposed the creation of a group called the Anbar Revolutionaries—and the placement of his severed head in the centre of the city failed to deter the more stubborn tribal sheikhs.[56] In fact, for some, the brazen intimidation inflamed several men enough that they declared an open revolt against what was then still al-Qaida in Iraq (actually under the Mujahidin Shura Council at the time).[57]

In September of 2006, a small time tribal sheikh named Abu Risha and a few tribal leaders in the Ramadi area formed the Anbar Salvation Council and called their growing rebellion the Awakening, or Sahwa movement. It was an explicit call for fellow tribes to 'wake up' and recognise the threat ISI posed to tribal tradition and autonomy. The use of these somewhat nebulous terms—salvation and awakening—and their implied link to the preservation of tribal traditions so intertwined with Arab identity would

---

[56] Montgomery, Gary, and Timothy McWilliams, eds, 'Al-Anbar Awakening, Vol II: Iraqi Perspectives', Quantico: Marine Corps University Press, 2009, p. 55.

[57] In reality, this was the third organised tribal coalition that rose up against the group. The third time was the charm.

frustrate the propagandists of the Islamic State media department for some time to come.[58]

In its original public declaration in September 2006, the Sahwa movement unequivocally embraced the very ethos of Sunni tribal society, and surprisingly, reconciliation with the Americans and the Shi'a state. This abrupt turn, a dramatic change of viewpoint regarding an unpopular occupational force and a government that upended the historical Sunni rule of the country, was an immediate and existential threat to any Islamic State dream of Sunni unity and in-group coherence.[59] Once Sunnis could be found both in the resistance and in the government, the Islamic State's identity appeals would fall flat, and give lie to the crisis that Haroro Ingram argues is central to identity messaging. A foundering in-group identity and the injection of confusion into what should be a simple process of individual self-identification led to a reduction in legitimacy that J.M. Berger argues is the driving force behind in-group hostility and violence towards the out-group.[60] To put it simply, the defection of Sunnis to the perceived enemy would make the Islamic State movement's campaign of terror and insurgency hard to justify to its own fighters, as well as to its extensive local and global support network.

At first the Islamic State's leadership ignored the Sahwa, even though it had been killing its leaders and men since the fall of 2006. Eventually, it fought it openly, claiming that the tribes had 'sold their religion for money' and killing important Sahwa figures. The killing of Abu Risha on the first day of

---

[58] Newton, Allen, 'The Awakening Movement: A Narrative-level Study of Mobilization', *Small Wars & Insurgencies* 28, no. 2 (March 2017), pp. 267–290, https://doi.org/10.1080/09592318.2016.1233641; Cottam, Martha, and Joe Huseby, *Confronting Al-Qa'ida: The Sunni Awakening and American Strategy in Al-Anbar*, Lanham: Rowman and Littlefield, 2016, pp. 94–113; Kramer, Nicholas, 'Waking up to the truth about the Sunni Awakening', *War on the Rocks*, 23 Nov. 2016. The use of the term *sahwa* could also be a subtle mimic of the Islamic Awakening in nearby Saudi Arabia, which had some credibility in Islamist circles. The Islamic State had to be careful with smearing a term like *sahwa*, and this could be the source of their hesitancy. See Lacroix, Stéphane, *Awakening Islam: The Politics of Religious Dissent in Contemporary Saudi Arabia*, Cambridge: Harvard University Press, 2011.

[59] For a detailed examination of the political worldviews of all the actors involved in the Sahwa movement, see Cottam, and Huseby, *Confronting Al-Qaeda*.

[60] Berger, J.M., 'Extremist Construction of Identity: How Escalating Demands for Legitimacy Shape and Define In-Group and Out-Group Dynamics', ICCT—The Hague 8, no. 7 (2017), pp. 3–4.

Ramadan, 2007 was the start of a deliberate campaign targeting these leaders. The Islamic State celebrated by bragging that its patient operatives had spent a month planning the elimination, proving that there was no one they could not touch. Deriding the slain coalition leader as 'the imam of atheism and apostasy, Abdel Sattar Abu Risha, the head of the so-called Anbar Salvation Council, and one of the dogs of the bearer of the cross, Bush,' an ISI press release promised that although he was one of the first to fall, he would not be the last:

> In this regard, we announce the formation of Special Security Committees to hunt down and assassinate prominent tribal figures, who collaborated with the enemy and tarnished the reputation of their pristine tribes by cooperating with the soldiers of the cross and the Safavid government of Maliki. We shall publish the names of these collaborators and traitors from among the tribal chiefs, to expose them to our blessed tribes. We apologise for not providing the details of this courageous operation for security reasons, and for the sake of protecting the lives of our sons from our blessed tribes, who participated successfully in this blessed operation, either by providing information or logistical support.[61]

The killing of tribal sheikhs and Sahwa members went on for years, with an estimated 2,313 members killed, according to one study of the Islamic State assassination campaign.[62] Yet its campaign was more sophisticated than this, and offered incentives as well as threats. In the same message that marked the death of Abu Risha, ISI extended to the Sahwa the first public invitation for them to repent. Amir Abu Umar made the offer himself, acknowledging the Islamic State's stated priorities for that Ramadan: jihad and forgiveness.[63] Abu Umar repeated the offer in May of 2008, with deputy Abu Hamza offering repentance in April 2009 to those who approached the Islamic State before its security officials found them.[64] This invitation to repent apostasy—specifically

---

[61] Ministry of Information, Islamic State of Iraq, 'The assassination of Abd-al-Sattar Abu-Risha, who was killed on the first day of Ramadan, 13 September', al-Fajr Media, 14 Sept. 2007.

[62] Whiteside, 'The Islamic State and the Return of Revolutionary Warfare', p. 754.

[63] al-Baghdadi, Abu Umar, 'They plan and Allah plans', audio message, al-Furqan Media, Sept. 2007.

[64] al-Baghdadi, Abu Umar, 'Solid Cement Structure', audio message, al-Furqan Media, May 2008; al-Muhajir, Abu Hamza, 'The Second Audio Interview With Shaykh Abu Hamzah Al-Muhajir, May God Protect Him', audio message, al-Furqan Media, 20 Apr. 2009.

collaboration with an apostate government—became a staple of Islamic State strategic communications for the next six years.[65]

A key part of their strategy was focusing on killing the leaders, not the rank and file. The leaders of the group learned from their bitter experience of 2006–7 and they managed to refrain from destroying what could be a valuable social construct in the future and, in engaging the tribes, adopted the exact same program as the Americans. The use of the term 'jihadi *sahwa* councils', attributed to the Prophet but certainly informed by more recent events, is the giveaway. Many of these tribal elements would be forced to pledge allegiance to the Islamic State, on camera, in 2014.[66]

The Islamic State points out the irony, almost incidentally, in how the US and Iraqi government that gave up on the Sahwa movement that had served its purpose, would now have this weapon turned back on them. The Islamic State's understanding of the social dynamics of their environment seems to be spot on, and they had learned from previous errors, as discussed in the introduction, that caused a tribal backlash.

Chapter Three of the Fallujah Memorandum lays out four ways in which a tribal engagement strategy would benefit the ongoing state-building project. For one, the integration of sharia and military advisors in tribal elements would facilitate the 'easy expansion of Islamic State control and domination', and provide an excellent means to influence the local population—a very Maoist way to drum up public support. Additionally, engaging the tribal leaders would be a recognition of their importance to ISI, flattering them in a way that is culturally appropriate in rural Iraq, where tribal sheikhs serve an important societal function of honour and prestige. Their efforts would also integrate the tribal structure into the Islamic State, instead of subjugating it in the manner of an occupation. In this way, Zarqawi's direct successors modified the original idea posed in his speech in Chapter 2, where he said 'People follow the religion of their kings. Their hearts are with you but their swords are with

[65] Whiteside, Craig, 'Nine Bullets for the Traitors, One for the Enemy: The Slogans and Strategy behind the Islamic State's Campaign to Defeat the Sunni Awakening (2006–2017)', ICCT-The Hague, 7 Sept. 2018, https://icct.nl/publication/nine-bullets-for-the-traitors-one-for-the-enemy-the-slogans-and-strategy-behind-the-islamic-states-campaign-to-defeat-the-sunni-awakening-2006–2017/

[66] Al Jazeera, 'ISIL wins support from Iraq's Sunni tribes', 4 June 2015, https://www.aljazeera.com/news/2015/06/sunni-sheiks-pledge-allegiance-isil-iraq-anbar-150604074642668.html

Bani Umayyah [the Umayyad caliphs—considered to be a corrupt example], i.e., with power, victory, and security.'[67] Finally, negotiations with tribal sheikhs allowed the Islamic State to make amends for past behaviour through the means of tribal reconciliation, something that is still prevalent in Iraq. By changing its approach to the tribes, the Islamic State laid the foundations for its growing support in the years after 2010.

5.5a. The Fallujah Memorandum, December 2009/January 2010
Chapter 4

A symbolic head for a nation without a strong leader is very important because the symbolic head becomes the true leader, even if he does not have any official government position. Therefore, any society that does not have a symbolic head is susceptible to disagreement, disorder, and civil war. The impact of such a leader is obvious in Afghanistan and Iraq today. In Afghanistan, Mullah Umar—may Allah protect him—used to be the political symbol. He was symbolic because he exercised justice and provided security during his rule. Even when his emirate failed at the hands of the crusaders and their followers, he did not give up on or betray the people's cause. He still called upon people to fight the crusaders and promised that he too would fight to expel them. Through his words and deeds, he was always present in people's minds. The goal of fighting the enemy crusader was to re-establish the Islamic Emirate under Mullah Umar. A lot of people still prefer the idea of this emirate over the current traitor government. The limited access Afghanistan's Muslim society has to improved media technologies, which often functions as a double-edged sword [against the jihadis] by fuelling *fitna*, and the fact that Mullah Umar is still in Afghanistan leading the struggle against the crusaders, has helped cast him as a symbol of jihad. Therefore, it is difficult for any other group to compete with the symbolic leadership of Mullah Umar and rally people, because even considering rallying around any other group would be

[67] Zarqawi means that the people will do what they are told by those in control. This saying is more famously known as *Cuius regio, eius religio* (whose realm, his religion), from the principle established during the Peace of Ausburg (1555) that allowed rulers to choose religions for their states as a form of sovereignty. Zarqawi was arguing that once the Islamic State was established, his group could rule in the prophetic method. But under an established democratic rule, the Sunni would be indifferent to his group and hard to mobilise.

considered treason against jihad. In summary, Mullah Umar is a political symbol of the Muslim society in Afghanistan. Although the jihad in Afghanistan started as an individual effort, it was easier to unify [against the infidels] because the *mujahidin* had a common leader in Mullah Umar.

In Iraq, early jihadi efforts did not have a unified Islamic leadership and the Islamic leaders in Iraq were unable to pick up the mantle of leadership because they only passively observed the efforts made by the first *mujahidin*. Additionally, Iraq had advanced media resources available to its citizens. All this fuelled disagreements, disputes, and divisions among the *mujahidin*, as was the case with the *mujahidin* who fought the Soviets, where the absence of a unified leadership resulted in many groups fighting each other.

Therefore, it is very crucial to have an Islamic political symbol to lead the jihadi project to safety. This is what the national resistance factions realised when they tried to install Harith al-Dhari [leader of the Association of Muslim Clerics] to strengthen their political position and compensate for their weak military standing, which was disintegrating. The foolish media policies of the traitors in Iraq, who mirrored the media policies of the crusaders, entrenched the symbolism of Abu Musab al-Zarqawi—mercy be upon him—and *amir al-mu'minin* (commander of the faithful) Abu Umar al-Baghdadi—may Allah protect Him. The recurring press statements about the arrests and assassinations of the amir, his ministers, and associates helped establish their symbolic importance.

We need to prepare a vice amir in case something happens to our Amir Abu Umar al-Baghdadi—may Allah protect him. This vice amir can easily continue in his path without having to start from ground zero. We will have him issue some verbal statements, declaring the beginning of a certain battle or granting a pardon, for example. This will show that the character of the vice amir is ready for him to fill in as amir when needed, and make it easier for people and the media to accept him.

There is another important aspect of this, which is to bring to light other visible figures to support the main politically symbolic figure. Although such people are hard to find in a short time period, it would be possible if the Ministry of Legal Committees worked to settle citizens' problems and issues with the Islamic State. This is an important legal front of ISI, through which it can respond to anyone who doubts it, and which creates a bond between ISI and its citizens by providing needed legal direction and advice.

For example, the Kingdom of Saudi Arabia's legal councils helped strengthen the ties between the regime and citizens and strengthened their loyalty. That is why Ibn Khaldun—mercy be upon him—said, 'A state is stronger if it creates ties with its citizens through religion rather than clannishness. This is because religion, unlike clannishness, does not revolve around competition and envy.' The members of this committee need not have pledged allegiance to ISI—other people can be included. The committee should concentrate on legislation and general awareness and should constantly be informed of new developments. It should also set plans and goals for *dawa* [preaching Islam] to spread the Salafi methodology. Mawardi said, 'A state can be established by the strength and power of resources such as money or by the power of religion; the latter is more stable.'

That is why we see some unjust states using their *ulama* [scholars] to protect the state against their own unfair practices. When politicians face crisis, they look to *ulama* to fix what they broke. In contrast the nation of Islam can only be led by religion.

We caution that ISI should insulate this committee, this legal institution, from the influence of politicians so they cannot take advantage of it to serve their own interests. This would allow the committee to rule from a place of righteousness and not just as a face representing Islam.

5.5b. Analysis

In the scholarly field, there is a tendency to focus on charismatic leadership as the dominant force at the forefront of terrorist groups and insurgency movements.[68] However, charismatic leadership tends to emerge in nascent organisations and movements, and as such it is often volatile. This unpredictability emerges from charismatic leader-follower bonds' tendency to be emotionally based and rooted in a situational and organisational environment characterised by crisis. In many respects, Zarqawi emerges as the quintessential charismatic figure and, particularly in the final twelve to eighteen months of his life, he likely became more of a hindrance to the movement's attempts to stabilise. After his death, Abu Hamza and Abu Umar emerged as his successors. Neither were charismatic figures; rather, they appeared as comparatively stable, legal-

---

[68] Jordan, Jenna, 'When Heads Roll: Assessing the Effectiveness of Leadership Decapitation', *Security Studies* 18, no. 4 (2009); see also Carvin, Stephanie, 'The Trouble with Targeted Killing', *Security Studies* 21, no. 3 (2012); and Johnston, Patrick B., 'Does Decapitation Work? Assessing the Effectiveness of Leadership Targeting in Counterinsurgency Campaigns', *International Security* 36, no. 4 (2012).

rational types whose authority was based on the fulfilment of a process.[69] Although Abu Umar is often neglected in discussions about the Islamic State's leaders, he served in a difficult period and the precarious political fortune of the group likely impacted his legitimacy as the leader of a 'paper' state. This chapter of the memorandum displays an understanding of the importance of leadership in militant organisations, particularly the need to build up other potential leaders who could take the place of the amir if he was killed. This was prescient, as Abu Umar and Abu Hamza, his minister of war, were both killed within six months of the document's initial publication. Their leadership plan had not been enacted, and Abu Umar's successor Abu Bakr al-Baghdadi had to start from scratch with no name recognition. In fact, he did not make any speeches for two years, not until the summer of 2012, though this did not seem to harm the organisation. Fast forward to 2018, and the group is very cognisant of the need to have a smooth transition if Abu Bakr al-Baghdadi is found and killed. As a transnational entity, it will matter more than ever.

[Note: Chapter 5—Dealing with Dissidents is omitted from this excerpt. In it, the authors put forth the notion that the Islamic State could work with minorities in Iraq and offer protection in return for an alliance. This was legally supported by Islamic customs of taxation and protection for non-Islamic citizens, or *ahl al-dhimmi*. Although the Islamic State instituted this practice in their caliphate after 2014, in reality, its brutality towards minorities like the Yazidi compelled minorities to flee their rule almost without exception. This chapter did not play a major role in the rise of the Islamic State. The following serves as the conclusion of the Fallujah Memorandum and is presented without comment.]

5.6. The Fallujah Memorandum, December 2009/January 2010
Summary of Results and Advice

1) It is essential to immediately begin a serious quest to combine the efforts of ISI and other jihadi groups, especially since there are various other opposing projects, proving that the others are also working and preparing while the *mujahidin*, who have a common goal, are stable but unprepared.

---

[69] Ingram, Haroro and Craig Whiteside, 'The Caliph's Role in the (un)Surprising Resilience of the Islamic State', Foreign Policy Research Institute, 25 Oct. 2018, https://www.fpri.org/article/2018/10/the-caliphs-role-in-the-unsurprising-resilience-of-the-islamic-state/

2) Military strategy should change according to the circumstances. The strategy of global war across Iraq that was previously practiced is no longer effective. The more effective strategy is to focus on specific targets and to break bones.

3) It is important to preserve the leaders and the movement's capacity to protect against attrition by the Sahwa forces. This can be done by providing other means to promote ISI domination, such as the jihadi *sahwa* forces project.

4) Jihadi symbols are key, especially during this time. We previously mentioned that Amir Abu Umar built up a significant amount of symbolism through an effective press and media strategy. It is important to safeguard our ability to create and promote this symbolism in case something unexpected happens to him.

5) Dealing with the dissidents according to Islam and sharia law, while also making sure that the governors and officers are aware of the importance of this matter, as this area is very susceptible to error. This can be done by signing covenants such as the one the prophet—peace be upon him—signed with the Jews to face the common enemy.

PART III

THE CALIPHATE

'Part III: The Caliphate' covers the period of the Islamic State's greatest successes. It begins with three announcements by leader Abu Bakr al-Baghdadi: 'Announcement of the Islamic State in Iraq and al-Sham' delivered in April 2013 (Chapter 6), 'A Message to the *Mujahidin* and the Muslim *Ummah* in the Month of Ramadan' from 1 July 2014, and his Friday *khutbah* (sermon) in Mosul's al-Nuri Mosque three days later (Chapter 7). Chapter 8 explores how the Islamic State sought to mobilise English-speaking Muslims to its cause, a relatively new addition to its strategy, through two crucial messages directly adressing Western audiences. The first is Abu Muhammad al-Adnani's speech 'Indeed, Your Lord is Ever Watchful' from 22 September 2014, which has been linked to a surge in terrorist plots and attacks in the West. Second, 'The extinction of the grayzone' from issue 7 of *Dabiq* magazine captures Islamic State's central message to Western audiences. The next chapter features guidance for how to mobilise women in the movement, highlighting the importance of gender appeals in their propaganda (Chapter 9). Around this time the Islamic State's propaganda machine captured the world's attention, and so the final chapter of this section features the doctrinal guidance it offers its propagandists—'Media Operative, You Are Also a *Mujahid*'—providing rare insights into the practical inner workings of the group's media efforts (Chapter 10).

6

THE DECLARATION OF THE ISLAMIC STATE IN IRAQ AND AL-SHAM

When Abu Bakr al-Baghdadi (henceforth Baghdadi) took the reins of ISI in May 2010, his predecessors Abu Ayyub al-Masri and Abu Umar al-Baghdadi had brought the group from the brink of death and laid the strategic foundations for its resurgence. Under Baghdadi's leadership, ISI continued its revival, replenishing its stocks and methodically applying its strategy across Iraq. Meanwhile, by December 2010, the so-called Arab Spring was sweeping through the region and, by March of the following year, it had reached Syria. The Assad regime cracked down brutally on peaceful protests, and it was only a matter of months before war broke out, signalling what has become one of the greatest human tragedies in modern history. In January 2012, ISI members, under the title of Jabhat al-Nusra and the leadership of Abu Muhammad al-Jawlani, were sent from Iraq into Syria to join the war effort. Jabhat al-Nusra quickly built a reputation for its fusion of military prowess and outreach strategies, especially in the Aleppo and Deir ez-Zor governorates where it was most active, though suspicions quickly arose as to who or what was directing the group. Then, on 8 April 2013, Baghdadi released the following speech, in which he announced that Jabhat al-Nusra was operating as an extension of ISI in Syria, seemingly laying to rest any questions about the group's allegiances and direction. This reality was to be formalised in the changing of the group's name to al-Dawla al-Islamiyya fi al-'Iraq wa al-Sham, the Islamic State in Iraq and al-Sham (ISIS).

Three themes are particularly noteworthy in this speech. First, Baghdadi is clearly keen to use this opportunity to tell the story of his organisation from its inception up to this historic moment. In doing so, he sounds almost like a corporate CEO, presenting his organisation's brand to the market by laying out the core values and strategic direction that have remained consistent through its history while framing those aspects which have changed (for example, its name) as products of progress. Second, he directly addresses the people of Syria and Iraq, who now represent the primary constituents of ISIS's expanded strategic and operational scope, imploring them to stay true to their faith personally, collectively and politically. Third, his speech outlines the evolving relationship between ISIS and al-Qaida (AQ), now fronted by Ayman al-Zawahiri. The speech stoked personal, ideological, and strategic tensions between AQ and ISIS, resulting in a war of words and actions that intensified in the months and years that followed. Ultimately, this speech represents the beginning of what would become one of the most significant signposts in ISIS's trajectory: its usurpation of AQ as the flagship of the global jihad. What follows is an excerpt from al-Furqan Media's English translation.[1] The translation is noteworthy in itself because of how poor it is compared to English translations that would be produced by the group in later years, reflective of the increasing professionalism of its propaganda efforts and the benefits of attracting linguistically diverse members.

6a. 'Give Good News to the Believers'
The Declaration of the Islamic State in Iraq and al-Sham, 8 April 2013 Audio Speech for Amir al-Muminin Abu Bakr al-Hussaini al-Quraishi al-Baghdadi

O you who believe! be careful of (your duty to) Allah with the care which is due to Him, and do not die unless you are Muslims (102) And hold fast by the covenant of Allah all together and be not disunited, and remember the favor of Allah on you when you were enemies, then He united your hearts so by His favor you became brethren; and you were on the brink of a pit of fire, then He saved you from it, thus does Allah make clear to you His communications that you may follow the right way (103) And from among you there should be a party who invite to good and enjoin what is right and forbid the wrong, and

---

[1] al-Baghdadi, Abu Bakr, 'Give Good News to the Believers', translation by al-Furqan Media, 2013. This official English-language translation of Baghdadi's speech is very poor in quality which is noteworthy given how much official Islamic State translations improved in future years. The authors' edits to this translation appear in square brackets and were made sparingly to assist with intelligibility.

these it is that shall be successful (104) And be not like those who became divided and disagreed after clear arguments had come to them, and these it is that shall have a grievous chastisement (105) [Surah al-e-Imran]

Then,

We send a glad tiding to the Islamic Ummah in the midst of the events which we were established in it and for it [sic], Alhamdulillah and support and success is from Him, so I say seeking assistance from Allah Almighty: Ascending from a lower level to a higher level is from the graces of Allah Almighty on the Jihadi groups, and it is a proof for their blessed work, as decline and retreat is a proof for a malady, we seek refuge with Allah. And the high levels aren't so except by the grace of the level or levels that preceded it because it is the paver and grader[.] [A]nd this ascending is only thought by who is given a great deal of searching for the stances which please Allah Almighty so he goes to it quickly[.] [A]nd this ascending is only thought by who is given by Allah Almighty farsightedness and knowledge of public interests and what the Ummah is waiting from the mujahidin for the sake Allah Almighty. This ascending is only thought by whom Allah Almighty gave him the knowledge of the stances which enrage the Kuffar and apostates....

This ascending, superiority and sublimation needs that we overcome our feelings and minds because it is a Sharia demand, and the Sharia has a priority over both of them.

The names of the Jihadi groups aren't names revealed from the sky or names of tribes or clans which cannot be abandoned or changed or replaced, rather they are names that were founded due to the legitimate necessity, and the supreme legitimate necessity permits to cancel and replace it with others to be at the level of growth and sublimity. This ascending needs new names that carry the fragrant of Islam in its expansion and extending and spreading for the Ummah to carry the hope of returning. New names to forget the previous names, despite our sympathy with it, and it was so in the jihad of Iraq[.] [O]ur previous sheikhs—may Allah Almighty accept him—Allah Almighty have assisted them to take the jihad forward, the mujahid sheikh Abu Musab al-Zarqawi—may Allah accept him—Allah Almighty gave him success to inflict severe losses in the enemies of Allah Almighty from Kuffar and apostates[.] [A]nd beside that blessed work he worked to roundup whom he saw in them goodness, righteousness and sincerity in supporting the religion of Allah Almighty, so he declared in Iraq the name: 'Al-Tawhid wa Al-Jihad'[.] [A]nd the hearts got attached to that name, and the eyes looked at that group and its work, and the ears heard it's [sic] news.

And after that group had a presence in the media and battlefield, the sheikh moved to a superior location and higher level and gave Baya'a [allegiance] to the mujahid Amir of Al-Qaeda Organization sheikh Osama bin Laden may Allah accept him. And I have been told by who heard from the sheikh Abu Musab: 'When I gave Baya'a to sheikh Osama, I swear by Allah I didn't need from him money or weapons or men but I saw in him a symbol for the Ummah to support the religion of Allah Almighty so I became under his command'. So the blessed Baya'a to Al-Qaeda Organization happened.

From the requirements of this transfer that changing of that name: 'Al-Tawhid wa Al-Jihad' which jihad in Iraq was associated to it[.] [A]nd if it wasn't for seeking the pleasure of Allah Almighty and sublimation and supe-riority[,] and enrages the enemies of Allah[,] it was hard to give up the name 'Al-Tawhid wa Al-Jihad' by who established it and belonged to it, since it was the name of the group established by sheikh Al-Zarqawi in the land of the Afghans in the mid-nineties of the past century.

The hearts that associated with that name for the sake of Allah responded to that blessed expansion from the circle of Iraq to be associated to the global jihad circle, and jihad in Iraq became associated to the supreme new name 'Qaeda Al-Jihad Organization in Mesopotamia' when sheikh Abu Musab—may Allah accept him—gave Baya'a to Al-Qaeda Organization knew how much this Baya'a will cost Ahli Sunnah in Iraq and how much will it cost his mujahid sons and brothers but pleasing Allah Almighty was above all human assessments so Allah sufficed him the needs of the people....

But the high spirits was still searching to ascend the jihad to the places where Allah Almighty loves to gain his contentment and enrage His enemies, so the sheikh extended his hand to the working groups in the arena which hold the Aqeeda of Ahli Sunnah wa Al-Jamā'ah, and he conditioned on them not to leave the arms no matter what the nature of the Taguti government that will be formed until Allah decides between us and them with the truth or we are killed before that.

And the Amirs of those groups responded to the call of the sheikh and there was an agreement, and there was a determination[,] so there was a new formation and new name 'Mujahidin Shura Council'[.] [A]nd the group abandoned its name 'Al-Qaeda Organization' which terrorized the enemies of Allah Almighty[,] which has a global resonance and is associated to the name of the mujahid sheikh Osama bin Laden may Allah accept him[.] [A]lso the other groups gave up its names[,] may Allah give them the best reward for the Muslims and unite the ranks of the for the sake of Allah Almighty and for His sake they are fighting. And the way of continuing the ascending of the group for the mujahid sheikh Abu Musab Al-Zarqawi was interrupted when he Allah Almighty graced him with martyrdom after he had infused the methodology of superiority for the pleasure of Allah Almighty in the hearts of whom he left from commanders and Amirs. [S]o they resumed the march on his blessed footsteps so the mujahid sheikh declared Abu Umar Al-Baghdadi and his war minister the mujahid sheikh Abu Hamza Al-Masri Al-Mujahir may Allah Almighty accept them a new stage and blessed step and with the assistance of their brothers and the support of the good sons of the tribes and its sheikhs so the result of that was the Islamic State of Iraq Alhamdulillah.

After that the name of Mujahidin Shura Council faded away and disappeared. So it is the vision of the senior sheikhs who are concerned of uniting the ranks of the mujahidin and inflicting severe losses in the enemies of the religion to raise the clear Tawhid and like that are the high spirits seek to expand to the arenas of the land of Islam to clash with the enemies of Allah Almighty[.] So let the sheikh Al-Zarqawi be tranquil in his grave since the road which he walked in and set its features and guided to it those who came after him walked in it and we are following their tracks Allah willing. We have been left by who preceded us from our sheikhs on a road which we can only walk on their blessed footsteps since they have drawn for us a way that doesn't recognize borders and sketched for us a methodology that doesn't belong to a nation or race and its journey of ascending doesn't stop[.] [A]s for Iraq they have continued the journey of ascending by their declaration of the Islamic State[.]

[A]nd as for Al-Sham they have formed cells that are limited for preparation and aid waiting for a chance to continue the journey of ascending which has to continue, so when the situation in Al-Sham reached to the shedding of blood and violating honors, and people of Al-Sham called for help and the people of earth abandoned them[,] we were obliged to rise up to support them[.] [S]o we assigned Al-Golani[,] who is one of our soldiers[,] with a group of our sons[.] [A]nd pushed them from Iraq to Al-Sham to meet with our cells in Al-Sham. [A]nd set for them the plans and drew for them the policy of work and supplied them with half of what is in the treasury every month and supplied them with men who became experienced from the battlefields from Muhajirin and Ansar[.] [S]o they did well next to their brothers from the ardent sons of Al-Sham, and the influence of the Islamic State expended to Al-Sham and we didn't declare that for security reasons[,] for the people to see the reality of the State away from the distortion, forgery and fabrication of the media. [A]nd time has come to declare before the people of Al-Sham and the whole world that Jabhat Al-Nusra is only an expansion for the Islamic State of Iraq and part of it and we are determined after making Istikhara [contemplation] of Allah Almighty and consulting whom we trust in his religion and wisdom to continue in the journey of ascending of the group by passing all that will be said since the pleasure of Allah is above everything[.] [A]nd no matter what happens to us because of that so we declare keeping our trust in Allah abolishing the name of the Islamic State of Iraq and abolishing the name of Jabhat Al-Nusra, and joining them under one name 'The Islamic State in Iraq and Al-Sham' and also uniting the banner which is the banner of the Islamic State the banner of the Khilafah....

Your brother
Abu Bakr al-Husseini al-Quraishi al-Baghdadi.

6b. Analysis

As leader of the Islamic State of Iraq (ISI), Baghdadi, unlike its founder Abu Musab al-Zarqawi, shunned the spotlight, so the fact he even delivered this address is indicative of its importance to the movement. For context, while Baghdadi had issued a statement on 9 May 2011 eulogising Osama Bin Laden,[2] his first speech to be released as audio, 'Allah Will Not Allow Except that His Light should be Perfected', did not come until July 2012, over two years after he became ISI's leader.[3] Almost nine months later, in what was only his second address, Baghdadi would declare the establishment of the Islamic State in Iraq and al-Sham (ISIS). While on the surface its primary audience was the people of Syria and Iraq, there is little doubt that the leader and his inner circle understood the potentially seismic implications of this declaration for their relationship with AQ and, consequently, for the broader transnational jihadi milieu. Overall, one purpose lay at the heart of Baghdadi's speech: to convince audiences that the movement's successes reflect Allah's graces and so, with its latest triumphs formalised through changing its name

---

[2] al-Baghdadi, Abu Bakr, 'Statement on the martyrdom of *Mujahid* Sheikh Usama bin Laden', al-Fajr Media Center, 9 May 2011.

[3] al-Baghdadi, Abu Bakr, 'Allah Will Not Allow Except that His Light should be Perfected' Fursan al-Balagh Media 2012, https://azelin.files.wordpress.com/2012/07/shaykh-abc5ab-bakr-al-e1b8a5ussaync4ab-al-qurayshc4ab-al-baghdc481dc4ab-22but-god-will-not-allow-except-that-his-light-should-be22-en.pdf

to ISIS, it was strategically and jurisprudentially incumbent upon Syrians and Iraqis to support them.[4]

Building the ISIS Brand

Baghdadi's speech begins by priming his audience with carefully selected Quranic verses that establish a jurisprudential frame through which to interpret the rest of his message. An Islamic scholar with a PhD in jurisprudence, he chose these verses from Surah Imran that call for commitment to the faith and unity amongst the *umma*, particularly during times of hardship, to set up his argument that success and failure are products of Allah's graces: 'Ascending from a lower level to a higher level is from the graces of Allah Almighty on the Jihadi groups ... [while] decline and retreat is a proof for a malady'. The case Baghdadi is seeking to establish in these initial minutes of his speech should be clear: if success reflects divine approval and failure reflects divine disapproval, it logically follows that the *umma's* unification should be directed towards the former. He then paints the picture of an ascendant movement whose changes in name are merely signposts on a journey that reflects an unwavering commitment to not only establishing the caliphate but doing so by applying the divinely guided method.

At the dawn of a new era for his organisation, Baghdadi uses this speech to construct 'Brand ISIS' by identifying its core pillars, which have remained unchanged and the symbols, such as its name, which have necessarily evolved as part of its advancement. Three core pillars sit at the heart of ISIS's brand: its *manhaj*, or methodology ('...they have drawn for us a way that doesn't recognize borders and sketched for us a methodology that doesn't belong to a nation or race...'), a creed of perpetual war ('...its journey of ascending doesn't stop...') and its definition of success and failure ('...[that] the people and land be ruled by the laws of Allah Almighty without anyone other...'). Throughout the speech, Baghdadi reinforces ISIS's historical commitment to these core pillars. While the pillars remained unchanged, the

---

[4] For a range of analyses of Baghdadi's speech see Bunzel, Cole, 'Introducing the Islamic State of Iraq and Greater Syria', Centre for Strategic Communication at Arizona State University, 9 Apr. 2013; Joscelyn, Thomas, 'Al-Qaeda in Iraq, Al-Nusrah Front emerge as rebranded single entity', *Long War Journal*, 9 Apr. 2013; and Zelin, Aaron, 'Al-Qaeda Announces an Islamic State in Syria', The Washington Institute for Near East Policy, 9 Apr. 2013.

group's name changed once again in order to appropriately symbolise its progression over time:

> The names of the Jihadi groups aren't names revealed from the sky or names of tribes or clans which cannot be abandoned or changed or replaced, rather they are names that were founded due to the legitimate necessity, and the supreme legitimate necessity permits to cancel and replace it with others to be at the level of growth and sublimity. This ascending needs new names that carry the fragrant of Islam in its expansion and extending and spreading for the Ummah to carry the hope of returning. New names to forget the previous names, despite our sympathy with it...

Perhaps aware of the attention which his speech was likely to draw, at least in the jihadi circles that made up his primary audiences, Baghdadi used this opportunity to present the story of the group's evolution and solidify its reputation. Sicco Van Gelder's *Global Brand Strategy* argues that a brand's 'reputation' is the product of contextual, intrinsic, and associative qualities, and all three are evident in Baghdadi's speech.[5] Contextual qualities, which relate to an organisation's history, lineage, and founder story, are reflected in how he presents the historical lineage of the group, tracing it from its founder Zarqawi, through the Iraqi insurgency, to its emergence as ISIS. Each anecdote is presented as another 'part of the history of our blessed jihad'. Associative qualities, on the other hand, concern the traits linked to a brand because of their relationships with other organisations. Baghdadi's reflections on Zarqawi's decision to align with bin Laden's AQ as well as the various ways in which his organisation has worked with other jihadi groups and tribes throughout its history (for example, the Mujahidin Shura Council) are clearly designed to highlight how those associations boosted its reputation. Finally, intrinsic qualities are those characteristics that a brand comes to embody in the eyes of its audiences. Throughout the speech, Baghdadi solidifies ISIS's intrinsic traits by reinforcing the idea that his movement has remained unwaveringly committed to its core values to 'enrage the Kuffar and Apostates' and ensure that 'the people and land be ruled by the laws of Allah Almighty without anyone other than Allah'. This tone is what makes his speech sound almost like that of a corporate leader trying to convince the market of his organisation and brand's advantages over its competitors—something that certainly got the competition's attention.

---

[5] van Gelder, Sicco, *Global Brand Strategy: Unlocking Branding Potential across Countries, Cultures & Markets*, London: Kogan Page, 2010.

Challenging AQ

On the surface, the ISIS declaration may seem like a relatively matter-of-fact account of how Baghdadi directed his subordinate Jawlani to take members of the group, still ISI at the time, across the border to support the Syrian war effort. Issues around authority and the legitimacy of any action, especially involving violence, are of paramount importance to jihadi groups because such concerns have significant jurisprudential consequences. So, rather than Baghdadi stumbling nonchalantly into a feud with AQ, it seems more plausible that an intent of his speech—even if a secondary one—was to challenge Zawahiri's authority to coax a response from him. It is hard to believe that the ISIS leader and his inner circle were ignorant of the implications this speech would have on Zawahiri's authority and AQ's role in the most important jihadi theatre of the time: Syria.[6] While security may have been part of his rationale for not revealing that Jabhat al-Nusra was an extension of his movement, Baghdadi also indicates that he wanted to allow Syrians and other *jihadis* to interact with the group without the baggage of preconceived notions and '...the distortion, forgery and fabrication of the media...' that such an association might entail. For him to now suggest that Jabhat al-Nusra was in Syria under his leadership, as an extension of his organisation, placed AQ on the sidelines of the war in Syria and painted Zawahiri as out of touch. Even if Baghdadi did not intend to challenge AQ and its head, it was an almost inevitable consequence of such an inflammatory declaration.

Baghdadi clearly wanted to achieve certain goals with this speech, among them gaining recognition for Jabhat al-Nusra's efforts in Syria, demonstrating the practical implementation of his group's *manhaj*, endorsing ISIS's agenda and promoting its 'brand'. These also need to be considered from the strategic perspective of the ongoing war in Syria. Jurisprudentially, there is clear guidance in the holy texts that demands unity of the *umma* during times of crisis and Baghdadi was clearly seeking to leverage this with his speech. In Syria, there had been calls for years for the disparate groups fighting the Assad regime to unify and Baghdadi was presenting ISIS as the best option for unification. He concludes his speech by calling upon Syrians to stay true to

---

[6] For analyses of the war in Syria see Lister, Charles, *The Syrian Jihad: Al-Qaeda, the Islamic State and the Evolution of an Insurgency*, London: Hurst, 2015; Dagher, Sam, *Assad or we burn the country: How one family's lust for power destroyed Syria*, New York: Little Brown and Company, 2019.

their faith and 'not make democracy the cost for the thousands who were killed from you'. From the perspective of the transnational jihad, there had been considerable tensions between AQ central and its affiliates on strategic issues concerning chains of leadership, the merits of publicly acknowledging their allegiance to AQ, and when to formally establish Islamic governance.[7] The ISIS declaration significantly deviated from AQ's preferred position on crucial issues by essentially positioning Baghdadi as a senior authority of the faith while also declaring an Islamic state beyond the borders of Iraq, with his organisation positioned at the head of the global jihad. The timing of the announcement also seemed to be taking advantage of an audio recording by Zawahiri, who only two days earlier had declared,

> ...our people in the Levant, you must unite in the issue [of *tawhid*].... Do your best to make the fruit of your jihad, Allah permitting, a jihadi Islamic State that spreads justice and consultation, and protects the rights and has conscience; a state that becomes a brick in the structure of the return of the rightly-guided Caliphate on the methodology of the Prophet, Allah permitting.[8]

In the same speech, Zawahiri lauded ISI: 'Now the facts are clear and obvious, that those who defended Islam, jihad and Sunnis in Iraq are the honourable *mujahidin*, and on top of them, the blessed Islamic State of Iraq, which is still, by the grace of Allah, standing and didn't change its creed and didn't back out or budge from the constants [fundamentals] of Islam despite this dirty war that is waged against it'.[9] He goes onto describe ISI as '...the rock against which the American project in the region was destroyed, which aimed at dividing Iraq, then Saudi Arabia, and ending [sic] with dividing Egypt. What saved Muslims from this satanic American plan is the honourable *mujahidin* of Iraq, and on top of them, the Islamic State of Iraq. So, may Allah reward them on behalf of Iraq and Muslims in the best way.'[10] The picture that emerges from this is of a mix of top-down and bottom-up factors, which ISIS sought to leverage with the strategic opportunism that is a recurring theme

---

[7] Lahoud, Nelly, Stuart Caudill, Liam Collins, Gabriel Koehler-Derrick, Don Rassler, and Muhammad al-'Ubaydi, 'Letters from Abbottabad: Bin Ladin Sidelined?', CTC at West Point, 3 May 2012, https://ctc.usma.edu/letters-from-abbottabad-bin-ladin-sidelined/, last accessed 18 Dec. 2018.

[8] al-Zawahiri, Ayman, 'Unity in the Issue of Tawhid', As-Sahab Media Productions, 6 Apr. 2013.

[9] Ibid.

[10] Ibid.

throughout its history. The impact of Baghdadi's speech would be measured by the response it was able to coax from its rivals. It would be the spark that ultimately changed the landscape of the transnational jihad.

Aftermath

The response to Baghdadi's speech was swift and its implications seismic for the global jihad. On 10 April 2013, Jawlani released an audio statement indicating that he did not have prior knowledge of Baghdadi's decision, although he would broadly comply with it, while reaffirming his allegiance to Zawahiri's AQ and refusing to change Jabhat al-Nusra's name. Clearly Jawlani wanted to distinguish his organisation from ISIS and report to Zawahiri's higher authority while remaining (perhaps begrudgingly) respectful to Baghdadi's call. Zawahiri took almost a fortnight to respond, and when he did on 23 May 2013, he chastised both men, demanding that Baghdadi reverse ISIS's name change and narrow its focus on Iraq while insisting that Jabhat al-Nusra was an AQ affiliate in Syria, thus, while independent, it was ultimately subordinate to his leadership.

If Zawahiri thought this would put the issue to rest he was sorely mistaken. Baghdadi and the spokesperson of ISIS's media apparatus, Abu Muhammad al-Adnani, delivered a series of scathing critiques of AQ and its leader. On 15 June 2013, Baghdadi released an audio message rejecting Zawahiri on jurisprudential and strategic grounds, and he was followed days later, on 19 June, by Adnani, who released an audio message criticizing the AQ chief.[11] Indeed, Adnani would play an increasingly central role in the propaganda battle via four speeches that largely focused on defending ISIS's *manhaj* while condemning AQ for its misguidance: 'They shall by no means harm you but with a slight evil',[12] 'This is not our methodology nor will it ever be',[13] 'This is

---

[11] al-Baghdadi, Abu Bakr, 'Remaining in Iraq and the Levant', al-Furqan Media, 15 June 2013.

[12] al-Adnani, Abu Mohammed, 'They Shall By No Means harm you but with a Slight Evil', Fursan al-Blagh Media Translation Section, 2014, https://azelin.files.wordpress.com/2013/07/shaykh-abc5ab-mue1b8a5ammad-al-e28098adnc481nc4ab-al-shc481mc4ab-22they-will-not-harm-you-except-for-some-annoyance22-en.pdf, last accessed 18 Dec. 2018.

[13] al-Adnani, Abu Mohammed, 'This is not our Methodology nor will it ever be', al-Furqan Media, 2014, https://azelin.files.wordpress.com/2014/04/shaykh-abc5ab-mue1b8a5ammad-al-e28098adnc481nc4ab-al-shc481mc4ab-22this-is-not-our-manhaj-nor-will-it-ever-be22-en.pdf., last accessed 18 Dec. 2018.

the promise of Allah'[14] and, 'Sorry, amir of al-Qaida'.[15] During this period, ISIS increasingly augmented this campaign with messaging that highlighted its spectrum of politico-military activities and the legitimacy of its *manhaj*. For example, on 8 August 2013, ISIS's al-I'tisam Media Centre released the first of a fifty-video series titled 'A Window Upon the Land of Epic Battles' showcasing a diverse spectrum of ISIS activities across Syria and Iraq, from tribal engagements and rule of law activities to military operations. The tit-for-tat propaganda war between ISIS and AQ led inevitably to violence between the two groups and, on 2 February 2014, AQ formally and belatedly disassociated itself from ISIS.

Ultimately, success or failure would be presented as a marker of the legitimacy and divine sanction of one group over the other. This was, after all, the metric Baghdadi had established for his own group when calling for unification and announcing ISIS. At the time of his April 2013 speech, it would have been absurd to think that, within a little over a year, ISIS would control swathes of territory across Syria and Iraq, announce the establishment of its caliphate and replace AQ as the flagship of the global jihad.[16] Indeed, by early January 2014, such a prospect would have seemed even more ridiculous as ISIS forces were forced to retreat eastward in Syria by a coalition of rebels while simultaneously receding westward in Iraq due to pressure from Iraqi military forces. And yet, by July of that year, ISIS would transform into the Islamic State and Baghdadi would appear for the first time in public as its caliph.[17]

---

[14] al-Adnani, Abu Mohammed, 'This is the Promise of Allah', al-Furqan Media, 2014, https://jihadology.net/2014/06/29/al-furqan-media-presents-a-new-audio-message-from-the-islamic-states-shaykh-abu-mu%E1%B8%A5ammad-al-adnani-al-shami-this-is-the-promise-of-god/, last accessed 18 Dec. 2018.

[15] al-Adnani, Abu Mohammed, 'Sorry, Amir of al-Qaeda', al-Furqan Media, 2014, https://jihadology.net/2014/05/11/al-furqan-media-presents-a-new-audio-message-from-the-islamic-state-of-iraq-and-al-shams-shaykh-abu-mu%E1%B8%A5ammad-al-adnani-al-shami-sorry-amir-of-al-qaidah/, last accessed 18 Dec. 2018.

[16] McCants, Will, 'How Zawahiri lost Al Qaeda', *Brookings*, 19 Nov. 2013.

[17] Some of the research that appears in this text was supported by the Australian Research Council [DE140101123].

7

THE CALIPHATE RISES

On 29 June 2014, Abu Muhammad al-Adnani announced that ISIS was now to be known as the Islamic State, that the caliphate had been established, and that Abu Bakr al-Baghdadi had been nominated as its caliph. On the same day, the Islamic State released a powerfully symbolic video of Adnani standing with one of its most iconic military commanders of the time, the red-bearded Umar al-Shishani, at the recently bulldozed Sykes-Picot border between Iraq and Syria. This triumph represented the culmination of over a decade and a half of struggle. From near total decimation in the aftermath of the Sahwa in Iraq and, only months earlier, the pincer movement of its rivals on either side of the Syria-Iraq border, the Islamic State could now revel in its greatest feat yet, achieved through a mix of shrewd strategising, ruthless opportunism, and calculated patience—the same traits that arguably drove its decision to declare a caliphate. In the days that followed Adnani's announcement, Baghdadi gave two speeches in the space of four days that capture the Islamic State's triumphalism and its push to unequivocally position itself as the centre of gravity for the Muslim world with the caliph as its sole authority. It is these speeches which feature in this chapter.

What follows are excerpts from al-Hayat Media Center's English-language transcripts of Baghdadi's audio message, released on 1 July 2014 and titled 'A Message to the Mujahidin *and the Muslim* Ummah *in the Month of Ramadan', and the* Friday khutbah *(sermon) he personally delivered in Mosul's al-Nuri Mosque on 4 July 2014.[1] The former was clearly designed to position the Islamic State as the*

---

[1] The abridged transcripts that appear in this chapter are drawn from official Islamic

twenty-first-century standard bearer of the caliphate and, as such, he plays upon a range of psychological, theological, strategic, and historical levers in making his case to the global umma. *Among other things, he reinforced Adnani's earlier claims that the Islamic State was more than just the flagship of the global jihad but the sole authority for the world's Muslims, who were now jurisprudentially obliged to support it. If the purpose of the 1 July audio was to outline the case for its caliphate, Baghdadi used his first video appearance as leader to project himself as caliph. The Islamic State-produced video of his Friday* khutbah *was steeped in powerful symbolism, captured not only in the speech's location, but in the new calpih's words, image, and behaviour. In the process of adopting this new mantle, his performance capped a larger effort to secure himself as the most successful leader of the Salafi-jihadi movement since its founding, the true heir to bin Laden's legacy, and the Islamic State in a chain of revolutionary leaders that stretched back to the Prophet himself.*

7.1a. 'A Message to the *Mujahidin* and the Muslim *Ummah* in the Month of Ramadan', 1 July 2014
From Amirul-Mu'minin Abu Bakr al-Husayni al-Qurashi al-Baghdadi

....So let the world know that we are living today in a new era. Whoever was heedless must now be alert. Whoever was sleeping must now awaken. Whoever was shocked and amazed must comprehend. The Muslims today have a loud, thundering statement, and possess heavy boots. They have a statement that will cause the world to hear and understand the meaning of terrorism, and boots that will trample the idol of nationalism, destroy the idol of democracy and uncover its deviant nature.

So listen, O ummah of Islam. Listen and comprehend. Stand up and rise. For the time has come for you to free yourself from the shackles of weakness, and stand in the face of tyranny, against the treacherous rulers—the agents of the crusaders and the atheists, and the guards of the jews.

O ummah of Islam, indeed the world today has been divided into two camps and two trenches, with no third camp present: The camp of Islam and faith, and the camp of kufr (disbelief) and hypocrisy—the camp of the Muslims and the mujahidin everywhere, and the camp of the jews, the crusa-

State English-language translations. With the exception of omitted text, no additional edits were made to the transcripts by the book's authors.

ders, their allies, and with them the rest of the nations and religions of kufr, all being led by America and Russia, and being mobilized by the jews.

Indeed the Muslims were defeated after the fall of their khilāfah (caliphate). Then their state ceased to exist, so the disbelievers were able to weaken and humiliate the Muslims, dominate them in every region, plunder their wealth and resources, and rob them of their rights. They accomplished this by attacking and occupying their lands, placing their treacherous agents in power to rule the Muslims with an iron fist, and spreading dazzling and deceptive slogans such as: civilization, peace, co-existence, freedom, democracy, secularism, baathism, nationalism, and patriotism, among other false slogans.

Those rulers continue striving to enslave the Muslims, pulling them away from their religion with those slogans. So either the Muslim pulls away from his religion, disbelieves in Allah, and disgracefully submits to the manmade shirk (polytheistic) laws of the east and west, living despicably and disgracefully as a follower, by repeating those slogans without will and honor, or he lives persecuted, targeted, and expelled, to end up being killed, imprisoned, or terribly tortured, on the accusation of terrorism. Because terrorism is to disbelieve in those slogans and to believe in Allah. Terrorism is to refer to Allah's law for judgment. Terrorism is to worship Allah as He ordered you. Terrorism is to refuse humiliation, subjugation, and subordination [to the kuffār—infidels]. Terrorism is for the Muslim to live as a Muslim, honourably with might and freedom. Terrorism is to insist upon your rights and not give them up.

But terrorism does not include the killing of Muslims in Burma and the burning of their homes. Terrorism does not include the dismembering and disembowelling of the Muslims in the Philippines, Indonesia, and Kashmir. Terrorism does not include the killing of Muslims in the Caucasus and expelling them from their lands. Terrorism does not include making mass graves for the Muslims in Bosnia and Herzegovina, and the slaughtering of their children. Terrorism does not include the destruction of Muslims' homes in Palestine, the seizing of their lands, and the violation and desecration of their sanctuaries and families.

Terrorism does not include the burning of masājid [mosques] in Egypt, the destruction of the Muslims' homes there, the rape of their chaste women, and the oppression of the mujahidin in the Sinai Peninsula and elsewhere.

Terrorism does not include the extreme torture and degradation of Muslims in East Turkistan and Iran [by the rāfidah], as well as preventing them from receiving their most basic rights. Terrorism does not include the filling of prisons everywhere with Muslim captives. Terrorism does not include the waging of war against chastity and hijab (Muslim women's clothing) in France and Tunis. It does not include the propagation of betrayal, prostitution, and adultery.

Terrorism does not include the insulting of the Lord of Mightiness, the cursing of the religion, and the mockery of our Prophet (peace be upon him). Terrorism does not include the slaughtering of Muslims in Central Africa like sheep, while no one weeps for them and denounces their slaughter.

All this is not terrorism. Rather it is freedom, democracy, peace, security, and tolerance! Sufficient for us is Allah, and He is the best Disposer of affairs.

{And they resented them not except because they believed in Allah, the Exalted in Might, the Praiseworthy} [al-Burūj: 8].

O Muslims everywhere, glad tidings to you and expect good. Raise your head high, for today—by Allah's grace—you have a state and khilāfah, which will return your dignity, might, rights, and leadership. It is a state where the Arab and non-Arab, the white man and black man, the easterner and westerner are all brothers. It is a khilāfah that gathered the Caucasian, Indian, Chinese, Shāmī, Iraqi, Yemeni, Egyptian, Maghribī (North African), American, French, German, and Australian. Allah brought their hearts together, and thus, they became brothers by His grace, loving each other for the sake of Allah, standing in a single trench, defending and guarding each other, and sacrificing themselves for one another. Their blood mixed and became one, under a single flag and goal, in one pavilion, enjoying this blessing, the blessing of faithful brotherhood. If kings were to taste this blessing, they would abandon their kingdoms and fight over this grace. So all praise and thanks are due to Allah.

Therefore, rush O Muslims to your state. Yes, it is your state. Rush, because Syria is not for the Syrians, and Iraq is not for the Iraqis. The earth is Allah's. {Indeed, the earth belongs to Allah. He causes to inherit it whom He wills of His servants. And the [best] outcome is for the righteous} [al-Aʿrāf: 128]. The State is a state for all Muslims. The land is for the Muslims, all the Muslims.

O Muslims everywhere, whoever is capable of performing hijrah (emigration) to the Islamic State, then let him do so, because hijrah to the land of Islam is obligatory.

Allah (the Exalted) said, {Indeed, those whom the angels take [in death] while wronging themselves—[the angels] will say, 'In what [condition] were you?' They will say, 'We were oppressed in the land.' The angels will say, 'Was not the earth of Allah spacious [enough] for you to emigrate therein?' For those, their refuge is Hell—and evil it is as a destination} [An-Nisāʾ: 97].

So rush, O Muslims, with your religion to Allah as muhājirīn (emigrants). {And whoever emigrates for the cause of Allah will find on the earth many [alternative] locations and abundance. And whoever leaves his home as an emigrant to Allah and His Messenger and then death overtakes him—his reward has already become incumbent upon Allah. And Allah is ever Forgiving and Merciful} [AnNisā': 100].

We make a special call to the scholars, fuqahā' (experts in Islamic jurisprudence), and callers, especially the judges, as well as people with military, administrative, and service expertise, and medical doctors and engineers of all different specializations and fields. We call them and remind them to fear Allah, for their emigration is wājib 'aynī (an individual obligation), so that they can answer the dire need of the Muslims for them. People are ignorant of their religion and they thirst for those who can teach them and help them understand it. So fear Allah, O slaves of Allah.

O soldiers of the Islamic State, do not be awestruck by the great numbers of your enemy, for Allah is with you. I do not fear for you the numbers of your opponents, nor do I fear your neediness and poverty, for Allah (the Exalted) has promised your Prophet (peace be upon him) that you will not be wiped out by famine, and your enemy will not himself conquer you and violate your land. Allah placed your provision under the shades of your spears. Rather, I fear for you your own sins. Accept each other and do not dispute. Come together and do not argue. Fear Allah in private and public, openly and secretly. Stay away from sins. Expel from your ranks those who openly commit sin. Be wary of pride, haughtiness, and arrogance. Do not become proud on account of gaining some victories. Humble yourselves before Allah. Do not be arrogant towards Allah's slaves. Do not underestimate your enemy regardless of how much strength you gain and how much your numbers grow.

I also remind you to attend to the Muslims and the tribes of Ahlus-Sunnah (the Sunnis) with goodness. Stay awake guarding them so they can be safe and at rest. Be their support. Respond with kindness if they do you wrong. Be gentle with them, giving them as much pardon as you can. Persevere, endure, and remain stationed. Know that today you are the defenders of the religion and the guards of the land of Islam. You will face tribulation and malāhim (fierce battles). Verily, the best place for your blood to be spilled is on the path to liberate the Muslim prisoners imprisoned behind the walls of the tawāghīt. So prepare your arms, and supply yourselves with piety. Persevere in reciting the Quran with comprehension of its meanings and practice of its teachings. This is my advice to you. If you hold to it, you will conquer Rome and own the world, if Allah wills...

7.2a. Exclusive Coverage of the Friday *Khutbah* and Prayer in the Grand Masjid of Mosul, 4 July 2014
al-Khalifah Ibrahim, Amir al-Mu'minin of the Islamic State

....So this is the basis of the religion, a book that guides, and a sword that aids. Indeed your brothers the mujahidin, were blessed with victory by Allah tabaraka wa ta'ala [blessed and exalted] and were blessed with consolidation after long years of jihad, patience, and fighting the enemies of Allah. Allah guided them and strengthened them to establish this goal.

Therefore they rushed to announce the Khilafah and appoint an Imam. This is an obligation upon the Muslims—an obligation which was abandoned for centuries, and disappeared off the face of the Earth. So many Muslims were ignorant of it and are sinful for abandoning it.

It is always obligatory upon them to establish it. So now they have established it, to Allah is all praise and from Him are all blessings. I was burdened with this great matter. I was burdened with this trust, this heavy trust.

I was appointed as a leader for you, although I am not the best of you, nor am I better than you. Therefore, if you see me upon truth, then aid me. And if you see me upon falsehood, then advise me. Obey me as long as I obey Allah in your regards.

And if I disobey Him, then I have no authority over you in such. I will not promise you as the kings and rulers promise their followers and subjects with luxury, comfort, security, and leisure. Rather I promise you with what Allah tabaraka wa ta'ala promised His believing slaves.

{Allah has promised those who have believed among you and done righteous deeds that He will surely grant them succession [to authority] upon the earth just as He granted it to those before them and that He will surely establish for them [therein] their religion which He has preferred for them and that He will surely substitute for them, after their fear, security, [for] they worship Me, not associating anything with Me. But whoever disbelieves after that— then those are the defiantly disobedient} [An-Nur: 55].

He ta'ala also said, {So do not weaken and do not grieve, and you will be superior if you are [true] believers} [al 'Imran: 139].

He ta'ala also said, {If Allah should aid you, no one can overcome you} [al 'Imran: 160].

He ta'ala also said, {and incumbent upon Us was support of the believers} [Ar-Rum: 47].

He ta'ala also said, {And to Allah belongs [all] honor, and to His Messenger, and to the believers, but the hypocrites do not know} [al-Munafiqun: 8].

This is the promise of Allah.

So if you want the promise of Allah, then fear Allah and obey Him. Obey Allah al-'Adhim [the Almighty] in every matter and in every condition. Adhere to the truth and hold on to it in matters you like and dislike.

If you want Allah's promise, then perform jihad fi sabilillah, incite the believes [sic], and be patient upon this hardship. If you knew what was in jihad of reward, honor, loftiness, and might, in the Dunya and Akhirah [world and hereafter], none of you would sit back or remain behind, abandoning jihad. It is the trade that Allah guided to.

He saved the people from humiliation by it. And He attached honor to it in the Dunya and Akhirah [world and hereafter]. [It is that] you believe in Allah and His Messenger and strive in the cause of Allah with your wealth and your lives. That is best for you, if you should know. He will forgive for you your sins and admit you to gardens beneath which rivers flow and pleasant dwellings in gardens of perpetual residence.

That is the great triumph. And [you will obtain] another [favour] that you love—victory from Allah and an imminent conquest; and give good tidings to the believers} [As-Saff: 11–13]. I end here, and I seek forgiveness from Allah for me and you....

7b. Analysis

That the reclusive Baghdadi not only released two messages in the space of a few days but appeared in public for the first time is testament to the importance of this moment in the historical and strategic trajectory of the Islamic State movement. Consider the immense risks associated with just releasing a message, let alone revealing Baghdadi to the world in Iraq's second largest city and within the walls of its most iconic landmark. With global attention transfixed, who better to declare 'O Muslims everywhere.... You have a state and a *khilafah*' so 'rush O Muslims to your state' than the supposed caliph himself who, days later, would present himself as the embodiment of piety as he conducted the Friday *khutbah*. After all, the legitimacy of a caliphate is in part a measure of the caliph's worthiness (and vice versa), so Baghdadi's appearance was going to be a key component in demonstrating the credibility of the group's agenda. Moreover, his speeches did not occur in a communications vacuum but rather represented the crest of a wave of propaganda months in the making.

Remaining...

In the early months of 2014, Islamic State began to build momentum behind its military efforts across Syria and Iraq, using its propaganda machine to not only amplify the reach and impact of its actions but also to target geographically disparate and linguistically diverse audiences. In May 2014, al-Furqan Media released 'Clanging of Swords, Part 4', which showcased Islamic State's military operations across Iraq.[2] It contained all the trademarks of the movement's long-form videos: powerful imagery interwoven with an overarching narrative that tells the story of the group's actions in the field, pursuing the caliphate through adherence to the prophetic methodology. The Islamic State's propaganda machine was being fed with its real world successes—powerful stories and imagery depicting the application and results of its *manhaj*. In turn, its propaganda amplified its reach and impact in the field, with the purpose of boosting its legitimacy and credibility as a politico-military and ideological force.[3] The Islamic State's messaging through the first half of 2014 focused on demonstrating how its politico-military efforts were both jurisprudentially sound and practically effective.

June 2014 would prove perhaps the most successful in the movement's history, as it captured Mosul on 10 June 2014 followed, in subsequent weeks, by Tal Afar and stretches of territory across Ninewa, Salah ad-Din, and Kirkuk in Iraq, as well as Syrian territories between Deir ez-Zor and the Syria-Iraq border. At a local level, Islamic State deployed tactical messaging in the lead up to and during these operations to coax support (or acquiescence, at least) from local populations and to intimidate local security forces. For regional and global audiences, Islamic State cast itself as a movement comprised of men and women from all over the world who were committed to an agenda that extended well

---

[2] Islamic State, 'Clanging of the Swords, Part 4', al-Furqan Media, Jihadology, 17 May 2014, https://jihadology.net/2014/05/17/al-furqan-media-presents-a-new-video-message-from-the-islamic-state-of-iraq-and-al-sham-clanging-of-the-swords-part-4/, last accessed 18 Dec. 2018.

[3] For analyses of Islamic State's propaganda strategy, especially during this period, see al-'Ubaydi, Muhammad, Nelly Lahoud, Daniel Milton, and Bryan Price, *The group that calls itself a state: Understanding the evolution and challenges of the Islamic State*, West Point, NY: Combating Terrorism Centre, 2014; Berger, J.M., Jessica Stern, *ISIS: The State of Terror*, New York: Ecco, 2014; Ingram, Haroro, 'The strategic logic of Islamic State information operations', *Australian Journal of International Affairs* 69, no. 6 (2015), pp. 729–752; and Winter, Charlie, 'Documenting the virtual "caliphate"', *Quilliam*, 2015.

beyond Syria and Iraq. For example, video footage of the Camp Speicher massacre, released on 12 June, was followed several days later by the al-Hayat Media Center's 'There is no Life Without Jihad', featuring British and Australian militants calling for their fellow Muslims to migrate to Islamic State-controlled territories.[4] During this period, the group increased its efforts to reach out to English-speaking audiences with the launch of online magazines Islamic State News[5] and then Islamic State Report.[6] The breadth of themes captured in these magazines was designed to showcase the full spectrum of the Islamic State's military and governance activities, with articles like 'Fresh Produce Injects Life into Halab Market',[7] 'Maliki's Forces Humiliated while Islamic State Stockpiles on War Booty',[8] 'On Patrol with the Office of Consumer Protection',[9] and 'On the Beat: ISR Examines how the Islamic Police Safeguards Ar-Raqqah and their Importance in State Building'.[10] Its capture of Mosul was the cover story in the Islamic State Report's third issue under the headline 'Islamic State Liberates the City of Mosul',[11] while the cover of its fourth issue showed its militants at the border of Iraq and Syria with the text reading 'Smashing the Borders of the Tawaghit'.[12] The Islamic State's magazines merely reinforced the themes already prevalent in its video and social media messaging, while its regional and trans-

---

[4] 'There is no Life without Jihad', al-Hayat Media, 19 June 2014, Jihadology, https://jihadology.net/2014/06/19/al-%E1%B8%A5ayat-media-center-presents-a-new-video-message-from-the-islamic-state-of-iraq-and-al-sham-there-is-no-life-without-jihad/, last accessed 18 Dec 2018.

[5] Islamic State's al-Hayat released three issues of Islamic State News through June 2014.

[6] Islamic State's al-Hayat released four issues of Islamic State Report through June 2014.

[7] Unidentified author, 'Fresh Produce Injects Life into Halab Market', Islamic State News, no. 2, 2014, p. 1.

[8] Unidentified author, 'Maliki's forces humiliated while Islamic State Stockpiles on War Booty', Islamic State News no. 3, 2014, p. 2.

[9] Unidentified author, 'On Patrol with the Office of Consumer Protection', Islamic State Report, no. 1, 2014, p. 4.

[10] Unidentified author, 'On the Beat: ISR Examines how the Islamic Police Safeguards Ar-Raqqah and their Importance in State Building', Islamic State Report, no. 2, 2014, pp. 5–6.

[11] Unidentified author, 'Islamic State Liberates the City of Mosul', Islamic State Report, no. 3, 2014.

[12] Unidentified author, 'Smashing the borders of the Tawaghit', Islamic State Report, no. 4, 2014.

national propaganda helped to elevate largely local issues and events onto a global stage. The Islamic State's propaganda machine during this period of success put out content with tactical, operational, and strategic intent, producing tailored messaging for local, regional, and global audiences that typically catered to the unique linguistic and contextual nuance of each.[13]

Then, in the final week of June 2014, Adnani delivered an uncompromising address announcing the establishment of the caliphate and the obligation of all Muslims to support their caliph. The purpose of the statement was to unequivocally present the case for Islamic State's legitimacy as the bearer of the caliphate standard and Baghdadi as its caliph. He did so by describing how the group had adhered to jurisprudential guidance in both declaring the caliphate and in selecting Baghdadi (now Caliph Ibrahim) as its head:

> ...the shūrā (consultation) council of the Islamic State studied this matter after the Islamic State—by Allah's grace—gained the essentials necessary for khilāfah, which the Muslims are sinful for if they do not try to establish. In light of the fact that the Islamic State has no shar'ī (legal) constraint or excuse that can justify delaying or neglecting the establishment of the khilāfah such that it would not be sinful, the Islamic State—represented by ahlul-halli-wal-'aqd (its people of authority), consisting of its senior figures, leaders, and the shūrā council—resolved to announce the establishment of the Islamic khilāfah, the appointment of a khalīfah for the Muslims, and the pledge of allegiance to the shaykh (sheikh), the mujāhid, the scholar who practices what he preaches, the worshipper, the leader, the warrior, the reviver, descendent from the family of the Prophet, the slave of Allah, Ibrāhīm Ibn 'Awwād Ibn Ibrāhīm Ibn 'Alī Ibn Muhammad al-Badrī al-Hāshimī al-Husaynī al-Qurashī by lineage, as-Sāmurrā'ī by birth and upbringing, al-Baghdādī by residence and scholarship. And he has accepted the bay'ah (pledge of allegiance). Thus, he is the imam and khalīfah for the Muslims everywhere. Accordingly, the 'Iraq and Shām' in the name of the Islamic State is henceforth removed from all official deliberations and communications, and the official name is the Islamic State from the date of this declaration.[14]

Put simply, Adnani was presenting the case under a Salafi-jihadi reading of Islamic law for why the Islamic State establishing its caliphate and selecting its caliph was legally sound. In doing so, the implications for groups fighting in

---

[13] For more see Whiteside, Craig, 'Lighting the Path: The evolution of the Islamic State media enterprise (2003–2016)', *ICCT Research Paper* 2016; and Winter, Charlie, 'ISIS' offline propaganda strategy,' Brookings Institution, 2016, https://www.brookings.edu/blog/markaz/2016/03/31/isis-offline-propaganda-strategy/

[14] al-Adnani, Abu Mohammed, 'This is the Promise of Allah'.

not only Syria and Iraq but around the world was simple: 'We clarify to the Muslims that with this declaration of *khilafah*, it is incumbent upon all Muslims to pledge allegiance to the *khalifah* Ibrahim and support him. The legality of all emirates, groups, states, and organisations, becomes null by the expansion of the *khilafah's* authority and arrival of its troops to their areas.'[15]

If Adnani's statement was to present the Islamic State's case to the world, the purpose of Baghdadi's 'A Message to the *Mujahidin* and the Muslim *Ummah* in the Month of Ramadan' was to show him getting on with running the caliphate. After all, according to the Islamic State's, the jurisprudential case was clear and beyond question: it was now the sole authority for the world's Muslims. Baghdadi wove psychosocial, jurisprudential, strategic, and historical layers of narrative and argumentation in this speech to shape how his audiences perceived not only him and his movement, but the world more broadly. To cut through the countless identities that make up the world's almost two billion Muslims, he conjured images of a bi-polar world, characterised by malevolent forces responsible for crisis (that is, all those who are not Islamic State-aligned Sunni Muslims) and those of purity (that is, Islamic State-aligned Sunni Muslims) who have solutions to that malaise (that is, the Islamic State itself):

> O ummah of Islam, indeed the world today has been divided into two camps and two trenches, with no third camp present: The camp of Islam and faith, and the camp of kufr (disbelief) and hypocrisy—the camp of the Muslims and the mujahidin everywhere, and the camp of the Jews, the crusaders, their allies, and with them the rest of the nations and religions of kufr, all being led by America and Russia, and being mobilized by the Jews.

Over this broad appeal that plays upon powerful psychosocial forces,[16] Baghdadi layered an historical perspective by arguing that '... the Muslims were defeated after the fall of their *khilafah* (caliphate). Then their state ceased to exist, so the disbelievers were able to weaken and humiliate the Muslims, dominate them in every region, plunder their wealth and resources, and rob

---

[15] Ibid.

[16] While this may seem crudely simplistic, it is important to recognise that the interplay of in-group, out-group, crisis, and solution contructs is an approach to persuasive communication that seeks to leverage powerful psychosocial and strategic forces. For more on these dynamics, see J.M. Berger, *Extremism*, Cambridge, MA: MIT Press, 2018; and Ingram, Haroro, 'Deciphering the siren call of militant Islamist propaganda: Meaning, credibility & behavioral change', The International Centre for Counter-Terrorim—The Hague 7, no. 9 (2016).

them of their rights.' The caliphate is thus presented as both a practical and symbolic mechanism for Muslim unification. Baghdadi also added a strategic perspective, addressing (if indirectly) accusations of terrorism by highlighting how the term is only attributed to those who 'refuse humiliation, subjugation, and subordination.... Terrorism is for the Muslim to live as a Muslim, honorably with might and freedom', while noting that the killing of Muslims is not considered terrorism. This narrative is designed to prompt audiences to see crisis, but then offer an empowering solution: 'O Muslims everywhere, glad tidings to you and expect good. Raise your head high, for today—by Allah's grace—you have a state and *khilāfah*, which will return your dignity, might, rights, and leadership.' Baghdadi went on to call for Muslims to rush to their state, because 'hijrah to the land of Islam is obligatory', weaving a strand of jurisprudence into his appeal. His call for specialists—'judges, as well as people with military, administrative, and service expertise, and medical doctors and engineers of all different specializations and fields'—not only reflects the practical requirements of consolidating this supposed state but also helps underscore its successes. After all, success and failure are a product of Allah's graces and the Islamic State's triumphs were framed here as the ultimate expression of divine approval. Baghdadi used his next speech to present himself as the embodiment of that success.

The caliph's 4 July 2014 address in Mosul is also best understood within the context of Adnani's statement delivered five days earlier. Regarding Baghdadi's ascent to the position of caliph, Adnani stated: 'The khalīfah Ibrāhīm (may Allah preserve him) has fulfilled all the conditions for khilāfah mentioned by the scholars. He was given bay'ah in Iraq by the people of authority in the Islamic State as the successor to Abū 'Umar al-Baghdādī (may Allah have mercy upon him).'[17] According to Adnani's description, Baghdadi satisfied the jurisprudential requirements for the position of caliph. When Baghdadi appeared in Mosul's al-Nuri Mosque to deliver the Friday *khutbah*, it was not to prove that he was caliph but merely to perform his role. The proof, as far as the Islamic State was concerned, was self-evident by satisfying the jurisprudential requirements. This highlights an important point. Unlike a charismatic leader, whose authority is characterised by emotion-based, leader-follower bonds, the position of caliph represents a unique fusion of legal-rational authority, based on adherence to 'law' or a legally-enshrined process, and traditional authority, based on established order and custom. On the surface, the

[17] Abu Mohammed al-Adnani, 'This is the Promise of Allah'.

distinction between charismatic, legal-rational, and traditional authority may seem like a superfluous detail, but the perceived basis upon which a leader is followed has significant implications for the stability of their authority over time. Authority based on a legal-rational or traditional rationale tends to be more stable than often volatile charismatic leadership. With hindsight, announcing the caliphate and its caliph was not only an opportunistic manoeuvre designed to establish the Islamic State as the premier authority of the world's Muslims but a means to strategically posture as a more stable and formal authority, at least compared to AQ, at the head of the global *jihad*.

It is useful to consider how Baghdadi was likely perceived by those who were either within the Islamic State or supportive of its agenda. From a jurisprudential perspective, the group was keen to emphasise that Baghdadi satisfied the conditions for becoming caliph. A year earlier, in July 2013, a biography of the caliph, reportedly authored by an Islamic State ideologue Turki al-Binali, had been posted on online forums, similarly emphasising that Baghdadi became the movement's leader after 'going through several phases', not to mention a long history of serving as a member of the group's shura council.[18] Indeed, this biography outlined many features of Baghdadi's life which would have deeply resonated with Islamic State supporters even before he formally became caliph. It highlights his prophetic lineage, as evidenced by 'al-Qurayshi' in his name, and his PhD in Islamic jurisprudence and experience as an *imam*, which underscores his position as a scholar. The text also noted his relationships with Iraqi tribes, especially in Diyala and Samarra, his experience as not only an organiser of insurgents but a fighter against US forces in Iraq, and his long history of service to the Islamic State movement.[19] The picture of Baghdadi presented in the pages of this biography is of a warrior-scholar who rose through the movement's ranks as his peers and superiors recognised his piety, humility, and commitment to the *umma's* cause. These are all traits that are traditionally revered in a leader in this sociocultural milieu. For those within the Islamic State well-versed on his background, but who may have never seen him before, these stories preceded his appearance, contextualising, for them at least, his first physical appearance.

---

[18] Islamic State, *Moments from the life Journey of our Master the Amir of the Believers*, July 2013, SITE Group, https://news.siteintelgroup.com/blog/index.php/categories/jihad/entry/226-the-story-behind-abu-bakr-al-baghdadi, last accessed 18 Dec. 2018.

[19] Ibid.

The Islamic State used Baghdadi's first appearance to demonstrate his legitimacy and piety, weaving layers of powerful symbolism into the event.[20] The choice of Mosul's Great Mosque of al-Nuri was symbolically powerful not only because of its prominent location in Iraq's second largest city but because it paid symbolic homage to Zarqawi as the movement's founder. As senior al-Qaida figure Sayf al-Adel states in *My Experiences with Abu Musab al-Zarqawi*: 'Abu Musab had an admiration for the character of the distinguished Islamic leader "Noor al Deen al-Zinky" who led the operation of liberation and change.... And his launch from al Mosul in Iraq had a major role in influencing Abu Musab to move to Iraq....'[21] During Zarqawi's first public speech in early 2004 (see Chapter 1), he had expressed a desire to replicate the twelfth-century ruler's campaign.[22] All of this contributed to the tremendous symbolic power of the setting of Baghdadi's speech, which was further reinforced by his physical appearance and behaviour. Baghdadi used the *miswak*—a stick used to clean the teeth—prior to delivering the *khutbah*, an action designed to mimic a reported habit of the Prophet Muhammad. From this to the black robes he wore, his slow ascent to the pulpit, and the delivery of the speech in classical Arabic, his image and behaviour during the Friday speech were engineered to show a man of great lineage, piety, and courage. The fact he was even delivering the sermon was itself symbolic, as it was the caliph's traditional duty to deliver the Friday *khutbah*. The majority of the sermon was devoted to satisfying required formalities but when he spoke of himself, he did not demand subordination from the *umma* or even present the case for his authority. Rather, he asked for their support:

> I was appointed as a leader for you, although I am not the best of you, nor am I better than you. Therefore, if you see me upon truth, then aid me. And if you see me upon falsehood, then advise me. Obey me as long as I obey Allah in your regards. And if I disobey Him, then I have no authority over you in such.

[20] For analyses written at the time see Hegghammer, Thomas, 'The Foreign Policy Essay: Calculated Caliphate', *Lawfare*, 6 July 2014; Atwan, Abdel Bari, 'A Portrait of Caliph Ibrahim', *Cairo Review of Global Affairs* (Fall 2015); McCants, Will, 'The believer: How an introvert with a passion for religion and soccer became Abu Bakr al-Baghdadi, the leader of the Islamic State', Brookings Institution, 1 Sept. 2015.

[21] al-Adel, Sayf, *My Experience with Abu Musab al-Zarqawi*, trans. L. Othman, ed. Haroro Ingram, 2015.

[22] Rasha al-Aqeedi highlighted how Baghdadi's appearance in the mosque would ultimately doom the iconic landmark. See Rasha al-Aqeedi, 'Mosul mourns its minaret, sort of', *American Interest*, 12 July 2017.

Baghdadi's purpose was to demonstrate piety and, in doing so, epitomise the values supposedly inherent to the position of caliph. At the time and in the years since, many criticised the ordinariness of his appearance and considered his speeches not to be particularly charismatic. This completely misunderstands his purpose as the movement's leader. The position of caliph is meant to be the pious, steadying hand of a calm, authoritative leader, supported due to the legal-rational and traditional requirements they have satisfied. While it may not have been clear at that point, the Islamic State had planted the strategic seeds that would help it weather the storms it would soon face as its boom turned to bust. But before these came, it continued its ascent.

...And Expanding

In the months after Baghdadi's speeches, the Islamic State's politico-military machine steamrolled on, capturing more territory in eastern Syria and securing the city of Mosul by expanding its grip on the surrounds. Holding not only territory but urban centres allowed the Islamic State to implement its own form of governance and promote these efforts with propaganda targeting local, regional, and global audiences. Its propaganda apparatus expanded and diversified in an effort to maximise the appeal of its messaging to linguistically diverse audiences. From this effort emerged the English-language magazine *Dabiq*,[23] the French *Dar al-Islam*,[24] and *Constantinople* in Turkish.[25] As its caliph had said, the Islamic State's primary aim since declaring its caliphate was to attract foreigners to its lands, and what followed was the largest influx of Islamist foreign fighters in modern history. Videos by the Islamic State's al-Furqan, al-Itisam, and al-Hayat media centres began to capture the world's attention, none more so than 'A Message to America', released 19 August 2014, which showed the execution of American journalist James Foley.[26] In less than a year, the Islamic State had transformed perceptions of the group—where President Barack Obama previously dismissed it as a 'jayvee [junior varsity] team',[27] US Defense Secretary Chuck Hagel now exasperatedly

---

[23] al-Hayat's *Dabiq* magazine ran for fifteen issues from July 2014 to July 2016.

[24] *Dar Al-Islam* ran for ten issues until August 2016.

[25] *Constantinople* ran for seven issues until August 2016.

[26] Islamic State, 'A Message to America', al-Hayat Media, August 2014.

[27] Contorno, Steve, 'What Obama Said About Islamic State as a JV Team', *Politifact*, 7 Sept. 2014, https://www.politifact.com/truth-o-meter/statements/2014/sep/07/barack-obama/what-obama-said-about-islamic-state-jv-team/, last accessed 18 Dec. 2018.

declared 'we haven't seen anything like this before'.[28] Perhaps the Islamic State overestimated its ability to intimidate its adversaries and underestimated the resolve of nations to defeat it, but by the end of 2014, a coalition of nations had formed to confront it. The message from the Islamic State at this time was that its supporters should prioritise *hijra* to its lands to engage in jihad in support of the caliphate. But as coalition strikes increased, it would be the Islamic State's charismatic spokesman who would lead the call for its supporters around the world, especially in the West, to act as operatives of terror behind enemy lines.[29]

[28] Wong, Kristina, 'Defense Secretary: ISIS Threat "Beyond Anything We Have Seen"', *Hill*, 21 Aug. 2014, https://thehill.com/policy/defense/215724-hagel-isis-beyond-anything-weve-seen, last accessed 18 Dec. 2018.

[29] Some of the research that appears in this text was supported by the Australian Research Council [DE140101123].

8

GLOBAL WAR

Abu Bakr al-Baghdadi's triumphant appearance in Mosul signalled the beginning of a period that was the peak of the Islamic State movement's second resurgence. For almost eighteen months, it consolidated (and in some pockets expanded) its territorial gains across Syria and Iraq. These successes in the field fuelled the messaging from its central media units, which churned out propaganda for multilingual, geographically disparate populations through various offline and online forums, backed by an unprecedented access to wealth, weaponry, and foreign fighters. Outside of its core territorial holdings across the Middle East's 'fertile crescent', the Islamic State and its caliph received pledges of allegiance from around the globe that allowed the movement to establish transnational provinces for the first time in its history. It was, by far, the most successful jihadi group in modern history when it came to territorial control, wealth, recruitment, and propaganda output. All this had been achieved against incredible odds that, as the months wore on, would only intensify. The United States and other Western nations had provided military and intelligence support to allies in the region but, as the movement's momentum grew seemingly unabated after the capture of Mosul, those efforts were formalised with the establishment of the Global Coalition Against Daesh in September 2014. It was in that month that spokesperson Abu Muhammad al-Adnani delivered the speech that opens this chapter: 'Indeed, Your Lord is Ever Watchful'.[1]

---

[1] The excerpts featured in this chapter are taken from official Islamic State translations. The source contained text in both rounded and square brackets. The authors have made minimal edits to the text.

Speaking for over forty-one minutes, Adnani set the scene of a global, multifaceted war against the only true defenders of Islam—the Islamic State—a war that required Muslims from every corner of the world to act on their behalf. The opening passages of his speech emphasised the extraordinary odds faced by the Islamic State and the centrality of the propaganda war at the heart of this epic clash. In the speech, the spokesperson warns of the 'sorcerers' who deceive the masses led by the 'mule of the Jews', President Barack Obama, and 'the uncircumcised old geezer', Secretary of State John Kerry. Since announcing its caliphate, the Islamic State's call to supporters was to perform hijra (migration) to its lands in support. However, with Adnani's speech came an explicit call for its supporters to engage in attacks at home, thus extending the frontlines of its war across the globe and behind the lines of its adversaries.

In the months after this rallying cry, terrorist attacks across France, the United States, Canada, and Australia suggested that Islamic State supporters had heeded Adnani's call. The January 2015 attacks, in which al-Qaida in the Arabian Peninsula supporters assaulted the Charlie Hebdo magazine headquarters and an Islamic State supporter held up a Jewish supermarket in Paris, particularly captured global media attention. A month later, the seventh issue of the Islamic State's Dabiq *magazine celebrated the attacks in its feature article titled 'The Extinction of the Grayzone', the opening section of which features next in this chapter, after an al-Hayat Media Center translation of 'Indeed, Your Lord is Ever Watchful'. It is significant not only because it cites Adnani's speech as the inspiration for a wave of terrorist attacks across the West, but also because it captures the Islamic State's key message to all Muslims, particularly those living in the West: Muslims must decide if they are aligned with the camp of Islam or the camp of disbelief, as the 'grayzone' between the two has disappeared. True Muslims, according to the* Dabiq *article, are faced with either travelling to Islamic State territories or attacking the Islamic State's enemies wherever they may be, else they themselves risk becoming legitimate targets of the group's attacks.[2]*

8.1a. 'Indeed, Your Lord Is Ever Watchful', 22 September 2014
Shaykh Abu Muhammad al-'Adnani ash-Shami

All praise is due to Allah, the Strong and Mighty. And may blessings and peace be upon the one sent with the sword as a mercy to all the worlds. As for what follows:

---

[2] The excerpts featured in this chapter are taken from official Islamic State translations. The authors' have made minimal edits to the text noting that the original text contained text in both rounded and square bracketed text by the original author/translator.

Allah the Blessed and Exalted said, {The people of Noah denied before them and the [disbelieving] factions after them, and every nation intended [a plot] for their messenger to seize him, and they disputed by [using] falsehood to [attempt to] invalidate thereby the truth. So I seized them, and how [terrible] was My penalty} [Ghāfir: 5].

And He the Exalted said, {And [remember], when those who disbelieved plotted against you to restrain you or kill you or evict you [from Makkah]. But they plan, and Allah plans. And Allah is the best of planners} [al-Anfāl: 30].

And He the Exalted said, {Those to whom the hypocrites said, 'Indeed, the people have gathered against you, so fear them.' But it [merely] increased them in faith, and they said, 'Sufficient for us is Allah, and [He is] the best Disposer of affairs.' So they returned with favor from Allah and bounty, no harm having touched them. And they pursued the pleasure of Allah, and Allah is the possessor of great bounty. That is only Satan who frightens [you] of his supporters. So fear them not, but fear Me, if you are [indeed] believers [Āli 'Imrān: 173–175].

Rejection of the truth, mockery of it, belying the people of truth, using falsehood in argumentation, plots, mobilization, intimidation, enmity, and war—all this is the condition of the disbelievers concerning the truth and the followers of the messengers since ancient times. The known factors of the battle are similar throughout the ages. Theirs is a conceited and brash encampment of falsehood, which demonstrates itself to be powerful, and subduing, one that no conqueror can dominate nor any defender withstand. But the reality is they are fearful and terrified, humiliated and left with a weak plan, shaken and defeated, despite their uninhibited movement throughout the lands. Their television and satellite channels as well as their sorcerers are in a state of alert day and night. They dispute by using sorcery, falsifying events, altering realities, and duping people. They deceive, incite, mobilize, and amass against the people of truth. They display the people of falsehood in every guise of strength, ability, force, and fierceness, in desperate and failed attempts to invalidate the truth, scare its followers, and defeat them. This is the case in every age and time.

You see the followers of the messengers in the opposite encampment with lower numbers, meagre equipment, and a weaker voice. But their strength can never be subdued. Their authority can never be broken. They are firm in every battle. And they are forefront in every encounter, having neither fear nor dread. In the end, they will have the triumph and victory. They are always and forever victorious, since the battle of Noah (peace be upon him) and until

Allah inherits the earth and those upon it. All this is due to their faith in Allah, the Mighty, the Compeller. From Him is their strength, and through Him is their authority. He is sufficient for them, and upon Him they rely. They are certain of His aid. And they returned having attained His favor and bounty. They do not fear anyone save Him.

O soldiers of the Islamic State, what a great thing you have achieved by Allah! Your reward is upon Him. By Allah, He has healed the chests of the believers through the killing of the *Nusayriyyah* [Alawites] and rāfidah [Shi'as] at your hands. He has filled the hearts of the disbelievers and hypocrites with rage through you. What a great thing you have achieved by Allah! Who are you? Who are you O soldiers of the Islamic State? From where have you come? What is your secret? Why is it that the hearts of the East and West are dislocated by their fear of you? Why is it that the chest muscles of America and its allies shiver out of fear of you? Where are your warplanes? Where are your battleships? Where are your missiles? Where are your weapons of mass destruction? Why is it that the world has united against you? Why have the nations of disbelief entrenched together against you? What threat do you pose to the distant place of Australia for it to send its legions towards you? What does Canada have anything to do with you?

O soldiers of the Islamic State and its sons everywhere, listen and comprehend. If the people belie you, reject your state and your call, and mock your caliphate, then know that your Prophet (blessings and peace be upon him) was belied. His call was rejected. He was mocked.

If your people fight you, accuse you with the worst of accusations, and describe you with the worst of all traits, then know that the people of the Prophet (blessings and peace be upon him) fought him, expelled him, and accused him with matters worse than those you have been accused with.

If the parties have gathered against you, then know they gathered against your Prophet before (blessings and peace be upon him). This is the established way of Allah, the Blessed, the Exalted. Or did you think that the people would greet you by saying 'Allah is the greatest' and 'There is no god but Allah'? And that they would joyfully bid you welcome?

...O America, O allies of America, and O crusaders, know that the matter is more dangerous than you have imagined and greater than you have envisioned. We have warned you that today we are in a new era, an era where the State, its soldiers, and its sons are leaders not slaves. They are a people who through the ages have not known defeat. The outcome of their battles is concluded before they begin. They have not prepared for a battle since the time of Noah except with absolute conviction of victory. Being killed—according to their account—is a victory. This is where the secret lies. You fight a people who can never be defeated. They either gain victory or are killed. And O crusaders, you are losers in both outcomes, because you are ignorant of the reality that none of us is killed but to resurrect the dead amongst us. None of us is killed but to leave behind him a story that awakens the Muslims from their slumber by its recount. And then you see the weak one of us—he who has no experience in fighting and thinks he cannot contribute anything practical on the ground, having no goal except to be killed, so that he can illuminate the path with his blood and thereby enliven the hearts with his story, generation after generation. He makes his body and remains a bridge for those who awaken after him to pass over. This person has realized that the life of his nation is through blood and the honor of his nation is through blood. So he went on with a bare chest and bare head towards death eagerly searching for life and honor. If he survives, he lives as a victor with freedom, might, honor, and authority. And if he is killed, he illuminates the path for those after him and goes on to his Lord as a joyful martyr. He has taught those after him that might, honor, and life are through jihad and being killed, and that humiliation, disgrace, and death are through submission and subservience.

O crusaders, you have realized the threat of the Islamic State, but you have not become aware of the cure, and you will not discover the cure because there is no cure. If you fight it, it becomes stronger and tougher. If you leave it alone, it grows and expands. If Obama has promised you with defeating the Islamic State, then Bush has also lied before him. Indeed, our Lord, the Mighty and Majestic, has promised us with victory, and here we are now victorious. He will grant us victory at every event. He is glorified and He does not fail in His promise....

O Muslims, America claimed when it first began this crusade, that it was defending its interests in Erbil and Baghdad and defending its citizens. Thereafter its blunder became clear, and the falsehood of its claims became obvious. It claimed that through its airstrikes it would save those expelled and left homeless in Iraq, and defend the civilians. Then it became clear to America that the matter was more dangerous and greater than it expected. So it started shedding crocodile tears over the Muslims in Shām (the Levant). It promised to save them and support them. It promised to save them from the terrorists. While at the same time, America and its allies remained watching the plight of the Muslims upon the hands of the Nusayriyyah. They watched with happiness seeing the killing, abuse, expulsion, and destruction, neither interested in, nor concerned about, the hundreds of thousands of dead, wounded, and imprisoned Muslims, and the millions displaced—including men, women and children—all over the world at the hands of the Jews, Crusaders, Rāfidah, Nusayriyyah, Hindus, atheists, and apostates, in Palestine, Yemen, Syria, Iraq, Egypt, Tunisia, Libya, Burma, Nigeria, Somalia, Afghanistan, Indonesia, India, China, the Caucasus, and elsewhere. Its sentiments were not stirred during the long years of siege and starvation in Shām, and it looked the other way when the deadly and destructive barrel bombs were being dropped. It was not outraged when it saw the horrific scenes of the women and children of the Muslims taking their last breaths with their eyes glazed over due to the chemical weapons of the Nusayriyyah—scenes which continue to be repeated everyday, exposing the reality of the farce of having destroyed chemical weapons belonging to its Nusayrī dogs, the guardians of the Jews. America and its allies were not emotionally moved or outraged by any of this. They closed their ears to the cries of distress from the weak, and turned a blind eye to the massacres carried out against the Muslims in every one of those lands for years and years.

But when a state emerged for the Muslims that would defend them, take revenge for them, and carry out retribution, America and the crusaders started shedding crocodile tears for the sake of a few hundred Rāfidī and Nusayrī criminal soldiers that the Islamic State had taken as prisoners of war and then executed. The hearts of America and its allies were broken by the Islamic State when it cut off the rotten heads of some agents, spies, and apostates. It was terrified and its allies were terrified when the Islamic State would flog and stone the fornicator, cut off the hand of the thief, and strike the neck of the sorcerer and the apostate.

So America and its allies rose in order to save the world from the 'terrorism and barbarity of the Islamic State' as they allege. They rallied the entire global media, driving it with false arguments to delude the masses and lead them to believe that the Islamic State was the root of evil and the source of corruption, and that it was the one killing and displacing the people, arresting and murdering those who are 'peaceful', demolishing houses, destroying cities, and terrorizing the women and children who were previously safe. The media portrayed the crusaders as good, merciful, noble, generous, honorable and passionate people who feared for Islam and the Muslims the 'corruption and cruelty of the Khawārij [a deviant, extremist sect] of the Islamic State' as they allege. To the extent that Kerry, the uncircumcised old geezer, suddenly became an Islamic jurist, issuing a verdict to the people that the Islamic State was distorting Islam, that what it was doing was against Islamic teachings, and that the

Islamic State was an enemy of Islam. And to the extent that Obama, the mule of the Jews, suddenly became a sheikh, mufti (Islamic scholar that issues verdicts), and an Islamic preacher, warning the people and preaching in defence of Islam, claiming that the Islamic State has nothing to do with Islam. This occurred during six different addresses he made in the span of a single month, all of them about the threat of the Islamic State....

O Sunnis of Iraq, the time has come for you to learn from the lessons of the past, and to learn that nothing will work with the rāfidah other than slicing their throats and striking their necks. They make themselves out to be helpless so that they can take power, they conceal their hatred, enmity, and rage towards Sunnis, they plot and conspire against them, and they trick and deceive them. They display false affection towards them and flatter them as long as Sunnis are strong. And they keep pace with them, compete with them, and work hard to weaken them when they are on equal footing.

But if one day they overcome them, they bare their fangs and reveal their claws, biting them, tearing them apart, killing them, and humiliating them. History is right there in front of you, O Sunnis, so read it. How many times have the rāfidah conspired against the Sunnis, and what do they do to them when they gain power?

Read their history and look at how they are in the present. Indeed, their idiot Nouri [al-Maliki] has shown you their true face, so do not let their new snake deceive you with his soft touch and sweet tongue. You have been stung through the hole of reconciliation before with Nouri, so beware.

Our dear people of Shām, you can see the reality becoming clearer day after day. Take a lesson from our people in Iraq, for history repeats itself. Indeed, the crusaders began building the Iraqi-safavid army by training its core in Jordan, with a few thousand soldiers, as they have decided to do today with regard to Shām. So what did the Sunnis get out of that army other than to have the rāfidah completely gain power over them? They tasted humiliation, disgrace, and many misfortunes at the hands of that army over a period of ten years. Furthermore, what did the sons of the Sunnis get out of joining that army other than apostasy from the religion of Allah, the destruction of their homes, and having their heads cut off? And those of them who lived, lived in continuous terror and a persistent state of fear, not knowing when he'd be taken by a bullet, or have his joints cut by an adhesive IED, or be deformed by an explosive or bomb, or be suffocated to death, or have a knife cutting his neck, or when he would return to find his home demolished, left in pieces after it was once whole. And for what would all this have been for? So take a lesson, O people of intelligence.

{And how many a generation before them did We destroy who were greater than them in [striking] power and had explored throughout the lands. Is there any place of escape? Indeed in that is a reminder for whoever has a heart or who listens while he is present [in mind]} [Qāf: 36–37].

So pay attention, O Sunnis. For the army that they have decided to prepare today by Āl Salūl (the Saudis) is nothing more than a new set of guard dogs for the jews, and a stick in the hands of the crusaders to be used against Islam and the mujahidin. Therefore, we advise the mujahidin in Shām to target anyone who joins that army or intends to join it. And he who has given his warning is free of blame.

As for the sahwah councils and their political sponsors, they will not be able to hide their reality after today. Their reality, that they are the sahwah councils and the shoes of the crusaders, will emerge very clearly.

So rally around the mujahidin, O Sunnis of Shām, and stop your sons from joining the army and the sahwah councils, for what good is there in an army built by the crusaders which they then train on the laps of the tawāghīt. So prevent your sons, and whoever of them refuses to listen, let him not blame anyone but himself if there comes to him a day in which he digs his grave with his own hands, his head is cut off, and his house is demolished. And the blessed one is he who learns from the lessons of others....

Let us not forget before ending to praise our mujahidin brothers in the bold Sinai Peninsula, for hope has emerged in Egypt and good news has loomed with their blessed operations against the guards of the jews, the soldiers of Sisi, the new Pharaoh of Egypt. Carry on upon this path, for it is the correct path, may Allah bless you....

And to our brothers the muwahhidīn in beloved Libya, until when will you remain dispersed and divided? Why do you not gather your groups, unify, unite your word, and solidify your ranks? Why do you not identify who is with you and who is against you? Your division is from Satan....

We also call out to the muwahhidīn in the robbed land of Tunisia, follow the footsteps of your brothers in Egypt....

As for Yemen, then O alas for what has come upon Yemen. Alas! Alas for Sanaa. The rafidī houthis have entered it, but the car bombs have not roasted their skin, nor have the explosive belts and IEDs cut their joints. Is there not in Yemen a person who will take revenge for us....

....So O muwahhid, do not let this battle pass you by wherever you may be. You must strike the soldiers, patrons, and troops of the tawāghīt. Strike their police, security, and intelligence members, as well as their treacherous agents. Destroy their beds. Embitter their lives for them and busy them with themselves. If you can kill a disbelieving American or European—especially the spiteful and filthy French—or an Australian, or a Canadian, or any other disbeliever from the disbelievers waging war, including the citizens of the countries that entered into a coalition against the Islamic State, then rely upon Allah, and kill him in any manner or way however it may be. Do not ask for anyone's advice and do not seek anyone's verdict. Kill the disbeliever whether he is civilian or military, for they have the same ruling. Both of them are disbelievers. Both of them are considered to be waging war [the civilian by belonging to a state waging war against the Muslims]. Both of their blood and wealth is legal for you to destroy, for blood does not become illegal or legal to spill by the clothes being worn. The civilian outfit does not make blood illegal to spill, and the military uniform does not make blood legal to spill. The only things that make blood illegal and legal to spill are Islam and a covenant (peace treaty, dhimmi [contract], etc.). Blood becomes legal to spill through disbelief. So whoever is a Muslim, his blood and wealth are sanctified. And whoever is a disbeliever, his wealth is legal for a Muslim to take and his blood is legal to spill. His blood is like the blood of a dog; there is no sin for him in spilling it nor is there any blood money to be paid for doing such....

...will you leave the American, the Frenchman, or any of their allies to walk safely upon the earth while the armies of the crusaders strike the lands of the Muslims not differentiating between a civilian and fighter? They have killed nine Muslim women three days ago by striking a bus transporting them from Shām to Iraq. Will you leave the disbeliever to sleep safely at home while the Muslim women and children shiver with fear of the roars of the crusader airplanes above their heads day and night? How can you enjoy life and sleep while not aiding your brothers, not casting fear into the hearts of the cross worshippers, and not responding to their strikes with multitudes more?

....O Allah, America, France, and their allies transgressed against us. They came with their legions to fight us out of their enmity for your religion. They prevent us from establishing your religion and your hudūd (fixed punishments), and ruling by what you revealed. O Allah, you know our weakness. We have no way to deal with their airplanes. O Allah, you have said what is true, 'So do not weaken and do not grieve, and you will be superior if you are [true] believers' [Āli 'Imrān: 139]. O Allah, we have believed in you and relied upon you. You are sufficient for us and the best disposer of affairs. O Allah,

America and its allies disbelieve in you and associate partners with you. O Allah, you have placed them above us by their airplanes. O Allah, you know we have no power nor strength against their planes except through You. O Allah, do not let them be above us while You are above them. O Allah, do not let them be above us while we are higher than them.

8.2a. 'The Extinction of the Grayzone', February 2015
Issue 7 of Dabiq *magazine, unidentified author*

The Endangered Grayzone

The grayzone is critically endangered, rather on the brink of extinction. Its endangerment began with the blessed operations of September 11th, as these operations manifested two camps before the world for mankind to choose between, a camp of Islam—without the body of Khilāfah to represent it at the time—and a camp of kufr—the crusader coalition. Or as Shaykh Usāmah Ibn Lādin (rahimahullāh) said, 'The world today is divided into two camps. Bush spoke the truth when he said, 'Either you are with us or you are with the terrorists.' Meaning, either you are with the crusade or you are with Islam' [Interview—4 Sha'bān 1422H].

The operations quickly exposed the different deviant 'Islamic' movements, the palace 'scholars', and the deviant du'āt, not to mention the apostate tawāghīt, as all of them rushed to serve the crusaders led by Bush in the war against Islam. And so, the grayzone began to wither[.]

But the fiery zeal of the broken Muslim Ummah began to cool by the hazy events known as 'the Arab Spring' as well as the lack of a body representing Islam (the Khilāfah) then. The Muslims saw the same aforementioned movements, scholars', callers, sects, and even the apostate tawāghīt get involved in 'supporting' the cause of the oppressed Muslims in Shām. And so confusion spread, and the withering of the grayzone was slowed or almost halted. Once again, the heretical call to the gates of Hellfire—the religions of the tawāghīt—was answered by many of the ignorant.

Then came the announcement of the Islamic State's expansion to Shām followed by the subsequent announcement of the Khilāfah... bringing the grayzone to the brink of permanent extinction... by reviving the great body of Islam and so no Muslim had any excuse to be independent of this entity embodying them and waging war on their behalf in the face of kufr. Now, a stance of 'neutrality' or 'independence' would doom him, as it entailed major sin, which would cause him to commit greater sins until he could commit kufr for the sake of his sinful interests, as the scholars stated, 'The reward for sin is another sin,' and 'Sins are the gateway to kufr' [al-Jawāb al-Kāfī—Ibnul-Qayyim].

The destruction of the grayzone is comparable to the division resulting from the Islamic message when it was first conveyed by the Messenger (sallallāhu 'alayhi wa sallam). As the angels said when they appeared before the Prophet (sallallāhu 'alayhi wa sallam) while he was sleeping, 'Muhammad is a divider' and 'Muhammad divided the people' [Sahīh alBukhārī]. For this reason, the mushrikīn would warn the Arabs against the Prophet (sallallāhu 'alayhi wa sallam) by saying, 'You have come to our lands. The matter of this man amongst us has grown severe. He has divided our jamā'ah (community) and scattered our strength. His words are like that of a sorcerer. He divides between a man and his father, a man and his brother, a man and his wife. We fear for you and your people what he has brought upon us. So do not speak to him nor listen to a word from him' [Ibn Hishām]. They would also say, 'He divides between a man and his religion ... a man and his clan' [Ibn Hishām] and 'He severed the bonds between us' [Ibn Hishām].

Rasūlullāh (sallallāhu 'alayhi wa sallam) came with al-Furqān (the Qur'ān, the divider between truth and falsehood) by which he divided his people into two opposing parties—the Muslims versus the mushrikīn—who then fought each other on the Day of al-Furqān (the Battle of Badr), where Rasūlullāh (sallallāhu 'alayhi wa sallam) slaughtered his mushrik [polytheist] adversaries by his sword.

And when a grayzone formed and a 'masjid' was established for it, Allah (ta'ālā) revealed to His Messenger (sallallāhu 'alayhi wa sallam) al-Fādihah (the Exposer, Sūrat at-Tawbah) by which the grayish were exposed as well as their harmful 'masjid'. Rasūlullāh (sallallāhu 'alayhi wa sallam) went on to demolish this 'masjid'... again ridding the Ummah of the destructive gray movement, as the grayzone was the hideout of the hypocrites, {Indeed, the hypocrites [think to] deceive Allah, but He is deceiving them. And when they stand for prayer, they stand lazily, showing [themselves to] the people and not remembering Allah except a little, wavering between them, [belonging] neither to the believers nor to the disbelievers. And whoever Allah leaves astray—never will you find for him a way} [At-Tawbah: 142–143].

And a sword was also revealed to deal with the grayish hypocrites if they openly exposed their dark hypocrisy. {O Prophet, fight against the disbelievers and the hypocrites and be harsh upon them. And their refuge is Hell, and wretched is the destination} [At-Tawbah: 73]. {If the hypocrites and those in whose hearts is disease and those who spread rumors in alMadīnah do not cease, We will surely incite you against them; then they will not remain your neighbors therein except for a little. They are accursed; wherever they are found, they are to be seized and massacred completely. This is the established way of Allah with those who passed on before; and you will not find in the way of Allah any change} [al-Ahzāb: 60–62].

And so, the hypocrites buried their heads in the sand, fearful of being exposed... They remained so until the wars of apostasy, when most of the Arabs apostatized from Islam. Then the hypocrites came out and rushed to join the open camp of falsehood, until the sword against apostasy—Abū Bakr as-Siddīq (radiyallāhu 'anh)—took his famous stance and forced them back into the religion by the edge of his blade. Again, the hypocrites concealed themselves until other fitan [trials] struck the Ummah, including the murders of al-Fārūq 'Umar, 'Uthmān, and 'Alī (radiyallāhu 'anhum)... fitan that gave birth to deviant sects and parties, which in turn provided cover for the hypocrites desperately seeking another grayzone to operate from.

And so, the hypocrites began to speak out brazenly, as Hudhayfah (radiyallāhu 'anh) said, 'Indeed, the hypocrites today are worse than those at the time of Rasūlullāh (sallallāhu 'alayhi wa sallam); those ones would hide their hypocrisy, as for today, then they openly declare it [al-Bukhārī].

And just as the Islamic message carried by the Prophet (sallallāhu 'alayhi wa sallam) split the former jāhiliyyah into two opposing camps, the Islamic State—by its very expansion to Shām—split the different factions in Shām including those with jāhilī [primitive] and 'ummī (blind) goals. The former War Minister Abū Hamzah al-Muhājir (rahimahullāh) was asked, 'Some people accuse you of being the cause for the Sahwah mission, how correct is this claim?' He replied:

'We have previously asserted that the true cause behind the Sahwah mission was the establishment of the Islamic State. This is what began to be apparent these days, for after the announcement of the State, the Islamic mission conflicted with the nationalist mission adopted by almost all colors of the spectrum in Iraq, and this is what all the different jabhāt ad-dirār (harmful fronts) which were announced and formed have declared openly and repeatedly. It is not strange for all these different assemblies to form after the announcement of the Islamic State for they were truly formed only to wage war against it, secretly and openly.'

'Indeed, the rancor and envy of the carriers of Āl Salūl's banner [the Surūriyyah] burned after losing their piece of the cake, after their hope for nationalist rule was demolished, and after they realized we would spill our blood and dismember our corpses cheaply so as to not allow the fruit of jihād to go to waste and so Iraq would not once again be ruled by something besides the Sharī'ah of ar-Rahmān. And because the reality of their armies [the Surūrī factions] is a lie especially after the sincere ones in their ranks joined us, their only option was to stand with the occupation against the Islamic State because the nationalist mission, which they argued for, gathered support for, and unified for, is the same mission desired by the occupation. The only condition is to be its agents, and this they had offered before for nothing in return from the occupation except a few dirhams and some security, which the occupation and its allies began to deprive them of' (The First Interview).

The different factions in Shām—as occurred in Iraq—began to split into two camps: the Islamic State versus the Sahwah backed by the crusaders, apostate regimes, and deviant movements... and those who tried to preserve the grayzone for different partisan interests found the grayzone withering rapidly before them, as their sincere soldiers abandoned them to join the Islamic State while their sick-hearted soldiers rushed to join the Sahwah factions. This division found its way quickly into different lands, as sincere mujāhidīn saw their former leaders fearful of losing power and influence rushing to futilely resuscitate the grayzone, even if it necessitated supporting the interests of the secularist, nationalist, and heretical parties waging war against the Islamic State on behalf of the crusaders and Arab apostate regimes. The grayzone—for these leaders—was a place to continue existing as independent parties and thereby preserve their own power. The Khilāfah's establishment finally pushed the sincere mujāhidīn to abandon their former leaderships, who were too busy burying themselves alive in the garbage dump of history.

This revival of the Khilāfah gave each individual Muslim a concrete and tangible entity to satisfy his natural desire for belonging to something greater. The satisfaction of this desire brought life back to the zeal latent in Muslims' hearts and when this entity embodying them was threatened by the crusaders, attacks were immediately carried out by the zealous Muslims in different kāfir lands in a way uniquely different to all attacks before. For years, different jihād organizations had called for individual attacks to be carried out against the crusader homelands, but their calls were met with minimal response. After the revival of the Khilāfah, numerous attacks were carried out in a period of months. This is something that the crusaders should deeply reflect over[.]

Europe was struck by attacks that killed multitudes more of kuffār than those killed in the recent Paris attacks. The 2004 Madrid operation and the 2005 London operation together killed more than 200 crusaders and injured more than 2000. Europe also witnessed an attack against 'free speech' when a mujāhid assassinated Theo Van Gogh for mocking Allah (ta'ālā), His verses, His religion, and His Messenger (sallallāhu 'alayhi wa sallam). So why was the reaction to the recent attacks much greater than that of any previous attack? It is the international atmosphere of terror generated by the presence of the Islamic Khilāfah… It is the lively words contained in the Khilāfah's call. When its spokesman Shaykh Abū Muhammad al-'Adnānī ash-Shāmī (hafidhahullāh) made his call to Muslims everywhere, ordering them to carry out attacks against the crusaders wherever they may be found, his call was answered immediately, with different individual operations executed within hours[.]

And of those who answered the call recently was the brave mujāhid Abū Basīr al-Ifrīqī (Amedy Coulibaly—rahimahullāh). It was the address 'Indeed, Your Lord Is Ever Watchful' that moved him most. He had given his bay'ah to the Khilāfah beforehand—immediately upon its announcement—and sat in wait for instructions from its leadership, while never traveling to Iraq nor Shām. It was the living and breathing entity of Islam, which he pledged allegiance to, that inspired his soul. He met with the Muslims and mujāhidīn in France, calling them to give bay'ah and defend the Khilāfah, while refuting the doubts spread against it. He provided others—including the two mujāhid brothers, Cherif and Said Kouachi (rahimahumallāh)—with money and weapons so as to call to jihād under the banner of the Khilāfah.

And thus, the time had come for another event—magnified by the presence of the Khilāfah on the global stage—to further bring division to the world and destroy the grayzone everywhere….

8b. Analysis

If Baghdadi's speeches in the previous chapter mark the beginning of Islamic State's peak, the sources featured here emerged at the zenith of this period, with the group strategically pivoting to globalise its struggle as a means to position itself for the unprecedented coalition effort against it. Adnani's speech plays off an array of motivational levers designed to mobilise Islamic State supporters against its enemies. It is useful to break the speech down into three parts.

The Peak of Islamic State's Second Resurgence

First, Adnani opens with a series of Quranic verses, most notably a reference to the story of Noah, which he draws upon throughout the speech as an historical and cosmic analogy for the challenges facing the Islamic State. These opening verses prime his audience to understand the group's struggles as a continuation of the perpetual battle between truth and falsehood. Notably, he places the information war at the heart of the conflict, declaring:

> They dispute by using sorcery, falsifying events, altering realities, and duping people. They deceive, incite, mobilize, and amass against the people of the truth. They display the people of falsehood in every guise of strength, ability, force, and fierceness, in desperate and failed attempts to invalidate the truth, scare its followers, and defeat them. This is the case in every age and time.

Contrasting with these powerful actors and forces, which coalesced for the sole purpose of destroying Islam, Adnani then describes Islamic State as 'the opposite encampment with lower numbers, meager equipment, and a weaker voice' but with truth on its side and thus a fearlessness and commitment that assures they 'are always and forever victorious, since the battle of Noah (peace be upon him) and Until Allah inherits the earth and those upon it'. He poses a series of questions designed to encourage his audience to reflect on the rationale driving powerful nations from around the world to come together to fight a comparatively smaller and weaker opponent in the Islamic State. For Adnani, the answer is simple and repeated throughout history from the time of the Prophet Muhammad: Islam.

Second, he launches into a wide-ranging attack on the credibility of Islamic State's adversaries, especially targeting the West. Dismissing consecutive US Presidents Bush and Obama as liars, Adnani condemned the United States for watching the deaths of Muslims around the world 'with happiness'. He goes on to argue:

> its sentiments were not stirred during the long years of siege and starvation in Sham, and it looked the other way when the deadly and destructive barrel bombs were being dropped. It was not outraged when it saw the horrific scenes of the women and children of the Muslims taking their last breaths with their eyes glazed over due to the chemical weapons.

Leveraging the media attention that had been devoted to the Assad regime's brutality and the limited response of Western nations,[3] Adnani uses these

---

[3] Mass torture and killings, including the use of chemical agents, were widely reported by media outlets and human rights organisations since 2011. For example, see UN News, 'As Syrian death toll tops 5,000, UN human rights chief warns about key city', *UN News*, 12 Dec. 2011, https://news.un.org/en/story/2011/12/398082-syrian-death-toll-tops-5000-un-human-rights-chief-warns-about-key-city; Ki-moon, Ban,

highly emotive examples to argue that the West only acted 'when a state emerged for the Muslims that would defend them, take revenge for them, and carry out retribution, America and the crusaders started shedding crocodile tears'. This passage is not only designed to smear the credibility of Western nations but seeks to reinforce the Islamic State's credibility as an actor that is filling the 'responsibility to protect' (R2P) void.[4] Adnani does not limit his attack to the West's apparent hypocrisy with regards to protecting human life, he also mocks Western leaders for presenting themselves as representatives of Islam. He paints the picture of a global media conspiracy that sought to present the coalition as protectors of Islam and Muslims, with Obama and Secretary of State John Kerry as its chief spokespersons. For example, he mockingly describes Kerry as 'the uncircumcised old geezer' who 'suddenly became an Islamic jurist' and Obama as 'the mule of the Jews' who 'suddenly became a sheikh ... an Islamic preacher, warning the people and preaching in defense of Islam, claiming that the Islamic State has nothing to do with Islam.' On this occasion, his intent was to demonstrate the absurdity of non-Muslims preaching to Muslims about their religion.[5] In contrast, Adnani suggests that it is the Islamic State that has demonstrated a consistent commitment to its *manhaj* and protection of Muslims.

While the opening and middle parts of the speech focus on providing his audiences with an historical, global, and cosmic perspective on the Islamic

---

'Crisis in Syria: Civil war, global threat', *United Nations Secretary General*, 25 June 2014, https://www.un.org/sg/en/content/sg/articles/2014-06-25/crisis-syria-civil-war-global-threat; Amnesty International, '"Death Everywhere": War crimes and human rights abuses in Aleppo, Syria', Amnesty International, 2015; and Taub, Ben, 'The Assad Files: Capturing the top-secret documents that tie the Syrian regime to mass torture and killings', *New Yorker*, 18 Apr. 2016.

[4] For a broader consideration of the jihadi 'responsibility to protect' appeals, see Ingram, Haroro, 'Jihadist "Responsibility to Protect" Appeals: Propaganda wars for the moral high ground', *ICCT*—The Hague, 14 Mar. 2019.

[5] The issue of how to refer to the self-described 'Islamic State' and what that meant for its relationship to Islam led many world leaders, including then President Obama and Secretary Kerry, to strategically avoid using the term 'Islamic State' and engaging in rhetoric about what constituted 'true' Islam. Some commentators warned at the time that such rhetoric may inadvertently undermine the efforts of allies in the region, see Hamid, Shadi, and Will McCants, 'John Kerry won't call the Islamic State by its name anymore. Why that's not a good idea', *Washington Post*, Dec. 29, 2014.

State's situation, he closes by addressing specific audiences around the world. In doing so, Adnani demonstrated an awareness and understanding of events and issues impacting the *umma*, while implicitly weaving those current events into a broader historical and cosmic context. Initially addressing various Sunni communities across the Middle East and North Africa, he extends his rallying cry to the West, specifically calling for attacks against American, Australian, Canadian, and French populations. He dismisses the distinction between civilian and military targets on the basis of both reciprocity (that is, Muslim civilians are killed in Islamic State territories) and their blanket status as disbelievers. Adnani opens his speech by positioning the Islamic State as the primary protectors of Muslims in the region and implores fellow Muslims to help protect their state, asking, 'How can you enjoy life and sleep while not aiding your brothers, not casting fear into the hearts of the cross worshippers, and not responding to their strikes with multitudes more?' Then he concludes by doubling down on this sentiment, lamenting the strategic advantage of the coalition's airpower. The message is clear: defend your state as it defends you.

In its immediate aftermath, Adnani's address received praise, while supporters online expressed a determination to actively counter anti-Islamic State propaganda. In some regards, Adnani's speech represents a milestone in the leadership's efforts to actively direct the propaganda activities of its supporters. More disturbingly, in the weeks and months after it, terrorist attacks perpetrated by individuals apparently inspired by the Islamic State occurred in Australia,[6] Canada,[7] the United States,[8] and France.[9] While it is not appropri-

---

[6] Two reportedly Islamic State-inspired attacks in Australia occurred in the months following Adnani's address. On 24 September 2014, an 18-year-old man attacked and seriously injured two police officers with a knife in Melbourne, Australia. He was killed by the officers. On 15 December 2014, a 50-year-old man attacked a café in Sydney, Australia. The siege lasted approximately seventeen hours, resulting in the deaths of three people including the hostage-taker. Both attackers claimed to be inspired by Islamic State.

[7] In October 2014, two reportedly Islamic State-inspired attacks occurred in Canada. On 20 October 2014, a 25-year-old man used a vehicle to attack two Canadian military personnel in Quebec, killing one and injuring the other. On 22 October 2014, a 32-year-old man attacked Parliament Hill in Ottawa, killing one and injuring three.

[8] On 23 October 2014, a 32-year-old man used a hatchet to attack four police officers in Queens, New York.

[9] Two terrorist attacks in France were apparently inspired by Islamic State in the months

ate to draw speculative causational links between Adnani's address and these attacks, the Islamic State's propaganda machine certainly took full advantage and sought to amplify their impact, especially via its English-language magazine *Dabiq*. During this period, the Islamic State's successes on the battlefields of Syria and Iraq were being promoted globally by a propaganda apparatus functioning at full steam. Its apparent ascendency in the field contributed to a narrative that politico-military success reflected divine favour. For the first time in its history, the Islamic State began to establish provinces outside of Iraq and Syria in late 2014, accepting pledges from groups that satisfied its requirements. Meanwhile, its media unit continued to attract global media attention with a video entitled 'Healing the Believers' Chests'.[10] In the same month, militants attacked the offices of Charlie Hebdo in Paris, motivated by the satirical newspaper's publication of the image of the Prophet Muhammad. Despite the attackers claiming allegiance to al-Qaida in the Arabian Peninsula, Islamic State supporters at the time claimed the attack was inspired by Adnani's speech. The following month, the cover of *Dabiq*'s seventh issue featured a photo of two elderly French Muslims holding 'Je Suis Charlie' signs with the words 'From Hypocrisy to Apostasy: Extinction of the Grayzone' beneath them.

Of the fifteen issues and hundreds of articles that appeared in *Dabiq* magazine over its two years of publication,[11] the opening section of the twelve-page article 'Extinction of the Grayzone' features in this chapter for three key reasons. First, it centers on what may be the central overarching claim of Islamic State propaganda—that the world is divided between the camp of Islam and the camp of disbelief—and explicitly applies it to the context of Muslims living in the West. It positions the establishment of its caliphate alongside the September 11 attacks as pivotal moments in the modern day elimination of the 'gray' area of Islamic moderation and compromise between the poles of Islam and disbelief: 'a stance of "neutrality" or "independence" would doom him [Muslims], as it entailed major sin, which would cause him to commit

---

following Adnani's address. On 20 December 2014, a 20-year-old man attacked police officers in Tours. On 22 December 2014, a 38-year-old man used a van to attack pedestrians in Nantes, killing one and injuring nine. On 21 December 2014, a 40-year-old man carried out a vehicular attack in Dijon, injuring thirteen.

[10] 'Healing the Believer's Chests', al-Furqan Media, 15 Feb. 2015.

[11] For analyses of Islamic State's English-language magazines see Ingram, Haroro, 'Islamic State's English-language magazines, 2014–17', *ICCT*—The Hague, 2018.

greater sins until he could commit kufr for the sake of his sinful interests.' The article uses historical and cosmic narratives as a context for contemporary events to offer additional justification for what the Islamic State claims to be jurisprudentially valid, strategically impactful, and historically proven solutions to that crisis: 'a sword was also revealed to deal with the grayish hypocrites if they openly exposed their dark hypocrisy'. According to the article's unnamed author, the establishment of the caliphate not only created the conditions within which compromise was utterly unacceptable but compelled true Muslims (that is, Islamic State-aligned Sunnis) towards action while making Islam's enemies fearful. As the article asserts,

> This revival of the Khilāfah gave each individual Muslim a concrete and tangible entity to satisfy his natural desire for belonging to something greater. The satisfaction of this desire brought life back to the zeal latent in Muslims' hearts and when this entity embodying them was threatened by the crusaders, attacks were immediately carried out by the zealous Muslims in different kāfir lands in a way uniquely different to all attacks before.... This is something that the crusaders should deeply reflect over[.]

The article goes on to argue that the unprecedentedly large response of Western governments to Islamic State-inspired terrorist attacks when compared with previous attacks was due to the establishment of its caliphate and Adnani's own charisma, exaggeratedly suggesting that regarding the spokesperson's orders 'to carry out attacks against the crusaders wherever they may be found, his call was answered immediately, with different individual operations executed within hours'.

The second reason for including the excerpt from this article is that it showcases a variety of propaganda strategies typical of Islamic State messaging. For example, the article does not name the author, while the bulk of its contents consist of quotations from the Quran or summations from *hadith*. This propaganda strategy is designed to give readers, typically young Muslims with little knowledge of Islamic jurisprudence, the sense that what is written is not only inherently credible but foretold. Another commonality in Islamic State propaganda that features prominently in this article is the implicit and explicit analogies drawing connections between the Prophet Muhammad and the Islamic State's actions. For example, 'just as the Islamic message carried by the Prophet... split the former *jahiliyyah* into two opposing camps, the Islamic State... split the different factions in Sham including those with *jahili* and *ummi* goals.' Such messaging is designed to highlight that Islamic State is replicating the Prophet's method.

Finally, *Dabiq's* seventh issue was arguably the issue in which the magazine came into its own, something that is reflected in the new sections it introduced and the way in which it synchronised with Islamic State's broader messaging efforts. The first issue of *Dabiq* published in 2015, issue seven sought to leverage prominent current events. For example, the 'Foreword'[12] highlighted the execution of two Japanese journalists—Kenji Goto and Haruna Yukawa—while its opening article, 'The Burning of the *Murtadd* Pilot',[13] provided a justification for its execution of Jordanian pilot Muath al-Kasasbeh, which featured in the video 'Healing the Believers' Chests'. Indeed, the issue even contained an advertisement promoting the video, describing it as 'the video that set crusader hearts on fire and left them burning in rage'.[14] Aside from 'The Extinction of the Grayzone', two other articles were devoted to praising Amedy Coulibaly, who had participated in the January 2015 attack on a kosher supermarket in Paris. They were titled 'A brief interview with Umm Basir al-Muhajirah'[15] and 'The Good Example of Abu Basir al-Ifriqi'.[15] *Dabiq's* seventh issue also featured sections previously unseen in the magazine: 'Among the Believers Are Men', which eulogised Islamic State foreign fighters; 'From the Pages of History', which drew historical lessons that were deemed pertinent for resolving contemporary problems; and 'To Our Sisters', featuring content specifically for the women among the Islamic State audience. The subsequent issues of *Dabiq* largely followed the style and format set out in its seventh issue.[17]

The Islamic State's Global Insurgency

Adnani's charisma and eloquence proved to be a powerful propaganda tool itself as the Islamic State's spokesman rapidly became the face of the group

---

[12] Unnamed author, 'Foreword', *Dabiq*, no. 7, 2015, pp. 3–4.

[13] Unnamed author, 'The Burning of the *Murtad* Pilot', *Dabiq*, no. 7, 2015, pp. 5–8.

[14] Unnamed author, 'New Release', *Dabiq*, no. 7, 2015, p. 67.

[15] Unnamed author, 'A Brief Interview with Umm Basir al-Muhajirah', *Dabiq*, no. 7, 2015, pp. 50–51.

[16] Unnamed author, 'The Good Example of Abu Basir al-Ifriqi', *Dabiq* no. 7, 2015, pp. 68–71.

[17] Ingram, Haroro, 'Islamic State's English-Language Magazines, 2014–17: Trends & Implications for CT-CVE Strategic Communications', ICCT-The Hague, vol. 8, no. 15 (2018), https://icct.nl/wp-content/uploads/2018/03/ICCT-Ingram-Islamic-State-English-Language-Magazines-March2018.pdf, last accessed 18 Dec. 2018.

during a period when its propaganda efforts had captured global attention. For its part, *Dabiq* magazine became a key forum through which Islamic State propagandists would increasingly call upon Muslims in the West to commit terrorist attacks at home. As the coalition applied increasing pressure on the Islamic State in its territories, the movement increasingly sought to stretch the frontlines of the conflict from the Middle East to the streets of London, New York, Paris, and Sydney. The Islamic State had expanded its campaign from Iraq and Syria to the world. However, the peak of its second resurgence would not last long. By the end of 2015, it was clear that the group's momentum had stalled and by the middle of 2016 its leaders were warning of hard times ahead.

WOMEN IN THE ISLAMIC STATE

In late January 2015, supporters of the Islamic State circulated a document called 'Women in the Islamic State: A manifesto and case study' on a password-protected forum used by jihadis. While its author was unidentified, the text was attributed to the outreach wing of the Khansa' Brigade, an all-women policing unit operating inside the caliphate at the time. The first and only of its kind, the treatise clarified a number of issues regarding the role of women in the Islamic State that had hitherto been obscured by sensationalist media reportage and deliberate misinformation. The text is split into three sections. The first portion deals specifically with 'modern' preoccupations like feminism, education, and science, and sets out an Islamic response to these 'corruptions'. The second part is purportedly based on the author's (or authors') eyewitness account of life in the territories controlled by the Islamic State back in 2014, providing dispatch-style reportage on the state of women in the cities of Mosul and Raqqah, while the last part is a diatribe against Saudi Arabia, comparing the lot of women living in Islamic State-held Syria and Iraq with the lot of women in the Arabian Peninsula. Only the first section is included below.

9a. Women in the Islamic State: A Manifesto and Case Study, January 2015

Introduction[1]

Praise be to Allah, who revived for us the Islamic State, and on His Prophet be the best prayers and most complete peace. Praise be to Allah, who has

---

[1] This original translation of this excerpt of the manifesto was prepared by Aymenn

restored [the Islamic state] to us after decades of humiliation and surrender, when the Ottoman Caliphate fell and its place was filled by Arab and non-Arab systems that collaborate with the enemies of the path, and Muslim societies were occupied militarily, economically and ideologically. And pure Islamic thought derived from the Book and the Sunna became a strange notion, distant from the reality of the people and their life, and Western colonialism was able to spread its filthy culture and atheistic, materialistic thought among the Muslims wherever their lands were. And from that time, true Islamic society disappeared, that [society] which was conscious of this worldly life and met the divine requirement of worship: 'I did not create jinn and men except that they should worship Me.'

And with the rise of the sun of the caliphate, and as the star of guidance becomes clear, this labyrinth that the generations of Muslims lived in for long decades has come to an end. Also coming to an end is the time of imitating the stronger—that is, the victorious Westerner—in their way and methodology of life, whether in regards to aspects of society, education, economy (the management of wealth), medical or industrial, and the other aspects of human life. This is so, and the clearest sign of independence from this disbelieving West is the change from the usurious paper currency that the Muslims became accustomed to, to the dinar and dirham currency in the way of the Prophet (peace and purest salutations be upon him), through which people set the prices and circulated it among themselves. Reliance on this truest form of wealth has wrought great economic benefits. Indeed, the greatest consequence of the imposition of this currency is ridding the Muslims of the usury that plagues he who deals in the paper currencies, because the laws of the global system that govern the printing of these paper monies are based on usury. As such, there are no exchanges without interest on any part of the earth, except those that take place within our Islamic State! And all the banks of the world are connected with each other by chains of transactions that do not please the Lord of men, and all that has been because of the tyranny of capitalism, which has been forcibly imposed on the people.

Therefore, the Islamic society that the Islamic State has begun to form in Iraq and al-Sham is a society fundamentally based on the worship of the one true

---

Jawad al-Tamimi. An alternative translation was prepared by Charlie Winter in 2015 and can be found here: https://therinjfoundation.files.wordpress.com/2015/01/women-of-the-islamic-state3.pdf

Allah, and anything that conflicts with this objective is consigned to hell. And this Islamic society, in its fledgling stages, needs more time and effort from us so that we can restore it to how it was in the time of the rule of the Prophet and the Rightly Guided Caliphate, with each person in their correct place. Among those people is the Muslim woman, for she is a member of Islamic society. There was a role for her back in those days, and today too she must have a role, in line with the requirements of sharia and the regulations of Islam.

In this missive, we will outline her true role, far removed from the disturbances of the present day that have abused her nature and religion until she and we have forgotten the reason for her existence on this Earth. This document relies, in all its pillars, on the Quranic and Prophetic guidance, the splendour of which guided man after he fell into darkness and loss, with complete faith that is unperturbed by any doubt about the truthfulness of these two sources in every time and place. This is undisputed, except by those who reject the guidance of Allah, and only disbelievers reject the guidance of Allah.

We will draw attention to two things.

First, it should be clearly understood that this message is a personal effort of some of the female supporters of the Islamic State, and must not be attributed to [the Islamic State] or its leadership. Second, it should not be considered a constitution or something that the state wishes to implement with regards to women.

This message has been written for three purposes.

1. To affirm knowledge regarding the role of the Muslim woman and the desired life she must lead to be happy in this world and the Hereafter.
2. To affirm the reality of the good, dignified lives of women living under the Islamic State in Iraq and al-Sham, refuting the doubts stirred up about harassment, based on evidence and witness testimonies from some of the Muslim women who are living there.
3. To expose the fake *tawhid* in the Arabian Peninsula that calls for individual protection of the woman, her religion, and her rights. You can ask any Muslim brother or sister about the reason for comparing this land with the Islamic State, and I say with praise of Allah Almighty:

It is not hidden to those of intelligence that theirs is a deceptive model of Islam that has been set before Muslims as an example, not only regarding women, but also on the issues of economy, education, and politics. But the authentic will be distinguished from the imitation, with Allah's permission.

And by Allah, we ask Him to benefit us as He is the one who grants success on the straight path!

Manifesto for Muslim Women

The message for Muslim women does not differ from the message for the Muslim society in any regard. Rather, it is derived from it and taken from it with affirmation. Its foundations and ideas are built on the basis of the two noble sources of guidance, following the first who followed its *da'wa*, starting with Maryam and Asiyya and ending with Khadijah, Fatimah, and A'ishah and the mothers of the believers, women of the Companions, and the followers whose lives were recorded in heavenly ink. May Allah be pleased with them and make them pleased.

And the principle of this message is that woman, as with man, was created to populate the Earth, but, as Allah Almighty wished, she was created from Adam and for Adam. For there is nothing greater for her than fulfilling the role assigned to her and imposed upon her by her Creator, the right of her husband over her: 'And among His signs is that He created for you partners from yourselves that you might find tranquillity with them and He has placed between you affection and mercy'.

So He defined the role and explained the purpose when He said, 'that you might find tranquility with them'.

In the hadith: 'If the woman prays her five prayers, fasts her month, remains chaste, and obeys her spouse, it is said to her: enter Paradise from any gates of Paradise you wish'. Narrated by Ibn Haban and authenticated by Albani.

But the problem today is that women are not fulfilling their true roles, those that are in line with her character and nature. There is one main reason for this—they are confronted with an image of man that is not true. There is a proliferation of quasi-men who shoulder no responsibility towards their *umma*, religion, and people, or even towards their homes and sons for whom their women provide. But this notion has not entered the minds of many. This is because men serve women like them and they are not able to distinguish themselves from them based off the two features that Allah Almighty mentioned in His book: 'Men have charge over women because Allah distinguished some over others and by the virtue of what they have spent from their wealth.'

And that is the great right of the husband: 'Were I to order someone to prostrate before another, I would order the woman to prostrate before her husband.' But regretfully women today do not realise this, in general, except those upon whom Allah has mercy. If all the men were to be men, then the women would all be women!

And in light of all this, it is incumbent upon Muslim women to refine themselves and raise their daughters according to what Allah their Creator has dictated, which will allow the Muslim household to arise, and, in turn, a Muslim society for the Lord of the Worlds to arise.

So, while Islam hands the reins of leadership over to man, it grants woman the honour of implementation. This is in line with the nature of mankind and something to which it has become accustomed—a leader who commands, considers, and assesses, and others who obey and implement his commands. It is on this basis that human society has functioned since ancient times, and it is on this basis that even 'liberal' states and 'free' people function today.

This is the right of the husband and that is the right of the wife. These are the roles that have been written, 'and engage with them fairly', not through emphasis and composure, but rather in *ihsan* [goodness] and grace. The righteous man must not exploit his position of command to abuse his authority and inflict harm. The Muslim man is distinguished by his gentleness and sympathy towards the weak. This is the character of righteous men—even disbelievers—to show contempt for harming women and fault those who do, condemning them and accusing them of malice.

The correct place for woman in society is one of serenity, among her children and family, nurturing, teaching, preserving, and raising the future generations. This is not possible if she is ignorant or illiterate, and Islam does not dictate that education or culture be barred to woman.

The greatness of this position and its secrets is the divine provenance of the mother, and this is her great right. The counsel given to children is to be devoted to her, and this has distinguished the righteous from others: 'And in devotion to my mother, He did not make me a wretched tyrant'. And the prophetic wisdom is: 'Paradise is under the feet of mothers'. Narrated by Ibn Majah and deemed authenticated by Albani.

Indeed, bearing the child of Adam, and breastfeeding and nurturing him is a difficult task, one that, in his wisdom, Allah entrusted to the wife of Adam, for what He granted her in terms of her natural and moral disposition makes her suitable for the arduous task He imposed upon her. And on her the Lord has bestowed a great reward, such as she could not find in any other position, no matter how much effort she exerts or how much she excels, she cannot be recompensed for this great role, no matter what a child does for their mother: 'Not one iota of it'.

The Failure of the Western Model for Women

The model of the disbelievers in the West failed the moment woman was supposedly 'liberated' from the prison of home. Problems began to ensue, one after another, greeting morning and evening those who treated their garbage understanding and the waste of their minds as a religion, instead of sharia and the ordained methodology for life. This is evidenced by the falsehood of what they have adopted and defended. We have seen some governments earmarking salaries and compensation for the woman who returns to her household and raises her children, labelling the position that of 'mistress of the household.'

Here, we will not enumerate the evil outcomes faced by those societies that 'liberated' woman, for these are not hidden from the distant observer, let alone those in close proximity. But we do want to expound on women's essential secret, their sedentariness, silence, and steadfastness, and its opposite, the movement and unpredictability that is in man's nature and in which he was created. When the roles become mixed and overlap, and human existence in its two halves—male and female—enters a state of action and instability, the foundations of society are shaken, its pillars weakened, and its edifice destroyed.

It suffices those considering the issue to be aware of the Prophetic hadith that encourages women not to go out [for prayer], though this is the greatest command, while it urges, even obliges, men to go out to pray with the congregation five times, day and night.

Indeed, Allah Almighty's command for the woman to stay put can only be good, for He is the Creator of man and knows what makes their worldly life and Hereafter right, and Allah knows what you do not.

How the Soldiers of Iblis Expelled the Muslim Woman From Paradise

In the story of the creation of Adam that Allah the Exalted conveys in the beginning of Surat al-Baqarah, among others, while the two ancestors of man were living in Paradise, their enemy Iblis deceived them, forcing them out of Paradise and onto the difficult Earth, which in no way resembles Paradise, for this world only resembles it in name. There, the two suffered and became weary in a way they never had while dwelling in Paradise.

Today, the soldiers of Iblis are carrying on the deed of their father (may Allah curse him), disguised as 'development', 'progress', and 'cultural enrichment'. These are nothing but temptation cloaked in the garb of ideas and intellect, through which they hope to send the daughters of Adam from their gardens and the protection of their husbands to the furnaces of toil and the torments of labour and weariness. They have achieved this, to some extent, by distorting four notions, which they used to penetrate the minds of Muslim women and toy with their emotions.

Sedentariness:

'And stay in your homes': This divine command is no longer welcomed among some women, whose hearts have been pierced by the arrows of Iblis' temptations. The silence of the home is no longer Paradise, and the heat of the Sun outside is no longer fire.

This, by Allah, is due to a fault in senses and apathy of feelings, for the skin whose owner is no longer made ill by the fire must be treated and cured.

Her enemies, the soldiers of Iblis, have a distorted idea of stability that is natural to her and her disposition, labelling her 'idle', 'stupid', and 'backwards', among other epithets.

'He considers me to have erred, and he is the one who has gone astray, and he considers him to be erroneous, when man prays!'

Work:

That which is outside the house is work, while that which is inside is not, and so the woman who stays inside is 'lazy' and 'uncultured' and does not contribute to development.

This matter was discussed earlier.

Knowledge:

They have claimed that the knowledge of this life is the most important, and that the knowledge of the Hereafter—the knowledge of sharia—is not knowledge at all! So, the woman must seek this lowly, worldly knowledge on mountain peaks and valley floors. She must traverse the Earth to obtain this knowledge in its Western abodes and to sit amidst those who are 'cultured'. She must examine the braincells of the crow, grains of sand, and the arteries of fish! But that the *umma* can be saved, future generations reformed, justice spread, and the flag of Islam raised.

However, as our eminent *'ulama* have stated, if woman learns to read and write, and to understand the commands of her religion alongside some worldly knowledge, that is sufficient for what is required of her—for her to fulfil the role for which she was created. There is no need to jump from here to there, attaining qualifications and titles, and there is no need to prove that her intelligence exceeds that of man.

Beauty:

'O sons of Adam, We have brought down garments to cover your private parts and adornments.' Even according to Allah there is ugliness. But by the decoration of the soldiers of Satan those parts become places of beauty and attractiveness.

And just as he expelled the two forebears, he snatches from woman her clothes, trying too to expel her from the Paradise of veiling and modesty. He encourages her to pay huge sums to change Allah Almighty's creation, as she asks surgeons to change the shape of her nose, ears, and jaw. Enveloped in a cloud of shame, those pins (a current fashion among women) hang from perforations in the pulp of her ear, she has shaved some parts of her hair but not others, and she has grown her fingernails in an unseemly way that is not pleasing to onlookers.

This is the civilized behaviour, modernism, and style that Iblis displays in his fashion houses and beauty salons.

The 'Secondary' Position of Woman

The fundamental position for the woman, as we have made clear, is in her home with her husband and children. But sometimes, some may be required to go out and serve the Muslim society under certain circumstances that we will explain, Allah willing. (This is aside from the things that the woman needs to do, travel, visiting people, hospitalisation and so on.) Going out under these certain circumstances is exceptional, and not the norm, as in the case of man.

The woman can go out to serve the community in a number of places. Among the most important are:

1. Obligatory jihad. If the enemy attacks her country and the efforts of the men are not sufficient, and if the lordly *ulama* authorise it, as some of the distinguished women did in the jihad of Iraq and Chechnya, with much sorrow, as the men were lacking even as they were present.
2. Most often a woman goes out to seek knowledge, and the most important is the knowledge of religion.
3. A woman may go out as a doctor or teacher to benefit other women, but this must be done within the regulations of the law, without exception.

It is preferable, however, for a veiled sister to remain in seclusion, guarding society from behind the lines. This has always been the most difficult role—the producer, the most important figure in the media work, has always organised matters from behind the scenes.

The Difference Between 'Seeking Knowledge' and 'Seeking Sustenance'

The two are always mixed up by 'enlightened', 'cultured', and 'developed' denouncers. But we say that seeking sustenance—employment, in the modern terminology—is something Allah assigned to man, for what He granted him the physical and mental ability, and he must care for the women who are in his trust, whether they be wives, daughters, or sisters, depending on the circumstances.

Islam was never a friend of ignorance and has only striven to eliminate it. The true illiteracy is the religious illiteracy that the Muslims of today live in, and which must be expunged from men, women, the elderly, and children. We say to these 'developed' people: seeking knowledge is not only useful, but is sometimes necessary, but turning away from learning religion is among the nullifiers of Islam.

Earthly knowledge, much of which is not important in the everyday lives of Muslims, is outlined and explained above. What is not important is a waste of time, and so a waste of man: 'O son of Adam, you are nothing but a number of days. If one day goes, part of you goes.'

Just because we say 'stay in your house', it does not mean that we are encouraging illiteracy, backwardness, or ignorance. Rather we realise the distinction between seeking employment—something that has become desirable since the 'liberation' of women—and seeking knowledge, which she has been commanded to attain.

Suggestions for Educating Muslim Women

Many of our girls have lost years to secular societies, pursuing fields of knowledge that are not related to religion and contribute nothing. These studies extend over many years, preventing them from marrying until they are complete. We have seen the social and material problems that emerge when marriage is abandoned or delayed too late—going against the guidance of the Prophet.

Here, we sketch out an educational program for our girls, one that starts at age seven and continues until they are fifteen, or slightly younger. It will cover different theoretical and practical fields, depending on the girls' age and level, determined by their mental and physical capabilities.

This suggestion is just a quick, simple outline, not an in-depth proposal, just to give you an idea.

Ages 7–9: This will include three programs. One religious, covering doctrine and jurisprudence, one a language class for studying the language of the Qur'an (reading and writing), and a knowledge class, which will teach the basics of arithmetic and the natural sciences.

Ages 10–12: This will involve a more in-depth religious program focusing on jurisprudence, particularly jurisprudential matters that relate to women and rulings on marriage and divorce. In addition to this and the language and knowledge classes, skills can be taught, such as weaving, textiles, or the basics of cooking.

Ages 13–15: At these ages, there will be more emphasis on sharia and practical skills, including knowledge on how to raise children. Here, the knowledge program should be limited to the fundamentals, with the addition of a new program teaching Islamic history and the life of the Prophet and his followers.

Nine is the age at which, according to sharia, a girl is considered a woman old enough to marry. Most women, before she is too contaminated, would marry at sixteen or seventeen, at the peak of their youth and vigour, while Muslim men would not delay beyond the age of twenty.

Suggestions for Women Required to Serve Society Outside the Home

Women have gathered nothing but thorns from the harvest of 'equality' with men. According to equality, they are granted the same amount of work and days off as men, despite their monthly affliction and longer-term issues like pregnancy, with no regard for the nature of her life and her responsibility for her husband, children and parents.

So, if a Muslim woman is compelled to work outside the home and benefit others, we must offer recompense for the services required of her, and her home and children must be safeguarded during her absence.

Here are our suggestions:

– The work must be appropriate to her and her capabilities, and she should not be entrusted with what she cannot endure or what is difficult for her to carry out.

– Her work days should not exceed three a week, and these should not extend so late in the day that she is absent from her house for a long time.
– Her circumstances should be taken into account when it comes to issues of necessity—if her child is sick or husband travelling, and so on—and she should be given adequate leave.
– She should be permitted at least two years of maternity leave, in which she will nurture and breastfeed her infant, and she will not return to work until the child is able to rely on itself for the important things.
– Her place of work should have an area where she can leave children who are not yet of school age and check on them occasionally to prevent the problems that arise from leaving infants alone, or entrusting them to the care of another.

[Remaining text omitted]

9b. Analysis

The origins and character of the Islamic State's female support-base have long been the subject of intensive media and academic discussion.[2] For the most part, analyses have focused on the issue of motivation, asking why women would want to join an organisation like the Islamic State.[3] The text featured above does not hold the answer to this question. Instead, it offers us something else: an argument for why they should.

[2] Dearden, Lizzie, 'How Isis Attracts Women and Girls from Europe with False Offer of 'Empowerment', *Independent*, 5 Aug. 2017, http://www.independent.co.uk/news/world/europe/isis-jihadi-brides-islamic-state-women-girls-europe-british-radicalisation-recruitment-report-a7878681.html, last accessed 18 Dec. 2018; Moshiri, Nazanine, 'Fears Grow Over ISIL Recruitment of Tunisia Women', *Al Jazeera*, 9 June 2016, http://www.aljazeera.com/news/2016/06/tunisia-worry-fear-grows-young-women-join-isil-160609060147143.html, last accessed 18 Dec. 2018; Dancel, Raul, 'Philippines Arrests Top Female ISIS Recruiter', *Straits Times*, 18 Oct. 2017, http://www.straitstimes.com/asia/se-asia/philippines-arrest-top-female-isis-recruiter-ex-wife-of-radicalised-singaporean, last accessed 18 Dec. 2018.
[3] See Saltman, Erin Marie, and Melanie Smith, '"Till Martyrdom Do Us Part": Gender and the ISIS Phenomenon', Institute for Strategic Dialogue and International Centre for the Study of Radicalisation, https://www.isdglobal.org/wp-content/uploads/2016/02/Till_Martyrdom_Do_Us_Part_Gender_and_the_ISIS_Phenomenon.pdf, last accessed 18 Dec. 2018; Hoyle, Carolyn, Alexandra Bradford, and Ross Frenett,

When it was first published—and at the time this chapter was written—most discussions around women in the caliphate were based on insights gleaned from social media accounts used by a small sliver of the group's Western female supporters.[4] The focus has primarily been on their putative roles as recruiters,[5] propagandists,[6] and combatants.[7] While the 'real-life' narratives of these individuals should not be discounted, neither should they be taken at face value. Much of what they claimed online was a deliberate attempt to exaggerate and sensationalise.[8]

'Becoming Mulan? Female Western Migrants to ISIS', Institute for Strategic Dialogue, https://www.isdglobal.org/wp-content/uploads/2016/02/ISDJ2969_Becoming_Mulan_01.15_WEB.pdf, last accessed 18 Dec. 2018; Camber, Rebecca, '"Jihadi Bride", 17, Married an ISIS Fighter Over SKYPE and Plotted to Launch UK Attack with Firearms and "pineapple" Hand Grenades Shipped from Syria', *Daily Mail*, 26 July 2017, http://www.dailymail.co.uk/news/article-4731152/Girl-17-arrested-plans-launch-attack-UK.html, last accessed 18 Dec. 2018.

[4] For example: Manrique, Pedro, Zhenfeng Cao, Andrew Gabriel, John Horgan, Paul Gill, Hong Qi, Elvira M. Restrepo, Daniela Johnson, Stefan Wuchty, Chaoming Song, and Neil Johnson, 'Women's Connectivity in Extreme Networks', *Science Advances* 2, no. 6 (2016); Huey, Laura, and Hillary Peladeau, 'Cheering on the Jihad: An Exploration of Women's Participation in Online Pro-*jihadist* Networks', The Canadian Network for Research on Terrorism, Security and Society, http://www.tsas.ca/wp-content/uploads/2018/03/TSASWP16–07_Huey-Peladeau.pdf, last accessed 18 Dec. 2018.

[5] Linning, Stephanie, 'Family of British Jihadi Bride who Left her Glasgow Home to Join Isis say they are 'Sickened by her Twisted Evil' after she Wrote a Poem Praising Tunisia Terror Attack', *Daily Mail*, 30 June 2015, http://www.dailymail.co.uk/news/article-3143292/Family-British-jihadi-bride-left-Glasgow-home-join-Isis-say-sickened-twisted-evil-wrote-poem-praising-Tunisia-terror-attack.html, last accessed 18 Dec. 2018.

[6] Moore, Charlie, and Julian Robinson, 'German Girl Facing the Death Penalty for Running Away to Join ISIS in Iraq Reveals how she was Groomed by a Girl Online and Arranged to Marry a Jihadist after Arguing with her Parents', *Daily Mail*, 4 Oct. 2017, http://www.dailymail.co.uk/news/article-4947820/German-girl-joined-ISIS-reveals-groomed.html, last accessed 18 Dec. 2018.

[7] Winter, Charlie, and Devorah Margolin, 'The *Mujahidat* Dilemma: Female Combatants and the Islamic State', *CTC Sentinel* 10, no. 7 (2017), pp. 23–28.

[8] Winter, Charlie, 'Women of the Islamic State: Beyond the Rumor Mill', Jihadology, 31 Mar. 2015, https://jihadology.net/2015/03/31/guest-post-women-of-the-islamic-state-beyond-the-rumor-mill/, last accessed 18 Dec. 2018.

By way of contrast, the above excerpt of the Khansa' manifesto does not pretend to offer its readers a 'realistic'—and thus idealised—account of what it is like to live in the Islamic State. Instead, it offers a series of conceptual guidelines regarding what exactly constitutes the 'ideal' Muslim woman. As such, it is a more credible lens through which to determine what the Islamic State actually thinks about its female supporters.

Writing in typical Islamist patois laced with references to the Qur'an and *hadith*, the authors of the manifesto spend much of their time explaining why women should live sedentary lives, spending most, if not all, of their time at home.[9] They hold that this is the 'great right' for women and that the only reason they are not doing it now is 'Western colonialism', which continues to spread 'filthy culture and atheistic, materialistic thought among the Muslims' everywhere. This status quo, they write, need not persist: the Islamic *umma* was recently liberated from the throes of existential crisis by 'the rise of the sun of the caliphate' and so, the lot of Muslims the world over irrevocably transformed. Because of the ascendant Islamic State, Muslim women could now live life as they 'should', returning to the fundamental essence of their being.

Before discussing what exactly this 'return' would look like, the authors elaborate on the issues from which their proposed system provides sanctuary, specifically focusing on what they mean for women. In particular, they ruminate on the scourge of education, something that is, they hold, the principal cause of the ills against which they are railing. Directly because of the insidious spread of Westernised curricula in Muslim-majority countries, women are said to be abandoning their religion to study the material sciences—that is, frivolous explorations into 'the brain cells of the crow, and grains of sand, and the arteries of fish'—and the pursuit of employment. Thus, they hold, foreign values are being internalised across entire populations of Sunni Muslims, sullying their purity and giving rise to things like feminism, the 'Western model for women' that leaves men emasculated and women unsure of how to live because they are presented with an 'image of man that is not true'.

Having established the contours of the gender crisis, the authors present their simple solution: the Islamic State. They contend that, by living in the caliphate and immersing themselves in the hypermasculinity of its men,

---

[9] See also Lahoud, Nelly, 'Empowerment or Subjugation: An Analysis of ISIL's Gendered Messaging', UN Women, June 2018, http://www2.unwomen.org/-/media/field%20office%20arab%20states/attachments/publications/lahoud-fin-web-rev.pdf?la=en&vs=5602, last accessed 18 Dec. 2018.

Muslim women will be able to right the cultural wrongs being afflicted on them in the rest of the world. Indeed, the woman who goes to live in the Islamic State is, fundamentally and automatically, a better *muslima*: there, 'righteous' and in a state of 'stability', she is preoccupied not with the aberrations of modernity but with the obligations of sound religiosity; and, there, 'veiled' and 'in seclusion', she need not concern herself with employment, scientific education, or physical adornments. Instead, she can live a purportedly 'natural', harmonious life, childrearing and homemaking, maintaining society 'from behind the scenes'.

While ideally women are to be housebound, their seclusion should not be total. Recognising this, the authors point to three occasions on which Muslim women living in the caliphate are permitted to leave their homes. First, they concede that women are unable to be optimal wives or mothers if they are steeped in 'illiteracy, backwardness, and ignorance', so some rudimentary education is necessary. Starting when they are seven years old and ending when they are fifteen, 'or slightly younger', they are permitted to leave the household to learn basic life skills at school. Once adults, they can still venture out for education, but only in 'the sharia sciences'. Second, granting that the existence of some female professionals—principally doctors and teachers—is unavoidable even in the most pristine Islamic society, the authors hold that such women should be allowed to leave the house in order to do what is required of them, provided that they correctly adhere to the sharia. The last of their proposed scenarios refers to women's engagement in combative jihad. Pointing to the twin precedents 'of Iraq and Chechnya'—but not, interestingly, Nigeria[10]—the authors state that women can and should participate in combat if it has been declared permissible by the Islamic State's highest religious authority. Failing that, though, they must always aspire to stick to their 'true role', which is characterised by domesticated 'stability'.

To be sure, none of these ideals stray far from jihadi orthodoxy.[11] However, the Islamic State's actualisation of the ideology in Syria and Iraq between 2013

[10] Pearson, Elizabeth, 'Boko Haram and Nigeria's Female Bombers', Royal United Services Institute (RUSI) Newsbrief, 25 Sept. 2015, https://rusi.org/publication/newsbrief/boko-haram-and-nigeria%E2%80%99s-female-bombers, last accessed 18 Dec. 2018.

[11] See Lahoud, Nelly, 'The Neglected Sex: The Jihadis' Exclusion of Women from Jihad', *Terrorism and Political Violence* 26, no. 5 (2014), pp. 780–802; Cook, David, 'Women Fighting in Jihad?', *Studies in Conflict & Terrorism* 28, no. 5 (2005), pp. 375–384.

and 2017 was an unprecedented opportunity to test out, in earnest, this radical conception of how women should 'be'. The experiment did not last: much of what is discussed above was abandoned when the caliphate territories collapsed in 2017 and, by early 2018, the group had swapped out its message of secluded empowerment for overt calls to arms.[12]

By explicitly calling on women to engage in combat—the possibility of which is, of course, hinted at in the manifesto—the Islamic State broke with jihadi convention even more radically than its predecessors.[13] While al-Qaida in Iraq, Boko Haram in Nigeria and the Riyad us-Salihin Brigade in Chechnya all deployed women in their respective war efforts, and not without controversy, they were only ever involved in terrorist operations and suicide bombings; conventional warfighting was always left to the men. However, in early 2018, the Islamic State introduced a new ideal into the fray: women fighters who were neither terrorists nor suicide attackers, but regular soldiers; adjuncts to, not anomalies in, its military machine, that were spearheading 'a new era of conquests'—that is, fighting in explicitly offensive operations.[14] Only time will tell what happens next, but there can be no overstating the potential ideological significance of this development, even if it proves to be rhetoric alone.

[12] See Winter and Margolin, 'The *Mujahidat* Dilemma'; Charlie Winter, 'ISIS, Women and Jihad: Breaking With Convention', Tony Blair Institute for Global Change, 13 Sept. 2018, https://institute.global/insight/co-existence/isis-women-and-jihad-breaking-convention, last accessed 18 Dec. 2018.

[13] Davis, Jessica, 'Evolution of Global Jihad: Female Suicide Bombers in Iraq', *Studies in Conflict & Terrorism* 36, no. 4 (2013), pp. 279–291.

[14] The Islamic State, 'Inside the Khilafah 7', al-Hayat Media Center, Feb. 2018.

10

MEDIA JIHAD

*In April 2016, the Islamic State published a document entitled 'Media Operative,
You Are Also a* Mujahid' *via its official propaganda channel on the social media
platform Telegram. The identity of the author was not provided, but the text was
attributed to the group's central publishing house, al-Himmah Publications. A
'revised and updated' edition of a similar booklet that appeared in a video produced by the group the year before, it straddled the middle ground between 'jihadi
strategic studies' and more stereotypically exhortative propaganda.*[1] *The document
was conceived with a view to setting out the importance of propaganda and
eschewing the concerns of media operatives that they, as cameramen not gunmen,
were participating in a watered-down version of jihad.*[2]

10a. 'Media Operative, You Are Also a *Mujahid*', April 2016
Al-Himmah Publication

[Beginning text omitted]

The media is a jihad in the way of Allah. You, with your media work, are
therefore a *mujahid* in the way of Allah (provided your intention is sound).

---

[1] Lia, Brynjar, and Thomas Hegghammer, 'Jihadi Strategic Studies: The Alleged Al
Qaida Policy Study Preceding the Madrid Bombings', *Studies in Conflict and Terrorism*
27, no. 5 (2004), pp. 355–375.

[2] Anon, '*Mujahid, anta ayuha al-'ilami* [Media Operative, You Are Also a *Mujahid*]',
translation by Charlie Winter, 2017, the Islamic State: Al-Himmah Publications,
2015.

The media jihad against the enemy is no less important than the material fight against it. Moreover, your media efforts are considered to be among the many great forms of the rite of jihad. We will return to these later.

We have compiled this publication for the following reasons:

1) To shed light on the importance of the media jihad in the ongoing war between the forces of disbelief and the armies of faith, something especially critical given the rise and acceleration of the propaganda war that the Crusaders—led by America and its allies—are waging against the Islamic State today.

2) To remind of the greatness of the reward reserved for those on the frontlines of the media jihad and the abundance of the gifts Allah has prepared for them. This is in order to encourage them to compete in this arena for the satisfaction of Allah the Almighty.

3) To raise awareness among jihadi media operatives regarding the importance of their role and to bring their great responsibility to their attention, as well as to foster the forbearance they need to complete this weighty task, especially after Allah bestowed upon us an Islamic caliphate based on the Prophetic methodology.

4) To alert all media operatives to the need to win media victories as well as military victories, and to bring to their attention the importance of inflicting psychological defeats upon the enemy before material defeats—as they say, 'half of the battle is the media.'

5) To repudiate the mistaken view regarding media work that the jihad is confined to the literal understanding of fighting with material weapons alone! On the contrary, verbal weapons can actually be more potent than atomic bombs.

6) To prepare a new generation dedicated to carrying out this work, a generation that understands what is demanded of them and remains unsatisfied unless their efforts are up to the standard of the Islamic caliphate based on the Prophetic methodology—which is in existence today by the will of Allah alone—embodying everything that the term caliphate comprises.

Forms of jihad in which the media plays a role

i) Verbal jihad

Anas (may Allah be pleased with him) related that the Prophet (peace be upon him) said: 'Strive against the polytheists with your money, your souls, and your tongues' [Strong *hadith*, narrated by Ahmad and others].

Verbal jihad includes disputing with unbelievers and hypocrites, calling them to Allah the Almighty, intimidating them, threatening them with violence, pointing out their defects, and shedding light upon their deceptive ways. It is also a means with which to buoy the morale of soldiers, spread news of their victories and good deeds, encourage the people to support them by clarifying their Creed, methodology, and intentions, and bridge the intellectual gap between the *mujahidin* and ordinary Muslims, as well as many other things.

Sheikh Hamud bin 'Uqla al-Shu'aybi once said:

> And of the various types of jihad, there is jihad by the tongue and pen. This incorporates all that is said to strengthen the morale of the soldiers and shatter the spirits of the enemy, things like poetry, sermons and news regarding the triumphs of the Muslims and the defeats of their enemies—for example: crying *takbir* [the phrase 'God is great'] when attacking the enemy, enthusing and encouraging the armies as to the certainty of their victories and the defeat of their enemies, or praying for their victory and support [*The neighing of the horses in the explanation of the book of jihad from achieving the target*, by 'Abd al-Rahim bin Mawad].

Moreover, verbal jihad consists of 'inciting others to the jihad and providing clarifications of its requirements. It also includes shedding light on the deceptions peddled by detractors, exposing the deviances of secularists and hypocrites and responding to those who dishearten, alarm or discourage the Muslims from among the rulers' scholars and call for tolerance and coexistence with the unbelievers. Likewise, it involves defending the jihad and the *mujahidin* by painting a brighter picture of it, thereby responding to the frenzied media campaign against it' [*Presenting the servants with the rewards of jihad*].

ii) Jihad of the sword

The Almighty said: 'The believers are the only ones who have believed in Allah and His Messenger and then doubt not but strive with their properties and their souls in the cause of Allah. It is those alone who are truthful.'

And He (peace be upon him) said:

> Never a Prophet had been sent before me by Allah towards His nation who had not among his people His disciples and companions who followed his ways and obeyed his command. Then there came after them their successors who said whatever they did not practise, and practised whatever they were not commanded to do. He who strove against them with his hand was a believer: he who strove against them with his tongue was a believer, and he who strove against them with his heart was a believer and beyond that there is no faith even to the extent of a mustard seed [Related by Muslim].

Some criticise media operatives for engaging in verbal jihad whilst sitting on sofas in beautiful houses...

But by Allah no, they are at the forefront of the conflict, in the heart of the war, within the furnace of its battles. They participate alongside their brothers, fighting against the enemies of Allah on the Earth and raising aloft the flag of jihad. They share their daily bread and wander the land with them, sleeping rough alongside them... They are commendable and may Allah reward them.

Media work is a struggle of the soul without any doubt. Anyone who is not certain of this should look to the media brothers of the Islamic State—like their fighting brothers, their pure blood flowed, they tasted the ills of imprisonment in Crusader-apostate jails, they emigrated, supported and strove until the enemy recognised their clout before the friend. They are still steadfast, we certainly believe so but Allah knows best.

All things considered, it is no exaggeration to say that the media operative is an *istishhadi* [suicide bomber] without a belt! This decoration is well deserved.

Have you not seen the photographer, how he carries a camera instead of a Kalashnikov and races before the soldiers in raids, welcoming bullets to his chest with open arms?!

Have you not seen the brigades that disseminate videos and pamphlets? How they enter into the most dangerous and fortified areas to circulate the *mujahidin*'s productions in the heart of the hypocrites' den?!

Have you not see how dedicated the media operative is in gathering intelligence on the enemy's movements and following the work of the brothers as they monitor the news of the enemy? This is just as the Prince of the Believers 'Umar (Allah is pleased with him) used to do: if a delegation was sent by him, he monitored the edges of the city every day to gather news regarding the enemy's army, awaiting the news of their great calamity?! [From the statement of Shaykh Abu Mus'ab al-Zarqawi (Allah have mercy upon him) entitled 'From a soldier to his amir']

Many envisage that this work is simple! But they are not aware of the fact that all jihadi news—whether it is disseminated on websites or broadcast over a radio—has behind it an army of media operatives!

We consider the media *mujahidin* to be among those about whom the Prophet (peace be upon him) said: 'Allah will admit three people into Paradise for one arrow: The one who makes it, intending it to be used for a good cause, the one who shoots it, and the one who passes it to him' [strong *hadith*, narrated by Abu Dawud and others]. With the Will of the Almighty Allah, if one piece of news is produced, everyone who participated in the production and delivery of it is admitted to Paradise—that is not beyond Allah's capabilities and his mercy.

My media operative brother, let it be known that your verbal jihad is not limited to speech alone, but also comprises speaking, writing, printing, audio recording, and preparing scenarios for video recording and so on. All of this requires a significant amount of effort.

Let it also be known that, for you, verbal jihad is more important than jihad of the sword while, for the military-minded brother, jihad of the sword is more important than verbal jihad [From the words of Shaykh al-Islam Ibn Taymiyya]. This is what made us prioritise in our research the issue of verbal jihad instead of the issue of jihad of the sword.

iii) Incitement to jihad

Allah the Almighty said: 'O Prophet, urge the believers to battle. If there are among you twenty [who are] steadfast, they will overcome two hundred. And if there are among you one hundred [who are] steadfast, they will overcome a thousand of those who have disbelieved because they are a people who do not understand.' The Sublime One said: 'So fight in the cause of Allah; you are not held responsible except for yourself. And encourage the believer [to join you] that perhaps Allah will restrain the might of those who disbelieve. Allah is great in might and stronger in punishment.'

Similarly, there are many prophetic texts and writings about His (peace be upon him) deeds that incite others to jihad, detailing its rewards and gifts, explaining what Allah has prepared for the *mujahidin* and the martyrs, urging the believers to mobilise for fighting, filling them with love for their religion, hatred for their enemies, and desire for reward from Allah, and preparing them for victory, success and empowerment.

Incitement to jihad is a task for which all Muslims are responsible. Even if they are excused from fighting on account of an extenuating circumstance that renders them unable to engage in physical jihad, it is stipulated upon them that they must instead incite in order to warrant their lack of engagement. The Almighty said: 'There is not upon the weak or upon the ill or upon those who do not find anything to spend any discomfort when they are sincere to Allah and His Messenger. There is not upon those who do good any grounds for complaint. And Allah is Forgiving and Merciful.'

However, this obligation—incitement—is more incumbent upon Muslim media operatives than other Muslims.

Inciting others to join the jihad is tantamount to engaging in the jihad oneself, as is steering others towards it and opening their eyes to it. Indeed, the one who incites is a *mujahid* in the way of Allah the Almighty and he rightfully receives a reward for every brother that embarks upon jihad because of his incitement.

iv) Infuriating the enemy

The Almighty said:

> It was not for the people of Madinah and those surrounding them of the Bedouins that they remain behind after the Messenger of Allah or that they prefer themselves over his self. That is because they are not afflicted by thirst or fatigue or hunger in the cause of Allah, nor do they tread on any ground that infuriates the unbelievers, nor do they inflict upon an enemy any infliction but that which is registered for them as a righteous deed. Indeed, Allah does not allow to be lost the reward of the doers of good.

In this great verse from Surat at-Tawbah is a proclamation that everything that angers the enemies of Allah, be it speech or deed—anything at all—is a form of jihad in the way of Allah. This is especially clear because the expression 'infuriate the unbelievers' is included in the middle of the above text regarding the rewards for jihad and compensation for the *mujahidin*. Also, this noble verse is in the Surah of Bara'ah, which includes the last of the verses regarding jihad that incorporates a whole legislation for the most important issues of jihad.

Everything that causes anger and vexation to the enemy is jihad. As the Almighty said: 'Nor do they tread on any ground that enrages the disbelievers, nor do they inflict upon an enemy any infliction but that is registered for them as a righteous deed. Indeed, Allah does not allow to be lost the reward of the doers of good.' Furthermore, He (peace be upon him) said to Hassan: 'Satirising the unbelievers is harder for them than being shot with arrows.' This is in two authentic collections of the *ahadith* of A'ishah. It is also in the *hadith* of Bara'ah in the form: 'Satirise the idolaters, verily the Holy Spirit is with you' *Neighing of the Horses.*

Anyone who knows the Crusaders of today and keeps track of that which infuriates them knows well how they are angered and terrorised by jihadi media. They—the curse of Allah the Almighty be on them—know its importance, impact and significance more than any others!

How many times we have heard from our media operative brothers—the ones who were imprisoned in American jails before Allah allowed them to get out—how the Crusaders interrogated them with special and extensive attention for days on end, giving them special and cautious treatment because they recognised their great role in the battle.

We will relate to you—my media operative brother, may Allah protect and guard you from imprisonment, amputation and fracture—the story of an Arab *muhajir* brother who came to the Land of the Two Rivers to engage in jihad with the *ansar*. When he came to the land of jihad, an official received him and ascertained from him a level of media experience, so he asked him to work in the media department. The *muhajir* brother vehemently refused this order because he had made up his mind to engage in military work. When he was asked what his reasons were, he said, 'I want the thing that damages the enemies of Allah the Almighty the most, and I do not believe that the media would allow me to fulfil this desire.'

His amir did not force him on the issue and left him instead to work with his fighting brothers, during the course of which Allah the Almighty decreed that he be imprisoned by the Americans. When Allah freed him from his imprisonment, the brother returned to his work immediately, but this time he chose a new role—he demanded to work in the media! When he was asked about this about turn and reminded of his former position and demands, he said, 'I changed my mind when I witnessed how desperate the Americans were to arrest just one media operative, and how much more attention they paid to the media operatives than the military ones in their investigations, the latter of which received far less attention!

After I learned about the great vexation that the media causes the Crusader and apostate enemies of Allah the Almighty, the Almighty Allah determined that I should embrace the media with all my heart.'

v) Bringing glad tidings to the believers' hearts

The Almighty said: 'Fight them; Allah will punish them by your hands and will disgrace them and give you victory over them and satisfy the breasts of a believing people. And still the indignation of their hearts. For Allah will turn (in mercy) to whom He will; and Allah is All-Knowing, All-Wise.'

He (peace be upon him) said: 'The most loved people to Allah the Almighty are those that are most beneficial to other people, and the most loved acts to Allah the Almighty are those that bring happiness to the Muslim' [sound *hadith*, narrated by al-Tabrani]. He (peace be upon him) also said: 'Among the best acts are those that bestow happiness to the believer' [strong *hadith*, narrated by al-Bayhaqi].

Sufyan bin 'Ayyinah related that, 'It was said to Muhammad bin al-Manka-dar: "Which work is the most loved to you?" He said: "Bestowing happiness to the believer"' [From *Jewel of the closest ones* by Abu Na'im, and *The best of the best* by Ibn al-Jawzi].

In accordance with the above, the other side of jihadi media work is giving glad tidings to believers, for everything that angers the unbeliever or hypocrite pleases the honest believer—it is a double-edged sword.

May Allah bless you, O media operative and bringer of glad tidings. Imagine the scale of the happiness that enters the Muslim's heart—both the *mujahid* one and the one who remained behind—when they watch one of the *mujahidin's* videos regarding the victories and successes of the monotheists or the losses of the Crusaders and apostates. How much it pleases them to read the pamphlets and books of the Islamic State, and O how the audio materials that are broadcast over the radio delight them. And so on and so forth...

So heed the Muslims' prayers thanking Allah the Almighty and share in the reward! Or await the fulfilment of their prayers to you that they say in your absence:

'O Allah, support your servants the *mujahidin* and abandon the unbelievers and apostates... May Allah reward all who participate in this media work with the best of rewards.'

Say: *Amin.*

vi) Obedience to the ruler

The Almighty said: 'O, you who have believed, obey Allah and obey the Messenger and those in authority among you. And if you disagree over anything, refer it to Allah and the Messenger, if you should believe in Allah and the Last Day. That is the best way and the best in result.'

And He (peace be upon him) said: 'He who obeys me obeys Allah, and he who disobeys me disobeys Allah, and he who obeys the amir obeys me, and he who disobeys the amir disobeys me'.

In this context, the reasoning behind the idea of obedience is that the amir (or media official) apportioned out the work, spreading the roles in a way he deemed to be appropriate. He saw fit that you are in the media trench. If you obey him, you obey Allah and if you disobey him, then you disobey Allah.

We consider media operatives to be from a group of knowledge seekers that the amir devotes to the study of sharia science and education. In the Words of the Almighty: 'And it is not for the believers to go forth [to battle] all at once. For there should separate from every division of them a group to obtain understanding in the religion and to warn their people when they return to them so they are cautious.' Therefore, it is necessary for there to be a group devoted to studying sharia science and educating fighters on matters of religion. If we do not provide this group, ignorance will take root among the people and it would be but a few decades before this generation of fighters in the name of Allah the Almighty would be lost and you would not be able to find anyone to continue the journey. Even if you found some left, they would not be of the level required to manage the global conflict with the evil states of unbelief.

Therefore, it is upon you—O media operative of the caliphate—to be cognisant of the need for people in general and the *mujahidin* in particular to be aware of the issues facing the Islamic *umma*. It is upon you to guide them onto the path of mankind's salvation from unbelief, injustice, and corruption. This is your responsibility! Yes, you and no one else! The Almighty said:

'And let there be [arising] from you a nation inviting to [all that is] good, enjoining what is right and forbidding what is wrong, and those will be the successful one' ['Imran, 104].

vii) Declaring the truth

The Almighty said: 'There has already been for you an excellent pattern in Abraham and those with him, when they said to their people, "Indeed, we are disassociated from you and from whatever you worship other than Allah. We have denied you, and there has appeared between us and you animosity and hatred forever until you believe in Allah alone"' [al-Mumtahanah: 4].

The Messenger of Allah (peace be upon him) said: 'The best jihad in the path of Allah is to speak a word of justice to an oppressive ruler' [a sound *hadith* narrated by al-Tirmidhi].

This is because

jihad against the enemy vacillates between hope and fear. However, if the *mujahid* tries to order the ruler to do the right thing then he can be subjected to torture or sometimes death. Therefore, it is better than jihad against the enemy because the aspect of fear rather than hope here is greater, and because the injustice of the ruler has an impact upon many, and if it is restrained, then good reaches a myriad of people. Thus, it has a larger impact than killing one unbeliever [*Presenting the servants with the rewards of jihad*].

The faithful monotheist media operative says what is just and true in an era in which there are few companions of the truth and even fewer honest ones! He transmits to the simple people a true picture of the battle without exaggeration and with no lies, obeying his Lord, Who said:

So who is more unjust than one who lies about Allah and denies the truth when it has come to him? Is there not in Hell a residence for the unbelievers? And the one who has brought the truth and believed in it—those are the righteous. They will have whatever they desire with their Lord. That is the reward of the doers of good, that Allah may remove from them the worst of what they did and reward them their due for the best of what they used to do.

Following the example of the Truest of the Truthful Ones (peace be upon him) who said:

It is upon you to tell the truth, for truth leads to virtue and virtue leads to Paradise, and the man who continues to speak the truth and endeavours to tell the truth is eventually recorded as truthful with Allah, and beware of telling of a lie for telling of a lie leads to obscenity and obscenity leads to Hellfire, and the person who keeps telling lies and endeavours to tell a lie is recorded as a liar with Allah [Narrated by Muslim].

This is a time in which most—if not all—of the mainstream media is driven by daily lies and professionalised falsification. Enemy media operatives are contented to be the bugles of unbelief, immorality, and fraud, and they fight against the religion and chastity. They deserve—truly—the description 'magicians of the Pharaohs.'

This is the time of estrangement about which He to whom no falsehoods are attributed (peace be upon him) said: 'There will come to the people years of treachery, when the liar will be regarded as honest, and the honest man will be regarded as a liar; the faithful man will be regarded as a traitor, and the traitor will be regarded as a faithful man, and the Ruwaybidah will become vocal.' It was said: Who are the Ruwaybidah? He said: 'Vile and base men who comment on the affairs of the people' [Strong *hadith*, narrated by Ahmad and others].

viii) Fending off the intellectual invasion

The media operative brothers—may Allah the Almighty protect them—are charged with shielding the *umma* from the mightiest onslaught ever known in the history of the Crusader and Safavid wars!

They are the security valve for the sharia of the Merciful. They are warding off an invasion, the danger of which exceeds even the danger of the military invasion! It is an intellectual invasion that is faced by the Muslims in both their minds and their hearts, corrupting the identity of many of them, distorting their ideas, inverting their concepts, substituting their traditions, drying the headwaters of their faith and deadening their zeal... And there is no power except with Allah.

The primeval enemies of the Muslims—the Crusaders, the Jews, the Safavids, and the Secularists—understand that colonising the heart is even more successful than colonising the land and enslaving Allah's servants! That said, anyone who turns the pages of history will conclude that no power—regardless of their potential—could subjugate the Muslims and corrupt their identity as was the case with a great many states and statelets that merged and fused with the Great Powers, only to disappear entirely and become obscured under the cloak of others. Every military raid that befell the Islamic *umma* ended in the enemy's demise and shameful defeat. The enemy was left unable to take anything with them other than their injuries, after being taught a lesson by the Muslims that they would not forget. And the last of these lessons was learned by the United States—the Carrier of the Cross—and those in its orbit, taught at the hands of the heroes of the Islamic State less than four years ago.

As such, the enemy recognised that military successes against the Muslims are impossible, so they came up with the intellectual, socio-cultural raid. Through it, they succeeded to some extent in winning over many of our sons to their ways and machinations.

So who in your opinion—O media *mujahidin*—will repel this media invasion?!

We will leave the answer to you...

[Text omitted]

10b. Analysis

Propaganda-based influence warfare has proven to be as instrumental to the Islamic State's doctrine of insurgency as its kinetic counterpart and, as the above text indicates, the organisation is eminently aware of this. Its claim that 'verbal weapons can be more potent than atomic bombs' is extreme, but there remains an undeniable truth to it: in the wake of its 2014 capture of Mosul, the Islamic State did successfully reshape the character of the war it was fighting, seamlessly provoking intervention from the 'Crusader' West, mobilising tens of thousands more foreign fighters, and establishing itself as a caliphate—and it did this largely through propaganda.

The above document hints at how it set about achieving this. After whittling away its theological exterior, a set of highly pragmatic communication principles emerges. Together, they revolve around the same three core objectives identified in Casrten Bockstette's 2008 work on jihadi communication management techniques—propagating the ideology, defending the movement, and intimidating the adversary.[3]

Regarding the first—propagation of the Islamic State's ideology—the text's authors are unambiguous as to the role of media operations. 'The Islamic *umma* today', they write, 'is waiting for you to lead it by its hands to the sharia and rid it of the inferiority and injustice from which it suffers'. The implication is that, if presented with the 'right' information and the 'correct' narrative, people everywhere will invariably end up supporting the cause of the Islamic State. To this end, they frequently return to the idea of opening the eyes of the global Muslim *umma* to present it with a revolutionary new way of living Islam.[4] The subsection titled 'Giving glad tidings to the believers' emphasises this notion, stating that the Islamic State's message of 'Truth', which is, of course, overtly positive, brings 'pleasure' and 'delight' to all believers that are exposed to it. The idea is that, if they are made aware of the caliphate's 'creed, methodology, and intentions', then the ideology upon which it is founded becomes easier to digest—more distilled, more simplified, and more approachable. In that sense, it falls to propaganda to 'bridg[e] the intellectual gap' between the Islamic State and its constituents, to transmit 'to the simple people [...] a brighter picture' of what it means to participate in its global project.

The logic behind this is self-evident: by propagating its ideology, the group can accrue more supporters and, thus, enjoy greater military and financial clout, both in-theatre and outside of its immediate sphere of operations. To this end, its media strategists have deployed a series of strategic and tactical campaigns since 2014.[5] First, they constructed a uniform and centralised brand that revolved around three simple ideas: militarism, victim-

---

[3] Bockstette, Carsten, 'Jihadist Terrorist Use of Strategic Communication Management Techniques', George C. Marshall European Center for Security Studies, Occasional Paper Series, no. 20 (2008).

[4] Research on the motivations of foreign fighters demonstrates just how potent this promise can be. See, for example, Sheikh, Jakob, '"I Just Said It. The State": Examining the Motivations for Danish Foreign Fighting in Syria', *Perspectives on Terrorism* 10, no. 6 (2016), pp. 59–67.

[5] For more on the distinction between tactical and strategic propaganda, see Ellul, Jacques, *Propaganda: The Formation of Men's Attitudes*, trans. Konrad Kellen and Jean Lerner, New York: Random House Vintage Books, 1965; and Winter, Charlie, 'Framing War: Propaganda, the Islamic State and the Battle for East Mosul', *Cambridge Review of International Affairs*, under review.

hood, and utopia.[6] Then, having done so, they published tens of thousands of media products—videos, photo-essays, magazines, newspapers, books and more—through which they presented their movement as a real-world embodiment of this brand, a physical manifestation of jihadism's metaphysical promises.[7]

This flood of strategic content was syncopated with short-lived tactical campaigns that were geared towards further popularising the Islamic State as an idea. Usually manifesting as media-friendly videos, magazines, and leadership statements, this side of the group's outreach operations worked by forcibly commandeering the global information agenda, attracting and sustaining the attention of the international community through violence and high-quality production techniques.[8] Not only did this intensify the consternation of the Islamic State's enemies (something that is touched on below), it brought distant sympathisers closer into the group's narrative orbit—and, the closer they were, the more intoxicating the idea of it became.

The second objective identified in the text—the need to defend the Islamic State as a movement—essentially revolved around the production of counter-propaganda. The authors wax lyrical about the need to create a message that 'responds to the frenzied media campaign' and 'deceptive ways' of the enemy. Indeed, 'given the rise and acceleration of the propaganda war that the Crusaders—led by America and its allies—are waging against the Islamic State today', they hold that few things are more important than 'expos[ing] the deviances of secularists and hypocrites, responding to those who dishearten, alarm or discourage the Muslims [and] call for tolerance and coexistence with the unbelievers'. Giving legs to this idea, they frame everything that runs counter to the Islamic State's messaging as part of 'the mightiest onslaught ever known in the history of the Crusader and Safavid wars'. Hence, media jihad is framed not just as a war for the reputation of the

---

[6] Winter, Charlie, 'Apocalypse, Later: A Longitudinal Study of the Islamic State Brand', *Critical Studies in Media Communication* 35, no. 1, pp. 103–121.

[7] See, for example, Milton, Daniel, 'Communication Breakdown: Unravelling the Islamic State's Media Efforts', West Point: CTC at West Point, Oct. 2016, https://ctc.usma.edu/app/uploads/2016/10/ISMedia_Online.pdf, last accessed 18 Dec. 2018.

[8] Winkler, Carol K., Kareem El Damanhoury, Aaron Dicker, and Anthony F. Lemieux, 'The Medium is Terrorism: Transformation of the About to Die Trope in *Dabiq*', *Terrorism and Political Violence* (2016), pp. 1–20.

Islamic State as an organisation, but for the very existence and future of Islam as a religion. As such, the stakes could not really be higher, and inactivity would be catastrophic, for 'ignorance [would] take root among the people and it would be but a few decades before this generation of fighters in the name of Allah the Almighty would be lost and you would not be able to find anyone to continue the journey'.

For the Islamic State, strategic communication is more than a way to recruit new members; it is also a means with which to keep old ones on board by fending off the 'daily lies' of its adversaries, which are 'more dangerous to the *umma* and its men than the projectiles that are shot from planes'.[9] Despite the intensity of this purported threat, the group's defensive propaganda is usually characterised by restraint. Instead of directly repudiating its enemies' claims, it has tended to counter them obliquely, attacking the credibility of the institutions from which they were issued in order to entrench a conspiratorial attitude among supporters.[10] In that sense, this stream of its media operations is tripartite: it rebuffs countervailing narratives by simultaneously ignoring them, discrediting their sources, and presenting a direct alternative.[11]

The imperative to intimidate the enemy through media jihad, the third of the Islamic State's core communication objectives, is writ large across the

---

[9] For more on this, see Ingram, Haroro, 'Deciphering the Siren Call of Militant Islamist Propaganda: Meaning, Credibility & Behavioural Change', ICCT-The Hague, vol. 7, no. 9 (2016), https://icct.nl/wp-content/uploads/2016/09/ICCT-Ingram-Deciphering-the-Siren-Call-of-Militant-Islamist-Propaganda-September2016.pdf, last accessed 18 Dec. 2018; and Ingram, 'A "Linkage-Based" Approach to Combating Militant Islamist Propaganda: A Two-Tiered Framework for Practitioners', ICCT-The Hague, vol. 7, no. 6 (2016), https://icct.nl/wp-content/uploads/2016/11/ICCT-Ingram-A-Linkage-Based-Approach-Nov2016.pdf, last accessed 18 Dec. 2018.

[10] For more on the in-theatre application of this, see the section on information censorship in Winter, 'Totalitarian Insurgency', Center on Irregular Warfare & Armed Groups.

[11] An important exception to this rule came in the wake of the Islamic State's terrorist operation against the Reina nightclub in Istanbul, Turkey. The attack resulted in the deaths of a number of Sunni Muslims from the Arabian Peninsula, something for which the Islamic State was criticised by jihadis and non-jihadis alike in the days that followed. Unusually, it responded to this criticism with an editorial feature in *al-Naba*, its Arabic-language newspaper. See Anon, 'Illuminations on the Blessed Istanbul Operation', *al-Naba # 63* (2017).

above text. The strategic logic that underpins this idea—that war must not be waged through weapons alone—is alluded to in the first few pages, when the authors mention 'the importance of inflicting psychological defeats upon the enemy before material defeats'. Essentially, they are referring to the use of scare tactics before and alongside kinetic operations, media 'missiles' that, if calibrated correctly, can be as effective as military offensives because they 'shatter the morale of the enemy'. In this domain, the adversary is deemed to be particularly vulnerable. Indeed, the authors note that 'anyone who knows the Crusaders of today and keeps track of that which infuriates them understands how they are angered and terrorised by jihadi media'. While combative jihad undoubtedly remains important to this group, as does its media-based, intimidation-focused equivalent—it could even stand, at times, to be more impactful.

While most jihadis share this assessment—that 'half the battle is the media'—the Islamic State has taken it the furthest, becoming notorious for the hyper-violent execution footage it has drip-fed online since the mid-2000s.[12] In many cases, its executioners are foreigners that directly address people living in the states from which they originated, and, on occasion, they are children.[13] The intent is transparent: the group wants to maximise publicity, even when it is 'negative'. That is because these videos are not just about deterrence or provocation. Rather, they are borne of the same logic as 'propaganda of the deed' and seen as a way to weaponise mainstream news discourse and popularise the Islamic State brand.[14]

In 2014, soon after the group captured Mosul and declared its caliphate, this approach yielded tremendous results. For months on end, tales of its gruesome crimes dominated the global news agenda, elevating the organisation and its cause from being relatively unknown to centre stage. This rationale has

---

[12] For an early academic account of this, see Farwell, James P., 'The Media Strategy of ISIS', *Survival* 56, no. 6 (2014), pp. 49–55; see also Chouliaraki, Lilie, and Angelos Kissas, 'The Communication of Horrorism: A Typology of ISIS Online Death Videos', *Critical Studies in Media Communication* 35, no. 1 (2018), pp. 24–39.

[13] See, for example, Winter, Charlie, 'Shocked by the 'Cubs of the Caliphate'? Of Course You Are—That's Isis's Plan', *Guardian*, 6 Jan. 2016, https://www.theguardian.com/commentisfree/2016/jan/05/cubs-of-caliphate-isis-children-videos-propaganda, last accessed 18 Dec. 2018.

[14] For more on the logic of propaganda of the deed, see Bolt, Neville, *The Violent Image: Insurgent Propaganda and the New Revolutionaries*, London: Hurst, 2012.

also motivated its use of terrorism, which similarly leverages media notoriety to communicate a much-exaggerated sense of the group's omnipotence and ubiquity to both supporters and adversaries.[15]

Crucially, the impact of this particular aspect of its media jihad is multiplied many times over because, for the Islamic State, civilians living peacefully in adversary states are just as much enemies as the militaries fighting for the governments they live under. As such, they are considered legitimate targets in its war—psychological and otherwise.[16] It is this idea, not irrational barbarism, as policymakers often claim,[17] that lies at the core of its proclivity for ultraviolent execution videos and narrative-led terrorism, two of the most critical strings in its asymmetric bow.[18]

To be sure, none of the above ideas are new to the field of jihadi strategic communication. However, the extent to which they have been thought through and operationalised by the Islamic State is unparalleled—this document attests to that. The group's almost obsessive focus on shaping the information battlespace was especially apparent in the years that followed its caliphate declaration, when its material victories played an almost supplementary role to the propaganda victories in which they ultimately resulted. Nimbly navigating off- and online territories, the group adeptly used media activism to entrench itself in the minds of its supporters and its enemies. There

---

[15] Winter, Charlie, and Haroro Ingram, 'How ISIS Weaponized the Media after Orlando', *Atlantic*, 17 June 2016, https://www.theatlantic.com/international/archive/2016/06/isis-orlando-shooting/487574/, last accessed 18 Dec. 2018.

[16] The group has written at length about its intention to divide the world into 'Crusaders' and 'Muslims', thereby eliminating any sense of there being a 'gray zone'. See 'From Hypocrisy to Apostasy, the Extinction of the Grayzone', *Dabiq* #7, al-Hayat Media Centre, Nov. 2015.

[17] For example, Collinson, Stephen, 'Obama Unyielding on ISIS as Criticism Mounts after Paris Attacks', *CNN News*, 17 Nov. 2015, https://edition.cnn.com/2015/11/16/politics/obama-isis-strategy-paris-attacks/index.html, last accessed 18 Dec 2018; Johnson, Boris, 'Sign Me Up to Fight Islamic State's Demolition of the Past', *Telegraph*, 15 Mar. 2015, https://www.telegraph.co.uk/news/worldnews/islamic-state/11473832/Sign-me-up-to-fight-Islamic-States-demolition-of-the-past.html, last accessed 18 Dec 2018.

[18] For more on the concept of narrative-led strategy, see Nissen, Thomas Elkjer, 'Narrative Led Operations: Put the Narrative First', *Small Wars Journal*, Oct. 2012, http://smallwarsjournal.com/jrnl/art/narrative-led-operations-put-the-narrative-first, last accessed 18 Dec. 2018.

is no way to know whether it did this through intuition or learning, but it is incontrovertible that propaganda runs to the very core of this organisation, and has done so since the inception of its earliest predecessor.[19]

---

[19] See Whiteside, 'Lighting the Path', ICCT (2016).

PART IV

PURIFICATION

'Part IV: Purification' focuses on the Islamic State's most recent period of decline. It starts with a transcript of the video 'The structure of the *Khilafah*', which outlines the Islamic State's underlying organisational dynamics, a surprisingly resilient mechanism throughout its boom-bust history (Chapter 11). It then features Abu Muhammad al-Adnani's 'Those Who Lived in Faith, Lived Upon Evidence', the final speech of the Islamic State's charismatic media spokesman and one that flagged to its supporters the coming decline and the implications for the movement (Chapter 12). Next is Baghdadi's August 2018 speech 'And Give Glad Tidings to Those Who Are Patient', which offers important insights into how the movement's leadership sought to cohere the movement's politico-military and propaganda efforts during its period of decline (Chapter 13). The final two chapters are devoted to two statements released in 2019: an audio statement by then spokesperson Abul-Hasan al-Muhajir (Chapter 14), and a filmed statement by Baghdadi, the now guerilla caliph of the Islamic State (Chapter 15).

11

THE STRUCTURE OF THE CALIPHATE

'*The Structure of the Khilafah (Caliphate)*' *is a video published by al-Furqan Media on 6 July 2016 that attempts to explain the governing structure of the Islamic State.*[1] *The video's narrator goes into a great deal of detail about the relationship between the caliph and the Delegated Committee, bureaus, and provinces that fall under this leadership structure, and the ministries, committees, and offices that do the day-to-day work of administering its extensive territorial holdings in Iraq and Syria. The video was published in English and several other languages, fulfilling the exhortations jihadi theorists like Abu Musab al-Suri had advocated for decades—spreading the ideas of this Islamist project beyond Arabic speakers. The following is our transcript of the video and descriptions of the displays.*

11a. 'The Structure of the *Khilafah*', 6 July 2016
al-Furqan Media

'In the name of God, the Merciful, the Compassionate,[2] O *umma* of Islam, we have become determined to not repeat the tragedy and to not allow the fruit

---

[1] Video available at Aaron Zelin's Jihadology website. Islamic State, 'The Structure of the Caliphate', al-Furqan Media, 6 July 2016, Jihadology, https://jihadology. net/2016/07/06/new-video-message-from-the-islamic-state-the-structure-of-the-caliphate/, last accessed 18 Dec. 2018.

[2] The distinctive voice of Abu Umar al-Baghdadi, the deceased amir of the Islamic State

to be lost. For the believer is not bitten from the same hole twice. Indeed, the Islamic State will remain...'[3]

[Narrator]: It is a structure that has become more manifest than the sun in the middle of the sky. It was erected by the arms of defiant men and irrigated by the blood of the *shuhada* (martyrs) through patience, conviction, and hardened resolve. Its methodology is the guiding book and the aiding sword with respect to defending the religion and governing the worldly affairs. *Imama* was legislated in order to follow prophethood in upholding these two matters, and no era had ever been void of a *khalifa* or imam, until the people of Islam became squanderous, neglectful, chaotic masses overtaken by tribulations and enveloped with hostility. So the religion was lost and the lands usurped, but Allah sends forth for the *umma*, at the head of every one hundred years, a man who will renew for the *umma* its religion. Thus, the *khilafa* was announced and the *khalifa* given *baya* after years of religious famine and political barrenness. So the earth yielded crops and became green, the caravan proceeded forth, the religion returned, and the sanctities were defended. This is the land of the *khilafa*, and this is its structure. Its subjects are governed, justice is applied evenly, and the Lord of mankind is feared.

[Several graphics display the structure of the Islamic State governance as the narrator describes them:]

The governing structure consists of the *khalifa*, the Shura Council, the Delegated Committee, the *dawawin* [ministries/bureaus], the *wilayat* [provinces], and the committees and offices.

The *dawawin*: Bureau of Judgment and Grievances, Bureau of Hisbah [religious compliance police], Bureau of Da'wah [Islamic call or proselytisation], and Mosques, Bureau of Alms, Bureau of the Soldiery, Bureau of Public Security, Bureau of the Treasury, Bureau of Media, Bureau of Education,

---

of Iraq and predecessor to Abu Bakr al-Baghdadi, serves as the introduction of this video. Its release by al-Furqan distinguishes it as a centrally produced video by the top leadership, compared to the majority of releases, which are executed by local media offices with central media approval. The following Abu Umar quote—in Arabic but subtitled for the English audience—is an excerpt from a speech covered in Chapter 3.

[3] The narrator of this video is largely thought to be Canadian Mohammad Khalifa, who was born in Saudi Arabia before immigrating with his family to Toronto. He was the voice of many English-language videos produced by the group, often at the orders of Abu Muhammad al-Furqan, his amir.

Bureau of Health, Bureau of Agriculture, Bureau of Resources, Bureau of Spoils and Plunder, Bureau of Services.

The *wilayat*: Baghdad, Anbar, Salah ad-Din, Fallujah, Diyala, Shamal [north of] Baghdad, Janub [the 'belts' south of Baghdad], Ninawa, Kirkuk, Dijlah, Jazirah, Barakah, Khayr, Raqqah, Damascus, Aleppo, Homs, Hamah, Furat, Najd, Hijaz, Sinai, Barqah, Tripoli, Fezzan, Algeria, West Africa, al-Liwa al-Akhdar, Khurasan, the Caucasus, Aden-Abyan, Shabwah, Hadramawt, Sanaa, Bayda.

The committees and offices: the Emigration Committee, Committee for the Affairs of Prisoners and Martyrs, Office for Research and Studies, Administration of the Wilayat, Office for Public and Tribal Relations.

The head of its affairs is *Amir al-Mu'minin* [the Commander of the Faithful—referring specifically here to Abu Bakr al-Baghdadi], may God protect him, and he is the *khalifa*. He upholds and spreads the religion, defends the homeland, and fortifies the fronts. He prepares the armies, implements the *hudud*, enforces the people's adherence to the sharia rulings, and governs their worldly affairs. He is aided in all this by upright, qualified men. They are *ahl al-hal wa al-'aqd* [those qualified to elect or depose the caliph on behalf of the *umma*] and his shura council. The task of communicating orders once they've been issued, and ensuring their execution, is delegated to a select group of knowledgeable, upright individuals with perception and leadership skills, as the *khalifa* cannot himself personally carry out all the work of the state, for that is an impossible endeavour. So it's necessary for there to be a body of individuals that supports him, and that body is the Delegated Committee. The Delegated Committee supervises the following branches of state: firstly, the *wilayat*; secondly, the *dawawin*; thirdly, the offices and committees.

For with the expansion of the Islamic State, it became necessary to create effective ways to administer and supervise its territory. This led to the formation of the *wilayat*. They are regional divisions set up in order to facilitate the affairs of governance in the Islamic State. Each region is headed by a *wali* [governor] designated by the *khalifa*. The wali refers any serious matters to the Delegated Committee and governs the *wilaya*'s subjects. Justice is thereby secured and the needs of the people are met. The *wilayat* of the Islamic State, may Allah honour it, have reached thirty-five in number, of which nineteen are in Iraq and Sham, and sixteen are located distantly, spanning several global regions.

Secondly, the *dawawin*. They are places for protecting rights and are under the supervision of the Delegated Committee. They have offices in every *wilaya* that assume the maintenance of public interests and protect the people's religion and security. The *dawawin* are fourteen in number, and they are as follows.

The Diwan of Judgment and Grievances: It is a *diwan* that is presided over by a sufficient number of judges and is responsible for clarifying and enforcing the sharia rulings in matters of blood, family and marriage-related issues, wealth, and other matters, in addition to judging between the people.

The Diwan of Hisbah: It is a *diwan* that is responsible for overseeing the public by ordering them to perform good deeds when they are neglected, preventing them from evil deeds when they are committed, and obligating them with what is in accordance with the sharia.

The Diwan of Da'wah and Masajid: It is a *diwan* responsible for the *da'wah* to Allah. It is concerned with preparing and appointing imams and preachers and holding preparatory seminars and sharia courses, in addition to building and preparing *masajid* (place of worship).

The Diwan of Zakah [alms]: It is a *diwan* responsible for collecting the *zakah* and distributing it to those who deserve it, and is concerned with meeting the needs of the poor and needy in accordance with a structured work mechanism and guidelines set in place for this.

The Diwan of the Soldiery: It is a *diwan* responsible for managing the *khilafa*'s wars, guarding its fronts, planning and making the necessary preparations for military raids, and dispatching the divisions, brigades, and battalions, in addition to providing the *khilafa*'s army with trained personnel and individuals with military and administrative qualifications.

The Diwan of Public Security: It is a *diwan* responsible for safeguarding internal public security in the Islamic State and for protecting it from anything that would disrupt it, and for waging war against infiltration and against any spy networks.

The Diwan of the Treasury: It is a *diwan* responsible for the protection and safekeeping of the Islamic State's treasury, including wealth and reserves from the resources that Allah has bestowed on the Islamic State.

The Diwan of Media: It is the body responsible for any content released by the Islamic State, whether that content is audio, visual, or written.

The Diwan of Education: It is a *diwan* responsible for propelling the wheel of knowledge. Among its tasks is to regulate curriculums and courses in accordance with sharia frameworks and to locate the required personnel.

The Diwan of Health: It is a *diwan* responsible for developing the health sector and providing any means essential for preventing and treating sickness and disease.

The Diwan of Agriculture: It is a *diwan* responsible for the agricultural and animal resources and for maintaining food security for the subjects of the Islamic State.

The Diwan of Resources: It is a *diwan* responsible for the exploitation of oil, gas, and mineral resources.

The Diwan of Fay' [spoils] and Ghana'im [booty]: It is a *diwan* responsible for counting and safekeeping the wealth that Allah bestows on the Islamic State following battles, raids, and otherwise, for the *diwan* conducts the allocation of shares to those who deserve them.

The Diwan of Services: It is a *diwan* responsible for supplying water and electricity, paving and maintaining roads, and supervising and maintaining the public utilities in the Islamic State.

Thirdly, the offices and committees: They are bodies that deal with various matters and are comprised of specialised personnel. These bodies are supervised by the Delegated Committee.

The Hijra [migration] Committee: It is an office concerned with receiving those who immigrate to the Islamic State and with providing the various committees and *dawawin* with the personnel they require.

The Committee for the Affairs of Prisoners and Shuhada [martyrs]. It is a body that is responsible for resolving the affairs of Muslim prisoners and doing the utmost to save them. It is also responsible for looking after the families of the *shuhada* and caring for their children.

The Office for Research and Studies: It is concerned with researching sharia issues and expounding on any matters referred to it by various bodies.

The Administration of the Distant Wilayat: It is responsible for overseeing and managing the affairs of the *wilayat* outside of Iraq and Sham.

The Office for Public and Tribal Relations: It is a link between the Islamic State and the heads and dignitaries of the tribes in the *wilayat* of the Islamic State.

Upon Allah's spacious earth and beneath His sky, the Khilafa State spreads its shade. It has outlined the path of salvation and triumph for the Muslim generations, for the earth belongs entirely to Allah, and He causes to inherit it whom He wills of His servants, and the best outcome is for the righteous.

[Battle scenes and atrocities with the following captions, sung in the a capella style of the *nashid*]:

When war erupts, we march to it. We plunge into its flames and frights, as we are defiant and we are its fuel, which kindles its blaze. When war erupts, we march to it. We plunge into its flames and frights, as we are defiant and we are its fuel, which kindles its blaze. We've quenched our swords on blood of necks, so ask the nation of *kufr* about its affliction. Their lowly were gathered by terror and truth has dispelled their minds. We present to the battle its heroes and we wear the garments of war, we pound the forts and their ruins, and we sever, with sword, their attachments, steeds ... racing their riders and expelling traitors from the land, destroying all disgrace and lowliness, raising the forelocks to assassinate it [apostasy]. Unto eternity we stood and marched forth, seeking the beauties and their like. We yearn, with longing and love for them, to meet the honoured and whoever achieved. We purchased gardens and their surpluses, we've adored their aroma and sweet taste—through our Lord's *tawhid* we've arisen to it and we hope acceptance, how great it is!

11b. Analysis

The origins of this structure predate the establishment of the Islamic State in October 2006. According to conventional wisdom about the evolution of modern insurgency, the structure will become flatter, with less input from leaders and a general decentralisation of activities.[4] The Islamic State has turned this logic on its head, and nothing demonstrates this more than this video and the hundreds of other documents collected by scholar Aymenn al-Tamimi since 2013 for his archive of Islamic State administrative documents.[5] This research—a treasure trove for fellow scholars—includes examples of bureaucratic determinations on mundane issues from each of the *dawawin* described here.[6] Despite the security risks of building a highly structured organisation subject to enemy targeting, the movement's leadership used the transition from al-Qaida in Iraq to the Islamic State of Iraq to build a (at the time) national-level structure that would perform three important tasks: con-

[4] Metz, Steven, 'Why America Will Face Even Deadlier Insurgents in the Future', *World Politics Review*, May 3, 2019, https://www.worldpoliticsreview.com/articles/27813/why-america-will-face-even-deadlier-insurgents-in-the-future

[5] Aymenn al-Tamimi, 'The Evolution in Islamic State Administration The Documentary Evidence', *Perspectives on Terrorism* 9, No. 4, Special Issue on the Islamic State (August 2015), pp. 117–129, https://www.jstor.org/stable/26297420

[6] Aymenn al-Tamimi, 'Archive of Islamic State Administrative Documents', begun 27 January 2015 and now grown to four parts, can be found here: http://www.aymennjawad.org/2015/01/archive-of-islamic-state-administrative-documents and the continuation here: http://www.aymennjawad.org/2017/08/archive-of-islamic-state-administrative-documents-3

trol its members' use of violence, maximise the value of group resources, and expand territorial control into new areas.[7] According to scholar Jacob Shapiro, who calls this the 'Terrorist's Dilemma', the vehicle the leadership chose was the 'M-Form' organisational structure, which has a centralised set of departments that are replicated at multiple localities.[8]

It was the veteran jihadis—most with experience gained in al-Qaida camps in Afghanistan before 2001—that put together the blueprint for the future Islamic State. Accordingly, it should be no surprise that the original frameworks of Tawhid wal Jihad, al-Qaida in Iraq, the Mujahidin Shura Council, and the Islamic State of Iraq are all closely derived from that of al-Qaida Central, if not identical. According to captured documents, available in the Harmony Collection at West Point, al-Qaida's organisational chart in 1999 included the following departments: military, political (sharia), information, security, surveillance, foreign purchase, and an administrative and financial committee.[9]

In comparison, according to captured Mujahidin Shura Council and Islamic State of Iraq documents, the group's provincial governance in Anbar province had similar subunits by late 2006: military, legal (sharia), media, security, and administration. Missing a foreign purchase division, the leaders instead relied on elements of its administrative wing to conduct financing and run its lucrative extortion efforts that freed the leadership from outside influences and fundraising activities—a key imperative learned from Abu Musab al-Suri's lessons from the original Syrian uprising.[10] Anbar province's organisa-

---

[7] Johnston, Patrick B., Jacob N. Shapiro, Howard J. Shatz, Benjamin Bahney, Danielle F. Jung, Patrick Ryan, and Jonathan Wallace, 'Foundations of the Islamic State: Management, Money, and Terror in Iraq, 2005–2010', RAND Corporation (2016), p. 53.

[8] Shapiro, Jacob N., *The Terrorist's Dilemma: Managing Violent Covert Organizations*, Princeton, NJ: Princeton University Press, 2013, p. 94.

[9] Forest, James J.F., Jarret Brachman, and Joseph Felter, 'Harmony and Disharmony: Exploiting al-Qaeda's Organizational Vulnerabilities', CTC West Point, Harmony Documents AFGP-2002–000078 and AFGP-2002–000080 (14 Feb. 2006), pp. 61–63, https://ctc.usma.edu/app/uploads/2010/06/Harmony-and-Dishar-mony.pdf, last accessed 18 Dec. 2018.

[10] al-Suri, Abu Musab, 'Lessons Learned from the Jihad Ordeal in Syria', CTC West Point, Harmony Document AFGP-2002–600080, pp. 6–7, https://ctc.usma.edu/harmony-program/lessons-learned-from-the-jihad-ordeal-in-syria-original-lan-guage-2/, last accessed 18 Dec. 2018.

tion mirrored a similar structure at the national level, with the exception of a *shura* committee.[11] Captured documents confirmed that lower-level district organisation in the Anbar towns of Tuzliyah and Julayba were also organised exactly like their provincial parent.[12] To show the extent of the sophistication of the organisational structure in this early period, the Anbar provincial administrative amir in 2006–7 supervised a unit responsible for economic studies, loots and sales, aid and storage, human resources, inventory and audit, movement and maintenance, finance and accounting, and programme improvement and training.[13]

The announcement of the first 'cabinet' of the Islamic State in April 2007 demonstrated the beginnings of an evolution that built on the al-Qaida Central-influenced structure, with the following ministers: a deputy to the amir/war minister (long-time Zarqawi deputy Abu Hamza al-Muhajir), and public relations, public security, media, oil, sharia, martyrs and prisoners, agriculture and fishing, and health ministers.[14] A second slate in 2009 produced a new list of ministers in the same departments.[15] Tamimi notes that many of the titles (professor, doctor, engineer) of the individuals named in both slates give the impression of technocratic expertise, while also maintaining an impressive inclusion of diverse and important Sunni tribes (Janabi, Mashadani, Dulaymi, Jubouri) with a minimum of foreigners.[16]

In 2009, after being routed by pro-government Sunni militias the aforementioned (Sahwa) and other counterinsurgent forces two years earlier, Abu Umar al-Baghdadi created a tribal engagement office that financed and managed local efforts to recruit and co-opt Sunni tribal figures back into the Islamic State fold. Along with this political outreach, security detachments assassinated key Sahwa figures who refused to renounce their affiliation with the government or who were labelled as impediments to the destruction of the

---

[11] Johnston et al., 'Foundations of the Islamic State', p. 74.

[12] Ibid., p. 78, citing Harmony Documents MNFA 2007–000566 and NMEC 2007–632298.

[13] Ibid., p. 77, citing Harmony Document NMEC 2007–632298.

[14] al-Jubouri, Muharib, 'The Establishment of the first Islamic Administration of the Islamic State of Iraq', al-Furqan Media, 19 Apr. 2007.

[15] al-Baghdadi, Abu Umar, 'Declaration of the Second Cabinet Reshuffle for the Islamic State of Iraq', al-Furqan Media, 21 Sep. 2009, https://archive.org/details/Al-Tashkeelah-2-Le-Dwla-Iraq-Islamic, last accessed 18 Dec. 2018.

[16] al-Tamimi, Aymenn, 'The Evolution in Islamic State Administration: The Documentary Evidence', *Perspectives on Terrorism* 9, no. 4 (2015).

local Sahwa organisation by tribal rivals.[17] The survival of the tribal engagement office in the current structure of the Islamic State is vindication of both the importance and the effectiveness of this structural innovation. While Saddam had also flirted with tribal engagement during times of regime stress with limited results, the creation of this department by Abu Umar—an original member of the Iraqi Salafi movement—played a large part in ensuring access to the Sunni population and securing a comeback in later years.[18] The Islamic State's current structure (as of 2016–17) contains the same original departments of the early movement and many new ones, now that the organisation governs territory and tends to the needs of a real population.[19]

This video serves as more than a glimpse into a sophisticated insurgent organisation, one that, while innovative and well-developed, is not much different or advanced than another large-scale insurgency—the National Liberation Front (the Viet Cong, 1958–75).[20] The purpose of the structure is to run a shadow government, which is the defining feature of an insurgency—the desire to win out in a competition for a specific population's allegiance.[21] The efficiency and effectiveness of a governing system will eventually be reflected in the loyalty of elements of the contested population,

---

[17] Documents housed at the Captured Records Research Centre describe the office's function well, as detailed by an Islamic State operative. See Abu Khaldun, 'Synopsis of the Relations Committee in Baghdad's Southern Belt', CRRC document AQ PMPR-d-001–717 (2009); and Abu Khaldun, 'OPSUM from Abu Mustafa of Southern Belt trying to overturn Sahwa,' CRRC document AQ-POAK-d-001–695, 9 Sep. 2009.

[18] A detailed examination of the evolution of the tribal engagement office can be found in Whiteside, 'The Islamic State and the Return of Revolutionary Warfare', pp. 765–767.

[10] For more on the evolution of Islamic State governing structures, see Whiteside, Craig, 'A Pedigree of Terror: The Myth of the Ba'athist Influence in the Islamic State Movement', *Perspectives on Terrorism* 11, no. 3 (2017), pp. 8–10.

[20] There is a remarkable similarity between the two organisational structures, the careful blend of military and political leadership, as well as a penchant for secrecy and skill in counterintelligence, see Pike, Douglas, *Viet Cong: The Organization and Technique of the National Liberation Front of South Vietnam*, Cambridge, MA: MIT Press, 1966.

[21] Fall, Bernard, 'The Theory and Practice of Insurgency and Counterinsurgency', Naval War College Review (Winter 1998 [reprint from the April 1965 issue]), retrieved from http://www.au.af.mil/au/awc/awcgate/navy/art5-w98.htm

and the Islamic State's longevity to date, despite internal and external pressures, has a lot to do with the performance of the group's governing systems and philosophies.

Up until 2013, this meant the establishment of governing institutions to run the insurgent organisation. Did the Islamic State of Iraq's Ministry of Agriculture really function in 2007? This question was often used as a sarcastic punch line during this period at the expense of the group, but there is evidence that the ministry's management of stolen farms in parts of Iraq at this time was raising money for the organisation through harvesting in the same way that organised crime sometimes uses legitimate activities as a front for fundraising.[22] In fact, all of these ministries were functioning, some at very low levels, but these efforts paid dividends when opportunities and the environment favoured the group's endeavours after 2010.

Tamimi and Zelin both argue that the Islamic State's shadow sharia offices were the first to appear in contested localities in Syria, which provided cover for the group's security elements to quietly build a picture of rival jihadi and nationalistic resistance groups for future elimination, when the time was right. In this way, the Islamic State developed a doctrine for the subversion of existing local governance in the drive to create the contiguous caliphate in 2014.[23]

The establishment of the caliphate in 2014, a popular enough political goal that transcends the narrow Salafi trend, forced the Islamic State to consider how its ideas would translate beyond Iraq and Syria—areas where its core leadership had operated since 2002. With allegiances to Baghdadi flowing in from like-minded Salafi-jihadi groups around the world, the Islamic State leadership developed a hub and spoke model of a dispersed caliphate with non-contiguous provinces.[24] The geographic distance between the Islamic State and new affili-

---

[22] One of the authors was aware of Islamic State administered fish farms in the 'belts' south of Baghdad, stolen from Shi'a families who had left the largely Sunni areas out of fear. In retrospect, this information—viewed with some skepticism at the time— exemplifies the ways the Islamic State of Iraq stayed alive after its Sahwa setbacks. Stolen land deeds also played a role in the various ministries' fundraising. See: Knights, Michael, 'Al-Qa'ida in Iraq', *CTC Sentinel* 1, no. 7 (June 2008).

[23] al-Tamimi, 'The Evolution of Islamic State Administration', 2015; Zelin, Aaron 'The Islamic State's Territorial Methodology', The Washington Institute for Near East Research Policy, Research Note 29, Jan. 2016, https://www.washingtoninstitute. org/uploads/Documents/pubs/ResearchNote29-Zelin.pdf

[24] This model of future insurgency with its Maoist similarities, reliance on terror as propaganda of the deed, and dispersed territories held together by modern commu-

ates sharing the important name brand—one so carefully cultivated over a decade—would test the management skills of the group's leadership.

This video refers to outlying provinces and a new committee called the 'Distant Provinces Administration', but the cultivation of these armed groups as approved affiliates started long before the Islamic State officially accepted them. In the new provinces, the Islamic State's leaders communicated to prospective affiliates a series of requirements that had to be met to be declared a *wilaya*, or province of the Islamic State. The tasks were: broadcast their allegiance to the caliph, politically unify fragmented ideologically acceptable groups, select a leader and advisory council, control territory in order to implement the prophetic method of governance, and be accepted by the Islamic State leadership.[25]

For example, in January 2016, this process was beginning to occur in the Philippines as four Salafi-jihadi militant groups, largely defectors from the existing Abu Sayyaf group, were uniting under a pro-Islamic State coalition.[26] By March, the Islamic State's Philippine affiliate claimed its first attack, in the Mindinao city of Marawi, through the group's unofficial news agency, Amaq.[27] In June, the group recognised a veteran militant, former Abu Sayyaf member Isnilon Hapilon, as the amir of all Islamic State fighters in the Philippines, which had still not been awarded provincial status.[28] Instead, the Islamic State media department reported the activities as simply occurring in 'East Asia', without using the word province.[29] By 2017, the

---

nications, was predicted (with some degree of accuracy) by John Mackinlay in *The Insurgent Archipelago*, London: Hurst, 2009.

[25] Zenn, Jacob, 'The Islamic State's Provinces on the Peripheries: Juxtaposing the Pledges from Boko Haram in Nigeria and Abu Sayyaf and Maute Group in the Philippines', *Perspectives on Terrorism* 13, no. 1, Feb 2019, https://www.universiteitleiden.nl/binaries/content/assets/customsites/perspectives-on-terrorism/2019/issue-1/zenn—revised.pdf; for original guidance see: Islamic State, 'Wilayat Khurasan and the Bay'at from Qawqaz', *Dabiq*, Issue 7, al-Hayat Media Center, 12 Feb. 2015, p. 35.

[26] Gunaratna, Rohan, 'The Islamic State's Northward Expansion in the Philippines', Counter Terrorist Trends and Analyses 9:5 (2017), p. 2. Jade Parker and Pawel Wocjik pointed us to this source.

[27] Zenn, 2015.

[28] Islamic State, 'The Solid Edifice—The Philippines', 21 June 2016, accessed on Aaron Zelin's Jihadology https://jihadology.net/2016/06/21/new-video-message-from-the-islamic-state-the-solid-edifice-the-philippines/

[29] Zenn, 2015.

group's media began to use Islamic State-East Asia (IS-EA) to describe the efforts of Salafi-jihadi affiliated groups trying to build insurgencies in the disparate archipelagos of the Philippines, Indonesia, Malaysia, Myanmar, Thailand, Brunei, and Singapore.[30]

Tamimi points out in his analysis of this specific video that the Philippines is not the only prospective *wilaya* omitted from the list presented by the narrator. Bangladesh, Somalia, Indonesia, and Tunisia were also left out of the video, as was Wilaya Bahrain and Sahel (coastal Syria, not Africa).[31] This cannot be an oversight, considering the source of the video and its proximity to the leadership. In many ways, the conference of *wilaya* status to the far-flung Salafi-jihadi groups around the world that desperately wanted money, experience, and the name brand was subject to very strict requirements. Many prospective groups, like the Maute-Hapilon alliance in the Philippines, went to great lengths—including being nearly wiped out in the six month battle for Marawi and its aftermath—to meet the Islamic State's high bar, which required groups to unify, submit propaganda to the central office in Iraq/Syria, and attempt to achieve *tamkin* (political consolidation and administration of territory).

We will end this analysis with another of Tamimi's insightful observations about the video: there are often inconsistencies between the official titles of ministries, committees, and offices, as portrayed in the video, and the actual documents found in his archive of administrative sources. In some cases, this is a result of changes in the status of an office, as happened to Turki al-Bin'ali, who was identified as the 'chief religious advisor' of the Islamic State by the US government in a sanctions release. Cole Bunzel explains that Bin'ali was the amir of the Department of Research and Fatwas (*Diwan al-Buhuth wa'l-Ifta'*), then the Committee for Research and Fatwas (*Hay'at al-Buhuth wa'l-Ifta'*), and finally the Office of Research and Studies (*Maktab al-Buhuth wa'l-Dirasat*). This indicates a successive demotion of both individual and the office (from ministry, to committee, to office) and the removal of Bin'ali's

---

[30] Islamic State, 'Inside the Caliphate #3', al-Hayat Media Center, 20 Aug. 2017, accessed on Aaron Zelin's Jihadology, https://jihadology.net/2017/08/20/new-video-message-from-the-islamic-state-inside-the-caliphate-3/. Thanks to Pawel Wocjik for pointing this out to us.

[31] al-Tamimi, Aymenn, 'Observations on the new Islamic State video "Structure of the Caliphate"', 6 July 2016, http://www.aymennjawad.org/2016/07/observations-on-the-new-islamic-state-video

ability to issue fatwas, unfolding within an organisation struggling with ideological schisms following the establishment of the caliphate.[32] But in most cases, the discrepancies, which primarily concern the replication of these offices at the lower levels of the Islamic State structure, are more an example of the structural flux and legion of local peculiarities within an organisation fighting an insurgency in some places and conventional war in others. Regardless of these differences, understanding the structure of the Islamic State and how it has evolved is a task of fundamental importance for understanding how the group operates globally, and a critical task for those charged with defeating it.

---

[32] Bunzel, Cole, 'Caliphate in Disarray: Theological Turmoil in the Islamic State', *Jihadica*, 3 Oct. 2017 http://www.jihadica.com/caliphate-in-disarray/

12

DEFINING SUCCESS AND FAILURE

When the Islamic State's long-time spokesperson released his final speech in May 2016, it was becoming apparent that coalition efforts were taking their toll on the movement. The Islamic State's blitz across the Middle East's 'fertile crescent' through 2014 had stalled the following year and, slowly but surely, reversed. Unlike previous iterations of the group, it now had international provinces dotted across the Middle East, Africa, and Asia as well as supporters throughout the West who were willing to assist the movement from afar as propaganda 'fanboys' or attackers behind enemy lines.

The following excerpt is from Abu Muhammad al-Adnani's speech 'That They Live By Proof', translated and published by Islamic State's al-Hayat Media.[1] It is significant for three reasons. First, it draws stark contrasts between not only the credibility, but also the definitions and timelines of success and failure of the Islamic State and its opponents. Second, it offers important insights into how the Islamic State's leadership attempted to prepare the movement and its supporters for future losses. Third, as Adnani's final speech before he was killed in September 2016, it represents a significant signpost in the movement's evolution: the second decline in its almost two-decade-long history.

---

[1] The excerpt featured in this chapter is taken from an official Islamic State translation. The source contained text in both rounded and square brackets. The authors have made minimal edits to the text.

12a. 'That They Live By Proof', 21 May 2016
An Address by the Official Spokesman of the Islamic State
The Mujahid *Shaykh Abu Muhammad al-'Adnani ash-Shami*

All praise is due to Allah, the Strong and Mighty. May blessings and peace be upon the one sent with the sword as a mercy to the creation. To proceed:

Allah said, 'Indeed, the ones who oppose Allah and His Messenger—those will be among the most humiliated. Allah has written, "I will surely prevail, I and My messengers." Indeed, Allah is strong and mighty' (al-Mujadilah 20–21). And our Lord AWJ [the Mighty and Magestic] said about the Jews, 'And when your Lord declared that He would surely dispatch against them, until the Day of Resurrection, those who would afflict them with the worst torment. Indeed, your Lord is swift in penalty; but indeed, He is Forgiving and Merciful' (al-A'raf 167). Abu Hurayrah narrated that Allah's Messenger said:

> The Hour will not be established until the Muslims fight the Jews. The Muslims will continue killing them until the Jews hide behind stones and trees. Then the stone or the tree will say, "O Muslim, O slave of Allah, there is a Jew hiding behind me, so come and kill him"' (Reported by Muslim). He also narrated that the Prophet said, 'The Hour will not be established until the Romans descend upon A'maq. Then an army from the city, from among the best people of the earth on that day, will head out to them. When they form ranks for battle, the Romans will say, "Make a way between us and those who took slaves from our people so that we can fight them." So the Muslims will say, "No, by Allah, we will not make a way between you and our brothers," and will then fight them. One-third of them will retreat and Allah will never forgive them, one-third of them will be killed and they will be the best of shuhada, according to Allah AWJ, and one-third of them will never face any trials and will then reach Constantinople and conquer it' (Reported by Muslim).

So woe to you, O Crusaders, and woe to you, O Jews. Whenever you arise, parade, oppress, and transgress, Allah comes at you from where you did not expect, as His slaves afflict you with the worst torment. This is what our Lord has promised us and Allah does not go back on His promise, may He be glorified. America the incompetent, together with its allies, thinks that it can scare the believers or triumph over the mujahidin. Certainly not! Indeed, the crusader coalition came to Iraq 13 years ago, thinking that none would be able to overpower it and that strength is in numbers and equipment. Then, after only a matter of days, the idiot Bush announced an end to military operations, alleged that the war was over, and claimed victory in all his delusion, falsehood, and conceit, and with the utmost level of deception and arrogance. So we informed him that his war had not yet begun, and it was only a short time before Bush's lie and the mujahidin's truthfulness became apparent and their war on America and its allies erupted. Thus, the coalition's army was ground all over Mesopotamia and fell into the swamp of destruction, of which it would not get out, by Allah's permission. Then, after 8 years of a destructive war that devastated America's economy and exhausted its army, the mule Obama announced the crusader army's withdrawal from Iraq, falsely claiming another victory. We informed him, again, that the battle had not yet intensified and we swore to them, saying, 'If you leave, you will return.' So America and the mule of the Jews lied, while the mujahidin spoke the truth. And so here is the Islamic State, remaining, by Allah's grace, and here is the defender of the Jews and the Cross, America, having returned with its army, entangling its very own sons in a war with the mujahidin, promising itself and its allies the destruction of the Islamic State and the end of jihad.

So listen, O America! Listen, O Crusaders! Listen, O Jews! Our Lord AWJ said, 'And Our word has passed for Our slaves, the Messengers, that they would be supported and that Our soldiers would indeed prevail' (As-Saffat 171–173). 'Fight them, Allah will punish them by your hands, and He will disgrace them and give you victory over them, satisfying the hearts of a believing people and removing the fury of their hearts' (At-Tawbah 14–15). Indeed, we await what He has promised and we have confidence in Him. So your armies and your masses will never scare us. Your threats and your campaigns will not dissuade us. You will never be victorious. You will be defeated. Or do you think, O America, that victory is by killing one leader or another? Indeed, it would then be a falsified victory. Were you victorious when you killed Abu Mus'ab, Abu Hamzah, Abu 'Umar, or Usamah? Would you be victorious if you were to kill ash-Shishani, Abu Bakr, Abu Zayd, or Abu 'Amr? No. Indeed, victory is the defeat of one's opponent. Or do you, O America, consider defeat to be the loss of a city or the loss of land? Were we defeated when we lost the cities in Iraq and were in the desert without any city or land? And would we be defeated and you be victorious if you were to take Mosul or Sirte or Raqqah or even take all the cities and we were to return to our initial condition? Certainly not! True defeat is the loss of willpower and desire to fight. America will be victorious and the mujahidin will be defeated in only one situation. We would be defeated and you victorious only if you were able to remove the Quran from the Muslims' hearts. How impossible a feat! How far off a task it would be! Rather, we are the People of the Quran, who sell their souls for Paradise....

Listen, O Americans, and understand. What have you accomplished after these 13 years of war against the mujahidin in Mesopotamia, and what have they accomplished? Indeed, you came to Iraq with tens, or rather, hundreds of thousands, while we were only a few hundred, or rather, dozens, more or less. It was only three years before Rumsfeld declared resignation, incapacity, and defeat; and the mujahidin declared the establishment of the Islamic State. 'How many a small group was victorious over a large group, by the permission of Allah; and Allah is with those who persevere' (al-Baqarah 249). Thus, America was defeated, as its army faced ruin and collapse, except that it was rescued by the sahwat of treachery and shame.

Then came the established way of Allah AWJ of testing and trying the mujahidin, so the trial increased and the tribulation intensified, until consolidation was lost in the cities. But this only increased the mujahidin in patience and certainty. It occurred to America that it was the golden opportunity to run away. So Obama the Liar declared victory and withdrawal. O you failed, defeated mule! Where is your alleged victory? Where is the new map of the Middle East brought by America? Have you forgotten or do you feign to forget? Or is it us who have drawn it, with your ruin and end coming imminently? Where is the 'free, united' Iraq? Where is democracy? Do you deceive yourself, your people, and the world? Or do you now acknowledge the Islamic State? Where are the promised security, development, and prosperity? Were you lying, O America, or are you simply unable to fulfil promises? Have you made the world safer by waging war against us, America, or has fear and ruin become the norm? Let Canada, France, Tunisia, Turkey, and Belgium bear witness. Have you eradicated terrorism and extinguished the fire of jihad, or has it spread and risen, reaching into every land? Have you succeeded against the mujahidin, or have we declared the Khilafah and are we blessed, by Allah's grace, with consolidation!

Hold on, America; the war is not over and you have yet to win. By Allah's permission, you will be defeated, so wait. Wait, for our swords have not been sheathed, our arms have not become weary, and our resolve has not weakened. We have not become bored nor frail; rather, by Allah's grace, our strength has multiplied exponentially since the beginning of your war, America. Every day that passes, we gain strength, by Allah's grace, and you become weaker. We take firm steps forward, and by Obama's failed plan, you but stumble.

O Muslims! O Ummah of Muhammad! Sham has exposed them. The reality has become as clear to you as the sun. So whoever perishes, perishes by proof, and whoever lives, lives by proof. This is the whole disbelieving world that has gathered, joined in an alliance, and rushed madly into fighting the Islamic State. They made waging war against it, defeating it, and annihilating it their first priority. By what means? What is their goal? What is the reality? What is the rallying cry? Why have dozens of disbelieving nations gathered to wage war against the Islamic State? Why have America and its allies launched some 20,000 airstrikes against us? Yes. Some twenty-thousand airstrikes! Why do they spend billions of their wealth on their war against us? Why do they train and arm armies, gangs, and militias? Why do they carelessly send their sons from overseas to fight us? Why do they not train, arm, back, or support any fighters except those who are vetted? Ask them, if they would answer, or answer, if you can already comprehend.

The whole world has not come together to wage war against us except because we command the worship of Allah, alone without partner, and we incite others to do so. We make wala based upon it and we declare the disbelief of those who abandon it. We warn of shirk in the worship of Allah, and we are severe against it. We make enemies based upon it and we declare the disbelief of those who engage in it. This is our call. This is our religion. For this alone, we fight the world and they fight us...

O Muslims! Truly, the mujahidin are victorious—victorious by the sword and arrowhead, by the evidence and proof. This is the small group striking armies and nations of the world, enduring these long years. It did not enter any land except that the tawaghit were unable to crush it and end it therein. No army fought it except that it caused them to become weak, to bleed, and to weep. And indeed, the mujahidin have refuted all doubtful arguments, despite the mobilization of every evil scholar against them, and despite the use of every form of media. There remains no excuse for anyone after the war of Sham. The truth has appeared clearly for both the learned and the common-ers. There are only two armies, two camps, two trenches. It is the war between kufr and iman. It is the war of wala and bara. Any other war is nonsense, no matter the slogans raised by the disbelievers in their war, and no matter the goals they have claimed.

Where are the Kafir West's alleged defense of 'civilians' and protection of 'human rights' and 'freedom'? Indeed, the false and deceiving mask of nobility has fallen, showing its ugly face under the Nusayri [Alawite] barrels of death, destruction, and gas. America and its allies do not ache and feel pain, except when the mujahidin advance and gain victories. The world does not weep at the Russian and Nusayri massacres each day against the Muslims. The senti-ments in Europe, America, and other disbelieving nations are not moved nor shaken by the displacement of millions. They are not disturbed by the hunger, disease, suffering, and death of thousands of helpless and besieged children, women, and elderly people. America and its allies did not care about those in Ghutah, Zabdani, Madaya, and Mu'addamiyyah. They only cared about those besieged in the city of Khayr. So they were quick to aid them, throwing heaps of food each day to the Nusayriyyah. The people of Europe and other lands of kufr do not shudder at the Russian destruction of hospitals and residential zones, though they are afflicted by sleeplessness and insanity whenever the Islamic State decapitates some of the disbelievers, causing them to shiver, tremble, flare up, bombard, and rally. This, and their ears are deaf and their eyes are blind to what the crusaders, the Hindus, and the atheists do of massacres, crimes and atrocities against the Muslims in Burma, Turkistan, Indonesia, Kashmir, the Philippines, Palestine, Bosnia, Central Africa, Chechnya, the Sunnis of Iran, and the Muslims everywhere else. So it is not transgression, criminal, or terrorism unless it is perpetrated by a Muslim; just as it is not transgression, criminal, or terrorism if the victim is a Muslim.

Yes, O Muslims, 'That whoever perishes, perishes by proof, and that whoever lives, lives by proof' (al-Anfal 42). As for the evil scholars, the shuyukh of dollars and dinars, and the assembly of sorcerers, hypocrites, and agents, then the falsity of their fatwas, which they vomit, has become clear. The doubts they affirm have been unveiled and proven false, and they will not benefit their masters after today, by Allah's permission. They will fail, no matter how earnest and active they might be. Everyone knows their reality. When their masters gain strength and tighten their grip on the peoples' necks, they pass fatwas on the obligation of obeying them and the prohibition of disobeying them and waging jihad; no matter how much they have fallen into kufr, tyranny, wrong, and spreading corruption. Then, when the mujahidin gain a foothold in some city, ruling therein by what Allah revealed, their blood boils and they burst in anger, regurgitating their vomit and passing the fatwa to disobey the mujahidin and to fight them, expel them, and to uproot them, no matter the cost of Muslim blood, ruin, and destruction, and permitting—even recommending—seeking support from the kuffar in this regard. Yet whatever the disbelievers do to the Muslims of slaughter, torture, devastation, and displacement, these evil scholars are deaf, dumb, and blind. There is no fatwa, no condemnation, and no criticism. But when the mujahidin kill a kafir in a distant land or respond to some transgression, the donkeys of knowledge clamor and mobilize without shame to disavow, condemn, criticize, offer condolences, wail, and lament. All while the tawaghit rulers of usurped Muslim lands have not left a single nullifier of Islam, except having committed it, and these evil scholars have not left any 'evidence' in their defense, except that they altered its meaning, whitewashed it, and exploited it. The mujahidin do not practice a ritual, revive a sunnah, implement a ruling, or establish a hadd, except that the palace scholars find fault with them, revile them, criticize them, and spread suspicions in order to avert people from the cause of Allah....

O Muslims! Indeed, we do not wage jihad to defend a land, nor to liberate it, or to control it. We do not fight for authority or transient, shabby positions, nor for the rubble of a lowly, vanishing world. If our goal were one of these heaps of debris, we would not have fought the world with all its sects, creeds, and peoples. If we were able to avert a single fighter from fighting us, we would do so, saving ourselves the trouble. However, our Quran requires us to fight the entire world, without exception. We have done no more than to establish the law of our Lord. If it were an issue of choice, we would have changed. If what we follow or fought for were mere opinion, we would have recanted. If it were a whim, we would have replaced it. If it were a constitution, we would have modified it. If it were some fortune, we would have haggled. If it were but fate, we would have been content. But it is the Quran and the guidance of our Prophet....

We fight in obedience to Allah and to become closer to Him. And victory is that we live in the might of our religion or die upon it. It is the same, whether Allah blesses us with consolidation or we move into the bare, open desert, displaced and pursued. It is the same, whether one of us is carried off to prison as a captive, or spends the night with his family, safe and sound. It is the same, whether we are unharmed and take ghanimah or we are wounded or killed, as victory—according to us—is to live as muwahhidin, to disbelieve in taghut, to fulfill wala and bara, and to establish the religion. If this exists, then we are already, and under all circumstances, victorious. This is the reality, by Allah, and not mere slogans. Those who were truthful soldiers and leaders of the State wrote this with their blood. Whoever thinks otherwise, even if he is in our ranks, is not of us. He will inevitably be cast out or leave, even after some time....

Ramadan has come near, and it is the month of raids and jihad, the month of conquest. Prepare yourselves and get ready. Let each of you hope that he passes it fighting for Allah's cause, seeking and hoping for Allah's reward. Let all of you make it, by Allah's permission, a month of suffering for the kuffar everywhere; and we specifically direct this to soldiers and supporters of the Khilafah in Europe and America.

O slaves of Allah, O muwahhiddin! If the tawaghit have shut the door of hijrah in your faces, then open the door of jihad in theirs. Make your deed a source of their regret. Truly, the smallest act you do in their lands is more beloved to us than the biggest act done here; it is more effective for us and more harmful to them. If one of you wishes and strives to reach the lands of the Islamic State, then each of us wishes to be in your place to make examples of the crusaders, day and night, scaring them and terrorizing them, until every neighbor fears his neighbor. If one of you is unable, then do not make light of throwing a stone at a crusader in his land, and do not underestimate any deed, as its consequences are great for the mujahidin and its effect is noxious to the disbelievers.

It has reached us that some of you do not act due to their incapacity to reach military targets, or their finding fault with targeting those who are called 'civilians,' so they leave harming them, doubting the permissibility thereof. Know that inside the lands of the belligerent crusaders, there is no sanctity of blood and no existence of those called 'innocents'. This is not the venue for mentioning all of the evidences, for the list is too long; the least of which is dealing with them in just, as their warplanes do not distinguish between one who is armed and another who is unarmed, nor between a man and a woman. Know that your targeting those who are called 'civilians' is more beloved to us and more effective, as it is more harmful, painful, and a greater deterrent to them. So go forth, O muwahhidin everywhere! It might be that you attain great reward or even shahadah during Ramadan....

12b. Analysis

Adnani's 'That They Live By Proof' offers scholars and practitioners an important study in the mix of thematic continuities and adaptions that characterise the Islamic State's propaganda through its periods of fluctuating fortune.[2] In

[2] A long-term (multiyear) analysis of patterns in Islamic State's media output reveals a thematic 'hedging' strategy in which certain themes associated with periods of success (for example, statehood, conventional politico-military activities, calls to foreign fighters, 'building the ranks', and rational-choice appeals) versus periods of decline (for example, struggle and sacrifice, unconventional politico-military activities, purification of the ranks, 'just terror', and identity-choice appeals) tend to dominate dependent on strategic conditions. While so-called 'boom themes' dominate propaganda output during periods of success and 'bust themes' tend to dominate during periods of decline, the opposite themes do not completely disappear but are merely given less

contrast to Abu Bakr al-Baghdadi's speeches in Chapters Six and Seven, or Adnani's 'Indeed, Your Lord is Ever Watchful' in Chapter Eight, the strategic context of this declaration is a movement on the precipice of decline, facing the inevitability of its foreseeable future: hardship and devastation. The over-arching theme of Adnani's last speech is that one must rely on evidence (that is, 'proof') for understanding all matters—whether it is strategic, operational, politico-military, propaganda, or cosmic in nature—and use that to decide how to act.

His speech opens with a series of citations from the Quran and *hadiths*, reiterating prophecies meant to explain the ebb and flow of divine destiny before he moves on to the last thirteen years of American involvement in Iraq, contrasting America's 'say-do' gaps with those of the Islamic State. Adnani mocks the Bush-era faith that 'none would be able to overpower it [America] and that strength is in numbers and equipment' and states that 'it was only a short time before Bush's lie and the mujahidin's truthfulness became apparent'. According to Adnani, this dynamic continued as 'the mule of the Jews [Obama] lied, while the mujahidin spoke the truth'. This apparent credibility gap, which he is apparently seeking to expose, is a common theme in the Islamic State's messaging and more broadly reflects different definitions and timelines of what constitutes success and failure.

The Reason We Fight

Just as Adnani mocked the US for believing tangibles were the key to success, he argues that it is equally absurd that the Islamic State's loss of territory, resources, or even personnel be considered evidence of failure:[3]

> Indeed, victory is the defeat of one's opponent. Or do you, O America, consider defeat to be the loss of a city or the loss of land? Were we defeated when we lost

---

priority. This 'hedging' helps to facilitate strategic pivots in both the information and ground theatres while helping to maintain a sense of the movement's credibility and consistency as a politico-military actor over time. For more on Islamic State's use of 'hedging' and its implications, see Whiteside, Craig, and Haroro Ingram, 'In search of the virtual caliphate: convenient fallacy, dangerous distraction', *War on the Rocks*, 27 Sept. 2017.

[3] For a monitoring of the decline of Islamic State's territorial control through 2015–18 see, 'Islamic State and the crisis in Iraq and Syria in maps', *BBC News*, 28 Mar. 2018, https://www.bbc.com/news/world-middle-east-27838034

the cities in Iraq and were in the desert without any city or land? And would we be defeated and you be victorious if you were to take Mosul or Sirte or Raqqah or even take all the cities and we were to return to our initial condition? Certainly not! True defeat is the loss of willpower and desire to fight.

As Adnani defined what constituted failure for the Islamic State, he would go on to assert that victory was simply remaining committed to its *manhaj*. This manifests both collectively ('...whether Allah blesses us with consolidation or we move into the bare, open desert, displaced and pursued') and individually ('It is the same, whether one of us is carried off to prison as a captive, or spends the night with his family, safe and sound.'). The Islamic State's perpetual war and commitment to its *manhaj* is operationalised with a phased politico-military strategy.

Throughout Adnani's speech, contrasts are drawn between the West and the Islamic State, designed to highlight the credibility divide, the perpetual nature of their war, and the Islamic State's proficiency as masters of asymmetric warfare.[4] Regarding the latter, Adnani asserts 'you came to Iraq with tens, or rather, hundreds of thousands, while we were only a few hundred, or rather, dozens, more or less. It was only three years before Rumsfeld declared resignation, incapacity, and defeat; and the mujahidin declared the establishment of the Islamic State'. The ebb and flow of the Islamic State's fortunes are shown as having divine origins, as periods of decline are explained as 'the established way of Allah of testing and trying the mujahidin, so the trial increased and the tribulation intensified, until consolidation was lost in the cities'. These passages showcase the circularly reinforcing nature of the Islamic State's definition of success and failure, its commitment to perpetual war, and the phased politico-military strategy that enables it.

All of this leads to the theme central to his speech—from which it received its title—that 'whoever perishes, perishes by proof, and whoever lives, lives by proof'. For Adnani, all evidence indicates that the global coalition attacks on the Islamic State were motivated by its commitment to destroy Islam. The remainder of the speech is thus devoted to outlining the multidimensional nature of the war against Islamic State, of which violence is the crudest of weap-

---

[4] For more on Islamic State's politico-military strategy, see McCants, Will, *The ISIS Apocalypse: The History, Strategy, and Doomsday Vision of the Islamic State*, New York: St. Martin's Press, 2015; and Whiteside, Craig, 'New masters of revolutionary warfare: The Islamic State movement (2002–2016)', *Perspectives on Terrorism* 10, no. 4 (2016).

ons, though by no means the most destructive. Echoing a sentiment incessantly repeated in Islamic State propaganda, Adnani argues that information—the battle of hearts and minds—is the theatre that represents the heart of this war for *both* sides of the conflict. It is perhaps unsurprising that he points to the coalition's 'mobilization of every evil scholar' and 'use of every form of media' as powerful tools of war. It is here that he unequivocally establishes why the Islamic State fights and it is, naturally, in stark contrast to what he suggests are the motivations of the West:

> We do not wage jihad to defend a land, nor to liberate it, or to control it. We do not fight for authority or transient, shabby positions, nor for the rubble of a lowly, vanishing world. If our goal were one of these heaps of debris, we would not have fought the world with all its sects, creeds, and peoples. If we were able to avert a single fighter from fighting us, we would do so, saving ourselves the trouble.

This is not to say that he dismisses tangible indicators altogether. Adnani continually makes arguments that frame the Islamic State's use of violence as not only defensive but motivated by what could be interpreted as Islamic State's own 'Responsibility to Protect' (R2P) mandate.[5] Adnani would use R2P and the principle of reciprocity to justify attacks on civilians in the West, 'as their warplanes do not distinguish between one who is armed and another who is unarmed, nor between a man and a woman'. Indeed, he concludes his speech with a specific call to Muslims living in the West, again positioning them as operatives with a unique vantage point behind enemy lines. In stark contrast to earlier speeches that called for supporters to travel to Islamic State lands, Adnani frames engagement in 'just terror' as an imperative for Western supporters, reflecting a strategic pivot, both politico-militarily and in terms of propaganda activities, braced for the coming decline.[6]

---

[5] Ingram, Haroro, 'Jihadist "Responsibility to Protect" Appeals: Propaganda wars for the moral high ground', International Centre for Counter-Terrorism—The Hague (14 March 2019).

[6] For analyses of Islamic State directed and inspired activities in the West, see Vidino, Lorenzo, and Seamus Hughes, 'ISIS in America: From retweets to Raqqa', Program on Extremism, 2015; Nesser, Petter, Anne Stenersen, and Emilie Oftedal, 'Jihadi Terrorism in Europe: The IS-Effect', *Perspectives on Terrorism* 10/6 (2016); and Vidino, Francesco Marone, and Eva Entenmann, 'Fear Thy Neighbor: Radicalization and Jihadist Attacks in the West', ICCT, ISPI and Program on Extremism, 2017.

The Islamic State's Freefall

In hindsight, Adnani's speech represented a recognition from within the Islamic State that, by the middle of 2016, its leadership saw the writing on the wall. In the aftermath of the address, the military and intelligence pressures grew and fissures appeared within the Islamic State's politico-military and propaganda campaigns. What followed was a period of rapid territorial decline. This was manifest in more than just the loss of the land and havens from which it applied its governance initiatives, but also the loss of human capacity and revenue as it was displaced from populations formerly under its control. This had a quantitative and qualitative impact on the Islamic State's propaganda output,[7] and the apparatus suffered perhaps its most devastating blow yet with the deaths of Abu Muhammad al-Furqan and Adnani, respectively the mastermind and the master spokesperson of its propaganda efforts.[8] With its territorial losses and the faltering of its propaganda apparatus, it was tempting for some to suggest that the Islamic State was finished as a movement or, equally absurd, that it would somehow retreat online to buy time before rising again. In September 2016, however, its propaganda machine seemingly kicked back into gear with the release of a new flagship magazine *Rumiyah* (Rome), concentrating its various linguistic offerings in one format.[9] Drawing heavily on content from *al-Naba* to fill its pages, *Rumiyah* was published in a variety of languages with content in each issue tailored specifically for the linguistic audience being targeted. Rather than disappear completely or continue unsustainably, it seemed that the Islamic State's propaganda machine, in the aftermath of devastating strikes against its personnel, resources, and logistical networks, was streamlining.[10] As it had done before,

---

[7] Winter, Charlie, and Ingram, Haroro, 'Terror, Online and off: Recent trends in Islamic State propaganda outputs', *War on the Rocks*, 2 Mar. 2018.

[8] Wright, Robin, 'Abu Muhammad Al-Adnani, the voice of ISIS, is dead', *The New Yorker*, 2016, https://www.newyorker.com/news/news-desk/abu-muhammad-al-adnani-the-voice-of-isis-is-dead last accessed 18 December 2018.

[9] For an analysis of Islamic State's English-language magazines see Ingram, Haroro, 'Islamic State's English-language magazines, 2014–17: Trends & Implications for CT-CVE strategic communications', International Centre for Counter-Terrorism (The Hague), March 2018; Mahlouly, Dounia, and Charlie Winter, 'A tale of two caliphates: Comparing the Islamic State's internal and external messaging priorities', *Vox-Pol* (2018); and Ingram, Haroro, 'An analysis of *Dabiq*', *Australian Journal of Political Science* 51, no. 3 (2016).

[10] See Milton, Daniel, 'Down, but not out: An updated examination of the Islamic

the movement had now started to transition down the phases of its campaign strategy, increasingly reverting to guerrilla warfare and terrorism as it was routed from its urban strongholds and, at least in Iraq and Syria, back to the deserts, as Adnani had predicted. And, as before, its war was far from over—it was merely adapting.[11]

State's visual propaganda', *Combating Terrorism Center at West Point*, July 2018, https://ctc.usma.edu/app/uploads/2018/07/Down-But-Not-Out.pdf last accessed 18 December 2018.

[11] For a timeline of the Islamic State's fortunes throughout its history see Wilson Center, 'Timeline: the rise, spread, and fall of the Islamic State', 30 April 2019, https://www.wilsoncenter.org/article/timeline-the-rise-spread-and-fall-the-islamic-state 20 July 2019.

13

PATIENCE

After four years of intense, unrelenting pressure from the anti-Islamic State coalition and a variety of local actors across the Middle East and North Africa, by 2018, the movement was a hollowed-out shell of what it had been at the peak of its second resurgence. It now held only 2 per cent of the territory it controlled at its high point, and it was in this context that, after a year of silence, Baghdadi delivered the hour-long address 'And Give Glad Tidings to Those Who Are Patient' (21 August 2018), which features in this chapter. It is useful to contrast this speech with those from 2014 appearing in earlier chapters. The mood here is considerably darker, as Baghdadi seeks to persuade his movement to remain patient, committed, and unified during this time of 'purification'—the caliph reminds his audience that it is only during periods of tribulation that the true believers are separated from the pretenders so that the seeds of resurgence can be sown again. As evidence, he points to historical precedent and divine promise, assuring his listeners that only unwavering commitment to the movement's manhaj (method) *guarantees survival and, eventually, success. Here is the caliph calling for patience, not panic, from the rubble of his supposed caliphate.*[1]

---

[1] The excerpt featured in this chapter is taken from an official Islamic State translation. The source contained text in both rounded and square brackets. The authors have made minimal edits to the text.

13a. 'And Give Glad Tidings to Those Who Are Patient', 21 August 2019
Amirul-Muminin Shaykh Abu Bakr al-Baghdadi
Al-Hayat Media Centre Translation

...And so here before us are the deceptive years, as the dark night of tribulation, hardship, and suffering has increased in severity and engulfed the Muslims with its sorrow. After many centuries of the noble era had come to an end—an era that radiated among mankind with the da'wah of Islam and its rule in the land, with the Muslims being the masters of the dunya, as they were a people of strength, resolve, and defiance who, through their deeds of sacrifice, would record feats that would not be forgotten, and through their deeds of bravery and daringness, would record amazing tales—here we find them today in the books of loss and fragmentation, being torn to pieces by whims and desires, with the Christians tampering with their religion, and the nations of kufr roaming their lands after having usurped them and fenced them between borders of shame and humiliation. And the truthful muwahhidin have become sacrificial offerings which—from time to time—the tawaghit and their puppets offer to the grandsons of monkeys and pigs as a renewal of their pledge of obedience to them and a declaration of their allegiance to them. And any reasonable onlooker would now see nothing but a religion that has been put to loss, sanctities that have been rendered permissible to violate, and people refraining from speaking or listening to the truth and having fear of openly declaring the truth before mankind.

Thus, the deeds of this ummah came to resemble the deeds of those nations that had preceded it, deeds which its Lord had warned it against in His Book, and its scholars closely resembled their scholars. So the various forms of Jahiliyyah became many in our era, their evil became exacerbated, and their partisans gained dominance and became tyrannical. Indeed, these diseases present in the Ummah's body are a sure means of attracting disaster and misfortune, exacerbating distress and adversity, and enabling the enemy's dominance, and the Muslims will not find relief except by repenting truthfully, and returning and submitting to the Creator, and through the adherence to His commands and prohibitions by actualizing tawhid, forsaking shirk, and preventing any means that can lead to shirk. And likewise, by adhering to the Book of Allah and the Sunnah of His Messenger, and by clinging to them through knowledge and deed, and through reflection and understanding, like the understanding of the predecessors of this ummah, the noble Sahabah, and those who followed them in goodness. In this, there is success and salvation in the two abodes (that is, the dunya and the Hereafter).

Our Lord has clarified that the Book and the Sunnah are a means of protection from kufr and division for those who hold onto them. He says:

> And how could you disbelieve while the verses of Allah are being recited to you and among you is His Messenger? And whoever holds firmly to Allah has indeed been guided to a straight path. O you who have believed, fear Allah as He should be feared and do not die except as Muslims [in submission to Him]. And hold firmly to the rope of Allah altogether and do not become divided. And remember Allah's favor upon you—when you were enemies and He brought your hearts together and you became, by His favor, brothers. And you were on the edge of a pit of the Fire, and He saved you from it. Thus does Allah make clear to you His ayat that you may be guided (al 'Imran 101–103).

And our Lord forbade us and warned us against differing and becoming divided, saying, 'And do not be like the ones who became divided and differed after the clear proofs had come to them. And those will have a great punishment' (al 'Imran 105).

And in an authentic hadith, Abu Hurayrah narrated, saying:

> The Prophet said, 'Indeed, Allah is pleased with three things for you and He dislikes three things for you. He is pleased for you that you worship Him and do not ascribe partners to Him, and that you hold firmly to the rope of Allah altogether, and that you not become divided. And He dislikes for you [engaging in] gossip, asking too many questions, and squandering wealth.'

O Muslims, we are passing through days from among the days of Allah during which He distinguishes the evil from the good and the truthful from the liars, and likewise distinguishes the false claimants. And the sons of Islam in the Khilafah State, by Allah's grace, continue to make a firm stand, disavowing their own ability and strength and relying on their Lord, in the face of the alliances of kufr, which include Crusaders, Jews, atheists, murtaddin, and Majus. They have broken their sheaths, saddled their steeds, set up ambushes for their enemies, and lied in wait in every place of ambush. They did not listen to the criticism of any coward exhausted by a difficult lifestyle, the harsh nature of the path, and the intensity of its horrors, and they did not abandon that methodology they were pleased with. They followed it out of obedience to Allah while having certainty that this matter would lead to blood being spilled and the enemy viciously mobilizing against them, and to immense tribulation, including imprisonment, injury, and loss of limbs, and that its outcome would be conquest and consolidation—with Allah's permission—for the pious, muwahhid slaves of Allah. Our Lord, the Wise and Acquainted, says:

> Allah has promised those who have believed among you and done righteous deeds that He will surely grant them succession [to authority] upon the earth

just as He granted it to those before them and that He will surely establish for them [therein] their religion which He has preferred for them and that He will surely substitute for them, after their fear, security, [for] they worship Me, not associating anything with Me. But whoever disbelieves after that—then those are the defiantly disobedient (An-Nur 55).

And He informed us that the sifting of the believers' ranks would inevitably occur, saying: 'Or do you think that you will enter Jannah while such [trial] has not yet come to you as came to those who passed on before you? They were touched by poverty and hardship and were shaken until [even their] messenger and those who believed with him said, "When is the help of Allah [coming]?" Unquestionably, the help of Allah is near' (al-Baqarah 214). He also says, 'And We will surely test you with something of fear and hunger and a loss of wealth and lives and fruits, but give good tidings to the patient, who, when disaster strikes them, say, "Indeed we belong to Allah, and indeed to Him we will return." Those are the ones upon whom are blessings and mercy from their Lord. And it is those who are the [rightly] guided' (al-Baqarah 155–157). He also says, 'Or do you think that you will enter Jannah while Allah has not yet made evident those of you who fight in His cause and made evident those who are patient?' (al 'Imran 142).

He also says, 'And We will surely test you until We make evident those who strive among you [for the cause of Allah] and those who are patient, and We will test your affairs' (Muhammad 31). In his interpretation of this ayah, Imam at-Tabari states:

> [Allah says], 'We will surely test you,' O believers, with killing, and with jihad against the enemies of Allah, 'until We make evident those who strive among you,' meaning, 'Until My party and allies—those who wage jihad for the cause of Allah—among you, and those who are patient upon fighting His enemies know [this] and it becomes evident to them, and [until] those among you with knowledge of His religion are made apparent from those who have doubt and confusion regarding it, and the believers [are made apparent] from the munafiqin, and We will test your affairs and will then make evident the truthful among you from the liars.'

This marks the end of his words—may Allah have mercy on him.

Indeed, the scales of victory and defeat with the mujahidin—the people of iman and taqwa—are not based on the loss of a town or city, nor do they yield to what the creation possesses of advanced air power, missiles, or smart bombs, or their multitudes of followers and supporters, for the earth belongs to Allah and He causes whomever He wills to inherit it, and He supports whomever He wills. There is nothing except that our Lord has the grasp of its forelock, and most people will not believe, even if every believing, mujahid caller [to Allah] were to eagerly strive [to call them to faith].

Rather, both sides of these scales only yield to what the slave of Allah possesses of conviction in the promise of his Lord, [what he possesses] of steadfastness upon his tawhid and iman, his genuine desire to fight the enemies of the religion, and his refraining from turning back or retreating from that. So it is with this that the believers weigh the changes in any situations. If they abandon their religion, their patience, their jihad against their enemy, and their certainty in the promise of their Creator, they are defeated and humiliated. And if they hold firmly to it, they will attain honor and be victorious, even if after some time, for indeed, the final outcome is for the righteous.

So there is no path to bring honor to this religion after believing in Allah and singling Him out with worship except through waging battle, and through the love of attaining shahadah on His path, and by disgracing His criminal, disbelieving enemies everywhere. With this, the religion is established and given victory. And our Lord the Wise and Acquainted, at times bestows victory upon His believing slaves, and at times He tries them, deprives them of this blessing, and makes them taste tribulation due to certain wisdoms that He knows and has decreed.

Ibnul-Qayyim enumerated some of these wisdoms. He states, 'Among them is that the truthful believer is distinguished from the lying munafiq, for when Allah made the Muslims manifest over their enemies on the day of Badr and their reputation increased, there entered with them into Islam outwardly those who were not with them in Islam inwardly, so the wisdom of Allah required that He bring about a trial for His slaves that would distinguish between the believer and the munafiq. So the munafiqin raised their heads in this battle—meaning Uhud—and uttered that which they had been concealing, and their insinuations now became explicit statements, and the people became clearly divided into disbelievers, believers, and munafiqin, and the believers became aware that they had an enemy within their own house who would always be present with them, so they prepared and took precautions against them.

'And among [these wisdoms] is that if Allah were to always give victory to the believers over their enemies everywhere and always grant them consolidation and domination over their enemies, their souls would have transgressed and become arrogant. If He were to always grant them victory, they would be in the same condition that they would be in if He were to grant them a tremendous amount of rizq (wealth and sustenance). But nothing makes His slaves upright other than going through ease and difficulty, and comfort and hardship, and scarcity and abundance. So He is the one who manages the affairs of His slaves in accordance with His Wisdom. Indeed, He is Acquainted and Seeing of them.

'And among [these wisdoms] is that He prompts forth the servitude of His allies and His party both in ease and in hardship, and both with regards to that which they love and that which they dislike, and both when they are victorious and when their enemies are victorious over them. So if they are steadfast upon obedience and servitude concerning that which they love as well as that which they dislike, they are truly His slaves, unlike those who worship Allah on one edge, such as in times of ease, blessings, and health.

'And among [these wisdoms] is that when He tries them with being overcome, broken, and defeated, they become humbled and low, and are in need of honor and victory from Him, and victory only comes following humiliation and defeat. Allah says, "And already had Allah given you victory at [the battle of] Badr while you were lowly" (al 'Imran 123). He also says, "And on the day of Hunayn, when your great numbers pleased you, but they did not avail you at all" (At-Tawbah 25). So when He wants to bring honor to His slave, mend him, and grant him victory, He first breaks him, and His mending of him, His breaking of him, and His support [of him] are proportional to his humiliation and defeat.

'And among [these wisdoms] is that souls become hasty and tyrannical when they enjoy constant health, victory, and prosperity, and this is an illness that hinders them from being serious in their journey to Allah and to the abode of the Hereafter. So when their Lord, Owner, and Giver of Mercy wants dignity for them, He puts forth for them trials and tribulations that will be a cure for that illness that obstructs them from eagerly proceeding towards Him, and that trial and tribulation becomes like a doctor who gives a patient some bitter medicine to drink and cuts from him a painful vein in order to remove the disease from him. And if he were to leave him, the disease would overcome him until it had resulted in his death.

'And among [these wisdoms] is that shahadah is one of the highest of ranks with Allah. The shuhada are those who are special to Him, and they are those of His slaves who are brought closer to Him, and shahadah is the rank that immediately follows the rank of siddiqiyyah. He loves to take from among His slaves shuhada. Their blood is spilled for the sake of attaining His love and His pleasure, and they give preference to His pleasure and His love over their lives. There is no path to attaining this rank except by recognizing the means that lead to it, such as the enemy gaining dominance.' This marks the end of his words—may Allah have mercy on him.

Therefore, O muwahhid mujahidin guarding the frontiers, O sons of Islam and carriers of its banner in the era of estrangement, take the Book with strength, grasp the hot coals of sacrifice, and follow in the footsteps of the Messengers, the Prophets, and the siddiqin, 'those who convey the messages of Allah and fear Him, and do not fear anyone but Allah. And sufficient is Allah as a Reckoner' (al-Ahzab 39). Indeed, our Lord has brought us from their stories in His Noble Book that which contains a reminder, and He mentioned to us the condition of their peoples, as well as their statements, as a means of consoling all who tread the path of those whom Allah has guided, so that they may take guidance from them and hold onto that which they held onto. So we find the Noble Messenger, the Prophet of massacre and mercy, teaching his ummah and leaving for the following generations books filled with [the records of his] efforts and sacrifices so that those after him would follow his example and tread his righteous path, the straight path of Allah. His face was split open and his incisor was broken, his uncle, companions, and loved ones were killed, he was harmed by the slanderers [who slandered his wife, 'Aishah], he and his noble companions suffered hunger and hardship until they were severely shaken, and throughout his life and his da'wah they were afflicted with a degree of anguish and adversity that Allah had fixed and decreed for the people of iman and taqwa. In his Sahih, al-Bukhari reports that al-Khabbab Ibn al-Aratt narrated, saying:

> We complained to Allah's Messenger as he was reclining on his cloak in the shade of the Ka'bah. We said, 'Will you not seek aid for us? Will you not make du'a for us?' So he said, 'Indeed, [with regards to] those who came before you, a man would be taken and a hole would be dug for him in the ground and he would be placed in it, and a saw would be brought and placed on his head and he would be cut into two halves. And that which was on his bone and flesh would be combed with rakes of metal, but that would not turn him away from his religion. By Allah, this matter will surely be fulfilled, to the point that a rider would travel from San'a to Hadramawt not fearing anyone but Allah, and the wolves [he fears] for his sheep, but you are being hasty.'

The author of Madarij (i.e., Ibnul-Qayyim) states:

> When it became the case that the one seeking the straight path is pursuing a matter that most people turn away from and wants to tread a path upon which his companions would be of the utmost scarcity in numbers and might, and that people naturally feel lonely when isolated and desire the entertainment of a companion, Allah brought attention to the companions of [those who tread]

this path, and that they are those 'whom Allah has bestowed favor upon, of the prophets, the siddiqin (steadfast affirmers of truth), the shuhada, and the righteous. And excellent are those as companions.' Thus, He attributed the path to the companions of those treading it—and they are those whom Allah has bestowed favor upon—in order to remove from the one seeking the truth and seeking to tread the path the feeling of being isolated from the people of his era and from his own people, and so that he would know that his companions on this path are those whom Allah has bestowed favor upon and, therefore, would pay no attention to the opposition he faces from those who've turned away from it, as they are the ones who are diminished in status, even if they are greater in number, as was stated by some of the salaf [who said], 'Follow the path of truth, and do not feel lonely due to the small numbers of those treading it, and beware the path of falsehood, and do not be deceived by the multitudes of those who are ruined.' And whenever you feel isolated in your loneliness, look to those companions who have preceded you and be eager to catch up to them, and turn your gaze away from those other than them, for they will not avail you of anything before Allah. And if they call out to you as you are proceeding on your path, do not turn towards them, for should you turn towards them they will take you and obstruct you.

This marks the end of his words.

So congratulations to every individual following in the footsteps of those whom Allah has bestowed favor upon, being met with that which they were met with, and being patient just as they were patient, until he arrives at the pool (i.e. Kawthar), not having altered or changed.

Abul-Wafa Ibn 'Aqil states, 'If you wish to know where Islam [really] lies in relation to the people of any era, then do not look to their crowding at the doors of the masajid, nor to their loud proclamations of "Labbayk" at the mawqif (i.e., 'Arafah). Rather, look to their concurrence with the enemies of the Shari'ah.'

The imam of the Najdi da'wah states:

So can the religion be fulfilled, the banner of jihad be upheld, or the enjoinment of good and the forbiddance of evil be established except by loving for the sake of Allah, hating for the sake of Allah, having enmity for the sake of Allah, and having allegiance for the sake of Allah? And if the people were to agree on one way, and on having love without any enmity or hatred, there would be no furqan (means of separation) between truth and falsehood, nor between a believer and a disbeliever, nor between the allies of Ar-Rahman (the Most Merciful) and the allies of the Shaytan.

O Muslims, the Crusaders—and at their forefront, America—thought that this ummah was like a fragile, premature infant and had no descendants that ought to be feared in this era, and they believed that by destroying crops and cattle in their war against the Muslims they could ruin the hopes that glowed within the breasts of the mujahidin. But if one seeking plain facts were to examine the situation, he would realize what had become of America, the protector of the Cross, after she had entered the arena of direct combat with the sons of Islam for close to two decades. Here we find her, by Allah's grace, living the worst phase she has passed through in her modern history, as is being openly declared by her leaders, and [living] a condition that permits for her eradication to occur, with Allah's permission. She no longer even conceals her frustration over the tremendous amount of wealth she spent, and from which she gained nothing but regret. For with the spread of jihad, and with her fervent endeavor to curb it and stop it from spreading further, she is only bled faster in a state of misery as she suffers two matters that are even more bitter. And the sanctions she is imposing on her allies and is droning on about today—as is the case in the Turkish affair—and her demand for the release of the Crusader priest, and her demand being met with rejection, and the Russians and Iranians rebelling and not acquiescing to the sanctions that she dictates against them, and even North Korea exhibiting that she won't comply and describing America's approach as being akin to gangster politics—all this is a sign of regression and decline from her previous position, and a deliberate show of contempt from her allies due to the weakness they see in her. And indeed, her loss of intimidation and her weakness is due first to Allah and then to the mujahidin. And there is no consideration given to her haughtiness and to what she rants about, such as her alleged victory in having driven the Islamic State out of the cities and countrysides of Iraq and Sham, for Allah's earth is vast, war is competition (that is, victory alternates between both warring parties), and the battle has not come to an end.

...Do not be terrified or deceived by the multitudes of those who've relapsed, or those who dissent or discourage others. Adhere to the Jama'ah and beware of differing with your leaders. Let each man among you guard his front and let not Islam be attacked from your direction. So the doctor, media specialist, judge, preacher, accountant, security agent, and administrative specialist are all in jihad, and each one of them is persevering and remaining patient. He fulfills his duty regardless of the role he is given. And beware of those who seek to incite between you and your leaders, and to create hatred and revive slogans of Jahiliyyah among you. Hold firmly to the advice of your prophet, who said:

> And I order you with [adherence to] five matters that Allah has commanded me with; The Jama'ah, listening, obeying, hijrah, and jihad for the cause of Allah, for indeed, he who splits off from the Jama'ah so much as a hand span has removed

the collar of Islam from his neck until he returns, and he who calls out slogans of Jahiliyyah is indeed from the people of Hell.

They said, 'O Messenger of Allah, even if he fasts, and even if he prays?' He said, 'Even if he fasts, and even if he prays and claims that he is a Muslim. Therefore, call the Muslims with their names—with that which Allah has named them; Muslims, believers, and slaves of Allah.'

And rejoice over Allah's guardianship over you and His support for you even if there are few who give you aid and support, for it is reported in Sahih Muslim that the Prophet said, 'There will not cease to be a group from my ummah fighting upon the command of Allah, subduing their enemies, and not being harmed by those who oppose them until the [Final] Hour comes to them and they are upon that [affair].'

O soldiers of Islam and sons of the Khilafah in Sham, in Barakah, Dimashq, Raqqah, Khayr, Idlib, and Halab, have trust in the promise and support of Allah, hold firmly to His strong rope, and be worshipers at night and warriors during the day. Furthermore, rejoice and hope for good, for indeed, with hardship there is relief, and one portion of difficulty will not overcome two portions of ease. Indeed, the grandsons of Abu Basir and Muhammad Ibn Maslamah (i.e., the lone mujahidin) have pounced and have made the Crusaders, the criminal atheists, the Nusayriyyah, and the Sahwat of apostasy all taste a portion of the muwahhidin's might. So the battle between us and them has had its fire reignited, and its flames will continue to intensify and they will not be able to handle it, with Allah's permission. The Crusaders enticed the Nusayriyyah and the atheist Kurds and hurled them into the fires of a vicious war that will completely consume them, and they thought that they had confined the Islamic State to the town of Hajin and its surroundings, but it is contrary to what they think, and with Allah's ability and strength, they will not enjoy a single hand span of territory in the land of Sham. The Islamic State is not confined to Hajin, for the sons of the Sunnah are warriors who do not sleep in the face of injustice. Their souls refuse to live a life of humiliation and lowliness, for the era of subjugating the Muslims, devaluing their blood, and abusing their remains without any deterrent has come to an end. The era of shackling and enslaving [the Muslims] has come to an end, and the coming days are brimming with that which will harm the enemies of the religion and make their lives bitter.

Therefore, O armies of Iraq, O people of perseverance, it was in your land that the spark was lit, so launch one raid after another, and beware of luxury and comfort. Make every effort to unify your ranks, and prepare battalions that will charge headlong towards death. Make the lives of the Rafidah and murtaddin bitter, and annihilate them completely. Show Allah from yourselves that which is good, out of revenge for the religion and in support of those oppressed in the prisons of the Safawiyyin and murtaddin. By Allah, we have not forgotten you, O our imprisoned brothers and sisters. You have a tremendous right upon us, and we will not spare any effort to rescue you, so be patient and steadfast, turn to your Lord and Creator with much du'a, be urging with what you request, and ask Him to grant your brothers victory and facilitate relief for you that comes quickly. Draw on the sweetness of conviction to help you persevere over the bitterness of pain, and draw on the remembrance of Allah and the companionship of His Book—by memorizing it, pondering over it, and acquiring an understanding of it—to help you persevere over your loneliness, for these are the provisions of the muttaqin. And that day will surely come when you take revenge on those who torture you. You have a right upon us that you see from your brothers that which heals your breasts and mends the wounds in your hearts, with Allah's permission, for there is no good in a life in which Ahlus-Sunnah are humiliated, their sanctities are violated, and we continue to sit and weep like women, and as such, the filthy Rafidah will not see from us anything but harshness and might.

And as for you, O supporters of the Khilafah everywhere, in the media realm and on the battlefield, we give you glad tidings that the Islamic State is in the best of conditions, because it hopes for that which is with Allah, and what is with Allah is better and more lasting. Do not be alarmed by the campaign of intentional disinformation and defamation to which the enemies of Allah have devoted centers, committees, and significant numbers of trolls. Beware, O lions of information and warriors of media, of taking news from any source other than the Central Media of the Islamic State. Renew your covenants, make further sacrifices, and divert [the disbelievers] away from fighting the Islamic State, for indeed, the battle today is in your arena and you've been spared from all others, and your brothers are busy at work, so deter others from them and be a means of aid and support for them.

And we congratulate the fierce lions in the lands of the Cross—Canada, Europe, and elsewhere—on their noble deeds in support of their brothers. May Allah bless your endeavors and accept your tremendous heroism. Proceed and follow in their footsteps, O supporters of the Khilafah. Make whatever preparations are easy for you, place your trust in the Most High and Capable, select your targets, and carry out a strike that will tear out their hearts and make them lose their minds, for a piercing bullet, or a stab deep in the intestines, or the detonation of an explosive device in your lands is akin to a thousand operations here with us. So equip yourselves for your war, and ignite its fires so that its flames may consume the Crusaders and the murtaddin.

And during these numbered days [of Eid], I remind you, O soldiers of the Khilafah and its supporters, to revive the example set forth with the killing of Ja'd Ibn Dirham by slaughtering every secularist, atheist, and murtadd who wages war against Allah and His Messenger—and may Allah accept your slaughter.

Our Lord, forgive us our sins and the excess [committed] in our affairs, plant firmly our feet, and give us victory over the disbelieving people. And Allah prevails in His affair, but most people do not know. May Allah's blessings and peace be upon our prophet, Muhammad. And our final declaration is, 'All praise is due to Allah, the Lord of the creation.'

13b. Analysis

In 'A message to the *Mujahidin* and Muslim *Ummah* in the Month of Ramadan', in July 2014 Baghdadi declared: 'O Muslims everywhere, glad tidings to you and expect good. Raise your head high, for today—by Allah's grace—you have a state and khilāfah, which will return your dignity, might, rights, and leadership.' This stands in stark contrast to his August 2018 declaration, in which he proclaimed: '…And so here before us are the deceptive years, as the dark night of tribulation, hardship, and suffering has increased in severity and engulfed the Muslims with its sorrow.' The mood and themes of the 2018 speech reflect the harsh realities of the predicament facing the Islamic State.[2] As caliph, Baghdadi had presided over the movement's greatest achievements through the period of 2014–15, but now he stood at the helm as it slid into a steep, multi-year decline.[3]

A Well-Worn Path for Survival…

To rally the Islamic State movement in the aftermath of yet another boom-bust period, Baghdadi threads four themes through his speech: patience,

[2] Callimachi, Rukmini, 'ISIS leader Baghdadi resurfaces in recording', *The New York Times*, 22 August 2018, https://www.nytimes.com/2018/08/22/world/middleeast/isis-leader-baghdadi-recording.html last accessed online 30 June 2019.

[3] BBC News, 'Islamic State and the crisis in Iraq and Syria in maps', *BBC News*, 28 Mar. 2018, https://www.bbc.com/news/world-middle-east-27838034

purification, commitment, and coherence. The Islamic State movement's propagandists typically frame the boom-bust dynamic that characterises its history ('But nothing makes His slaves upright other than going through ease and difficulty, and comfort and hardship, and scarcity and abundance') as a testament to an unwavering commitment to its *manhaj*, regardless of ultimately superficial metrics of success like territory, lives, and resources. At the forefront of Baghdadi's speech is the notion that periods of bust are not only strategically important, but they are legitimised as divinely-ordained periods for much-needed purification, from which only the truest of believers emerge. In this time of most acute crisis, Baghdadi positions the Islamic State's heroic struggle within a broader cosmic context of the war between good and evil:

> O Muslims, we are passing through days from among the days of Allah during which He distinguishes the evil from the good and the truthful from the liars, and likewise distinguishes the false claimants. And the sons of Islam in the Khilafah State, by Allah's grace, continue to make a firm stand, disavowing their own ability and strength and relying on their Lord, in the face of the alliances of kufr.... They did not listen to the criticism of any coward exhausted by a difficult lifestyle, the harsh nature of the path, and the intensity of its horrors, and they did not abandon that methodology they were pleased with.

For the caliph, history offers precedence for not only the importance of hardship as a purifier of the faith and the faithful ('...trial and tribulation becomes like a doctor who gives a patient some bitter medicine to drink and cuts from him a painful vein in order to remove the disease from him') but a wellspring of examples, suggesting how to revive the *umma*'s fortunes. Naturally, the Prophet Muhammad is presented as the exemplar: 'So we find the Noble Messenger, the Prophet of massacre and mercy, teaching his ummah and leaving for the following generations books filled with [the records of his] efforts and sacrifices so that those after him would follow his example and tread his righteous path....' Midway through the speech, Baghdadi also uses history to remind his audience that, despite his movement's present predicament, two decades of war against the US ('the protector of the Cross') had resulted in a significantly weakened global superpower with diminished standing in the world. Patience is thus framed as not only a religious virtue but a pragmatic necessity for weathering short-term losses for the sake of longer-term success. Of course, the latter is achieved via commitment to the movement's *manhaj*.

Baghdadi devotes much of the second half of his speech to addressing specific communities around the world, and it is in these passages that he seeks to tackle the issue of sustaining coherent efforts—a significant problem for any global movement but especially one under intense strain. During times of triumph this was a comparatively easier task, as the Islamic State's chains of command were able to exert necessary influence across its areas of operations and its politico-military successes served as evidence that its strategy, vaunted by its propaganda machine, was effective. Now, with its leadership and mid-level bureaucracy devastated by military strikes, mounting losses in the field,[4] and a significantly diminished propaganda apparatus,[5] it became increasingly clear to the public that the Islamic State was struggling to maintain coherence across the movement.[6] One issue of particular concern to the group, which Baghdadi's speech addresses, was actions carried out by supporters without formal links to the Islamic State, who acted as amplifiers and even creators of propaganda. The caliph directs a warning to the movement's followers about 'the campaign of intentional disinformation and defamation' and the pitfalls of 'taking news from any source other than the Central media of the Islamic State'. The fact this issue is highlighted by Baghdadi himself is a testament to its strategic importance to the movement and is symbolic of the group's strug-

---

[4] Milton, and Muhammad al-'Ubaydi, 'The fight goes on: The Islamic State's continuing military efforts in liberated cities', Combating Terrorism Center: West Point, 28 June 2017.

[5] West Point's Combating Terrorism Center released a series of in-depth research reports based on captured documents and other primary source materials that provide detailed insights into Islamic State military, governance and propaganda departments during this period of decline. For example, see Dodwell, Brian, Daniel Milton, and Don Rassler, 'Then and Now: Comparing the flow of Foreign Fighters to AQI and the Islamic State', Combating Terrorism Center: West Point, 8 Dec. 2016; Milton, 'Communication Breakdown: Unravelling the Islamic State's Media Efforts', Combatting Terrorism Center: West Point, 10 Oct. 2016; Milton, and Muhammad al-'Ubaydi, 'The fight goes on: The Islamic State's continuing military efforts in liberated cities', Combating Terrorism Center: West Point, 28 June 2017; Milton, 'Pulling back the curtain: An inside look at the Islamic State's media organization', Combating Terrorism Center: West Point, 28 Aug. 2019; Almohammad, Asaad and Charlie Winter, 'From battlefront to cyberspace: Demystifying the Islamic State's propaganda machine', Combating Terrorism Center: West Point, 5 June 2019.

[6] For an in-depth analysis of the organisational characteristics of the Islamic State's media apparatus see Almohammad, Asaad, & Winter, Charlie, 'From battlefront to cyberspace: Demystifying the Islamic State's propaganda machine', Combating Terrorism Center at West Point, 5 June 2019.

gle to maintain coherence in its effort. Indeed, in the weeks following the speech, *al-Naba* magazine provided guidance to Islamic State followers on how to avoid succumbing to disinformation.[7]

...And Revival

Baghdadi is careful to paint a picture that is much more upbeat than the reality, in vague enough terms to avoid him sounding out of touch.[8] The entire speech, delivered during a bust period so similar to that of 2007–8, evokes striking parallels between this speech and Abu Umar al-Baghdadi's speech from 2007 that celebrated the fourth year of *jihad* in Iraq (see Chapter 3). Abu Umar talking about the health of the group was either him being deliberately deceptive at the time, or the speech was delivered before the bottom fell out of the then new Islamic State of Iraq. Baghdadi seems to have learned from his predecessor in this regard. His 2018 speech was designed to address a global audience and offer a more sophisticated defence of Islamic State strategy to its supporters around the world. These supporters are told to continue to rely on Islamic State media's interpretation of events, maintaining the practice of forsaking Western news in favour of the voice of the caliphate. Interestingly, Baghdadi carefully points to where the military focus of the group will be: as before, it was to be in Iraq, where the 'spark was lit'. Despite the more global approach, in light of new affiliates around the world to attend to, the local focus on Iraq will not change. The caliph's attempt to justify the ambitious new strategy to his audience, despite these obvious contradictions between past and present, local and global, is not unsurprising for a group that managed to achieve what had been considered impossible before 2014.

To sell his message of resilience in the face of an even more devastating defeat than the group's 2007–8 decline, Baghdadi followed his precedessor Abu Umar's lead regarding communications during a strategic downturn, centring his speech on the woes of the great enemy—the US. He gives considerable attention to the decline of US global influence, and the ways in which its hegemony was being tested in Asia, Europe, and the Middle East. In doing

---

[7] BBC Monitoring, 'Islamic State gives tips to supporters about online behavior', *BBC Monitoring*, 6 Sept. 2018, https://monitoring.bbc.co.uk/product/c2006ylx

[8] Wilson Center, 'Timeline: the rise, spread, and fall of the Islamic State', 30 April 2019, https://www.wilsoncenter.org/article/timeline-the-rise-spread-and-fall-the-islamic-state last accessed 20 July 2019.

so, he underpinned his point that continued resistance against the US is not only feasible, but eventually will lead to victory. What was most helpful to Baghdadi, however, was the small kernel of truth he relied on, so necessary for propaganda to ring true in the ears of supporters: his observation that the Islamic State movement had been defeated before and rose back from irrelevance. He just had to convince supporters and fighters alike that it would happen again.

14

A GLOBAL INSURGENCY

The release of statements by Islamic State's senior leaders entails an extraordinary amount of risk for the individuals involved and the organisation more broadly. The strategic calculus that must occur within the group's ranks weighs the potential benefits of senior leaders acting as messengers at a given strategic moment against the risks. Of course, the risks vary, depending on the form the propaganda takes, with a written statement being potentially less risky than an audio statement. The greatest risk is associated with an audio-visual release, in which the slightest over-sight could have catastrophic consequences. In 2019, two of Islamic State's most senior figures would step forward to deliver statements that sought to reshape how strategic conditions were perceived by the Islamic State's friends and enemies, while also boosting morale amongst its supporters. Their overarching message was simple: stay the course, our movement has been here before, and we will rise again.

The excerpt featured in this chapter is from an official translation of an audio statement mde by Islamic State's spokesperson Abul Hasan al-Muhajir, titled 'He Was True to Allah and Allah Was True to Him', released 18 March 2019.[1] The excerpt features the second half of Muhajir's address, beginning with him mocking the contradictory statements of anti-Islamic State coalition officials. The similarities between Muhajir's statement and Adnani's speeches in structure, theme, and argumentation contribute to a sense of consistency in message that contrasts with

---

[1] The excerpts featured in this chapter are taken from official Islamic State translations. The sources contained text in both rounded and square brackets. The authors have made minimal edits to the text.

the often confused messages emanating from its Western rivals. Muhajir then ties together events on opposite ends of the earth, weaving them into an emotionally compelling narrative, one in which the slaughter of Muslims in Baghuz, Syria, and Christchurch, New Zealand were symbolic of an enemy conspiracy and hypocrisy as well as reminders of the righteousness of Islamic State's global insurgency.

14a. 'He Was True to Allah and Allah Was True to Him', 18 March 2019
*English Translation of the Audio Statement by the Official Spokesman
of the Islamic State
The Mujahid Sheikh Abul-Hasan al-Muhajir*

...O brothers in Tawhid, builders of glory, and guardians of the Khilafah, may Allah bless your jihad and your pursuit. You have delighted the chests and irritated the kuffar, and for your efforts, every believer is thankful. Every Muslim knows the rank of the people of good deeds, glorifies their work, and anticipates their vanguards and seeks to join them. So, continue the march; following the footstep of the first predecessors among the muhajirin and ansar, may Allah be pleased with them all.

O people of Islam, the epic battles and their effect in the Wilayat of the Islamic State are no longer obscured. By Allah's grace, the sons of the Khilafah continue to prove that they are the firm and solid rock on which will break the alliance of kufr, by Allah's permission and strength. They will retreat from the lands of Muslims in disgrace and shame, trailing behind them the woes of humiliation and dishonor in outright exposed scandal where each of them will be putting the blame on the other. Here is America, the enemy of Islam and its people, after it demolished the houses of the people of the Sunnah and exterminated them in cold blood and upended the land to the evilest of who walked on the ground among the Iraqi Rafidah and the mushrikin of Sham, it announced a fake victory that has no connection to reality, despite the fact that they are certainly aware about the nature of the battle and its dimensions with the sons of the Islamic State. The chiefs of its parties, who oppose the policies of their obeyed fool, did not remain silent or turn a blind eye to what is really happening on the ground and the field actualities and their fluctuations, to the point where the politicians of the cross and the house of decadence called the 'White House' started living in pandemonium and contradictions, which makes it impossible for the follower to understand what they meant by the word victory that they are talking about. Nonetheless, this is delirium and recklessness of the imams of kufr who took a liking to or were coerced to validate just like the people of Nuh, Aad and Thamud, the Pharaoh, and Abu Lahab.

So outlandish that a victor cannot make an official visit to a country that he claims has established peace and stability. In fact, he was only able to make a stealthy visit like a coward thief fearing harm and fled in quick steps fearing the reaction and lamentation of his people for spending $7 trillion on a country that he can only visit in secret. America, the contemporary deity of heathens, has accepted what is less than the victory that they talked to people about. The Andrews Air Force Base meeting gathered more than 80 countries, and one of its final resolutions was that: 'It is not about winning the war, rather, it is winning the peace.' That meeting was followed by the resignation of the American emissary and its presidential representative in the Crusader coalition for the war against the Khilafah, the despicable one who hates the people of the Sunnah, the so-called 'McGurk' in protest over the claim of victory over the Khilafah and the intention to withdraw from Sham. The Islamic State still constitutes a real threat, as he said, and a danger for the region. His master quickly denigrated his dreams, humiliating him and stating that he never knew him before and that he is one of the remnants of the failed Obama policies and there is no need for his hallucinations and what he says and accusing him of seeking publicity and the limelight before his departure. Soon after, the Roman dog re-emerged with an audacious report that proves the opposite of the victory he claims, and the developed countries can not engage in endless wars, while admitting the failure to undermine the steadfastness and the determination of the Khilafah soldiers. He started to cast blame on the countries of the coalition for not committing to send enough supplies and soldiers to solidify the bases of the government of the Iranian Rafidah militias in Iraq, in fear of the sudden emergence of the Islamic State and its recapture of the territories from which it was ousted. They are expecting this, and they are divulging it and do not keep it secret. Moreover, they think when the withdrawal occur or not, the Islamic State will regain those regions in less than a year, as it was stated by their Ministry of Defense and was confirmed by the commander of their forces in the Middle East, the Crusader [Joseph] Votel who confirmed that the end of the war against the Islamic State is still far away. He added, during a hearing before Congress, that 'the Islamic State soldiers have not surrendered yet and are still ready to resume fighting'.

This was followed by National Security Advisor Bolton, during a television interview hosted by one of the news networks a few days ago. While being questioned about the claim of his master of 100% victory and what was stated by the Crusader Votel, this bungling fool came up with a third account and added more confusion to the clarity of his master, stating: 'The threat of the

Islamic State is still standing and the Islamic State soldiers are still dispersed in Syria and Iraq and the Islamic State is growing in other areas of the world.'

What is the reason behind this fear and apprehension, if not that they are convinced that the state of the Khilafah has become a reality, the danger of which cannot be ignored or denied. It was not a faction, organization, or a party content to subsist on the crumbs of sponsors or to knock on the doors of the Crusaders, begging and seeking their approval or for them to remove it from the list of what they call extremism and terrorism. No, the Islamic State has become, and all praise is due to Allah, the hope of the Ummah and the mighty castle held high in the heart of the Ummah, taking a straight road, allowing no reproach, and fearing not the blame of blamers. This is its army, the companies of its battalions touring Iraq, Sham, Khurasan, West Africa, and other Wilayat, awaiting the hour of decision. Twelve-thousand will not be defeated due to a lack of numbers, by Allah's permission. So die in your rage, O Crusaders and murtaddin [apostate]. Die in your rage. To hell with you, O America, and the alliance of demons with you, from the Arab and non-Arab tawaghit. Do you think that with your tyranny and destruction of the civilization of mankind and your extirpation of Sunnis that you will impose a reality or a bitter agreement? Or did you think that the scenes of weak and poor refugees leaving from the siege of death in Baghouz in Sham, or the pictures of women, children, and elderly would weaken the sons of the Khilafah, its army, and supporters? No, by Allah, this era is not yours and there is no security for you, just seas of blood and body parts, O tawaghit of the East and West.

The delusions that fettered the sons of Islam throughout the past centuries have been stripped away and shattered under the will and might of the extraordinary heroes of the Ummah and their noble leaders the day they sacrificed themselves for their religion, the elevation of the Khilafah's structure, and the glory of the Muslims. The Islamic State has been victorious. Yes, the Khilafah was victorious the day that its soldiers and sons stood firm, and they still are like steadfast mountains. They still proclaim their unshakable belief and proud doctrine, not paying heed to their enemy even when chained between their hands. The machines of destruction and death that you possess, America, have not been able to steal the belief and certainty that is in their hearts. How strange you are! Have you not become tired while you were trying in vain to eliminate the mujahidin and their state? Haven't the flames raging in Manbij and southern Hasakah stopped you? But the heroes doubled back to strike Manbij again. You are going down in failure and collapse, yet, still blustering of victory without consideration. Stop, for the mujahidin were but a few hundred before the conquest of Mosul, and today they are thousands upon thousands. They inevitably will achieve victory if they persevere and fear Allah.

...O people, everyone saw the incident of the massacre at the two mosques in Crusader New Zealand. We will reflect on that incident. One is not surprised when he sees the criminal murderers from the leaders of kufr and the governments of rida' as they adorn the victims of the two mosques with crocodile tears. The traitorous representatives of the wretched tyrannical councils and organizations that have surrendered to their enemy compare the killing of those worshipers with the Shari'ah-compliant jihad that the sons of the State of Islam are undertaking to establish the religion and repel the aggression of the Safavids, the Crusaders, and the murtaddin and turn them back from the Muslims' lands. It is as if the allies of kufr in Iraq, Sham, Khurasan, and other Wilayat of the State of Islam, are striving intensely to fill the needs of the people, to teach them about their religion, to grant them resources and wealth, and drop flowers on their heads. As if they never once announced that the mosques no longer hold sanctity for them. We never heard grief or lamentation from these murtadd representatives for their masters' massacres. It is the exact opposite. They are the ones who initiate and point to the weaknesses of the Muslims, striving intently and creatively in this regard. Here is Baghouz in Sham today. The Muslims are still burned to death inside of it, harmed by shelling from known and unknown weapons of mass destruction. This is not a surprise, but what our Lord told us of in His book about the hate of the kuffar and their resentment of Muslims, to suffice and heal those who desire their rights and request guidance. What they have done to the Muslims throughout the ages and centuries is too much for a Muslim to differentiate. So pay no attention to their lies. This massacre in the two mosques is nothing but a catastrophe among past and future catastrophes that will be followed by scenes of suffering from all who approach living among the mushrikin. What they call for and claim in their promotion of rights and freedoms is a lie. Let the scene of killing in the two mosques be enough to awaken the supporters of the Khilafah residing there, to seek vengeance and take revenge for their religion and the sons of their Ummah who are being slaughtered everywhere on Earth under the support and blessing of the nations of the cross and the governments of rida' and subservience.

We bring glad tidings to the Muslims in the East and the West, that the Khilafah, by Allah's grace, is only strengthened and solidified to bear hardship and burdens by the intensity of the Crusader campaign, and to ascend to the rank of leadership of the Ummah, by Allah's permission. Since the disappearance of the rule of their state as a result of the damage from consecutive Crusader campaigns, the Muslims have not witnessed their mujahidin sons engaging in an open war on several fronts and various areas under a single command and banner, exhausting the Crusader nations and their minions, the collaborator murtadd governments. Every time the Crusaders think they have imposed their influence and stolen the abode of Islam, the conquerors appear in another region in a war brought on by the sons of the Khilafah and their leaders, after Allah's grace, to rival the enemy, frustrate him in every part of the world, and drain his energy and capabilities. This tireless work is what is required of every son of the Khilafah, to expend all that they can until Allah the Exalted wills conquest.

...What needs to be addressed and warned about is what is being done by the mouthpieces of kufr from the grandsons of Ibn Saba and Musaylimah the liar, who belong to the tawaghit of the region and their apostate governments, and their urgent attempts to erase the truth and say that the Khilafah was made to submit and became of the past and an example to later ages. The fact remains, if the Islamic State loses some towns and cities in some of its Wilayat, Allah grants it conquest in other Wilayat in imbalanced hit-and-run battles in which they drag the enemy with all that he owns, following a policy of eradication and scorched earth. This is what the atheist immoral media does not show. Because the Muslim victim is not satisfied with anything but the religion of Allah in law and methodology and refuses to submit to the nations of kufr with their councils and laws that are imposed on mankind.

O tribes and Sunnis in Sham in general, and east of the Euphrates in particular, for a long time the Islamic State has warned and cautioned against the mistake of joining the ranks of the Kurdish atheists and made clear the atheism of this apostate sect, its disavowal of the divinity of Allah, and its socialism and licentiousness with possession and dignity, with its putrid jahilliyah call for Kurdish nationalism as a basis for its establishment of its so-called state. These three principles, upon which this damned sect is based, which are atheism and kufr itself, require no further clarification. Thus, we repeat and remind the Sunni tribes east of the Euphrates, whose sons are still in the ranks of those criminal atheists and who have not learned their lesson from the sight of those who have been killed at the hands of the Khilafah soldiers, to prevent their sons and urge them to repent before we get to them and to disavow those who do not seek repentance. What reason do you have to fight the mujahidin?

You were blessed with Allah's Shari'ah and His rule for years. As for you, O atheist Kurds of Sham: By Allah, you have waged a war for which you are neither qualified nor capable. Bear the consequences. Reassess and save yourselves if you can. Look at Iraq. America, with its aircraft that you worship, will avail you nothing. Indeed, our battle with you has not seen its fiercest fighting yet. You have seen some of the Khilafah soldiers' raids and their strikes in your regions. How many heads of tribes have been cut off, commanders of a security headquarters have they choked and killed, gatherings of shame have they blown up, and evil curs have they slaughtered on a checkpoints. So, expect it to be a holistic war that will not leave anything behind.

O lions of the Khilafah and men of the State in Raqqah, Barakah, and Khayr, leap like hungry lions, avenge the blood of your brothers and sisters, and declare a raid of revenge that will extirpate the roots of the people of kufr and atheism from Sham. Make these like the days of Zarqawi that will eliminate the ranks of the Crusaders and apostates. Seal the explosive devices, spread the snipers, and launch explosive attacks using boobytraps. There is no good in living a life while honors are humiliated and sanctities are violated, and while the ardent Sunni youth are restrained by a bunch of atheists who were handed by the worshipers of the cross the rule of an Islamic land which they destroyed, killed, and displaced its people. Make sure that the shoes and servants of the Crusaders understand that the blood of the shuhadaa and their families will not go to waste.

O Sunni tribes of Iraq, is it not time that you understand the massive plots woven against you? What did the traitor murtaddin gain from the agent politicians in the past decade? Nothing but rejection, being chased by arrest warrants, and accusations of terrorism and corruption. Becoming apostates did not arbitrate them with their lords, and they lost their religion and material gains for nothing. You have denied taking the path of righteousness, and you know about the wrath and hatred of the Rafidah who were unleashed to humiliate and expose you to all shades of disgrace.

...O Sunni people of Iraq, the Islamic State is your lifeboat and your impenetrable fortress against the Iranian Safavids expansion, so repent before it is too late and learn a lesson from others. No matter how long it might take, the Islamic State is coming back to the areas it departed, by Allah's will. Today, you see how Allah's protection is surrounding the soldiers of the Khilafah despite the flocks of airplanes and mobilization. They are still visible to their enemies, and are perfecting their ambushes to attack their rabble and crush their gatherings. They have taken an oath to make this land green and prosperous. Let the Rafidah know that the home of the Khilafah, Baghdad, will not be a second Tehran or any Qum, and that battles that will turn the hair of children grey wait them.

O solders of the Khilafah in Iraq, Sham, Khurasan, Yemen, East Asia, West Africa, Libya, Sinai, Somalia, and everywhere, prepare for the war and be diligent about it, grasp the opportunity, move the brigades, and make prolong the battle. Your enemy would not stand that. And do not be horrified by the noise made by the alliance of kufr and its cause to eliminate the Khilafah and curb its influence, for Allah will preserve it by your unity and adherence around His tight rope. Nothing will harm it or make the life in it horrible, not even the tons and tons of what it has been through so far. This is only the beginning of the road and the first step of the rebound and an approval for the coming conquest, by Allah's permission.

We are an ummah that will die only by being killed, and you are only arrows striving and intent on a target. If so, then there is no escape from death. Du'a are not for those who embrace it because it is victorious, who embraces it to lead followers, who embraces it to achieve his ambitions and to trade them in the market of invitations to be bought and sold. Rather, they are for those with living hearts turned toward Allah, pure from Him from every defect, not desiring rank, goods, or profit. They seek His face and hope for His satisfaction. The believer fears for himself and asks the Lord for perseverance in His religion and a favorable outcome. This a path worn by hardship, long exile, separation from family and friends, and the trampling of the soul with the possibility of harm, such as imprisonment, fracturing, and dismemberment—I seek Allah's protection from that.

Amirul-Mu'minin Abu Bakr al-Husayni al-Qurashi al-Baghdadi, may Allah preserve him, urges you to fear Allah in private and public, and may the tongue of one of you constantly remembering Allah be near to his Creator and Lord. He also urges you to abandon something that you have long been called to avoid and beware of, which has a pivotal role in the battle: it is the communication devices. Their risks have multiplied and disasters because of them have become common. So let not one of you make himself or his brothers a target of his enemy. There is no harm if a job that can be accomplished with those devices in two days is accomplished without it in one week instead.

Emphasize, alert, and beseech the mujahid in all of his words and his affairs to seek the reward which will come to him while he is encamped, if he has good intentions and performs the act well. Be earnest in taking precautions and being on guard and expect reward for obedience to your commanders and for angering the enemies of Allah and breaking off from them in anger. Fear Allah in your religion. Your religion is never accepted if you do not fear Allah and preserve the sanctity of brotherhood with other Muslims.

As for you, O men, women, and child captives everywhere, persevere in truth and know that the end of all the affairs of the believer is good. How could it not be for a believer? If Allah wants to test a believer, then afflictions will strike him, such that erases the sins and raise his rank in the afterlife, of which man may not realize how to reach or hope for. It suffices to say that it is an abandoned road and a clear Sunnah...

14b. Analysis

Just under forty-five minutes in length, this statement came at an important time for the Islamic State. Strategically, its last sliver of territory in Syria was about to be lost as footage emerged from Islamic State's official Amaq News Agency, showing trench-based fighting, in which everyone that remained in Baghuz—men, children and, significantly, women—was participating. The Islamic State's attempts to defend its last holdout now saw the coalition-backed and Kurdish dominated Syrian Democratic Forces (SDF) seizing and holding most of its remaining territories. Around the world, media reporting portrayed Baghuz as the last pitiful death rattle of a failed enterprise.[2] Debate raged about its implications for the anti-Islamic State coalition effort.[3] Amidst these events, on 15 March 2019, a terrorist attack targeting Muslims in Christchurch, New Zealand, killed fifty-one men, women, and children, as the attacker livestreamed the murders. In his first statement since September 2018—published within days of the Christchurch tragedy—it is clear that Muhajir wanted to leverage current events to inject the Islamic State's agenda into the media discourse with a speech that, in many ways, mirrored the structure, themes, and style of his predecessor Adnani.

[2] Callimachi, Rukmini, 'ISIS caliphate crumbles as last village in Syria falls', *New York Times*, 23 Mar. 2019; 'Islamic State group defeated as final territory lost, US-backed forces say', *BBC News*, 23 Mar. 2019.

[3] For a variety of perspectives, see Browne, Ryan, 'Top US general in Middle East says fight against ISIS "far from over"', *CNN*, 7 Mar. 2019; Callimachi, Rukmini, and Eric Schmitt, 'Splitting with Trump over Syria, American leading ISIS fight steps down', *New York Times*, 22 Dec. 2018; Ingram, Haroro, and Craig Whiteside, 'Do great nations fight endless wars? Against the Islamic State, they might', *War on the Rocks*, 25 Feb. 2019; Donald Trump, 2019, *State of the Union 2019*, 5 Feb. 2019.

Patience and Certainty

The first half of Muhajir's statement, which does not appear in the featured excerpt above, focuses on establishing the thematic and jurisprudential focus of his speech via a series of quotes and excerpts from the Quran and *hadiths*. The spokesperson's opening lines capture this succinctly:

> Jihad is the apex of Islam and its pinnacle. Jihad, in our time, is an obligation on every individual, and it is second only to believing in the oneness of our Lord, the Great and the Exalted. Because of this, it has become an obligation on the holders of the banner of jihad to equip themselves with what will assist them against its hardship and bear its tribulation. The servant's sharpest weapons are patience, certainty, and fear of Allah. These are the only effective and lasting tricks in his hand.

Dozens of references to the Quran and *hadith* follow, designed to unequivocally establish in the minds of his listeners the cosmic, historical, and jurisprudential proof that the Islamic State's current tribulations are evidence of the righteousness of its path. They also served as proof of the need for steadfastness along that path as only the truest of believers will demonstrate, and the inevitable rewards for such commitment.

Having primed his audience, the second act of Muhajir's statement pivots to address the contemporary issues at hand. It is at this point that the featured excerpt begins. Echoes of Adnani's 2015–6 statements can be heard, in terms of both content and argumentation; the notion that victory is measured in commitment, that the battle is far from over, and that Islamic State's enemies are, once again, deceiving themselves and the world about their predicament.[4] Events in Baghuz and Christchurch are held up as examples of an overarching effort by the West to destroy Islam, observing dissonance in the way the international community responded to the death of innocent Muslims. 'Here is Baghouz in Sham today', he said, where 'the Muslims are still burned to death inside of it, harmed by shelling from known and unknown weapons of mass destruction'. Yet no one was paying it any attention. Instead, all eyes were on Christchurch, which is 'nothing but a catastrophe among past and future catastrophes that will be followed by scenes of suffering from all who approach living among the mushrikin'. Regarding the grief expressed by Western leaders following the Christchurch attack, Muhajir declared 'one is not surprised when he sees the criminal murderers from the leaders of kufr and the govern-

---

[4] See Chapters 8 and 12.

ments of rida' as they adorn the victims of the two mosques with crocodile tears'. Muhajir considers such expressions hypocritical, given the role of Western nations in the war on the Islamic State: 'It is as if the allies of kufr in Iraq, Sham, Khurasan, and other Wilayat of the State of Islam, are striving intensely to fill the needs of the people, to teach them about their religion, to grant them resources and wealth, and drop flowers on their heads'.

This is part of Muhajir's broader effort to reframe the coalition war against the Islamic State as a war against Sunnis designed to facilitate Shi'a and atheist domination while emphasising the lack of consistency and credibility exhibited by Western leaders. Speaking of the 'pandemonium and contradictions, which makes it impossible for the follower to understand', the spokesperson mockingly drew attention to the claims and counterclaims of victory by US officials that led to:

> The resignation of the American emissary and its presidential representative in the Crusader coalition for the war against the Khilafah, the despicable one who hates the people of the Sunnah, the so-called 'McGurk' in protest over the claim of victory over the Khilafah and the intention to withdraw from Sham.

Muhajir seemed to relish highlighting how President Donald Trump[5] 'quickly denigrated his [McGurk's] dreams, humiliating him and stating that he never knew him before and that he is one of the remnants of the failed Obama policies and there is no need for his hallucinations and what he says and accusing him of seeking publicity and the limelight before his departure'.[6] To reinforce this sense of confusion, Muhajir cites US Central Command chief General Joseph Votel[7] and US National Security Advisor John Bolton[8]— that 'bungling fool'—who similarly declared that 'the threat of the Islamic State is still standing and the Islamic State soldiers are still dispersed in Syria and Iraq and the Islamic State is growing in other areas of the world'. For Muhajir, the absurdity of Trump declaring victory over the Islamic State was best evidenced by the fact that the president was unable to:

---

[5] Bowden, John, 'Trump defends foreign policy decisions amid personnel resignations', *The Hill*, 22 December 2018, https://thehill.com/blogs/blog-briefing-room/news/422625-trump-rips-grandstanding-isis-envoy-mcgurk-following last accessed 30 June 2019.

[6] Callimachi, and Schmitt, 'Splitting with Trump over Syria, American leading ISIS fight steps down'.

[7] Browne, 'Top US general in Middle East says fight against ISIS "far from over"'.

[8] Samuels, Brett, 'Bolton: "The ISIS threat will remain"', *Hill*, 10 Mar. 2019.

make an official visit to a country that he claims has established peace and stability. In fact, he was only able to make a stealthy visit like a coward thief fearing harm and fled in quick steps fearing the reaction and lamentation of his people for spending $7 trillion on a country that he can only visit in secret. America, the contemporary deity of heathens, has accepted what is less than the victory that they talked to people about.

Trump's tacit 'acceptance' of the fact that the Islamic State had not been defeated had, Muhajir claims, already started to rend the coalition apart. He said that the president had 'started to cast blame on the countries of the coalition for not committing to send enough supplies and soldiers', something that meant it was on the brink of collapse. The Islamic State was poised to make the most of this—it would, according to Muhajir, 'regain those [lost] regions in less than a year'.

Seas of Blood and Body Parts

For Muhajir, the Islamic State was the real victor in all this. Despite the tribulations it still faced, 'the state of the Khilafah has become a reality, the danger of which cannot be ignored or denied'. That alone, he said, constituted success. For the first time in centuries, he went on, Muslims the world over had been empowered and, for this reason, 'the Islamic State has been victorious.' When it seized Mosul, it had 'but a few hundred' fighters, but in early 2019 numbered in the 'thousands upon thousands'. The implication is that this victory was incontrovertible, permanently altering the course of the global jihadi project. All this was cause for defiance, something that Muhajir embodied as he again echoed his predecessor Adnani:

> So die in your rage, O Crusaders and *murtaddin* [apostates]. Die in your rage. To hell with you, O America, and the alliance of demons with you, from the Arab and non-Arab *tawaghit* [tyrants]. Do you think that with your tyranny and destruction of the civilization of mankind and your extirpation of Sunnis that you will impose a reality or a bitter agreement? [...] No, by Allah, this era is not yours and there is no security for you, just seas of blood and body parts, O *tawaghit* of the East and West.

The speech concluded, as is characteristic of Islamic State statements, by addressing specific audiences. Speaking to audiences in Syria and Iraq, Muhajir called on listeners to 'make these like the days of Zarqawi' and 'seal the explosive devices, spread the snipers, and launch explosive attacks using boobytraps'. To the so-called soldiers of the caliphate around the world, Muhajir directed calls for preparation and action ahead of a generational battle. The overarching message to all was clear: the Islamic State would continue to fight its global insurgency no matter what the cost. As part of this, defeat in one place would always be met with advances in another. At its lowest point since early-2014, Muhajir was unequivocally confirming that the Islamic State movement was involved in a global insurgency, one in which the conditions of a prolonged war afforded it strategic advantages:

> the Muslims have not witnessed their mujahidin sons engaging in an open war on several fronts and various areas under a single command and banner, exhausting the Crusader nations and their minions, the collaborator murtad governments. Every time the Crusaders think they have imposed their influence and stolen the abode of Islam, the conquerors appear in another region in a war brought on by the sons of the Khilafah and their leaders, after Allah's grace, to rival the enemy, frustrate him in every part of the world, and drain his energy and capabilities.

After his closing remarks, the statement ends with Muhajir passing on an unusual message from Baghdadi, urging supporters of the Islamic State to be more careful in their use of communications technology, warning that 'their risks have multiplied and disasters because of them have become common'. In an extension of the theme of patience, he warns that 'there is no harm if a job that can be accomplished with those devices in two days is accomplished without it in one week instead.' For the so-called caliph to offer what is essentially operational advice seemed peculiar but, with hindsight, it foreshadowed what was to come. Baghdadi's advice at the end of his spokesperson's speech seemed like an attempt to demonstrate that he was an engaged commander. After all, it was becoming increasingly clear that within the Islamic State, factional schisms were not only intensifying along strategic and jurisprudential lines but Baghdadi was increasingly being blamed as the leader in absentia.[9] The stage was now set for the caliph without a caliphate to appear for the first time since his triumphal address in Mosul almost five years earlier. It would be his final appearance.

---

[9] Bunzel, 'Ideological Infighting in the Islamic State', *Perspectives on Terrorism* 13(1), 2019, pp. 13–22; al-Tamimi, Aymenn, 'Dissent in the Islamic State: "Hashimi Advice" to Abu Bakr Al-Baghdadi', *Aymenn Jawad Al-Tamimi*, 4 January 2019, http://www.aymennjawad.org/22199/dissent-in-the-islamic-state-hashimi-advice-to; and al-Hashimi, Hesham, 'Criticism and analysis of the book "Enough extending hands to pledge bay'ah to al-Baghdadi"', European Center for Counterterrorism and Intelligence Studies, 29 March 2019.

15

THE GUERRILLA CALIPH

On 29 April 2019, six weeks after the publication of Muhajir's audio statement, the Islamic State released a video titled 'In the Hospitality of Amirul-Mu'minin.' *It featured Baghdadi sitting in a simply furnished room, addressing three subordinates—presumably senior commanders. At a minimum, the video was a proof of life for the caliph who had long been rumoured to be critically injured or dead after eight months of silence. Of course, the video was intended to achieve much more than that. Its release answered many questions about how the Islamic State intended to evolve its portrayal of the caliph to complement the plummeting fortunes of his organisation. In only his second ever appearance on film, Baghdadi reassured supporters and countered critics from within the group and the broader global jihadi milieu, affirming that he remained very much at the helm as the guerrilla caliph of a global insurgency.*

For the final chapter of this book, Baghdadi's statement appears in full.[1] Three features are particularly noteworthy. First, the caliph uses the speech to demonstrate that he is very much aware of and closely monitoring not only global events and issues but the fortunes of personnel within his organisation. Second, his physical appearance in the video was markedly different to his last appearance in 2014. Gone were the formal black robes, now replaced with military camouflage and an AK-74 by his side. Baghdadi was made to look equally comfortable in the role of

---

[1] The excerpt featured in this chapter is taken from an official Islamic State translation. The source contained text in both rounded and square brackets. The authors have made minimal edits to the text.

guerrilla commander in 2019 as he had been playing the political and spiritual leader in 2014. Third, he was projecting his authority as not just the leader of Islamic State but 'amirul-mu'minin' (commander of the faithful). While his forces no longer held territory in Syria or Iraq, Baghdadi had overseen the movement's extraordinary transnational expansion and his physical appearance and words would provide a much-needed morale boost across the group and help to counteract detractors. Less than six months later, Baghdadi would be killed in a special forces raid on his hideout in northern Syria. What follows is his final speech.

15a. 'In the Hospitality of Amirul-Muminin, the *Khalifah* of the Muslims', 29 April 2019
Ibrahim bin Awwad al-Badri al-Hussayni al-Qurashi al-Baghdadi al-Furqan Media[2]

All praise is due to Allah. May Allah's peace and blessings be upon the Messenger of Allah, his family, his companions, and everyone who follows his guidance.

As for what follows: Indeed, the battle for Islam and for its people with the Cross and its people will be a long battle. Although the battle of Baghouz is over, it demonstrated the savagery and brutality of the nation of the Cross against the Muslim *umma*. At the same time, it demonstrated the bravery, tenacity, and steadiness of the Muslim *umma*. This steadfastness has jolted the hearts of the Crusaders and amplified their rage and rancor against the steadfast of the Muslim *umma*.

All praise is due to Allah, and to you, brothers, the amirs and *walis*, who took turns in this *wilaya* until being chosen by Allah, as we consider them, but Allah is the ultimate judge. The first of them was your brother Abu 'Abdul-Rahman al-'Anqari at-Tamimi, who is from the Peninsula of Muhammad (PBUH). Then your brother Abu Hajar 'Abdul-Samad al'Iraqi at-Talibi took charge of the leadership; he sacrificed his life and wealth. Then your brother Abul Walid as-Sinawi succeeded him, who was then succeeded by your brother 'Abdul-Ghani al-'Iraqi. The last one was your brother Abu Mus'ab al-Hijazi, who is from the Peninsula of Muhammad (PBUH).The steadfastness, poise, and determination of these brothers were the reason the *mujahidin* and the subjects there remained steadfast, in spite of the small size of this spot and the immense size of the vicious Crusader onslaught and the smother-

[2] This speech was transcribed by Jackie Lobban from the English translation of al-Furqan Media's video (8 June 2019).

ing siege. Through the perseverance of these men, the people of Islam in this spot persevered.

We should not forget to mention your brothers the media knights; prominent among them are Abu 'Abdullah al-Ustrali, Khallad al-Qahtani, from the Peninsula of Muhammad (PBUH); Abu Jihad ash-Shishani, Abu Anas Fabien al-Faransi and his brother Abu 'Uthman, may Allah have mercy on them. We should also not overlook the courage and bravery of the Shari'ah Committee members, prominent among whom is Abu Raghad ad-Da'jani, from the Peninsula of Muhammad (PBUH).

We should not forget to mention your brothers who bore the heaviest load in this battle, the military personnel, including amirs and soldiers, battalions and brigades, and those who did their best to arrange and take care of their affairs and needs during battle; prominent among whom are your brothers Abu Yasir al-Baljiki and Abu Tariq al-'Iraqi, among many more others. If we fail to remember them, they will not suffer any loss, since Allah knows them best. May Allah have mercy on them and accept their deeds. May He reward them with goodness on behalf of the Islamic *umma*. They confronted the Crusaders in this battle, demonstrated their utmost capability, and proved to the entire world that the *mujahidin* have the upper hand when fighting *kuffar*. They upheld the truth they represent.

We give Allah praise and attribution, that your *mujahidin* brothers in the Islamic State, starting with [the] Baiji, Mosul, and Sirte battles and on through Baghouz, did not abandon their faith, nor did they give away land to the *kuffar* except over their corpses and torn body parts. May Allah reward them with goodness and may He accept their deeds. All of them have been the reason for the steadfastness of this *umma* in this small stretch of land. We ask Allah to accept their dead as *shuhada*, heal their wounded, release their captives, and accept their offerings. By Allah's permission, their brothers will not forget these sacrifices, such an offering, or these contributions. They will avenge them and never forget them as long as they are alive. This battle will have a sequel, by Allah's permission.

May Allah reward the brothers in all the *wilayat* for their blessed, unified raid to avenge their brothers in Sham, which amounted to ninety-two operations in eight countries. The significance this has is that it indicates the *mujahidin*'s unity of rank, their steadfastness, their awareness, their perception of the requirements of the battle, and their understanding of the reality they live in.

We congratulate your brothers in Libya for their steadfastness and their blessed raid entering the town of Fuqaha, despite their withdrawal from it, may Allah reward them bountifully. They have shown their enemies that they are capable of the holding the reins of the initiative, knowing that the battle today with their enemies is a battle of attrition. We recommend all of them to fight their enemies and drain all that they have from their human, military, economic, and logistical resources and everything.

Our battle today is one of attrition and struggle for the enemy. They need to know that jihad is continuing until the Day of Resurrection, and that Allah ordered us to wage jihad and did not order us to achieve victory. We beseech Allah to bestow upon us and our brothers steadfastness, pertinence, success, and right guidance, for He is the best to protect and the best to help.

As for the *baya'ah* by your brothers in Burkina Faso and Mali, we congratulate them for this *bay'ah* and for joining the caravan of the *Khilafah*, may Allah protect them as well as our brother Abul Walid as-Sahrawi. We recommend them to intensify their attacks against Crusader France and its allies and to avenge their brothers in Iraq and Sham. They must know that the lives of the believers are equal in value. The humblest of them is entitled to the protection of all. They stand as one against their enemies. They need to realise that a Muslim to another Muslim is like one body; when one limb suffers, the whole body reacts with sleeplessness and fever.

We have also learned that Allah has guided several members of parties and organisations in Khurasan, so they pledged *bay'ah* to the *Khilafah* and joined the convoy of *mujahidin*. We ask Allah to grant all of us firm establishment, rightness, and success; to fulfil the pledge; and to provide support and aid to their brothers. I believe you have followed the news of Netanyahu taking over the reins of the Jewish government and the main event of the falls of the tawaghit of Algeria and Sudan. However, it is unfortunate and sad that people fail to realise, up to this moment, why they have taken to the streets and what they want? The moment they substitute a *taghut*, another *taghut*, more criminal and crueler to Muslims, takes over. We keep telling and reminding them that the only effective method against such *tawaghit* is waging jihad for the sake of Allah. *Tawaghit* may be contained by jihad, and with jihad come pride and dignity. The only effective method against those *tawaghit* is the sword. They need to return to the Almighty and Exalted Allah. They need to pursue sharia ways to replace the systems and *tawaghit*, so the religion will be in its entirety for Allah.

As for your brothers in Sri Lanka, they have healed the *muwahiddin*'s chests with their *inghimasi* operations that unsettled the Crusaders in their Easter celebration to avenge their brothers in Baghouz. The number of casualties from among the Crusaders has reached or exceeded 1,000 between killed and wounded. This, by Allah's permission, is only part of the vengeance that is awaiting the Crusaders and their quislings. All praise is due to Allah, for among those killed were some Americans and Europeans.

We also congratulate the *muwahiddin* in Sri Lanka on their *bay'ah* and on them joining the *Khilafah*. We advise them to hold tight to the firm rope stretching from Allah, to unite their ranks and message, and to be a thorn in the side of the Crusaders. We ask Allah to accept the *inghimasi* brothers as *shuhada*, and to grant success to their brothers to complete the blessed march they have begun. Also, we should not forget your brothers' blessed operation in the Peninsula of Muhammad (PBUH) in az-Zulfi, and we ask Allah it be followed by another one. And we advise their brothers to avenge the *muwahiddin* in the Peninsula of Muhammad (PBUH) and to strive to continue down the path of jihad against the as-Salul tawaghit, may Allah damn them.

[The video concludes with footage of Baghdadi conversing with three men, presumably meant to be senior commanders. The following subtitle appears, stating 'Amirul-Muminin—may Allah preserve him—directs to double the work and intensify the strikes on the Crusader and *murtaddin* and their assistants'. The caliph is then shown being handed reports and conversing with the individual seated closest to him about their contents.]

15b. Analysis

The strategic concerns within the Islamic State about the convergence of several worrying dynamics—the wholesale loss of territorial control,[3] internal schisms along strategic and ideological fault-lines,[4] and accusations that

---

[3] Wu, Jin, Derek Watkins, and Rukmini Callimachi, 'ISIS lost its last territory in Syria. But the attacks continue', *New York Times*, 23 Mar. 2019, https://www.nytimes.com/interactive/2019/03/23/world/middleeast/isis-syria-defeated.html. Despite losing territorial control of all its urban centres by early 2019, persistent reports of resurgence in pockets of Syria and Iraq have persisted. For example, see Wallace, Brandon, 'ISIS Resurgence Update—April 2019', Institute for the Study of War, 19 Apr. 2019.

[4] The pressures of decline exposed deep fractures within the Islamic State along the lines of strategic and jurisprudential differences of opinion, with dissenting factions even publicly airing their concerns about Baghdadi being a caliph *in absentia*. Indeed, a former Islamic State jurisprudential official even authored a book arguing for withdrawing allegiance to the caliph. For more see Bunzel, Cole, 'The Islamic State's Mufti on Trial: The Saga of the "Silsila 'Ilmiyya"', *CTC Sentinel* 11, no. 9, Oct. 2018, https://

Baghdadi was absent if not dead[5]—led to the release of an audio-visual statement featuring Baghdadi, the group having decided that the enormous personal and organisational risks associated with such a communiqué were worth it. It is no coincidence that the two times Baghdadi appeared on film were the two most important moments in the movement's recent history, bookending its caliphate era. The first, of course, was when the caliph triumphantly ascended to the pulpit of Mosul's al-Nuri Mosque in 2014.[6] The second was with this video release, signalling that the Islamic State had once again settled into the battle rhythms of an insurgency but, this time, on a global scale.

Allah Ordered Us to Wage Jihad...

The presentation of 'In the Hospitality of *Amirul Muminin*' is telling. Without the slick production that typically characterises Islamic State propaganda, the simplicity of the video featuring Baghdadi directs the audiences' attention entirely towards the caliph, his words, and performance. The focus of the video is Baghdadi, who is seen addressing three members of staff, giving viewers the impression of a spontaneously recorded insight into the inner workings of the Islamic State's central command.[7] He looks at ease as the

---

ctc.usma.edu/islamic-states-mufti-trial-saga-silsila-ilmiyya/; Bunzel, 'Ideological Infighting in the Islamic State', *Perspectives on Terrorism* 13(1), 2019, pp. 13–22; al-Tamimi, Aymenn, 'Dissent in the Islamic State: "Hashimi Advice" to Abu Bakr Al-Baghdadi', *Aymenn Jawad Al-Tamimi*, 4 Jan. 2019, http://www.aymennjawad. org/22199/dissent-in-the-islamic-state-hashimi-advice-to; and al-Hashimi, Hesham, 'Criticism and analysis of the book "Enough extending hands to pledge bay'ah to al-Baghdadi"', European Center for Counterterrorism and Intelligence Studies, 29 Mar. 2019.

[5] For more on the debate regarding the death of senior Islamic State leaders and the merits of targeted killings, see Ingram, Haroro, and Craig Whiteside, 'Don't kill the caliph', *War on the Rocks*, 2 June 2016; Hamming, Tore, 'Kill the Caliph! The Islamic State's evolution from an integrated to a fragmented group', *Jihadica*, 20 May 2019.

[6] See Chapter 7.

[7] The Islamic State's internal security practices would disallow regular meetings of the type depicted in the video. More likely was the use of a courier system designed to limit exposure. Indeed, its organisational structure is air-gapped to prevent exposure that could lead to catastrophic loss. For more, see Cruickshank, Paul, 'A View from the CT Foxhole: Edmund Fitton-Brown, Coordinator, ISIL (Daesh)/Al-Qaida/

guerrilla caliph, sitting on cushions, his head covered by a black *ghutra*, wearing a khaki-coloured waist-coast, charcoal grey *thawb*, and a camouflage ammunition belt, AK-74 assault rifle by his side. The video concludes with Baghdadi examining reports and issuing directives.

Baghdadi's appearance reveals much about how the group was looking to adapt the image of its caliph to complement its strategic transition back into an insurgency. Historically, the political, military, and spiritual roles associated with the position of caliph allowed Islamic State propagandists to highlight certain aspects of his authority over others, depending on the strategic conditions at the time. While in 2014, Baghdadi was presented as the spiritual and political leader guiding the masses, in 2019 he was very much the *mujahid* amir, pulling the political and military strings of his global insurgency. By naming and praising commanders before providing commentary on contemporary events and issues, he was showing himself to be an engaged leader who was acutely aware of the strategic, organisational, and contextual nuances of the campaign ahead. This was also a not so subtle shot at detractors within his organisation who accused Baghdadi of being an absent leader focused on self-preservation, oblivious to the changes occurring within his own organisation, let alone beyond that.

It is important to highlight that the portrayal of Baghdadi's authority was not limited to his military role, despite the video's focus on that aspect of the caliph's responsibilities. The use of the term *amir al-muminin* (commander of the faithful) in the title of the video, an honorific that Muhajir also used to refer to Baghdadi in his March 2019 statement,[8] is an implicit acknowledgement of the continuation of the caliph's spiritual authority, as well as his political and military role. The title also sends a broader message to the global jihadi milieu that, with Baghdadi very much alive and in charge, he maintained his status as the Commander of the Faithful. The Afghan Taliban and its own *amir al-muminin* Mullah Mohammad Omar once faced this same challenge, struggling with how to maintain and project his status while essentially leading an insurgency on the run. When Baghdadi first positioned himself as *amir al-muminin*, al-Qaida countered by pointing to Mullah Omar's authority well

---

Taliban Monitoring Team, United Nations,' *CTC Sentinel* 12, no. 4 (April 2019); and Djani, Dian Triansyah, 'Letter from the Chair of the Security Council Committee re: ISIL,' United Nations Security Council, 15 Jan. 2019.

[8] See Chapter 14: Global Insurgency.

into 2015, apparently unaware that he had died in 2013.[9] Despite the risks associated with showing the caliph in person, Baghdadi's video appearance demonstrated that supporters and detractors alike could rest assured that he was alive and commanding his forces. Indeed, his appearance may have been especially important for ensuring that the 'true believers'—whether those continuing the fight overtly or operating covertly within populations formerly under the Islamic State's control—remained committed to the cause.[10] The Islamic State must compete within the global jihadi milieu for its claims of authority to be recognised, something that requires a synchronised effort to promote its *manhaj* (methodology), in-field results, and the authority of its leader in a compelling way. The Islamic State took an enormous risk showing Baghdadi to the world at this time and, whether connected or by coincidence, within six months he was dead. Into the void stepped a new guerrilla caliph, Abu Ibrahim al-Hashimi al-Qurashi, who would now be charged with leading the Islamic State's global insurgency.

...And Did Not Order Us to Achieve Victory

Baghdadi's 2019 appearance has to be understood in context—for many years, at least since 2016, the Islamic State's media department had been preparing its supporters for an imminent period of decline, working in close partnership with its leadership.[11] Indeed, the caliph's speech was not the panicked response of a leader in distress but the latest message in what had been an ongoing

[9] Islamic State propagandists, like Adnani, would ridicule Al-Qaida for pledging allegiance to a dead amir. For example, see Roy, Olivier, and Tore Hamming, 'Al-Zawahiri's Bay'a to Mullah Mansoor: A Bitter Pill but a Bountiful Harvest,' *CTC Sentinel* 9, no. 5, May 2016, https://ctc.usma.edu/al-zawahiris-baya-to-mullah-mansoor-a-bitter-pill-but-a-bountiful-harvest/

[10] Ingram, Haroro, 'How ISIS Survives Defeat: Propaganda and Decisive Minorities,' *Oxford Research Group* (blog) 26 Sept. 2016, https://www.oxfordresearchgroup.org.uk/blog/how-isis-survives-defeat-propaganda-and-decisive-minorities

[11] For analysis of the Islamic State media department and interactions with leadership since Zarqawi, see Whiteside, Craig, 'Lighting the Path: the Evolution of the Islamic State Media Enterprise (2003–2016),' International Centre for Counter-Terrorism—The Hague 7, no. 11 (2016). For the state of the media department post-caliphate, see Munoz, Michael, 'Selling the Long War: Islamic State Propaganda after the Caliphate,' *CTC Sentinel* 11, no. 10, Nov. 2018, https://ctc.usma.edu/selling-long-war-islamic-state-propaganda-caliphate/

dialogue with supporters to be patient and stay true to the cause. Within two years of capturing Mosul, then-spokesperson Adnani's May 2016 speech presaged this moment, conceding that territory had been lost and hinting at the likelihood of a return to insurgency.[12] This was followed by *al-Naba*'s many editorials, Muhajir's April 2018 speech,[13] and a series of articles in *al-Naba* explaining the Islamic State's approach to insurgency strategy.[14] While rare, Baghdadi's video appearance emerged as an exclamation point to a media strategy that reminded Islamic State supporters to remain committed to the cause during this latest period of decline, until the foundations could be laid for another resurgence. But there are significant risks associated with having leaders act as messengers and this messaging strategy may, ultimately, have contributed to the killing of the Islamic State's two most senior leaders.

Baghdadi's death punctuated a devastating period for the Islamic State in which it lost all the territory it once controlled across Syria and Iraq, its leadership suffered crippling losses, and its ranks were ravaged by war. His was not only the longest tenure as top leader of the movement but also the most brutal with slavery, rape, torture, and genocide all brazenly used as weapons in bloody campaigns that razed the societies of friends and foes alike. Baghdadi's successor, Abu Ibrahim, has taken the reigns at a crucial moment in the Islamic State movement's history when it once again faces seemingly insurmountable odds. While the Islamic State is significantly weaker now than at its peak through 2014-15, it is comparatively stronger in both capabilities and networks compared to other periods of decline in its history. Indeed, the Islamic State movement is well-positioned to exploit opportunities that may emerge from distracted adversaries in no small part due to its global network of formal and aspiring provinces. In short, Baghdadi may be dead but the story of the Islamic State movement is far from over.

---

[12] See Chapter 12. https://smallwarsjournal.com/jrnl/art/abu-muhammad-al-adnani%E2%80%99s-may-21-2016-speech

[13] al-Muhajir, Abul Hasan, 'By their Example Be Guided', 22 Apr. 2018; Bunzel, Cole, 'Divine Test or Divine Punishment? Explaining Islamic State Losses', *Jihadica*, 11 Mar. 2019, http://www.jihadica.com/author/cole-bunzel/

[14] See the numbered series starting with: Islamic State, 'Allah will come up with a Nation', and 'Toppling the Cities as a Temporary Methodology of the *Mujahideen*', *al-Naba* #179, 25 Apr. 2019, p. 3 and p. 9, respectively. Available at Aaron Zelin's Jihadology website https://jihadology.net/2019/04/25/new-issue-of-the-islamic-states-newsletter-al-naba-179/

CONCLUSION

Over fifteen chapters, *The ISIS Reader* has featured milestone texts, video transcripts and speeches from the Islamic State movement, drawn from its tumultuous multi-decade history. In doing so, it has told the 'inside story' of the Islamic State's struggle, from a wandering band of jihadis in Afghanistan to the Islamic State in Iraq, from near decimation in 2010 to its triumphant declaration of a caliphate in 2014, and, finally, from its global expansion across Asia, Africa, and the Middle East to its return to beleaguered insurgency in 2018–19. Presenting this trajectory in the Islamic State's 'own words' offers essential insights into the complicated mixure of personalities, strategic logic, opportunism, success, and failure that shaped its fortunes. Several recurring trends emerge from this study that are pertinent for scholars wishing to understand the movement and strategic-policy architects seeking to devise strategies to confront it.

One of the most significant is the group's strategic culture of critical reflection and innovation, evidence of which continually emerges and re-emerges throughout its history. As outlined in 'Part I: Join the Caravan', this strategic culture was evident from very early in the movement's history and has been crucial for understanding not only how it has achieved success but managed failure and learned from both to adapt to future challenges. For example, while the Islamic State's successes through 2013–15 are extraordinary by any standard, they are even more remarkable given the movement's almost total decimation less than a decade earlier. The means by which it did this were laid out in 'Part II: *Baqiya*!', which explored the movement's strategy to re-establish its networks in Iraq and implement a plan of survival that simultaneously set the foundations for a future resurgence. This strategic opportunism, so often displayed throughout its history, is only possible because of the strategic

303

culture that informs the movement's posture as a politico-military force. Too rigid, and the movement risks being sluggish and incapable of adapting to changing circumstances. Too fluid, and it risks fracturing during periods of boom and especially in times of bust. The Islamic State has demonstrated that commitment to its *manhaj* is more than just an abstract obligation to the divine—it is a pragmatic commitment to a strategy that its leaders believe will bring the movement success and, ultimately, herald the End Times. This feeds directly into the next trend.

Far from being ashamed of the turbulent, boom-bust dynamic that characterises its history, the Islamic State's leaders and propagandists promote these ebbs and flows as a divine gift designed to test the movement's commitment to applying its *manhaj*. With its creed of perpetual war and its gauge of success being adherence to its *manhaj*, not material strength, these otherwise rhetorical abstractions are operationalised in the field by the group's application of a phased politico-military strategy of revolutionary warfare.[1] As examined throughout 'Part III: The Caliphate', during periods of supremacy, the Islamic State transitions from unconventional to more conventional governance and warfare strategies as it reaches force symmetry, then superiority, by outcompeting its opponents in the field. During periods of weakness, it moves back through those strategic phases from conventional operations to guerrilla warfare and terrorism strategies. It is important for scholars and practitioners to not focus disproportionately on the ideological rhetoric of the group alone and, in doing so, underestimate the pragmatism that is in fact the real trademark of the movement's history. That pragmatism is borne not only from the abovementioned strategic culture that seems to be encouraged within its ranks but the harsh realities of fighting multidecade wars against materially superior opponents.

Another quality to emerge from this study is the central role afforded to propaganda as a mechanism by which the Islamic State movement competes against foes who are conventionally superior to it by almost any measure.[2]

---

[1] Whiteside, Craig, 'New masters of revolutionary warfare: The Islamic State movement (2002–2016)', *Perspectives on Terrorism* 10, no. 4 (2016), http://www.terrorismanalysts.com/pt/index.php/pot/article/view/523/1036

[2] Ingram, Haroro, 'The strategic logic of Islamic State information operations', *Australian Journal of International Affairs* 69, no. 6 (2015); Winter, Charlie, 'Media Jihad: The Islamic State's doctrine for information warfare', International Centre for the Study of Radicalisation and Political Violence, 2017.

CONCLUSION

While the Islamic State movement is not unique in the strategic importance it places on messaging,[3] the group distinguishes itself from others in its veneration of the practice. Given the limited resources at the group's disposal compared to its coalition of foes at any time in its history, including when it was at the peak of its powers in 2014–15, the fact that it devotes the resources, time, and personnel that it does to propaganda reveals how central this is to its strategy. Its leaders have long demonstrated a deep appreciation for the power of words and images to shape how local, regional, and global audiences perceive the group and its enemies. Pragmatically, messaging acts as a force multiplier for the Islamic State's actions by presenting its system of control as superior and, potentially, a force nullifier for the actions of its enemies. It also deploys propaganda to influence how friends, foes, and neutrals perceive events and issues more broadly, blending words and actions to present a system of meaning that it hopes its target audiences will adopt.

The Islamic State itself once stated that the purpose of its messaging was to 'light the path' and 'revive negligent mind', and these are useful sentiments for scholars and practitioners to keep in mind.[4] Strategic messaging does not create 'the path'—actions in the field must do that—but it can be used to bring into focus certain things over others, shaping how circumstances and actors are perceived and, consequently, whom populations choose to support. The psychological impact of the Islamic State's propaganda stems not only from its manipulation of ideology, but also how its use of words and images leverage broader contextual factors—that is, events and issues that are pertinent to its audiences—to resonate with them. The more that scholars and practitioners focus disproportionately on certain elements of the Islamic State's propaganda efforts (for example, its use of social media, and English-language sources), the more limited our understanding of its strategies will be and, in turn, any countermeasures are less likely to be effective.

---

[3] For example read insurgency doctrines such as al-Muqrin, Abdel Aziz, 'A practical course for guerilla warfare', pp. 83–180, in *Al-Qaida's doctrine for insurgency*, trans. Nigel Cigar, Washington D.C.: Potomac, 2009; Guevara, Ernesto, *Guerilla Warfare*, Lincoln: University of Nebraska Press, 1998; Irish Republican Army, *Handbook for Volunteers of the Irish Republican Army*, Boulder, CO: Paladin Press, 1985; Taber, Robert, *War of the Flea*, Dulles: Potomac Books, 2002; Tse Tung, Mao, *On Guerrilla Warfare*, trans. Samuel B. Griffith II, Chicago: University of Illinois Press, 2000.

[4] Whiteside, Craig, 'Lighting the Path: The evolution of the Islamic State media enterprise (2003–2016)', International Centre for Counter-Terrorism, 2016.

Finally, what should be clear from this study is that Islamic State has a history of telling its supporters exactly what it intends to do. Each chapter reveals how the group used its leaders' speeches, its doctrine, and propaganda messaging to inform its audiences of its current activities, shed light on its history, and provide projections about how it intended to exploit opportunities and weather coming storms. While there is no question that the Islamic State's propaganda offers an inevitably jaundiced perspective and, on many occasions, engages in blatant misinformation, the materials the movement produces nevertheless offer vital insights into its inner workings—insights that we ignore at our own peril.

Some may suggest that we risk succumbing to Islamic State propaganda by engaging with its sources. This ignores the fact that the movement needs to convince potential supporters of not only the jurisprudential and religious veracity of its agenda, but its pragmatic ability to achieve those goals in the real world against powerful enemies. Credibility becomes an important commodity, especially amongst local populations willing to accept lethal certainty as an alternative to (often equally lethal) uncertainty. Others may dismiss engaging with primary sources as we have done here as an act of sympathy for Islamic State or, even worse, a naively dangerous act that can lead to radicalisation. Such positions, however, are based on a fundamental misreading of how and why propaganda 'works'. This blinkered attitude has all too often resulted in problematic research outputs and informed shoddy operational, strategic, and policy decisions. It is imperative that primary sources act as the foundation upon which our understanding of phenomena such as the Islamic State movement is based, not just as window dressing. Certainly, access to materials that articulate how to construct weapons or plan attacks should be limited, where appropriate and possible, but to deny academic and practitioner access to these materials is not only of little value but counterproductive. Ultimately, democracies should be willing to expose 'dangerous ideas' to the light of public debate rather than inadvertently giving their authors the perverse credibility that they crave, the kind that comes with being subjectively censored. On the basis of both principle and pragmatism, it is essential that the mentality and culture around engaging with primary source materials produced by extremist groups, including but by no means limited to those covered in this book, shifts to one of critical enquiry and engagement. Successfully countering such movements and the individuals they inspire depends upon it.

GLOSSARY

This glossary defines the below terms according to the Islamic State's interpretation, re-appropriation and usage, not according to how they are used in mainstream discourse.

amiliya inghimasiya	'Plunging operation'—an assault-style suicide operation.
amiliya istishhadiya	'Martyrdom-seeking operation'—a suicide operation or bombing.
amir (*umara*)	'Commander'—describes leaders of units, administrative divisions or groups.
amir al-muminin	'Commander of the faithful'—an honorific used to refer to the caliph.
ansar	'Supporters'—usually refers to local group members, as opposed to foreign members, who are termed *muhajirin*.
Al Salul	An historic label used pejoratively in reference to the Saudi royal family.
al-wala al-bara	'Loyalty and disavowal'—a prominent concept among jihadis which holds that one has to be unflinchingly loyal to Islam and unflinchingly opposed to all things and activities associated with disbelief.
baya	'Pledge of allegiance'—in this context, denotes a pledge to the caliph.
dawa	'Proselytization'.

dua	'Invocation'—a prayer of supplication or specific request.
ghanima (ghanaim)	'Spoils'—used in reference to items (guns, ammunition, money, clothing, etc.) taken from the enemy after or during an attack.
hijra	'Migration'—the act of travelling to join the Islamic State in Syria, Iraq, or any other conflict zone in which it is operational.
iqamat al-hudud	'Establishing the *hudud* punishments'—implementing religiously mandated punishments for certain crimes such as adultery, theft and banditry (e.g., amputations and beheadings).
jihad	'Struggle'—used in this context to refer to war against disbelievers and apostates with a view to spreading the rule of Islam.
jund al-khilafa	'Soldiers of the caliphate'—refers to Islamic State fighters.
junud al-dawla	'Soldiers of the state'—refers to Islamic State fighters.
khalifa	'Caliph'.
khilafa	'Caliphate'.
kafir (kuffar)	'Disbeliever'—someone who does not follow the religion of Islam as it is interpreted by the group in question.
khariji (khawarij)	'Kharijite'—refers to an early sect in Islamic history. It is applied to anyone considered an 'extremist' by both moderate Sunni Muslims and even some jihadis.
kufr	'Disbelief'.
majusi	'Zoroastrian'—used in reference to Iran and its proxies, like *safawi/safawiyin*.
muhajir (muhajirn)	Someone who engages in *hijra* (see above).
mujahid (mujahidin)	One who engages in jihad. For the Islamic State, this refers to soldiers and leaders alike.
munafiq	'Hypocrite'—refers to someone who claims to be a true Muslim but is not implementing or following Islam's rulings fully or properly.

munasir (*munasirin*)	'Supporter'—refers to supporters around the world (i.e., online). In the Islamic State's territories in Syria and Iraq, it also was used to describe civilian supporters of the caliphate (i.e., administrative workers).
murtad (*murtaddun*)	'Apostate'—refers to someone who has "willfully" left Islam. Used to describe Muslim opponents of the Islamic State in general and Western-aligned Middle Eastern governments in particular.
mushrik (*mushrikun*)	'Polytheist'—someone that associates others with Allah.
nusayri (*nusayriya*)	Derogatory reference to Alawites, derived from Ibn Nusayr, the man reputed to have founded the sect. Syria's ruling Asad family are Alawites, so the term is used to refer to all supporters, workers, and soldiers associated with the Syrian regime.
rafidi (*rawafid/rafidiya*)	'Rejectionist'—a pejorative used in reference to Shia Muslims in Iraq.
safawi (*safawiyun*)	'Safavid'—refers to the Iranian dynasty that ruled according to Shia Islam. Used by the Islamic State to describe Iranian and Iran-backed forces in Syria and Iraq.
Sahwa	Refers to Sunni tribes, or Awakening forces, that fought the Islamic State of Iraq in the 2000s. In the 2010s, it was used to describe all non-state Sunni forces fighting against the Islamic State.
sahwa	'Awakening'.
shahid (*shuhada*)	'Martyr'—someone killed in the cause of Islam (whether as a fighter on the battlefield, as a suicide bomber, or as a civilian in an airstrike).
sharia	Islamic law.
shari'i	Adjective describing something that is 'legitimate' or in accordance with Islamic law.
shirk	'Polytheism'.

majlis shura	'Consultation council'—the entity charged with designating the leader of the Islamic State and top-level strategic decision-making.
manhaj	'Methodology'.
taghut (*tawaghit*)	'Tyrant'—refers to Middle Eastern governments and their rulers.
tawhid	'Oneness' or 'monotheism'.
ulama	'Scholars'—plural of *alim*, refers to individuals recognised by the Islamic State as having acquired religious authority through learning.
umma	'Community'—refers to the global community of Muslims.
wali	'Governor'—refers to leaders of Islamic State provinces.

INDEX

INDEX

Qutb, Sayyid, 20

Ramadi, Iraq, 65, 74, 86, 87, 132
rape, 82, 87
Raqqah, Syria, 106, 199
Rashidun Caliphate (632–61), 29, 30, 35, 111, 115, 119, 188, 201
al-Rawi, Manaf, 36 n.26
Reina nightclub shooting (2017), 228 n.11
responsibility to protect (R2P), 192, 259
revolutionary war, 130–34
al-Rishawi, Abu Risha, 86, 137–9
Riyad us-Salihin Brigade, 213
Rumiyah, 111 n.12, 260
Rumsfeld, Donald, 252, 258
Russia, 253, 271
Ryan, Michael, 130

Sa'd ibn Mu'adh, 29
Saddam Hussein, 39, 44, 61, 68, 243
Saddam University of Baghdad, 60
Safavid Empire (1502–1736), 139, 183, 224, 225, 227, 283, 285
Safiyyah, 29, 33
Sahel, Syria, 246
al-Sahrawi, Abul Walid, 296
Sahwa (2005–13), 11, 54 n.6, 55, 64, 86, 87, 107–118, 125–9, 134–41, 145, 161, 242
    Alliance of al-Mutayyabin (2006) and, 60
    Baghdadi (Abu Umar) on, 66 n.23, 86, 87
    'Extinction of the Grayzone' on, 188, 189
    extra-judicial killings, 113 n.15
    Fallujah Memorandum and, 107–118, 125–9, 134–41, 145
    Islamic Army in Iraq, relations with, 63

public declaration of (2006), 60, 68, 86, 138
Ramadi, capture of (2007), 87
Shi'a, relations with, 138
Tunisi, attacks on, 88 n.54
Utaybi on, 71, 74, 87
Sa'id ibn Jubayr, 101
Saint Jean sur Richelieu ramming attack (2014), 193 n.7
Salafi-jihadism, 4 n.2
    Badri and, 60
    nationalism and, 114 n.18
    Zarqawi and, 3, 13, 19, 20, 21, 42
Salah ad-Din, Iraq, 73, 168
Samarra, Iraq, 35, 66
Saraya al-Ghuraba, 71
Saraya al-Jihad, 71
Saudi Arabia, 70, 73, 74, 158, 184
    Grand Mosque seizure (1979), 20
    legal councils, 142
    Sahwa, 138 n.58
    Wahhabism, 20
    women in, 199, 201
September 11 attacks (2001), 186, 194
al-Shafi'i, Abu Abdullah, 124
al-Shami, Abu Anas, 19–20, 21–2, 32, 34, 35, 36 n.26, 68, 90 n.57
al-Shami, Jarrah, 87
Shapiro, Jacob, 241
sharia
    Adnani and, 99, 100, 105
    Baghdadi on, 151
    dawawin and, 238, 239, 244
    Fallujah Memorandum on, 116, 119, 123, 127, 136, 140, 145
    hudud, 73, 185, 237
    Naji and, 5
    Utaybi and, 20
    Zarqawi and, 27
Sheikhayn, 70 n.33
Shi'a Islam, Shi'a Muslims